Field of
Oleander

Field of Oleander

GEORGE B. ERONINI

ARPress
ILLUMINATING IDEAS
EMPOWERING VOICES

ARPress
45 Dan Road Suite 5
Canton MA 02021

Hotline: 1(888) 821-0229
Fax: 1(508) 545-7580

Ordering Information:
Quantity sales. Special discounts are available on quantity purchases by corporations, associations, and others. For details, contact the publisher at the address above.

Printed in the United States of America.

ISBN-13:   Paperback   979-8-89330-793-1
                  eBook   979-8-89330-794-8

Library of Congress Control Number: 2024904729

Table of Contents

Prologue

Arrival

"Unbelievably luxurious," Raymond Karr grandiosely quipped as he sat spread out alone in the back seat of the unmarked black Lincoln taxi. His arrival in the United States as a young F-1 student had remained by far the happiest and most memorable in his life. The experience was simply extra-ordinary for him, having stepped out of a Pan Am jumbo jet, cleared both Immigration and Customs, and out of JFK airport terminal in an early sunrise clear blue sky, to board the taxi.

Exhilarated Raymond loved and inwardly appreciated everything – the hovering of planted trees and shrubs from the gentle breeze that blew, the busy pedestrians clamoring to get to their destinations, even the taxicab driver himself, a Cuban immigrant, about 38, toned white with a square jaw that was covered with a three-day old beard, and wildly bushy eyebrows, who had just conned him into hiring the taxi. Raymond thought the driver's flat nose was a perfect carve out of the alphabet m.

In spite of Raymond's exuberance, the driver's futile struggle to communicate in English language stunned him and caught him off guard. It was his first encounter ever with a non-English speaking white man. But he was able to figure it out when the driver added 'jes' to the end of every question he asked or every answer he gave, which was his pronunciation of yes. "Ne-hay-ra" was Nigeria. What mattered to him was that the driver knew which local airport he was headed, which was La Guardia.

While the Lincoln cruised along, every single object that stood or moved on that windless autumn morning fascinated him. He would later tell friends it felt like he was just born, and sometimes he seriously theorized on the ecstatic idea that he must have been the only human that ever felt such heightened excitement about anything, period. He recently described the experience as god-awesome, and the memory always left him covered with goose bumps. In his Oral Presentation class, he seized the opportunity to thank his God for that overwhelming experience, asking Him to bless anyone who ever felt the same way or who will ever experience such a ravishingly exciting moment. He had vowed to declare heaven if he ever felt that excited again.

Mediocre by social standards, Raymond was a six feet tall, twenty-nine-year old, medium built with bow-legs that curved right from his pelvic girdles. In high school his friends constantly joked that he was long not tall, and openly taunted him for what they dubbed a 'seismic' penis. His short nappy hair naturally receded a half-inch back from his forehead. He looked like a typical African with dull eyes, standard nose and disproportionately large lips. He had no luck with girls and seldom scored with them, believing that they somehow found him naturally unattractive.

He attended mostly all-boys schools by chance or by providence. One time his mother was about to transfer him to a co-ed high school, which excited him greatly, but then it was converted to an all-boys school that semester after forty years as a gender mixed school. He was devastated by his continued hard luck with girls.

Despite his difficulty in wooing over the opposite sex, Raymond knew and loved beautiful women, so much that he easily could be a great judge in a beauty contest. Unfortunately, the few girls who showed interest in him he found extremely unattractive, and he often ran away, literarily. The most memorable was a lanky girl with k-legs and facial bumps, who threw herself at him in a nightclub. He wound up going home with her and during sex had a mid-orgasm shutdown. He had affinity for hairy women, esxhibited especially by thick feminine eyebrows. He almost always fantasized romance with one and it became a core motivational force driving him to succeed financially.

Raymond Karr's American dream was created rather than born and was with him from conception. He never recalled ever being taught or told about America to know it was everything he wanted in the world. All he could remember was that he woke up one morning when the family resided in Aba, a commercial town in Eastern Nigeria, to find the entire nursing staff from the local hospital openly weeping. A beloved president had been assassinated. They said his name was

John F. Kennedy. Raymond's grandpa, an uneducated farmer, chose to affectionately reference him by his middle name, but instead of what Raymond later came to learn was "Fitzgerald", his grandpa pronounced it "Farraday".

Raymond's first question, as he saw his own mother, a nurse, crying was "Is it America?" How the concept of America came to his mind remained a mystery to him growing up. It was 1962 and little Raymond was only three or four. Back then in Africa, dates and times were mostly for the record-keepers. Raymond didn't even think he could remember any other incident at that early age other than this. He was deeply saddened. Something had gone terribly wrong in America. His mother's tearful explanation made no sense but whoever Kennedy was had to do with America and that was all that mattered for little Raymond, enough to make him sad.

From then on, anything that mentioned America deeply touched Raymond Karr's heart and he emotionally rooted for it. He was the staunchest ally of whoever named his side 'America.'

That was how he became fascinated with the State of Israel. In elementary school, during recess, you couldn't pay little Raymond enough money to be on the side opposing 'America' when they played games, any game, be it soccer or tag or sprint race. Before soccer games, each team with little rascally, soccer star wannabes had to choose a country to represent and since everyone would like to choose America, a simple penny coin toss settled it. That was until a volunteered penny mysteriously vanished, causing misery to 7 year old Jude Atufuo, a slightly obese boy with dark chocolate skin and crocodile eyes, who became one penny poorer. From then on, in order not to endure the bitter lessons from *Fat Jude Experience*, now their euphemism for stolen money, a flattened soda bottle cover took over as coin. The winner would choose to represent America and was expected to win, and for some mysterious reason, whether by design or providence, often did. The unfortunate loser of the coin toss would then choose another country, usually Nigeria or England.

Even in street boxing challenges, first choice was always Dick Tiger, a legendary Nigerian boxing champion, over John Fulmer, the British boxer, who lost a title fight to the Nigeria's price fighter. If you won, you were Dick Tiger and if you lost, you would carry the unenviable cross of John Fulmer. So it was better to chicken out and become a coward than to box and lose. One can always fight another time and redeem cowardice but the label of John Fulmer was there to stay.

Raymond Karr still remembered a childhood song when they would pretend to perform magical acts. The lyric was "Come and See American Wonder, Come and See American Wonder." Children would clap and sing over and over again for about six times or so, before unfolding whatever magic. Alternatively, they would say, "In the name of Alaska," which all the children, who were still struggling to read up to z in their alphabet lessons, ignorantly pronounced 'Alasaka.' That would suffice for a magical incantation. Any performance deemed extra-ordinary the children attributed to American Wonder. As a so-called magician, if you didn't sing 'American Wonder,' you couldn't fool children spectators into believing you performed a magical act. But if you genuinely recited the magic song, every child would clap and make-believe despite the ridiculously obvious hideaway.

In his youth, Raymond used to think he was one of the most amazing magicians because he sang the song with so much flair that other children preferred to see him at the makeshift 'magic' stand.

Other perennial songs of his youthful days included his all-time favorite:

Who will buy my lily with the color white? Who will buy my lily with the color red? This color gives you glory, red, white and blue'.

And this was even long before he became aware the song happened to be mentioning the three colors that were also emblematic of the American flag.

Raymond was crushed when at that young and naïve age of about seven he learned that the Queen of England, the legendary Queen Elizabeth II, was not the ruler of America. One of his wild dreams was to visit Her Majesty when he grew up and go to America. When he learned England had nothing to do with America sovereignty-wise, young Raymond was no longer interested in their famous childhood favorite subjects like Buckingham Palace, London, Trafalgar Square, etc. He no longer had the desire to recite *'Pussycat, pussycat, where have you been? I'd been to London to see the Queen.'* When airplanes and their contrail lines crossed their city, while other children waved and chanted "Queen Elizabeth," his lone and overwhelmed voice chanted

"America."

Memories from Geography lessons introduced Raymond Karr, via map, to cities like Los Angeles, San Francisco, Santa Monica, and states like New York, Texas, Arizona, etc. He would open up the map and just stare and wonder at the fanciful names of cities across America.

Time magazine further opened Raymond's eyes about the political events in America, especially in Washington, DC. When Raymond was in junior high school, he and his younger brother would save their pocket money until it was enough to buy *Time*, which they patiently took turns reading multiple times. When savings did not add up, they were both highly motivated to walk miles to the library just so they could read their favorite magazine. Ultimately, it became the catalyst for Raymond Karr's dream of one day living in Washington, DC.

When the Eastern Airlines Boeing 727, a much smaller aircraft that Raymond Karr boarded at New York's LaGuardia airport landed at DC National airport after just one hour flight, a next on the taxi line cab with a heavy-set African-American female driver with a deep feminine voice, one of Raymond's initial surprises, drove him to 13th & G Streets, the original campus of Strayer University. His already super love fest with his newfound land deepened. Never mind the jet lag, the chilling temperature, the rip off from the Lincoln Continental driver, who gave him back a ten dollar bill after conning him into signing over his five hundred-dollar travelers check for the luxury ride from JFK to LaGuardia. To hell with all. Raymond Karr was in Washington, DC, for Christ's sake – the home of the President of the United States of America, and the seat of global politics. He started to relish the notion that he was breathing in the same air space with Mr. President.

Everything Raymond read from *Time* magazine during his early teens was coming to mind in bits and pieces – the finely defined rotunda of the colossal Capitol Hill, the coveted White House, Presidents Nixon and Ford, Watergate, Thomas P. (Tip) O'Neil, Governor Reagan, Bob Dole of Kansas, the Iran hostage saga, the Camp David accords. He remembered one of the many fascinating stories he read in *Time* about the outcome of the US presidential election, headlined 'Kissinger Out, Vance In.' The article went on to narrate the choice of then President-elect Carter to replace Secretary of State Henry Kissinger with his own choice, Cyrus Vance, to head the State Department.

The article was of keen interest to Raymond Karr because he never appreciated Gerald Ford's taking over the office from Richard Nixon and he was glad to see President Ford defeated by Jimmy Carter. But that was purely for a childish and nonsensical reason that President Ford's first name, Jerry, was also the first name of one of Raymond Karr's secondary school team leaders, or 'prefects', as they dubbed it, whom he passionately resented because of his pompous attitude and heavy handedness.

Moreover, back in the '70's, Nigeria was constantly plagued by military coup d'etat. He naively felt that Vice President Ford duplicitously plotted to kick Nixon out of office to become president over a 'minor issue' he had read about regarding secret taping of the opposition party at the Watergate hotel in Washington, DC. For that, he never warmed up to President Ford. But one quote by the ex-president constantly amused him and that was his humorous "I'm a Ford not a Lincoln" statement when he took office. That resentment lingered in him until he came to the United States to surprisingly learn the ex-president was actually a mild-mannered gentleman conservative and played football in college.

Equally fascinating to him was that the 1980 U.S. presidential election was heating up between Ronald Wilson Reagan, then governor of California, and Jimmy Carter, the incumbent president. He was heavily rooting for Ronald Reagan because he felt President Carter's overly pragmatic approach to foreign policy weakened America's resolve in the world. He believed that such weakness led to, among several other developments, the Soviet invasion of Afghanistan with impunity under General Secretary Leonid Ilyich Brezhnev, and Iran under Ayatollah Ruhollah Khomeini forcefully seizing American diplomats in Teheran as hostages without fear of reprisal. Though such a nice person, who ultimately became the first US president to visit Nigeria, he thought Governor Reagan was more poised to deal with such rogue State behavior.

While overly excited Raymond Karr stood on the street corner of the steady Washington traffic reminiscing all of these issues, and he knew he was actually in the most important city in the world, the steadily awakening awesome feeling heightened like his heart was about to melt away into Nirvana. As he'd sometimes phrase it, *oh it felt so bloody damn good it's indescribable.* A few times he comically displayed exuberance that must have aroused suspicion of stage-one insanity. His very first encounter with an actual American in Washington, DC was a mentally unstable sixty-two year old, full bearded African-American man in a rumpled brown suit and purple neck tie, who used his black fedora to solicit donations. Unsuspecting Raymond asked for direction to Strayer University but got an incoherent response from the pan handler. American accent was a great new challenge to him but an appearance of a beggar in a complete suit he found both astonishing and fascinating.

In summing up that incredible moment, Raymond imagined he would beg to differ and cautioning the astronaut who landed in the moon or to the politician who won an election or became president, or others who landed big paying jobs or lucrative movie contracts, to take no offense but he just didn't believe they felt quite like him. His experience, he thought, was the epitome of a love affair with new environment he had found himself in.

Challenges of a constantly changing world eventually tempered Raymond Karr as he began to pursue academic and financial obligations that were necessary for the road to success in America. It was all moving slowly but steadily in the right direction for him, year after year, until the months leading to the fall of 1990, a whole decade since his arrival in the United States.

Chapter 1

Associates

Everything spelled doom and gloom in that awful autumn in the distraught mind of Raymond Karr.

It all began on a windy Sunday evening in early September. The cloudy sky obscured the sun, which was poised for an early setting, with its subtle orange color rays indicating its westerly location and its readiness to vanish for the day. The cold temperature had been unexpectedly harsh from the wind that had been blowing all day, scattering leaves, sometimes in miniature swirls, on the streets and corners of Washington, DC and its suburbs. There had been a slight rainfall around noon but the atmosphere only left a constant hint of more to come, making the case to be handy with an umbrella.

Inside his dimly lit living room, which was his favorite of the newly furnished four-bedroom duplex home, Raymond sat lazily alone on a reclined upholstered chair, legs stretched out and crossed, a toothpick tucked in his thick lips. With a remote control that practically yearned for a new set of batteries, he stretched out his hand and randomly flipped television channels to see if any of the programs could interest him. Occasionally, he would pause to thud the remote control on the floor to energize the batteries then would look around to admire or critic the environment he had single-handedly decorated.

Hanging on the white-painted wall directly facing him was a brilliant color photograph of the White House Rose Garden, which always fascinated him, and on the wall behind him a large Nelson Mandela portrait he usually glanced at whenever he needed to be inspired. With lifeless plants that included four pots of red and yellow poinsettia, a pot on each of the four corners of the walls, the living room left a splendiferous impression to anyone who valued the art of interior decor.

Finding nothing of interest to him on television, he frustratingly tossed the remote control on the floor close to the base of his chair, knowing there was a good chance that sooner or later he might be needing it again. He yawned, heaved himself up and checked with the clock on the mantelpiece which struck at six-fifteen p.m.

Sitting back, he joined his fingers at the back of his head and stared blankly at the ceiling, his mind delving into his lackluster success after a decade in the land where he was certain most dreams do come true.

In addition to a season of many woes, he was thinking, particularly the loss of a close football game by his beloved Washington Redskins, he was in a desperate search for any other form of entertainment and that prospect too seemed virtually unattainable. He knew he was financially restrained and earlier when he checked his pocket, he counted only eleven dollars and some loose change, which could only hold him until the middle of the week.

Last Friday, he had received an official letter from his bank warning him of an overdraft fee that had left his checking account in the red. He had felt slightly relieved that the bank at least honored the check. But when he settled down to assess his prospect for an income, it dawned on him that he had no realistic hope of balancing his checkbook anytime soon. His only bank account could be in jeopardy and he might never be able to cash checks without having to pay a fee, which was the only reason he had struggled very hard to maintain the account.

He had also been deserted by Rebecca, his thirty-year-old live-in lover, who three days ago had packed up and left. She took their eight-month-old boy, Charles, as well as Shawna, her seven-year-old daughter from a previous relationship. They had quarreled as usual, and he had nagged her over sloppiness, but this time she had decided she had had it up to her chin and felt it was time to spit for good.

Occasionally, Raymond's remorseful mind would shift to Rebecca. She was sloppy and she was a convenience taker. She would use household items and carelessly toss them away, often where Raymond had to search for some time before finding them. It was one of several bad habits he so disliked about her, but to hell with all. He was now dearly missing everyone. Sure she nagged constantly, he thought, and her mouth was the sharpest object since the invention of razor blade, but he wanted her back.

But most urgently of all, he needed to make a fast break at some dough and soon.

The constantly revolving world of agony seemed to be awfully near the breaking point following the Redskins loss, which always set him off in a bad mood. Two weeks earlier, his tenant pal, James, had traveled overseas, promising to introduce him to a business that would brighten his financial future upon his return.s

"What you need is a business trip with me. You're a masquerade of a man befitting of immense wealth, therefore shouldn't have to be poor. I'll take you along with me one of these days," he had said to Raymond during one of their many discussions on how best to achieve financial success.

Raymond always thought about it, but what business and why dodge the answer whenever he asked? He was certain James fully understood his limits as far as setting up a legitimate racket was concerned, as well as his moral limitations. James also was very much aware of a no-gimmicks status that surrounded his financial obligations.

Raymond's real problem was that he was heavily indebted with medical bills, utilities bills, and a staggering two months behind in his mortgage payment, therefore was in no mood for futility. His ultimate ambition to gain admission into George Washington University medical school was still a driving force in his life, but that too was gradually fading away before his very own eyes.

All his thoughts at the moment variably hovered on how to salvage his numerous fiscal challenges, ignoring the CBS *Sixty Minutes* program on television. The import-export arrangement with a Swiss company was looking like his only shot at raising the funds for GW Medical. However, waiting on that to materialize into profit, he knew, was like sowing an apple seed and waiting to harvest its fruits. It always depressed him whenever he deliberated on the time and probability of succeeding in the racket.

While in deep thought, he fell asleep and had a nightmarish déjà vu dream that caused him to shake himself awake. In the dream, he had been playing a soccer game with his friends of his teenage years at their favorite field, which belonged to the college of education near his home. The usual wild twist in dreams had occurred whereby all of a sudden, all his playmates had vanished and he found himself stranded in the middle of the field watching horrifyingly as Oleander plants grew rapidly around him. He had tried to run home only to find he was hopelessly impeded as the poisonous plants had metastasized throughout the soccer field, worst of all encroaching harrowingly like savage zombies.

He now stood in the middle of a dangerous field. Field of Oleander.

When he awoke, he reminisced the first time he had the same dream. He was a young and naïve fourteen-year-old, vulnerable with all the flawed characters of unruly adolescents. Along with his colleagues, he was debuting in knuckle headedness, well past the experimenting ages of scorching harmless insects and stray frogs. They escaped dormitories to attend movies at the theater, whiled away crucial study times to talk about girls and daydreamed of sexual encounters with hot chicks in the neighborhood, quarreled over who held the bragging right of nailing a new dame, sometimes fist-fought over checker games.

He vividly recollected that he had drifted into convulsion because he had let himself ride the dream along and Oleander trees outgrew his height and began to converge like monsters to attack him. His mother, Ma Lucy, awoken by the noise of his loud murmuring, had hurriedly switched on the light and rushed to his bedside. She had observed his fixated eyes looking dull and lifeless and had violently shaken him awake with a big scream for neighbors to help in the wee hours of the morning. Nurse Beatrice next door, the hospital's resident anesthetist, thirtyish and fair complexioned, though heavy set was curvaceous and attractive with a flat stomach, had just returned from an emergency call and had heard Ma Lucy's scream, and rushed in to inquire and offer help. Because she was single Raymond had often daydreamed of sex with her.

Since there was no medical interpretation or diagnosis, only fever, Ma Lucy resorted to intense prayers to counter its lingering aftereffects of mini hallucinations.

Acting upon the advice of one of the family friends, Ma Lucy had reluctantly consulted the town's soothsayer, a lanky old man with discoloring veins throughout and a bulging Adam's apple who, after telling her it was a subtle sign of a bad future occurrence, dutifully admonished Raymond. "Choose your associates carefully, son," he had said in a rattling high-pitched voice and cleared his throat, which he seemed to be doing at the end of every sentence. He then charged Ma

Lucy a yam tuber and two cobs of raw maize for his service.

Raymond, waking up to a similar bad dream, harbored some doubts that in his adulthood, strong and tested, was going into the same hallucination as when he was young and cowardly to ghost stories, had he not forced himself to wake up. Nonetheless, he felt glad to have awoken rather than chancing it.

But just as when the dream had first occurred, he awoke with the same surreal feeling – cold sweat, slight fever that evaporated immediately, and the feeling of blood rushing to his head.

Now wide awake and shaking off the bad dream, irking loneliness returned to claim a better part of his evening.

Determined not to give up the quest for at least a brighter evening, he knew he'd have to reach out and touch someone. He dragged the telephone with its long cord to his chair and called up his best pal, Dennis. It went to voicemail. Disappointed, he reluctantly left a message that he had called.

Just as he was about to doze off again a surprising solid knock came from the door. It was a moment of uncertainty for him, but nonetheless a welcoming feeling. He sprang up and, walking halfway to the door, he stood still to wonder. For a wound-leaking quiet evening of a Redskins loss in the little suburban town of Riverdale and the entire nation's capital, who might that be?

His curiosity half evaporated when he suspected Dennis could be the possible guest. He lazily walked to the door and the moment he peeped through the pinhole, there stood the spoken about devil. Just what he needed at the moment. What a great relief, he thought.

"Commissioner!" Dennis said with visible enthusiasm. The nickname 'Commissioner' was their own affectionate name for each other.

"Commissioner, I just hung up the phone on your answering machine," Raymond said. As he held the door open by its knob, a sudden cold wind surged in against the panel, forcing him to hold firm as he opened and waited for Dennis to step inside.

"Oh really? I tried calling but got busy signals. I was wondering if you'd found a new sweetheart and gotten busy with her," Dennis said with an inquisitive look in his eyes.

Dennis was dressed to kill. Six feet, slim to average weight, light brown skin and a noticeable square jaw, he was handsome with a touch of flamboyance in him that always seemed to vanish in the presence of women. He wore a gray flannel suit and an off-white-colored silk shirt. A silver broach pinned his slim black tie against his shirt, giving him an image of a playboy. His shiny black Giorgio Brutini shoes matched perfectly and caught Raymond's attention. His mood was unusually upbeat for a Sunday evening when the Cowboys had just left town and stolen a victory in RFK stadium. He made straight to the chair, his attention admiringly focused on the new coffee table Raymond had just squeezed out of a ten-month layaway plan.

He sat down on the loveseat.

"Big Masquerade! Now, that's what I call a real beauty. How come you haven't told me about this?" Dennis said, bending forward to inspect the clay base and glass-top coffee table.

Both friends were Ibos, and their tribesmen often used the term "Masquerade" in elevating one's social status. Masquerades in the Ibo land were believed to possess supernatural powers, mythical as it may sound. And so when a person was deemed to have achieved something extraordinary, that person was praised and called a masquerade.

"I told you about this November last year when I first made a down payment on it," Raymond said.

"Oh yeah, I remember! I'll get me one exactly like this, but it'll have to be in another week or two," Dennis said, stood up and reached out to feel the clay-like, rectangular piece that supported the chrome. "This is a real masterpiece," he said and ran his fingers around the edge of the glass.

He sat back on the loveseat and loosened his tie. He remained silent for a moment, his mind busy thinking. Can't wait to show off my house in just a couple of weeks, he said in his mind. He had dreams of his own and now surely a way to achieve those dreams. But at the moment he'd keep it to himself, knowing if he bragged publicly and fell short in the end, his prestige was sure to follow.

Raymond brightened the chandelier to the max and it further

exposed the beauty of the entire newly decorated living room. He took pride in the decoration but sometimes regretted spending a better portion of his meager income to achieve it.

The home was Raymond Karr's first real taste of the American dream. Actually, it was a desperate search for recognition from critics, and to rekindle the diminishing respect of friends and relatives who expected better from him. It sort of quelled the lingering narrative out there that somehow his much-talked-about ambition to attend George Washington Medical School was doomed. He felt aggrandized by the temporary 'masquerade' achievement of obtaining a mortgage for his own home.

But he was well aware that all was about to go down the drain, barring some kind of divine intervention of which hitting the lottery jackpot would be a prayed for one of it.

With four bedrooms and one and a half baths, the three-level, English colonial had a large, concrete outdoor space for four cars to park. Adjacent to the car park was a half-court for basketball. The ground level had a ten-foot-high ceiling and a fireplace on the corner that separated the living room from the dining room, for Raymond Karr, an intoxicating possession. He had a wall-to-wall, peach-colored rug installed to match the set of tan furniture, and pairs of white window curtains with peach-colored lace between to complement the rug. To him, the house became a golden anchor for all of his emotions, pride, and priced possessions.

When the talk about the beauty of the house lost its priority, Raymond stood up and went straight to the kitchen for beer without asking his guest, for he knew it was a sure favorite. He stood in the middle of the kitchen and savagely batted down a fly that had been nagging him all day long. He frantically searched around, hoping it was a hit. Twice since the morning, he had been determined to kill it but whenever he armed himself with a rolled stack of newspapers, it seemed to vanish into thin air.

Finding nothing that looked like a dying fly, he sighed in disappointment, gave up his search and opened the refrigerator, concluding the fly was simply too stealthy for him. Lucky bastard, he had thought, you must have read the deadly writing on the wall.

He grabbed two Heineken beers by their bottlenecks and went

back to find Dennis playing a fetch-the-tennis ball game with Ogu, his friendly Cocker-Spaniel-Labrador mix breed. At the sight of the beer bottles, Dennis immediately abandoned the dog to sit back at his chair and complimented.

"A host who brings beer brings life," he said in their native language, a traditional overture by guests when presented with any form of welcoming refreshment, usually local cola nuts.

A sudden gesture as that from him after years of blending in a Western cultural environment further assured Raymond he was up to something, perhaps intriguing.

Raymond resisted the temptation to strike up a conversation about the big game loss. It had emotionally flattened him and adding salt to injury, he had no doubt that it would dominate the news outlets all week, making it a particularly long week. He knew he'd have to skip his favorite Channel Seven evening news since the anchorwoman, a diehard Dallas fan, was sure to rob it all in during newscast. In Raymond's honest opinion, Dennis and he should've been in it together but it was apparent from Dennis' upbeat mood that Raymond stood alone in the agony of the defeat.

Dennis took one of the green bottles from Raymond's hand. At twenty-seven, Dennis had developed a ferocious appetite for drinking beer, and had often been jailed for either driving under the influence or assault and battery charges against his gorgeous Jamaican-born girlfriend who, for some reason, had found him irreplaceable. They had met three years earlier at a friend's bachelor party.

Astonishingly, Dennis didn't have a beer gut. His flat belly and athletic features gave him an ultra-masculine physique.

"Ogu… out!" Raymond commanded the dog, pointing at the staircase that led to the bedrooms.

Ogu was just about grasping the Ibo tribal name Raymond had chosen to call him since he adopted the playful dog from a Filipina a few months back. She had named him Solomon but Raymond renamed him Ogu the Ibo tribe's pagan god of justice and ingenuity.

The dog sat still, panting, ears upright, and staring curiously at Raymond as if it was about to learn a new trick.

"Ogu let's go!" Raymond said and paced toward the staircase.

Ogu quickly jumped on the staircase and outran Raymond to the top of the nine steps while Raymond barely crossed the third. Ogu sat patiently by the closed door leading to the master bedroom and waited until Raymond came and opened. Ogu rushed inside and Raymond quickly shut the door behind him and went back downstairs to find Dennis already killing the remnant of his beer.

"Commissioner, you know you're a big masquerade, the refrigerator is always stocked up with goodies," Raymond said courteously.

"Ah huh, that's just what the doctor ordered," Dennis gestured and immediately stood up to take him up on his offer.

Raymond picked up his beer from the coffee table and went to the entertainment center. While sipping, he flickered the knob of the television set, unsure of what channel to choose.

"It's been a hell of a boring evening, we staying indoors tonight?" Raymond said inquisitively as Dennis was on his way back from the kitchen, fresh beer on hand.

"Hell no," Dennis said and paused to light a cigarette with a pack of matchsticks he searched out of his breast pocket. "Kilimanjaro Night Club would be re-visited tonight." He paused again, waved off the light on the matchstick and took a long drag. He then slightly angled his head away from Raymond and blew out a long string of smoke. "I liked what I saw last Sunday night."

"Did you catch any bird?" Raymond pressed.

"No, not exactly but I'm tracking one and she's likely to show up at the club tonight."

"How did you figure that?"

"From a reliable source."

"How reliable is this source, Dennis?"

Dennis, seemingly in a mental calculation of something, became silent for a few moments while Raymond finally settled for *America's Funniest Videos* on television. Usually, Raymond would always be in the forefront of discussion about women, and the first to suggest weekend night-out. But the deluge of financial handicap had taken over his every thought. Dennis, who never failed to have money problems of his own, strangely had assumed the forefront of spending money at the night club. Otherwise, why did he appear so confident?

"Do you remember the bartender at the Heritage hall?" Dennis said.

"Yes," Raymond said immediately and folded himself to listen.

"Well, I overheard her promise him she would come back this Sunday with her girlfriend whom he is madly interested in."

Raymond rubbed his chin. He knew that regardless of the situation, he would have no choice or, for that matter, a better alternative, and he simply submitted to the night-out at the Kilimanjaro.

"Commissioner, I'm down to my last ten bucks. I'm not sure I'd go fishing tonight," Raymond said, walking back across to the sofa to sip on his beer.

"Don't worry. I think I can cover us just in case we make a double catch," Dennis said.

"I'll have to shower and get dressed, but for now please continue with merry-making," Raymond said, heading for the staircase.

"Wait a minute," Dennis called out," There's something I'd like to tell you before you go up."

Raymond paused, already on the first step, still holding his beer.

"Or do you want to shower first?" He carefully placed his beer on the coffee table, his face suddenly discolored. He knew he had just jumped ahead of himself, something he just didn't want to do with his new secret plan to catapult himself into the labyrinth of wealth. At least not at the moment. But he was becoming too excited to hold it in, a nature so indicative of him. A secret in him was like a warm in the mouth.

Raymond carefully weighed his options, but just when he was about to decide, Dennis beat him to it.

"All right, why don't you just go ahead and we'll talk after," Dennis said, reaching for the pack of cigarettes in his breast pocket.

Raymond said okay and leisurely climbed up the stairs, thinking along the way. As soon as he opened the bedroom door, Ogu excitedly jumped on him.

It took Raymond well over half hour to shower and dress to his satisfaction. In the course of final touches, he was just about to pick up the Heineken beer when the phone rang. He picked up the receiver and Ma Lucy, his mother's tender, loving voice came on the line. His mother routinely called him every Sunday ever since she left to live with his younger brother, Eddy, whose furniture rental company had transferred him to Lexington Park.

"How are you, dear?" Ma Lucy said, speaking in Ibo.

"I'm quite fine, Ma. I had planned to call you after dinner, how are you?"

"Well, I'll be fine as soon as I learn you were in church today," she said and laughed.

Ma Lucy's laughter did not fool him. He knew his mother well enough to know she was very serious. Ma Lucy's main concern was always to be sure he attended church regularly. A devout Catholic with a righteous personality, she was the first wife of a polygamist. She had six children altogether, with the first three girls and the second three boys. Raymond was the first of the three sons, and she had always wished he would be the most successful, a wish she was afraid, but certain, kept slipping away.

"I went to church in the morning," Raymond lied and instantly hated himself. He had exaggerated and misrepresented in the past but lying to Ma Lucy about religion was way out of line. He smacked his forehead and in his mind called himself a stinking liar.

"Very good, my son… is Rebecca back yet?" she said.

Raymond had telephoned his brother, Eddy, the following day and hinted him about Rebecca's departure, and he had apparently informed Ma Lucy.

"No Ma, how's Eddy and his family?"

"They're all fine. But I'd like to know why she left. You know she has your son, who is also my grandson, so it's not a matter you can simply brush aside," she said.

Ma Lucy always wanted all members of the Karr family to be together, something that eluded her. There had been the usual breakdown typical of a polygamous family that left her with the sole responsibility of all six children. It must have been awfully difficult but miraculously she was able to see all through college, aided only with constant prayer, and an excellent nursing career that finally rewarded her with a position as a Superintendent of Nursing. The Karr children had their fair share of good parental nurturing from her alone, and on the down side, she had lost her last born.

Feeling the heat, Raymond decided it was time to end the conversation.

"Ma, why don't I call you tomorrow on this…I have a guest waiting downstairs and we were just on our way out the door when you called."

Raymond and Ma Lucy tossed the issue around for a minute or so before finally settling on Raymond calling her the next morning.

Replacing the receiver, Raymond picked up his beer and gulped the remnants of it, trashed the empty bottle, then continued with his grooming for a fishing night at the Kilimanjaro Night Club.

Having admired himself from the standing mirror, and satisfied his outfit was sure to turn heads, he picked up the pack of Wrigley spearmint gum he had left on the headboard compartment.

He found Ogu sleeping by the fireplace. Dennis was still drinking and smoking. He suspected Dennis was almost impatiently awaiting his return despite Dennis' eyes that were fixated at the television. Dennis cleared his throat four times, he counted, before breaking the silence.

"You really took your time getting ready, what took you so long?"

He explained how Ma Lucy had telephoned and had delayed him, and how she had tried to engage him in a prolonged conversation about his common-law's sudden departure.

There were six empty bottles of Heineken beer on the coffee table and one three-quart full which Dennis was sipping on. He dragged the last of his cigarette, examined it before crushing it on the full ashtray.

Dennis "Green Bottle" Metu also smoked a lot. Four years back, both men roomed for two years in a two-bedroom apartment high-rise in Adelphi. Their living room was constantly filled with smoke from his cigarettes, something Raymond did not miss upon separation. Dennis had tried at the beginning of every year to quit, but each attempted resolution had been handily defeated.

"Were you trying to tell me something?" Raymond said, now eager to hear what Dennis had to say.

"Yes, Commissioner, but I'd been thinking. We've been friends for a long time and I think I know you too well to rush you into something of this nature." He paused to smoke and looked at his wristwatch, blew away a heavy smoke then continued. "I know you'll strongly oppose, so there may not be any need for me to tell you about this."

Raymond noticed Dennis' uneasiness. His hunch hinted that Dennis' secret disclosure may have something to do with breaking the law, but he decided to listen anyway. After all, it was the same Dennis he knew so well that could hardly hold back on an exciting prospect. When they were roomies, once Dennis had received a letter of invitation to interview with the Law Offices of Sullivan, Leichtman & Goldstein as a mailroom supervisor. He trumpeted and showed the letter to every human he encountered but in the end, failed to land the job. Raymond had a quick flashback of another time when Dennis was accepted to drive one of Barwood's fleet of taxis, arguably the most prestigious such organization in the nation's capital. The news nearly pierced the eardrum of the hearing impaired.

So, Raymond knew if this was a legitimate deal, Dennis could barely hold back.

"There's an exploratory deal that I want to involve myself in," Dennis said and paused to light another cigarette with the one he had smoked down. "I don't want to reveal the details until I come back successfully. It'll have to involve a trip to Nigeria. If I asked you to join me now, you may discourage me somewhere down the line, and I don't want to be discouraged. So don't worry until I come back from this experimental deal," he said as he stubbed out the cigarette.

"Well, when are you leaving?"

"Tuesday…"

"Flight ticket?"

"Yup, everything is already fixed."

Dennis took out two Nigerian passports from his breast pocket, each tucked in the middle with a Nigerian Airline ticket. He held them up for Raymond to see, seemingly unwilling to surrender them for close examination.

"How come you have two passports?" Raymond said, his forehead wrinkled as he corner-eyed Dennis.

Dennis calculated his thoughts, turned his back at Raymond, before responding as he slowly walked away. "One of them is for someone who particularly asked me not to disclose this to you." Four steps away, he paused again with one hand in his side pocket and the other holding a cigarette, he turned to face Raymond. "Let me not dishonor the promise I made to him entirely. Let this issue stop right here. Don't mention it to anyone else."

Raymond promised and made no further inquiry. He didn't like the prospect, and he stood still while Dennis grabbed his beer and sipped, avoiding the curious look from his eyes. He felt no need for further questions, realizing Dennis uncharacteristically had probably made up his mind not to reveal any further detail until later.

Raymond cleared the empty bottles on the coffee table while Dennis chain-smoked. It was easy for him to predict the "exploratory deal" had shades clouding all over it. Dennis had never discussed a business initiative with him since they met seven years ago.

A part-time undergraduate student at the University of the District of Columbia, Dennis had been a full-time taxi driver, and knew nothing other than to drive his cab, go to school and party on weekends. The least available chance on a weekday was utilized for beer consumption. He was as kind to other people as he was to himself. He was often victimized by being excessively kind, having been ripped off several times. On one memorable instance, he fell prey to a concerted effort by a group of individuals who claimed to be in transit of an on-going vacation, who robbed him. He had accommodated all four of them overnight free of charge, and when they left, he lost his three-hundred-dollar gold chain, six hundred dollars in cash, and an Italian suit worth eight hundred. The agony of such experience could straighten up anyone but excessively kind and trusting Dennis Metu.

For the first few weeks after his ordeal, he became wary of strangers but eventually eased back to the good old all-too-kind, all-too-trusting Dennis that he was before. He couldn't help but consider it an insult to monitor his guests.

Raymond's unsettling mind hovered around Dennis' business initiative with a lingering sense of disappointment as he was gathering the empty bottles to be trashed in the kitchen's waste basket. His instinct cautioned him to be careful as Dennis probably sensed the wariness in him.

"Let's go," Raymond said as he wiped his hands with a paper towel.

Dennis stood up, picked up his beer and gulped down the remnants of what was left, then walked toward the kitchen to trash the empty bottle. Raymond stood by the front exit door, waiting to turn off the light. He held the door open and waited patiently like a doorman when Dennis came back from the kitchen. As Raymond was about leave, he switched off the light and shut the door, then leisurely walked outside.

The effect of a slight drizzling rain diminished Raymond's enthusiasm for the night-out. He loved rain at night but not before a night-out. To him it discouraged most girls from coming out, for he loved it when the girls crowded the nightclubs. Conversely, Dennis preferred fewer people for a different reason. There was always a chance one or two hot chicks might show up and fewer guys, if any, would show up to compete with him.

Raymond stuck his hand out to feel and gauge the strength of the rain. Satisfied an umbrella was unnecessary, he followed Dennis. Although it was barely raining, the atmosphere felt discouraging to him. If he weren't in the company of Dennis, he would have been tempted to cancel the night out. But his best pal was there to lighten up the ambiance.

The drive to Kilimanjaro night club, which was located in Adams Morgan area of DC's Upper Northwest, took about twenty minutes or so from Riverdale. The traffic flowed steadily and most Washingtonians, as always when the Redskins lose to Cowboys, stayed home to grieve. Dennis drove his girlfriend's '86 Chevy Camaro. Old but meticulously cleaned, the ride still maintained its sharp, sporty design, at least enough to instill confidence in both men.

The time on the dashboard clock struck at eight fifteen p.m. How he crooked the car out of her without her demanding to come along remained a mystery, but he usually did.

On their way, both men completely avoided the subject of an exploratory deal that Dennis had brought up, focusing only on the fun they were about to have at the nightclub.

"Do you think it's gonna be crowded at the club? Because I really wouldn't want to have to compete with any guy if I hook up with a honey," Raymond had said.

"I think it will be crowded with women so you wouldn't have to compete with anyone," Dennis had replied, a vague assurance Raymond knew but was encouraged by it anyway.

"As long as there's no bad-ass-mustache dude intervening, I'm good," Raymond said.

His hate for competition over women had begun to swell. He always caved easily, especially when the competitor was a mixed race African-American. Worse if the dude spotted a well-groomed mustache.

Dennis had laughed with mockery and had stared hard at Raymond. "One thing you really should quit doing is giving up easily. I'm telling you, girls aren't like that. It's whoever raps better. Men are all eyes but women are all ears. Ever heard of that?"

"It's not always the case, Dennis, I remember some time ago when I thought I was Romeo among three beautiful gals until a bad ass mustache dude showed up. I tried to compete but was treated like a humorless clown. I'm never gonna make a fool out of myself again, boy it was so embarrassing I had to scam."

"Did you ask any of them for her number?"

"I asked one of them. She gave me a number all right, to AT&T's cold lady."

Dennis had laughed hard in amusement. At one point they had been forced to a stop by a red traffic light. Dennis had sighed in frustration as he brought the Camaro to an abrupt stop. A late model BMW sedan had pulled next to the Camaro, also stopped by the red light. Both men had noticed the pleasurable spectacle then eyed each other. The Beemer was packed with four attractive black chicks. The girls, also driven by curiosity, had all looked inside the Camaro and, finding its contents unworthy of their time, quickly looked away. Dennis had been infuriated but managed to maintain a posture of indifference. Raymond had felt inferior all along.

When the light turned green, Dennis had dragged the Beemer into a road race. After a hotly contested speed maneuver, Dennis swerved the Camaro in front of the Beemer with braising close call, scaring the female driver into unnerving concession. Raymond, who had remained silent all through but inwardly approved Dennis' showmanship, saw the feeling of satisfaction in Dennis's quick mockery smile.

Afterwards, Dennis thumbed in the car's cigarette lighter and searched his breast pockets for the pack. Finding it, he lit one, replaced the lighter, let out a string of smoke from his nostril and inserted a Bob Marley cassette inside the tape. Raymond resisted the temptation to reach out and decrease the volume. Dennis, sensing Raymond wasn't too comfortable with the blasting of the reggae tune, gestured by twisting slightly the volume control and drove on, partly humming and partly singing off key.

Approaching Columbia Road, Dennis turned off the music and the loss of a big game by the Redskins dominated the rest of their discussion en route to the Kilimanjaro Night Club.

Some of the bitterness Raymond felt from the game loss were gradually dissipating, thanks to the enthusiasm of going to the night club for "bird watching."

Chapter 2

A DAMNING PROPOSITION

James Duru, Raymond's tenant-buddy who had just returned from his business trip abroad, awoke Raymond at three-thirty early morning, tapping three times on his left leg. Coming into the supposedly empty house, not knowing James had been back and was asleep in his own room, Raymond, too tired and lazy to climb the ten flight of stairs to his bedroom, decided to rest for a few minutes before carrying himself up. When he had unlocked his door and came inside, he turned on the light, switched on the television and crashed on the sofa, not minding what program or channel the set was showing. The last thing he remembered was switching off the light and taking off his shoes.

It had been a long, hard-partying Saturday night at a friend's house. He had had a great time, although the well-behaved ladies, mostly Africans, hardly drank alcohol and were overcrowded by overly aggressive drunken men by almost a four-to-one margin. And so there was no luck with the women.

Two African-American ladies had attended the party among few others but were closely held by their jealous and overprotective Nigerian boyfriends, who were fully aware that Nigerian men invariably were known to be predatory toward other guys' girlfriends. No way in hell they'd chance it with the bastard hyenas, one of them had vowed to the other. He wasn't to be blamed. When it came to women, Nigerians tended to move faster than their shadows. Such feeling of insecurity was prevalent in the African community and both men knew they also bore some guilt of such abhorrent behavior that was deemed a social anathema.

The only white girl, a short and fat, freckle-faced German in her late twenties, was the hot freak of the night. She wore a black strapless evening gown with cuts on both sides that exposed her bare legs up to her thighs. Her shoulder length golden blond hair was well-groomed and the firm bra she wore made her full breasts puff out provocatively like they were about to explode. Her attractiveness seemed to have increased as gradually as the party alcohol decreased.

When Raymond had initially observed her as she arrived at the party, she was shy and stood alone in one corner sipping her drink from a cocktail glass. But as the evening wore down and more intoxicated men began to show tremendous interest, her feminine flair erupted as she drew more and more attention. When she had noticed her stock was riding sky high, she called shots and felt like a queen bee. Raymond had stood no chance. She wasn't his type anyway, he had consoled himself, then paused to examine her sexuality. Or was she? Well…unless somehow, she accidentally wound up on his bed and left it carelessly. One-night stands could be fun-filled sometimes.

But unlimited supply of booze, as well as hilarious humor made out of riddles and jokes among friends, old and new, dominated the evening, and for the most part made carousing with girls somewhat irrelevant. Raymond, who had a few drinks of his own, just about his limit of four Heineken bottles, was still worn out from the dusk to daybreak dance party, and when he returned to his home at a few minutes past one o'clock the next morning, he was barely standing on his two feet.

Blood rushed to his head and his heart thumped as he sprang up to the creeping tap he felt on his leg. He shook his head awake while blinking off the fog in his eyes, before he recognized James's boyish round face. James substituted for a pajamas a plain white bed sheet he wrapped around his body which he tied at the back of his neck, a ghostly appearance given the only source of light came from the television.

"James!" Raymond said, reaching out for a handshake as he struggled to stand up.

"Ray Ray," James said jokingly and firmly shook Raymond's hand. "Ray the Karr man, the only Karr owner in Washington, DC and vicinity. You're the reigning masquerade, my friend."

"That's right," Raymond responded. "You were supposed to call me from the airport to pick you up. How did you handle the ride problem?" Raymond said, inwardly relieved that in the end he didn't have to worry about the laborious commitment of a long drive to Dulles airport, a good half hour trip to Chantilly, Virginia.

Ever since James had requested a ride from Raymond for when he arrived back from his travel and he had no choice than to accept, it had kept him on an edge to lookout for that dreadful phone call. Sometimes it even annoyed him outright that James would dare ask for such a laborious favor. But they were friends and had a good landlord-tenant relationship. After all what are friends for, Raymond had thought to himself, and that had helped somewhat in tempering his ambivalence.

James parted Dennis' hand as if it had bitten him. "I had to catch a taxi," he said unevenly as he went to turn on the light.

Both men sat down on the sofa and turned to face each other.

Ogu emerged from the kitchen, panting profusely and wagging its tail. Two weeks had passed since it had seen James, who had become fond of the friendly dog. James had moved in six months ago from a neighboring apartment complex following a court order to oust him for rent delinquency. He had come to Raymond on the recommendation of a mutual friend, and Raymond had agreed to rent him one of the bedrooms at a fee he could comfortably afford. He had become a part of the family.

Shrewd, sometimes overly ambitious, average height with a pot belly and light chocolate complexion, James had come to the United States fifteen years earlier to attend college. Just one year after his arrival, he had inquired and discovered that the easiest means of obtaining a green card was to be married to an American. He had vacillated, especially since both of his parents, along with the elders in his village, who attended his send-off party and donated generously in the hopes of him succeeding on behalf of the village, had succinctly cautioned him to stay miles away from American women. First, they'd lure him into a relationship that would cost the village one of its sons of hope and then they'd lock him down with marriage, and that would be all she wrote, they feared.

He had found that he could pay for a fake marriage with no strings attached. He'd quickly get a divorce upon receiving his green card, after all no one should be forced to stay in a matrimony plagued with irreconcilable differences. He had decided the benefit outweighed the risk and had taken two thousand dollars of his tuition funds to pay for the arranged marriage.

Through a close friend, he was introduced to Renee DeGrasse, a runaway preacher's daughter struggling to be independent from strict parenthood. She had jumped on it for the money and the deal was sealed. Although she was shapeless with an ugly face, she had firm big breasts, which was her only chance of attracting a man. But she never flaunted it. When the Justice of the Peace had told him to kiss her the day they exchanged vows at the municipal building, they had reluctantly touched bodies for the first time. He had felt her softness and kind of liked it. Then one day when she came to pick up the second installment of her three payments, he had been lured by the dangling of her braless breasts and he was completely taken. Sex had hit the spot, instantly igniting the flame of love and infatuation. The epiphany had caused him to move his marriage program from the column of *Sham* to that of *Real*.

They were separated at the time he came to live in Raymond's home, thirteen years after marriage.

Ogu placed its forelegs on James' knees, attempting to lick his hands as he was stroking the dog back and forth on its belly.

"So tell me, how was your journey?" Raymond curiously inquired.

"Wonderful…. Wonderful indeed, I had so much fun in Nigeria, man. That country is so much fun if you have money, especially Lagos."

"Wow, big masquerade. Business-wise, did you say you went on a business trip?" Raymond said, brushing Ogu aside as James stood up and stepped closer to him.

"Yes, Ray. I don't want us to discuss that aspect right now. I'd like to brief you on that during the day, but for now, let's just say that suffering may be virtually over. I think I may have blazed the trail of wealth."

Raymond, although would have preferred to dig right into that subject, made no further inquiry. But he was encouraged by James' acknowledgment of a successful business he presumed would benefit him financially.

Both men discussed the beauty of Lagos, the poor economic condition of Nigeria, and girls for well over half hour before returning upstairs to their respective bedrooms. Raymond went to the closet, undressed and tossed his clothes on the floor. Changing into his night clothes, he heard James' footsteps and then a gentle tap on the door.

"Ray-Ray?" James said.

"It's open, come right in," Raymond said as he walked toward the door.

James cautiously opened the door and immediately shook Raymond's waiting hand, his left hand securely holding the plain white bed sheet he had wrapped around him.

"I just couldn't wait to give you this," James said and handed Raymond a brown paper bag.

Raymond reached inside the bag and took out a black and gold custom-made traditional hat. His jaw dropped in elation as he examined the expensive boat-shaped hat which was something he had always wanted to own. James was well aware of that when he was deciding in Nigeria an ideal gift he would surprise his pal with.

"Oh my God," Raymond managed to mumble out of speechlessness and tightly hugged James, who was gladly surprised by how the joy and appreciation Raymond was exhibiting far exceeded his own expectation.

"I'll see you in the morning, Ray, and we'll discuss other equally important issues in detail."

"Man, I just don't know how I can thank you enough. This is marvelous. Thank you very much."

"Don't even mention, man, you deserve better," James said as he exited Raymond's bedroom.

They said goodnight again to each other and Raymond, shutting the door, returned to his bed. Staring blankly at the ceiling, he began to reflect on Dennis' business trip to Nigeria two weeks prior and now prospectively James' business trip to the same country. He also thought carefully of the promises both James and Dennis had respectively made to him, and how pessimism kept creeping into his mind each time.

Raymond woke up late Sunday morning at the loud sound of music James was blasting on the stereo downstairs. Stretching his arms and yawning, he took his watch from the headboard drawer and studied it. It was eleven thirty-three. The sun was shining brightly as its ray cascaded in shades of stripes through the glass window of his bedroom and fell on the upper part of the headboard. He lazily climbed out of the bed, grabbed his robe and stood before the mirror to wipe off the morning eyes. Satisfied, he went out to meet James in the living room. Halfway down the stairs, he was greeted by Ogu, whom he paused to rub its head and belly before proceeding. James sat on the floor selecting his favorite records.

"Good morning, James," Raymond said, feeling the same sense of elation that had lingered in him since he went to bed after seeing Jamse.

"Ah… Ray Ray, 'morning," James said indifferently.

James reached out to the set's knob and lowered the volume of the music.

"Did I wake you up? Was the music too loud?"

"Oh no, it was great."

Raymond really did enjoy the music he woke up to. James played 'Super Trouper' Raymond's very favorite from the Swedish group, ABBA.

On that Sunday, the NFL TODAY television sports program came on at half past noon, its usual time slot on CBS. The Washington Redskins were about to take on the New Orleans Saints, and both Raymond and James were ready to glue themselves to the set. They had finished a late breakfast of scrambled eggs fried with minced onion and sliced tomato. James had prepared it while Raymond set the dishes on the table and vacuumed the rug. They had enjoyed the meal, perhaps out of hunger, chowing it down with white toasts and a choice of tea, orange juice or both. Raymond had had both while James had settled on just the orange juice.

During breakfast, James had purposely restricted their conversation to their sharply divided opinions of the explosive conflict in the Gulf region. Raymond went along but anxious and hopeful that James would finally talk about his successful business trip. Twice Raymond timely caught himself tempted to introduce the subject but each time wisely decided it was best initiated by James.

"As you may already have known, James," Raymond began as he always did on the subject that was beginning to fascinate him, perhaps as much as the Skins game, "the United States had been pouring troops into Saudi Arabia while United Nations debated on resolution six hundred and sixty, the first of a dozen resolutions."

"What's that supposed to do with Saddam occupying Kuwait?" James, whose libertarian view of politics always clouded his judgment said, looking bewildered.

"It would require, among other things, Iraq withdraw unconditionally from Kuwait, and authorize the use of force to free the occupied country, if necessary."

James sighed and simultaneously rolled up his eyeballs. "Oh, c'mon, Ray, you believe Saddam will blink at that? Gimme a break, you really must love this country."

He had previously accused Raymond of being psychologically brainwashed with what he deemed 'white man's mentality' following Raymond's profound endorsement of the Republican Party as more economically productive for America. Raymond's solidarity with the president's military proliferation in the Persian Gulf had convinced him he had been right all along. Their debate ended unresolved, as always, and with a word of caution from James, who often became emotionally anti-America. "Be careful with your biased embrace of this country," he said with a sense of resignation. He paused to wipe his mouth with a sheet of paper towel which he had set on the table before their breakfast. "Be careful when you speak in support of Bush on this issue before anyone else, 'cause Saddam Hussein has promised he would unleash his terrorists on American soil against Americas and their sympathizers."

Suspecting the subject was beginning to cloud the euphoria, Raymond wisely chose to withhold any further comments.

James picked up his almost empty glass of orange juice and bottomed it up. Cupping his hand over his mouth, he belched loudly then cleared the breakfast table and gathered the dishes, before heading to wash them in the kitchen sink. Raymond took out the trash and while at it, walked the dog who tremendously benefitted from the sloppiness, sometimes generosity of the chowing two men.

Finally, they returned to sit in the living room to focus on the football game that had just begun. It was then that James saw the perfect opportunity to explain his successful trip, and ultimately invited Raymond to join him in his next bid.

After listening to James' business trip itinerary, Raymond braced himself and sat bewildered. He could barely conceal his look of disappointment and James read it like a page in a children's book. The deal was to courier illegal drugs from Nigeria to the United States. James talked indirectly, carefully choosing his words, especially when referencing the good to be couriered.

"All you'll need to do is on your way back, bring along the gold dust," James had said repeatedly.

Raymond, typically, never second-guessed what the courier business would involve when James had referred it as gold dust. Otherwise, what else could it possibly mean?

James had sensed accurately that Raymond had a thousand questions, however didn't want to entertain any, at least as of then. It would be too much information to land on a cowardly pragmatist like Raymond. "You bear the responsibility of accepting or rejecting the business offer, Ray," James said, attempting bring the subject to conclusion.

Scoreless after eleven minutes of play, the Redskins defense forced a fumble and recovered at midfield. Raymond jubilantly jumped off the couch where he was seating and high-fived James, who was seating on the arm of the loveseat, his face expressionless.

When Raymond sat back to watch his team's offense at play, James' mind was busy plotting his next move. He had to do more to convince Raymond the risk was worth the take. If he hoped on any success, he'd have to divert Raymond's interest from the game and fill his brain with the logic of shady business. However, if he continued, Raymond's thousand questions could be unleashed on him with strong doubt that he would field all the answers enough to satisfy a Thomas Didymus. He was now in a catch twenty-two. But he was heartened that Raymond had not out-rightly rejected anything, his major concern right from when he realized in Lagos that his own ticket to risk-free wealth ultimately depended upon his ability to successfully recruit others to become couriers.

Raymond, disappointed that his team only scored a field goal with their turnover, focused his thought to James' proposal, staring blankly at the television. *Choose your associates carefully, son*, he instantly recalled from the soothsayer. He had a sudden flashback of his adolescent nightmarish dream that preceded the eerie advice whereby he found himself alone in a field of Oleander poisonous plants.

The flashback was very brief and when he snapped out of it, he turned to James. "Well," he said casually, breaking the silence, "I would've considered taking you up on the offer if it wasn't for my other business engagements." But James knew that he was merely excusing himself and was using his meat business initiative to weasel out.

"Ray, this isn't taking up any of your time for your meat business. We're talking only a couple of weeks and bam you're rich. It's as easy as jumping on board the airplane and flying to Lagos, two weeks stay in Lagos and you're back here to pursue your business. What's not to consider about that?"

Just when Raymond thought he had heard enough mind-bugling information, James made a shocking revelation that sent a chill up his spine. The means to courier over the drug would be by swallowing it inside his intestine.

Raymond suddenly lost interest in the football game and fixed his eyes at James. That was something he had never imagined before. He began to wonder suspiciously what kind of human being James was. He was also wondering if James actually did send illegal and dangerous drugs down his intestine, the same track he gulped down Heineken beer. Or was he just trying to find a sucker who would gamble with his luck and possibly his life, and there was gullible Raymond.

James stood up, cleared his throat three straight times, each with two seconds pause, before excusing himself to go to the bathroom. As he was leaving, he cautioned Raymond to keep their conversation strictly confidential and to carefully think through the business proposal before deciding, knowing fully well he would press on if Raymond said no. Raymond remained silent and managed to re-focus on the still three-point game that was beginning to bore him.

On several occasions, James and Raymond had castigated drug usage and trafficking. They both had chastised the mayor of Washington for his involvement in the highly publicized arrest and prosecution for narcotics usage. As the game was no longer of his preliminary interest, Raymond's thinking began to disseminate to other remedies. Should he find a way to part with him and ask him to move out of his house? He felt that James had essentially become a drug dealer and therefore no longer worthy of his friendship or any kind of relationship whatsoever. He must have been crazy to have let in a criminal like James inside his home, let alone to live there. What if the DEA was staging a sting on James? Sure they'd know he lived there and would arrest everyone in the house. Chances were that they'd find drugs stashed somewhere in the house and certainly would arrest everyone. He'd go to jail and become evening news in Washington, DC for all to digest with their dinner. Friends would ask doubting questions and enemies would gossip.

Raymond began to flirt with a wild thought that James could be mentally unstable. To entangle with a criminal drug gang is crazy in itself but to dare to make that known to his landlord was absurd enough let alone the unthinkable suggestion that he joined him. Otherwise who else with a sane mind would act so irrationally?

That's it, James is definitely insane, Raymond concluded in his thought, and that's no hyperbole. He must kick James out of his house, and the sooner he did it the better. Gone was also his hope of a business trip that would brighten his financial future, at least not from his presumed confidant.

Raymond sat uneasily on the sofa, lost in deep, regretful thought. He had lost all interest in the football game. Ogu panted in from the kitchen with a wagging tail to demand petting strokes but he ignored it. When the dog attempted to jump its forelegs on his laps, he pushed it aside causing it to casually walk back to the kitchen in disappointment.

The sound of the bathroom door unlocking warned him James was about to come back downstairs and he felt his heart thump a little hard. He needed to come up with an immediate response to James' outrageous business proposal. His mind raced to figure out a means to instantly terminate their tenant-landlord relationship. Perhaps it would have to wait a little longer but he felt the urgency to act soon was clear and unambiguous.

James raced down the stairs as if there had been nothing other than the ordinary conversation and, rather than resume his seat on the arm rest, heaved himself in the loveseat. He placed his right leg over the arm rest and hummed a song, his face expressionless. Raymond pretended to be focusing on the game, aware his friendship with him had been inflicted with a lethal poison.

"If the Redskins can't handily defeat New Orleans, they can expect to watch Superbowl from the comfort of their super-luxury mansions," Raymond said wryly, hoping to divert James' attention so he could work on his desired approach to the jaw-dropping outrage he had just heard. James, facing the television and watching without interest, did not respond and kept up his humming. Raymond saw it as the opportunity he needed to think.

His busy mind was interrupted when James stopped his humming. He resisted the temptation to face James, who fired the inevitable question. "So, what is it, buddy, deal or no deal? I guess I should say money or continued poverty... because that's really what the choice is."

Raymond bit hard on his lower lip, turned to look at James, clenching and unclenching his fist in a difficult resistance of the urge to punch him. "Allow me some time to think it over, James," Raymond said with a trace of anger in his voice that surprised James.

James, his eyes now fixed back at the television screen, began to plot an exit strategy. The football game was still only a three-point lead for Washington with six minutes left before the end of third quarter.

With a loss of words to smooth out the menace he knew he had created, he decided to abandon the idea, removed his right leg from the arm rest, and stood up. "I want to take a shower. Can I borrow a soap tablet?" he managed to say, still facing the television in a deliberate bid to avoid Raymond's hard stare. But instead, Raymond felt an ease-up of the tension that had built up inside him.

"Sure. Let's go upstairs in the bathroom."

Raymond walked behind James to the bathroom, took out a tablet of soap from the mirrored cabinet and tossed it to him.

"Thanks, Ray."

"You bet," Raymond acknowledged without enthusiasm and went back to the living room, while James went to the bathroom.

Much of Raymond's attention was drawn into the football game, occasionally brooding over James' business suggestion after James had showered and re-joined him in the living room. They resumed discussions, but this time the subject shifted to other Nigerians who were successfully breaking into the world of financial security.

"You are a sympathizer of American economic dominance over

Africans and African Americans," James said as he sat uneasily on the arm of the loveseat. Moments later he stood up, sighed then started toward the kitchen. His comment was the kind of antipathy toward America that Raymond deemed preposterous, and he quickly rebutted it.

"Americans of all races individually tend to care more about getting rich than who is richer than them, although the race factor can't be completely neglected," he said curtly. But deep in his mind he would've liked to order James to leave his house immediately.

He reasoned that James, filled with passion in his unshakable belief, was getting a little irritable. Heated political debate over war didn't strike him as the best time to terminate their relationship, for it would obscure a legitimate reason which was James' involvement in narcotics. When he attempted to change the subject, James was hell bent on getting his ideological opinion across and kept on voicing uncompromisingly his opposition to America's decision to oust Saddam Hussein's army from Kuwait.

After a few more argument over who was right and who was misinformed, they knew that as usual they were getting nowhere near a consensus and James succumbed to changing the subject.

It was yet another jaw-dropper for Raymond.

"Your pal, Dennis Metu, was on the same flight with me," James said. "He traveled for the same business purpose as I did."

Raymond was jolted. "Dennis? Our very own Dennis Metu?" Raymond said, stunned as his forehead wrinkled.

"Yes sir, James said with unintended sarcasm."

Raymond, awe struck, stood up and walked aimlessly toward the door and then back to stand next to the sofa as if in a trance, arms folded and eyes fixed at James "No, I think you're mistaking him for—"

"Look, man," James quickly interrupted, "no need to argue. He should be home right about now, why don't you just call and ask him? Would I lie to you about that too?"

"How much is he getting paid for such a deadly gamble?"

"No less than ten grand."

"Are you telling me that for ten thousand dollars Dennis "Green

Bottle" Metu swallowed heroin inside his stomach?"

"For ten thousand dollars Dennis will swallow a live snake."

At that point the entire subject was beginning to get beyond Raymond's comprehension. Arms still folded, he sat back on the sofa trying to digest the commotion in his head. Even Dennis was involved in such an illegal and highly risky business of smuggling narcotics. He knew then it was the business adventure Dennis had talked to him about the night they were out to the Kilimanjaro Night Club. He also knew he couldn't wait to hear it all from Dennis himself.

Raymond shifted to the right end of the sofa to reach the telephone on the side table. Bracing himself, he dialed Dennis's number. After two rings and a pickup, a strange male hello voice came on the line.

"Is Dennis there?"

"Hold on."

Raymond overheard him call out three times for Dennis and his heart skipped a beat.

"He's asleep."

"Tell him Commissioner called."

"That who called?"

"Commissioner...just tell him it's commissioner and he'll know who it is."

"Okay."

Raymond hung up and stared at James who was listening attentively and by no means ready to divulge any more information about his journey until Raymond spoke to Dennis. James stood up and stared back at Raymond, feeling he had finally found a ploy that could jumpstart Raymond's interest in following through with the clandestine operation. He shifted to sit inside the loveseat, now ready to go full strength.

With the football game almost over with the Redskins about to secure a narrow victory, which disappointed Raymond as he thought his team was capable of doing better, James was on the phone speaking with someone else. Raymond, still in deep shock and utter disbelief of what he just heard, sat nodding either in approval or disapproval.

Interrupted by a call-waiting signal, James pressed the call-waiting button, and listened before asking the caller to hold for Raymond. He then switched back and terminated his conversation before switching over to the call-waiting line.

"Hello? Hang on," he said and handed Raymond the receiver. He knew it was Dennis on the line and wasn't going to keep him waiting, even for a second. There was some serious doubt to be erased.

When Raymond took over the receiver, he welcomed Dennis back to Washington and both men exchanged pleasantries. Raymond wisely held back the details of what James had told him regarding the prospect of a drug courier, only listened while Dennis talked about the wonderful time he had while in Lagos. At intervals Dennis would caution Raymond to not rush into things, emphasizing he would detail him in full when they met, as soon as possible.

"Just come on down as soon as you possibly can, Commissioner, I got news for you," Dennis concluded, suspecting James had probably exposed the illicit deal to Raymond.

After Raymond's phone conversation with Dennis, he felt a growing impatience to find out if Dennis indeed swallowed drugs inside his stomach. He shrugged and rushed upstairs to bath, completely abandoning the conclusion of the postgame show on television.

Curiosity engulfed Raymond as he drove his smoky 1982 Ford LTD sedan to visit Dennis at his Hyattsville apartment, a fifteen-minute drive from Riverdale. The clock on the dashboard showed four thirty-five and the wind, which had been blowing hard, eased up a bit on the sunny afternoon. There was no signs of an overcast and most trees were now devoid of leaves as the fall season was beginning to intensify. If it indeed turned out to be true that Dennis had run a drug courier, should he walk away from their years and years of friendship? Should he repay Dennis the forty-five dollars he owed him and let him understand in no uncertain terms that their friendship was over? That prospect he promptly shut down as he knew so well he did not have the money to pay the debt. If he had to wait to come up with forty bucks in order to end their friendship, it might as well last a lifetime. Yet he had to do something, but what? Ideas, good and bad, ran through his mind while he exceeded the speed limit in order to get to Dennis's apartment as quickly as possible.

On arrival, Raymond had no problem finding a space to park. He hurried out of the car and dashed to Dennis's apartment. The loud music greeted his ears from ten yards away suggesting there was a celebration of some sort in progress.

The brick building overlooked a big shopping mall, and was located in the middle of four other identical buildings. Each had two levels with tiny iron bar balconies on the second level. The complex lacked sophistication but the lawn was excellently manicured with flowers planted along the sidewalk facing the front of the buildings. Dennis occupied the top floor of the second entrance. The music blasted even louder as he climbed the stairs that Dennis shared with four other tenants.

He knocked hard on the front door. Aside from the loud noise, which he was sure must have outraged Dennis' neighbors, there were visitors loudly chatting at the top of their voices coming from inside the apartment.

The door opened and Dennis, smiling and filled with joy, stood aside to let him in.

"Raymond the Karr man!" Dennis said, as he firmly shook his waiting hand.

Raymond acknowledged with a 'yes' and made straight for an empty chair, ignoring the four merry-making guests who were themselves oblivious of Raymond's arrival. The shock he initially felt when he left his house had dampened but had yielded way for a heightened curiosity.

"Come on in and have a seat. Good to have you around, buddy."

The living room was moderately furnished, and a four-foot wall with an archway separated it from the kitchen and a dining area. There were a uniform sofa and a love seat, one facing the other. The black lacquer coffee table that held a bouquet of artificial roses was a mismatch with the solid oak entertainment center. The brown wall-to-wall carpet gave the room some modern accent with the matching color of the two window blinds.

Raymond, now seated, decided to pay attention to the other guests. He instantly recognized two among them. One whom he had forgotten his name was a former neighbor during his teen years. But he chose to leave it alone since he tended to not have recognized him either. They were all feasting and drinking Heineken beer. Dennis locked the door and introduced everyone. Raymond stood up from his chair and shook every hand. Dennis, satisfied he had performed his customary duty, went inside the bedroom and closed the door behind him. He had been on the phone when Raymond arrived and gone back to resume his conversation.

Raymond, feeling he had no choice, reluctantly joined the other guests in friendly conversation. After about twenty minutes, Dennis came out from the bedroom with a change of clothes. He dressed in a white African garment and a pair of black slacks, with casual traditional python skin shoes. All the guests paused to admire and compliment his outfit. Pulling a chair from the dining set, he sat next to Raymond and started speaking to him. Raymond leaned against the arm of the loveseat so he could hear Dennis as the loud music was such a hindrance.

"There's nothing like money," Denis began. "Believe me, Commissioner, our country can be heaven— if you have money."

"Oh really? Heavy masquerade," Raymond said, still very much curious and eager to be enlightened.

"I had so much fun I don't even know where to start," Dennis said. "What can I tell you? Where do I start? Is it the women, the chauffeured ride, and all the red carpet treatment from the extremely wealthy business connection, those whom we were sent there for?"

"Commissioner," Raymond said. "Firstly, I'd like to know more about our country's economic climate. I heard about the mass suffering due to the woeful economy."

"That's if you don't have the money. I mean, being an American resident alone can get you influence which will take good care of you wherever you go."

Dennis only told the fun part of the story, understandably due to the presence of his other guests. He had his preferences. Soon after their limited discussion, Raymond tuned in to the football late games on Dennis' television, and despite the loud music, he was anxiously determined to receive an update on the scores and highlights. Dennis graciously lowered the noise of the blasting music and increased the volume of the set but without enthusiasm, an obvious sign the game was at the very bottom of his priorities momentarily. He was geared up for music and beer but he knew Raymond loved football no matter what, and he had to be a gracious host.

The postgame show flashed the scores and highlights for the one o'clock games and showed the Redskins defeated New Orleans 20-17. Raymond, who already knew the score, still found himself relishing on the W for his team. It was a close game but a win is a win, he thought. After the early games scores had been highlighted, Dennis quickly switched off the television set and told Raymond he wanted to see him in private. His guests stayed on, noticeably too intoxicated to realize that their presence probably was no longer desired.

"We have to do something about this, but what? Do we ask them to leave?" Dennis said in a low voice. "We really have to do something."

As Dennis spoke, three of the guests were chatting on top of their voices, and the fourth, a fat man with patches of graying mustache, was snoring on the sofa, baldhead tilted backward and mouth wide open. Raymond noticed Dennis was watching intently, expecting the telephone to ring any moment, dragging the long cord along to every corner of the apartment he went to. He finally settled it on the floor close enough for his instant reach in case it rang.

"Expecting a call?" Raymond asked.

"Oh yes," he said, once again impatiently picking up the receiver and lifting it to his ear to ascertain it was still functional. Satisfied there was a dial tone, he reached for the pack of cigarettes on the dinette, selected one and tucked it between his lips.

One of the tired guests unexpectedly announced they were set to leave and Raymond knew it was a move that made Dennis happy. The drunken men exchanged handshakes with Dennis again and exited the apartment, dragging along the sleepy head, who appeared too drunk to make it on his own.

James quickly shut the front door and went directly to the stereo and switched it off completely. Once again, he went to the telephone on the floor and dragged the cord along and sat next to Raymond on the sofa.

"The war against poverty is over," Dennis said jokingly, facing Raymond. "I have discovered the highway to financial freedom."

Dennis exhibited sheer excitement as he took a drag off his cigarette.

"Now listen carefully", he said. "I've known you for a long time, and we've been friends and, some time ago, roommates. There's nothing about you that I don't know."

He paused for another drag of smoke and puffed off a mushroom cloud. "I'm fully aware of your unequivocal stance against drugs, and I too am against it."

As Dennis spoke, Raymond, uneasy, grabbed a bottle of beer from the six-pack container. Dennis paused to listen to the telephone again. Satisfied, he stood up and walked to the kitchen to find a bottle opener. He returned with the opener and a bottle of Heineken beer for himself. They sat back in their previous positions as Dennis opened his bottle and sipped.

"As I was saying, Ray, I'm against drugs, but my being against it doesn't help eradicate the drug epidemic. The fact remains that people are still getting rich off of it, and just because I picked up and delivered a small quantity for some little money will make absolutely no difference in the war against drugs. After all, I don't know where or how drugs came to be in existence. All I know is just pick up and deliver to an individual."

Raymond was lost in thought while Dennis talked about how important it would be for a quick strike for money in order to live a life of financial fulfillment in America. All the time Dennis was speaking, Raymond's imaginative thought couldn't bring him to the reality of involvement in a drug smuggling escapade. However, he was prepared to listen and, to Dennis' astonishment, had not completely shut the door on the issue.

Raymond was drinking his beer from a glass cup when the telephone rang. Dennis quickly picked up the receiver as if it was about to escape. After a series of one-word answers, and a promise to meet the caller later, he hung up. He took a final drag from his cigarette, crushed the butt on the ashtray containing smoked-out dozens of stubs, and turned to face Raymond.

"Guess who that was?" he said with a broad smile.

"Tell me."

"Kenneth Chukwu. He's coming up for the deal to be sealed."

Raymond was shocked but not surprised at the hint of Kenny in the same smuggling escapade. He hadn't seen Kenneth Chukwu in two years. He had stopped talking to Kenny because of his rumored addiction to crack cocaine. They had met at Strayer University almost a decade ago and had become good friends and, at one point, shared an apartment together. But when Kenneth got addicted to drugs, he avoided him knowing he would attempt to mitigate rather than give up his crack addiction pleasures.

"So, Kenny is still in this hemisphere. Where has he been hiding all these years?" Raymond said.

"Actually, I had run into him several times and each time he cautioned me to keep it a secret from you. You've got to promise me you're not going to tell him."

"Oh no… If he didn't want to see me, why should I want to see him?" Raymond said wryly.

"Remember the two air tickets and passports I showed you prior to my departure for Lagos?"

"Yes."

"Well, the other one was his, and he also asked me not to disclose it to you. He really must be afraid of you or something."

"How much money are you receiving for the run?" Raymond said, returning directly to the intriguing issue of drug courier.

"I don't know how much Kenny will collect, but my share is supposed to be fifteen thousand dollars."

For a moment, Raymond was thrown off guard. It was a highly unexpected profit and Dennis studiously looked at Raymond's face, realizing such an amount of money could sway any hard head.

"Run it by me again," Raymond said with a look of shock and awe.

"I said fifteen thousand. One five grand," Dennis said, demonstrating simultaneously by first raising one finger with his right hand and then five fingers with his left. Watching him reminded Raymond of a floor trader on Wall Street.

Despite Dennis' mentioning of a huge sum of money to be made, Raymond, impressed as he was, still wasn't even contemplating getting involved in drug smuggling. The risk would be astronomically high for him, certainly to his awareness. Besides he had doubts of his full knowledge of the deal. Fifteen thousand dollars just for a pay-off to a mere courier sounded inconceivable. Although it was a generally established fact that narcotics trafficking, dangerous and illegal as it was, meant fast bucks to pushers, only a king pin would profit so much in one typical transaction.

They discussed the issue for slightly more than an hour, Dennis trying hard to convince Raymond it was worth the risk, and Raymond making all kinds of excuses why it wasn't the deal for him.

"Well, Commissioner," Raymond began to conclude, "Needless to say, I'm uncomfortable with the whole thing, but I promise you I'll take a hard second look at the chances. Right now, my thoughts are emphasizing the consequences and I'll be waiting to hear Kenny's version of the whole affair."

It had been two hours since Kenny called to let Dennis know he was coming over. Dennis gulped down the almost half-bottle of Heineken beer he had been sipping. He covered his mouth to belch before picking up the telephone.

"I wonder what happened to Kenny," he said as he began to dial.

He was waiting for a pick-up from the receiving end when a hard knock came on the front door. He quickly hung up and dashed to open without first inquiring or looking through the pinhole.

Kenny was wearing a white sleeveless shirt tucked inside a grayish baggy pair of pants with tiny light gold stripes. The gold necklace around his neck and a gold wristwatch added a rich taste to his machismo. His dark skin uniquely blended with the dark sunglasses he normally wore, which among friends earned him the nickname GQ. He had changed for the better since Raymond last saw him two years earlier. The first three buttons from the top of his shirt were open, exposing a broad chest that made his total physique an imposing presence.

"Ta raaah!" Dennis said as he postured with both of his hands like a game show host and showcased Kenny who was making his way inside the apartment.

Kenny stopped in the middle of the living room apprehensive and staring at Raymond. He removed his sunglasses and folded his arms.

"Raymond the huge masquerade," he said jokingly. "Raymond

Karr. The only Karr dealer in Washington DC and vicinity."

Raymond nodded approvingly each time Kenny called his name, and he responded with a resounding 'yes', each time.

"This is a complete surprise, isn't it?" Dennis said with a broad smile and stood by the door, looking with admiration. He shut the door and went straight to the stereo to restart the almost outrageous music blast that he had shut off prior to his confidential discussion with Raymond. Kenny extended his hand to Raymond for a handshake, cautiously stepping forward.

"Good to see you again, Kenny. It's been a long time," Raymond said, sure to have been caught off guard.

Kenny sat beside Raymond on the sofa while Dennis knelt by the entertainment center, carefully selecting the albums he intended to play. Raymond began to quiz Kenny on his whereabouts since the past couple of years, pretending he knew nothing about his old pal's rumored drug addiction. Kenny made excuses that Raymond knew were patently false, explaining how he had traveled extensively over the past year, his tedious preparations for his graduation at the University of Maryland, and an ordeal with his ex-girlfriend, etc. etc.

He had been in the United States for almost four years. Straight out of high school and without any prior employment experience, he had been admitted by the University of Maryland to study business law. After his second semester, he had diverted his funds toward purchasing a used Plymouth Champ and got himself a part-time job at a local Roy Roger's restaurant. Savvy, ambitious, and ebullient, he managed himself well juggling between work and school and paying tuition and apartment rental with the money he made from his job. Mysteriously, somehow, the Immigration and Naturalization Service found out that he had illegally accepted employment and when they threatened to deport him, he quickly married his understanding African-American girlfriend who instantly granted him a work permit and ultimately his Green Card.

But he was also a risk taker, the kind of character that refutes the proverb, *A Bird in Hand is Worth More Than Ten in the Bush*. He believed there was sure to be more than just one and that only losers settled for less. Money reigned supreme in his calculus. He'd do anything for the money and he'd go the distance in his quest for more, laying all cards on the table for it. His motto was 'Show Me the Money.'

Dennis began blasting his music, forcing Raymond and Kenny to significantly raise their voices to hear one another as Bob Marley, Dennis' favorite, sang. Satisfied with his choice of music, Dennis went to the kitchen and in a few moments came back with three bottles of Heineken, as well as a saucer full of cashew nuts. He placed the saucer on the coffee table and gave each man an unopened bottle of beer. Kenny stood up to grab the opener from the dining table, but Dennis beat him to it and helped everyone. He took out a pack of cigarettes from his breast pocket, selected one and lit up. Amidst the thunderous reggae music, it became almost impossible to hear one another, so much that Kenny requested that Dennis decreased the volume, and Dennis obliged with an apology, before descending on the cashew nuts.

The celebration must have gone for almost two hours when darkness began to cast. It was almost 7:30 p.m. when Raymond left to use the bathroom. He came back to find that Dennis had completely shut off the stereo and was deep into discussions with Kenny. As soon as Raymond stepped inside the living room, Dennis announced that everyone would be discussing what he deemed 'a means to defeat malaise.' Raymond sat alone on the sofa while both Dennis and Kenneth sat next to each other on the love seat.

"Kenneth," Dennis began, a note of seriousness in his voice. "I've spoken to Raymond about our new found method to beat poverty, but he doesn't seem to believe it's safe and easy. I'd like you to reiterate the facts before him."

Kenny dropped back on the chair and drank his beer, crossing his legs. All Raymond was curious to see was the fifteen thousand dollars Dennis said he was about to receive as his pay off. Raymond wasn't interested in the business itself. He had been struggling to make ends meet and that struggle, although not entirely fruitful, had at least given him a mortgage to pay and just enough to cater to his family.

The details of the deal stunk in Raymond's honest opinion as badly as the drug itself after Kenneth concluded. All-expense paid travel to Nigeria, a two-week mandatory stay in Lagos with lavishing lifestyle never imagined before, swallow capsules of heroin and board the plane back into the United States. Kenneth had mentioned there would be a twenty-one-hour flight that would take off from Lagos airport to

Germany for a connection in Frankfurt. For Raymond, that alone would amount to a lifetime in hell. After a few moments of thought, Raymond didn't find it difficult to reject the plan but made no attempt to explain his reason to both men.

"Well, it's up to you. I can only make recommendations to whomever I consider to be a friend," Dennis said with a note of anger and frustration in his voice.

"The risk is just too much for me," Raymond said. "I don't intend to get involved, really sorry to say. But I sure appreciate your offering me the opportunity. That shows me you're true friends," he said, knowing in his mind he really meant to substitute 'friends' with 'enemies.'

Kenny, obviously disappointed, stood up, sighed and went to the bathroom. Moments later, he came back to find Dennis still trying to convince Raymond. "I assure you that your credentials as a new permanent resident would make your trip flawless as you don't fit a smuggler's profile. Besides, Dulles International Airport would be absolutely free of Customs harassment. Moreover, it lacked the necessary facility to detect ingested narcotics," Dennis said. His eyes met Kenny's and they both smiled mockingly when Raymond asked him if he was sure of having to be paid fifteen thousand dollars.

"Tell him," Dennis said and nodded to Kenny.

"Action speaks louder than words," Kenny said. "Well, to be sincere, I want you to be as rich as I am. I have whatever connection is required to bring you up to a financial update. All you'll have to say is yes and the ball will be rolling. I'd expect that time of contemplation is over. This is time to choose destiny."

"Raymond, I can't believe you're even thinking this over. Do you prefer struggling all your life?" Dennis said.

After a few more words of advice from both friends, Raymond decided to listen to what was involved, but searched his mind to find yet another way out of the pressure.

"You know my unequivocal stance on drugs," Raymond said. "Just tell me what is involved and I'll think about it over the next couple of days."

"If you're interested, you don't have two days," Kenny said.

"Well, tell me what's involved. Explain the details," Raymond said as he was reaching for a handful of cashew nuts. He tossed one in his mouth and chewed then sipped on his beer.

Dennis and Kenny looked at each other.

Kenny was about to speak when Dennis quickly cut him off. "Kenny, give him the juice now."

Kenny then turned to face Raymond. "If you stick around this evening, a guy will be calling on the phone when he reaches the hotel, and we'll go collect raw cash. You'll see,"

Raymond wasn't entirely convinced by Kenny's assurance. He just knew he didn't want any part of the deal no matter what. That was what counted, he thought as he chewed down the nuts.

Kenny glanced at his wristwatch and then began dialing a telephone number while Dennis looked on with anticipation.

"Hampshire Motor Inn on New Hampshire Avenue in Takoma Park, Maryland, please," Kenny said to the hotel's receptionist.

After a brief question and answer session with the party on the other line, Kenny hung up. Dennis, who was intensely observing, was inwardly beginning to feel concerned but managed to maintain a steady face, feeling a crucial need to conceal his skepticism from Raymond. Feeling a bit warm, he went directly to the stereo and switched on the music, but this time as low as the volume could play without being completely silent. He then proceeded to the kitchen to warm up a meal of boiled rice and potatoes with tomato stew, while Kenny and Raymond caught up on other issues not concerning the drug deal.

They were all sitting around the dining table eating and drinking Heineken, when at eight o'clock, the telephone rang. Dennis quickly stood up and dashed to pick up.

Kenny cautiously dropped the bowl of rice he was about to add to his depleted plate and fixed his stare at Dennis.

"Hold on for a moment," Dennis said and with his head motioned Kenny to come over.

He handed Kenny the receiver and Kenny while speaking turned to Dennis and showed him an ok sign. He spoke for about two minutes and hung up. He turned to Dennis again and smiled broadly at him.

"He's here," he said joyfully. "We're right on the money, buddy."

Hearing that, Dennis jump-crossed his legs and twisted around in a flawed imitation of a Michael Jackson dance move. "Don't worry I'm ok," he said as he struggled to pick himself off the floor. He checked his clothes for possible stains and dusted off his buttocks.

Both Dennis and Kenny hurried to the kitchen sink and washed their hands. When they came back, Dennis told Raymond he must wait for them. So Raymond sat and drank Heineken and listened to music as both men left.

Soon after Dennis and Kenny left the apartment, Raymond's real thought on the subject began as he sat alone in Dennis' apartment, wondering if indeed the entire event was real. He wondered why Dennis and Kenny so desperately wanted him in on the illegal operation. If they struck it rich, why on earth couldn't they invest their money on something legitimate rather than continue on the path of trouble. As for the money itself, he just couldn't wait to see for himself because he'd always known the deal with drug dealers. They often reneged on their promises to pay cash, and it had always resulted to violence. Somehow, he imagined, this could all turn out to be a set up by the police to bust a drug ring. Perhaps Dennis and Kenny may either have decided to work for law enforcement, or for that matter, could be walking into a trap set up by Drug Enforcement Agents.

The more he reminisced on sting operations he had witnessed on television, the more frightfully skeptical he became. He had strongly advised some of his friends, Kenny and Dennis included, to ostracize anyone involved in illegal narcotics of any kind, citing the dangers of being caught in the middle of circumstances and spending time and money just trying to prove innocence. It wasn't worth the enormous risk, he had emphatically cautioned.

And for heaven's sake, who could ignore the ugly violence during the drug epidemic –victims who were killed even by their own siblings, or friends who turned against each other. With the eruption of gang rivalry, who could be foolish enough to involve himself in such a despicable social atmosphere?

After a considerably lengthy soul-searching, he decided he just couldn't go along with it. Ever present in his memory was the gruesome and highly publicized double murder of Isaac Dillum, III, the first son to the beloved Mayor of Washington, DC, Mayor Dillum., along with his eleven-year-old daughter, Tisha Dillum. It was a shocker that gripped the nation's Capital and echoed beyond the country to other cities around the world. Particularly significant was that Washington, DC had a dubious honor as the murder capital of the world and the Mayor's predecessor had been busted in an FBI sting for smoking crack cocaine. Mayor Isaac Dillum, Jr. was affectionately nicknamed "Mayor Clean House." When he declared his candidacy for mayor, he held a broom stick and promised to use it as a symbol of what he intended to do with malfeasance if elected.

Isaac Dillum, III, a thirty-two year-old DC corporate lawyer was stepping out of his dark-gray Lexus when presumably two men armed with automatic weapons opened fire and then fled. The incident opened a gaping wound in the hearts of the Mayor and many DC residents, as well as members of the Metropolitan Police Department whose homicide detectives had still not found the killers. Speculations mounted but police suspected drug related murder for hire. Among the numerous speculations was the rumor that the Mayor's son may have been engaged in some form of illegal drug activity, but that rumor was being conceptualized from the cliché 'where there's smoke there's fire.' Homicide detectives remained mum on the subject.

The initial two hundred thousand dollars reward went uncollected. The FBI stepped in and upped the reward to five hundred thousand dollars. DC chapter of the American Bar Association tacked in another five hundred thousand, and still no credible tips. Doubling the reward money was another cool million by Friends of Dillum and the reward stood at a whopping two million dollars. The double murder still remained unsolved.

And so Raymond had a flashback at both the TV and print media photos of the slain lawyer and his young daughter, both covered with white sheets. He made up his mind to refuse the offer. Although faces of their corpses were not shown, he could only register in his memory the awkward position of Isaac Dillum, III with both legs still inside the Lexus lying face up on the ground as though his killers purposely positioned him as such to make a statement.

The sudden loud sound of the telephone ringing jolted Raymond. He was about to answer, but halted abruptly and decided to let it ring until the caller hung up. It stopped after six rings and was silent a brief moment before it began ringing again. He wondered who could be needing to reach Dennis so desperately. Nervous and suspicious, he paused to think. He remembered an unfortunate incident not so long ago when another acquaintance, Samuel Okoro, whose younger brother, Matthew, took on two jobs in order to pay the bills and to feed both men as Samuel was unemployed. Samuel later resorted to selling drugs but when DEA charged in on a sting, was apprehended along with his hard-working, law-abiding brother. The innocent young man became clearly a victim of circumstance. Both brothers had spent years in jail following a plea bargain. It was one instance where a completely innocent individual had paid for a crime only his brother committed.

Giving it a further thought, it wasn't Raymond's house so why shouldn't he answer the telephone? It could even be Dennis himself or his girlfriend calling.

The phone rang incessantly until Raymond began to feel compelled to pick up. It could be an emergency. When he finally answered, he disguised his voice.

"Who's this?" Dennis' voice sounded forceful and quizzical when he heard the strange high pitched voice that said hello.

Realizing it was Dennis, he reverted to his normal voice and explained that he hesitated to answer because of uncertainty, an excuse Dennis couldn't quite comprehend but left it at that anyway.

"You're being too damn timid, Ray, a whole mountain of a masquerade like you, but we'll be spending more time here than I expected. Do you mind waiting a little longer?"

His statement got Raymond worried now more than ever.

"Why?"

"I'll explain when I come back."

"How about if I go home and be back later?"

"Well, you can do that but try to be back in the next hour. It is 8:45 now, so be back at around 9:30, 10."

Raymond thought for a moment before answering. "Why don't you call me when you're done?"

"Okay. That'll work," Dennis concluded.

They hung up and Raymond immediately picked up his keys and left.

The cold wind that made the temperature fall below normal forced Raymond to run to where he had packed his car. Cruising along the brightly lit streets, he began to reflect on his last phone conversation with Dennis. What was going on? Why all of a sudden did Dennis decide he wasn't coming back right away? Could he have been a subject of a sting operation? He recalled the daily news broadcast of DEA sting and sensed nothing but trouble.

Making no sense out of his perception, he suddenly began to envision the worse and felt for his buddy Dennis. Kenny had landed him in trouble with the law. Fifteen thousand dollars would be enough to lure him into a sting. He had been financially troubled for a long time and needed to change his taxicab that had cost him a fortune to fix. That Raymond had purchased a house had lodged him in a desperate search for some kind of achievement of his own. He always mentioned that each time they talked about ways to succeed financially.

Now there's the prospect of going to jail. That would decimate him, especially as the bread and butter of his entire family of seven, all of them living in a remote village in Africa. He had sent money to his family members every now and then, none of it substantial. He had sent fifty dollars at the maximum and usually mailed five dollars to his ailing mother.

Raymond's drive back to his house was free of traffic but fraught with heightened speculation as he pulled into his garage. Lit only by a distant streetlight, the house looked deserted with no lights reflecting through any of the windows. When he inserted his key to open the door, Ogu emerged from behind and happily jumped on him, leash intact around its neck, unusual for the dog to be strolling outside alone with an unhooked leash. When he looked around, sure enough James appeared from the dark corner of the high wooden fence that separated the yard's basketball court. He had apparently taken the dog as an escort to the convenience store two blocks down the street, and when he saw Raymond's car pull into the driveway had let go of the desperate dog.

"What happened to you, Ray? I didn't think you were staying away this long," James said.

"We'd been partying," Raymond said as both men shook hands and walked side to side inside the house.

"Your masquerade caliber Redskins won the football game," James said.

"I know, and boy am I excited."

While inside the house, James locked the door as Raymond freed Ogu from its leash and went straight to the kitchen. He relieved James of the grocery bag he was carrying and placed it on the counter, leaving him with the responsibility of sorting out the groceries.

Raymond then went to the bathroom, and when he came out heaved himself in the middle of the sofa, the fate of Dennis very much in his mind. More than anything else, he wished Dennis would call him right away to ease the tension that was rapidly building up in him.

After putting away the groceries, James came out from the kitchen and sat on the left end of the sofa, right next to Raymond. Meanwhile, Ogu rested on the corner between the kitchen and the dining room.

An eerie silence fell inside the house as Raymond sat thinking about the plights of Dennis and Kenny. It was broken when James touched off on the issue that Raymond was certain to be part of no matter what—Persian Gulf.

"Once again, James, I still think it would be in the best interest of Saddam Hussein to back off and not face the wrath of a formidable Western military arsenal," Raymond said.

"Wait until body bags begin to arrive at their air bases. Ray, I don't think you know enough about the vaunted Republican Guards," James said and sighed. "Bush will learn the hard way never to mess with a warrior of masquerade proportion like Saddam."

Raymond had vowed to end discussions on the Iraq issue with James following a bitter argument over the United States' involvement. It didn't work. Nearly ten minutes into the argument, the ringing of the phone brought it to an abrupt end.

"I'll get it," James said and quickly grabbed the receiver.

Raymond watched James as he spoke enthusiastically to Dennis, recounting their experience in the flight from Frankfurt, Germany. The Lufthansa Airline plane had taken off from Murtala Mohammed Airport in Lagos and had connected in Frankfurt after a six-hour layover, where James, Kenny and Dennis had coincidentally met. They then flew together into Dulles International Airport in Chantilly, Virginia. The drive from Dulles to any location around Washington was no more than a half hour.

"Hold on for Ray," James said afterwards, and then passed the receiver to Raymond.

"Commissioner," Dennis' voice came on the line.

"Don't tell me— you're now in charge of the government," Raymond joked. He knew right away from the jubilant tone in Dennis' voice that he had been wrong thinking Dennis and Kenny had been trapped and busted by the cops.

"Well, leadership has finally reached my hand," Dennis said. It was a common joke for the two buddies when the going looked good and situation called for celebration. Raymond overheard Kenny's voice when Kenny asked Dennis to have Raymond come over immediately. There was also a third male voice, as well as the pounding of reggae music in the background.

"Commissioner, come on down because all hell has broken loose here tonight," Dennis said. "The guy we went to collect the money from is here now. He's very young, but he's a multi-millionaire. You should see him and meet him."

"Has he paid you completely?" Raymond said.

"Of course…. He even gave me an extra thousand bucks for appreciation."

Raymond's eyes nearly popped out of their sockets. That was something he had to see for himself and it was enough to stir his curiosity.

"Okay. I'm coming right over," he said and hung up, looked at his watch that showed the time was a quarter to ten p.m. then dashed out of the house.

Chapter 3

DILEMMA

Raymond, now wearing a tan spring jacket, which he always neatly folded and carefully placed in an infrequently accessed corner of the trunk of his car for whenever it was needed, reached Dennis' apartment at exactly ten p.m. It was as usual a less busy Sunday evening traffic and the drive was quick and effortless, and no hints of an overcast. The Redskins' victory was sure to dominate in every sports loving family's household dinner table. An intriguing invitation from Dennis to come over was overshadowing that aura of football victory celebration for him. In little less than fifteen minutes, he had luckily found the same space he had parked during his earlier visit and pulled in then proceeded along the usual path to Dennis' apartment.

Again, as always, yards away from the building, he heard the sound of music playing, which he had grown accustomed to whenever he approached the complex. But this time the noise was more civil than on his earlier visit. Whatever happened, Dennis had probably decided to take it easy with the menacing noise and for a change be a good neighbor.

Kenny opened the door, jubilant with a broad smile. Dennis and another African male with a boyish face were dancing without partners in a narrow space between the living room and the kitchen. Raymond suspected he was the young millionaire Dennis talked about on the telephone. They both turned to look at Raymond while he shook hands with Kenny.

"Commissioner!" Dennis said and reached for a handshake. He was about to formally introduce Raymond to his guest but the man abruptly halted, took a step backward looking astonished as he stared studiously at Raymond while steadily finger-waved at him.

"Wait a minute," he said. "Hey wait just one minute... I think I know this guy. Aren't you... Wait a minute."

Dennis and Kenny stood still watching the unfolding drama while Raymond, who shook hands with the man, wrestled with his memory to recall the now incredibly familiar face. They continued to shake nonstop as if their hands had been glued together, while trying to recall where they had encountered each other before.

"Don't tell me this is Dick," Raymond said, seemingly recalling the stranger's flat nose and ever youthful face.

"Raymond Karr?" the stranger quizzically refreshed his own memory.

He was Richard Bata, Raymond's high school colleague and a close associate during their final year. They had met when Raymond transferred from a neighboring high school and was subsequently appointed to lead the student body's social affairs. Richard was the captain in charge of the dorm unit that housed Raymond and another close associate, Robert Madu, the school's senior captain. The three had developed a strong triangular friendship and had often set high standards of self-discipline in the school.

At sixteen, Richard, whose friends affectionately called Dick, was the youngest of the trio, and his modesty often made him appear cowardly. When friendship turned sour, 'head' was added to his short name to his bitter dismay. He had often depended on Robert or Raymond to effectively enforce disciplinary measure for unruly pupils he knew were more than capable of slamming him to the ground in a fight. He had carefully avoided confronting arrogant and mean-looking students who he knew were definitely going to resist.

Richard, in Raymond's eyes, had changed in several other ways. He grew taller and looked more masculine. None of the three amigos had seen nor heard from each other since their final exams.

Richard sat next to Raymond, while Dennis and Kenny sat on the love seat listening to the two men talk about their past, also practically giddy with excitement over the spectacular and happy reunion.

Shortly afterwards, Dennis and Kenny left to buy more drinks from the nearby liquor store, while the two old boys continued to talk about their long past encounters. Richard had lived in Atlanta ever since he came to the United States eight years ago with a visitor's visa.

He had absconded and when US Congress passed the Illegal Immigrant Amnesty bill, he had taken advantage to become a green card holder. They touched on almost every issue, including how and why Raymond chose to come to America – academic opportunity.

About twenty minutes later, Dennis and Kenny walked in with hands full of assorted drinks. Dennis was carrying a case of their very favorite Heineken beer and a six-pack of Guinness Stout while Kenny cradled a ripping brown paper bag containing two bottles of red wine and a medium-sized bottle of E&J brandy.

Dennis went to the kitchen to restock the refrigerator. Kenny on the other hand, sat a bottle of wine and the brandy on the coffee table before proceeding to the kitchen with the second bottle of red wine. Moments later, they both came out with wine glasses.

Raymond drank the sweet red wine while the three guys pounded away the brandy.

The party went nearly into daybreak, everybody nearly or absolutely drunk, music blasting. There came the knock on the front door that Dennis had been expecting. He had stopped twice to listen amidst the loud music and had opened the door whenever he suspected someone had knocked, but to no avail.

Dennis opened the door and walking into the apartment was Annette, his Jamaican-born girlfriend, dark, tall and fleshy with killer shapely hips and an amazing flat stomach that was sure to make any woman jealous. She was accompanied by a tall slim, black lady in a tight, dark red mini dress. The low cut shoulder part of her dress exposed nearly half of her full breast, covering only from the nipples downward, her long legs sleek and elegant. Her seductive appearance could have made any man's heart thump. Annette introduced her as Darlene.

Raymond stood up and yielded to his seat, struggling futilely to keep his lusting eyes away from the girl's voluptuous body. Kenny followed with the same seat-yielding overture but specifically ushered it to Darlene, who sat and accidentally exposed her sexy pink underwear to the sneak peek of both standing men. Kenny's Adam's apple lodged up and then down. Raymond couldn't believe his luck.

Suddenly it was an environment of well-behaved gentlemen. They all introduced themselves and, one by one, shook Darlene's hand. The cold and reserved look on Richard's face betrayed him as he tried unsuccessfully to overcome shyness and sheer lack of confidence around women. It had dogged him since his teenage years. However, from the sentiment, as the impromptu party went on, it became crystal clear Darlene would become Richard's. Raymond later discovered Annette had arranged it on Dennis' request so Richard wouldn't need to do much. Annette had fixed all in place.

It was no longer an all-male get-together. Everyone sat down except Kenny, who decided it was time to switch the music from reggae and calypso to a more dynamic disco jam, thanks to the new party atmosphere.

The party continued until early morning. When it was over, Raymond wound up on his bed, courtesy of Annette, who drove all to their respective residences. They were all too drunk to drive.

Raymond woke up late Monday morning with a chronic headache and too lazy to do anything, still wearing the same clothes he wore overnight. He yawned and glanced at his wrist watch which showed the time was eleven-twenty a.m. Sitting upright on his bed, he began to reflect on the dramatic reunion with Richard the night before. Face to face was simply relishing with his high school pal in the USA, a place they both talked so much about as an ultimate dream during their teens, although Raymond was always more vocal and enthusiastic about America. What a moment of elation after so many years. Raymond's mind also reflected on Darlene, the voluptuous lady and her provocative outfit. He could only recall dancing non-contact with her once. It was an exciting recollection, but as intoxicated as he was, he wasn't so sure if he had conducted himself appropriately or made a fool of himself. He hoped he hadn't created an embarrassing moment for himself or anyone present at the time.

The telephone rang reminding him of his splitting headache. Luckily James picked up from the living room extension before the third ring. Moments later, James' gentle tap on the door was a hint it was for him.

"Where on earth did you go last night, Dennis' apartment?"

"You bet," Raymond said as he struggled to stand up from the wobbling waterbed.

"Go ahead get the phone and we'll talk later," James said and exited immediately without a pause. On the line was Richard calling to invite him over. They briefly discussed the time for both men to meet at Hampshire Motor Inn where Richard stayed. It was almost 12 noon Monday and since the day was halfway gone, they concluded that Raymond snapped it up. Richard's flight was scheduled to depart at 3 p.m. from Washington National airport, just three hours away.

Once Raymond hung up, he immediately began to mentally create a list of the subjects he would like to discuss with his young millionaire high school pal. Dick had become extremely wealthy and could be interested in establishing a business connection in Washington area, and he, Raymond, could be the man in charge. He also thought about inviting Richard to invest in his import business. After all, he'd been waiting to import some canned meat from Switzerland, but the label printing that included the product's bar code had been delaying the progress of shipping. They could expedite the transaction and embark on importing a larger quantity for a larger profit. They could purchase a fax machine and computer to begin a more formal business operation, going into partnership. That was if Richard would be interested, but he suspected it would take persistent pressure to persuade his pal to seriously consider such slow money-making opportunity than the fast buck his old Richard had gotten used to. He also knew he would have to present an impressive demonstration of overview of the business and the potential success. Hopefully, that could convince Richard.

He went to the bathroom, his headache still chronic, but found he had run out of aspirin. He decided a shower might at least help the slight hangover and then he could stop by the pharmacy to buy an over-the-counter painkiller.

The long shower did little to help his hangover but his spirit was upbeat. Having dressed, he needed to inform James but James had left with Ogu.

Having done his routine sanitation inspection in the kitchen, he left through the usual side exit that led to the garage. He nearly panicked when he noticed his car was not inside the garage but quickly recalled that Dennis' girlfriend, Annette, had driven him home last night. He went back inside and dialed up Dennis, who himself was still lethargic from the all-night party, and managed to convince him to come by and drive him to where he had parked his car.

Raymond drove from Dennis' complex to Hampshire Motor Inn, ten minutes away, where Richard was eagerly expecting his arrival. At the hotel, Raymond easily found a parking space and hurriedly proceeded to the front desk. Three young female employees in baby-blue uniformed dresses stood idling behind the counter discussing their slim chances of getting a raise. The fourth, a clean-shaven middle-aged black man, interrupted his reading and attended to Raymond. He spoke with a West Indian accent.

"Mr. Karr is here," the clerk spoke on the phone, and paused to listen. He simultaneously nodded his head as he said okay, then hung up.

"Room C 232 is located on the second floor of the next building to the left, just as you leave the door," he said, demonstrating with his hand as he spoke.

"Thank you very much, sir," Raymond acknowledged and walked away. He had no problem locating the room but climbing the steep stairs worsened the headache that had been nagging him ever since he woke up. Knocking three times on the door of room C 232, he felt a surge of excitement run inside him. He couldn't wait to discuss business ventures with Richard Bata, and in a few moments they would be talking one-on-one. This could actually be the big break he'd been hoping for.

Richard opened the door, dressed only in his underwear. He looked tired and sleep deprived. He stepped aside to let Raymond inside the single suite, which was furnished only with a queen-sized bed set, two nightstands, a guest chair, a dresser and a table with a cushioned wooden chair, all cherry oak.

"Boy did you take long, Ray," Richard said.

Raymond smiled and looked around as he stood between the television set and the tail end of the bed, while Richard locked the door. The sight of who was lying on the bed and under a brown comforter, covering everything except a pretty face, shocked Raymond. Richard had actually slept with Darlene.

Raymond stared hard at Darlene's sleepy face, aware she was totally nude under the sheets.

"I had to wait for Dennis to come pick me up," Raymond said after a pause to evaluate the authenticity of a medium-size painting of a hotel maid that was hanging on the wall. "My car was parked by his apartment complex."

Darlene's dark red mini dress was lying on the guest chair. Underneath the dress and half conspicuous was also her pink undies laced around the edges with a white material, and her black handbag. Raymond visually imagined her lying naked on the bed covered only with sheets. The thought of Richard fumbling with her large breasts trickled a slight surge of jealousy in him, but it was brief. His mind quickly returned to business. Richard approached the chair and picked up the clothing items, then invited him to sit down, before proceeding to the bed where he left his clothes. Raymond sat down while Richard dressed, pants first. Admittedly, Raymond just couldn't take his imagination away from the sight underneath the bed sheet although keenly aware his thoughts were perverted.

Bare chested, Richard carried other pieces of his clothes inside the bathroom and came out moments later fully dressed. He slipped his foot into one of the pair of his shoes and searched around for the other, which he found partially hidden under the bed.

"Let's go out to the balcony," he said in a low voice.

Before exiting the room, he first went to the bed and kissed Darlene once on her cheek as Raymond proceeded to the balcony. He came out and joined Raymond in the balcony, which also served as an outdoor hallway to the rest of the suites.

"How was she, Dick?" Raymond said with a note of sarcasm in his voice.

With his fingers, Richard made an okay sign while nodding approvingly. They stood side-by-side facing the trees while holding the railing of the balcony.

"Kenny told me you're interested in breaking into market business. When might you be ready to go?"

Richard's use of the word 'market' confused Raymond. He wondered if it was a coincidence that Richard knew what his intentions were. By asking him when he would be ready to go, it appeared to him that Richard was speaking of his own business in Atlanta. But

Raymond replied anyway.

"As soon as possible, but when did you have in mind?"

"First of all, did they explain to you what was involved?"

Raymond realized immediately his wealthy old buddy was talking about drug market. "Yes, but first I'd like us to discuss other kinds of business. How about an establishment in this region? I have some suggestions," Raymond inquired and apprehensively waited to see what Richard's reaction would be.

"Oh no, Ray, not anymore. I ran a boutique in Atlanta, and still do. It's a headache and little money to be African and do business in this country. I struggled for four years with no real money payoff. Only three years in this 'market' business and I'm a comfortable man. I'm about to hang it all up and return to Nigeria for retirement soon."

Raymond realized he had no chance of convincing Richard to divest in narcotics for anything else. However, he decided to press on, explaining the progress of his impending import business.

"Believe me, Dick, this isn't something small. It is so big we can become everything we'd always wanted to be. I'll personally guarantee its success," Raymond said. Richard was looking down while spoke.

After Raymond carefully detailed his intended import operation, it was obvious that Richard simply was not interested and would rather the drug market deal. Utterly disappointed, he gave up and tactfully changed the subject. They went on to talk about old school days, who they'd seen lately and when.

Shortly after, they walked back toward the suite, Richard leading the way. At the door, he stuck out his index finger to signal Raymond to wait at the door. Slowly, he twisted the door knob and peeked in to ascertain Darlene was properly covered under the sheet before letting in Raymond. When the road was clear, he told Raymond he could come in then went to the bedside and retrieve his black leather briefcase. Darlene had now completely buried herself underneath the sheet from head to toe, dashing Raymond's quasi hope of a possible pleasurable sight. Richard opened the briefcase and took out a white piece of paper and a pen, wrote down his Atlanta telephone number and handed it to Raymond.

"Whenever you're ready, call me," he said, replaced the pen and the pad and closed the briefcase.

"I'll call you in another week," Raymond said, feeling disappointed. "I have to leave now. I have a lot to do today." He stood up ready to leave even before he concluded.

Richard, also feeling disappointed from his own perspective, speechlessly walked Raymond to the door then loosely shook his hand.

"Ray," he said, breaking his silence "I'll take good care of you, and I'll make you see the obvious difference between my idea and yours. Just tell me when you're ready."

"Okay, mean masquerade, I'll call you."

It was 1:45 p.m. when Raymond, who glanced once more at the bed before exiting, left Richard's hotel suite for his first meal of the day at the International House of Pancakes, adjacent to the hotel.

The sunny and hot Wednesday afternoon was unusual for mid-September. The temperature must have risen to record 80's and the streets of Washington, D.C. were filled with people caught in the surprise of an Indian summer. Workers sat around parks, some having their lunch while watching pigeons flock around them. Motorists cruised along, top of convertibles lowered to savor the wonderful warm weather.

Dennis and Raymond were just concluding the busy day riding in the 1978 Ford Mercury Dennis used for his taxicab. They had left from Raymond's house at nine o'clock that morning, drove to Dennis's bank in Silver Spring where he deposited five thousand dollars in cash, and proceeded to downtown for some of his other errands.

Dennis had had a mini shopping spree, including the purchase of a five-hundred-dollar gold necklace. Their itinerary concluded with a visit in Silver Spring to a man who advertised his used BMW for sale in the classified section of the Washington Post. As an experienced former automobile salesman in his resume, Raymond was charged by Dennis with scouting a good deal for him, which meant a better car at a decent price. Raymond had called up to arrange a visual inspection of the car.

There was one pressing hitch hanging in Raymond's mind as they were driving along the highway. Dennis had only budgeted five thousand dollars for a car, while the 1986 BMW was advertised for seven thousand, five hundred dollars. Raymond thought it was simply hopeless to even make the trip. He had tried to convince Dennis they would have little or no chance to consummate the deal, but Dennis had insisted that they took a crack at it anyway and Raymond had yielded.

After missing directions several times and winding up at numerous wrong addresses, they finally arrived at the right place, a fairly new ranch house with a gray siding and stucco frontage perhaps constructed no more than five years ago. It was quite distinct from the neighboring colonials on both sides.

Parked in the driveway, front facing the street, was a silver 4-door BMW automobile tagged with a 'FOR SALE' sign on the windshield. The shiny paint and four new tires affixed with alloyed wheels had made the classy car look as impressive as a good used can could be.

"If the man agrees to five thousand dollars, we'll take it, regardless of how it runs," Dennis had said.

Raymond rang the doorbell and turned to Dennis. "Let's not get too excited, man. You wouldn't want to spend that much money on a car and wind-up paying mechanics just to get it running. We have to test drive it properly before making any offers."

"You're right, Commissioner," Dennis had said. "That's why I particularly chose you to find me a car."

The door had opened and standing beside it was a young man of Persian descent in his late twenties. He was wearing a blue checkered shirt and a brown pair of corduroy jeans. His long and bogus nose, his jet-black short hair, his thick eyebrows and his trim-lined mustache all made Raymond suspect he probably originated from Iran.

"Hello," Raymond had said as the man grimaced.

"You came for the car?" he inquired in a thick Persian accent, looking curiously at both Dennis and Raymond. He kept staring nervously at the two with a constant left to right to left look and then up and down as if they had come to arrest him.

"Yes sir," Raymond had said immediately. "That was me that called earlier and told you I was coming this afternoon."

"Well, a lot of people called and some came by and wasted my time for nothing. Did you know the price I asked for?" he said, now calm and concentrated his face at Raymond.

"Yes sir, we read it in the newspaper ad, but first though may I ask if the price is negotiable?"

"I'd rather not negotiate, but if you are reasonable, I may listen."

He definitely was the shrewd type, or he just didn't trust these strangers.

"Well, can we look at the car first?" Dennis said, scratching his forehead.

"Sure. I'll bring the keys." He closed the door and went inside.

Dennis and Raymond glanced at each other.

Both men walked back to the car to commence visual inspection.

"The interior is marvelous. It looks like a new car," Dennis said as they peeped inside through the shields.

"Oh yes," Raymond concurred.

As they took a walk around the car, the man came up and unlocked the driver's side door.

"Who is going to test drive?" he said, looking at both of us from the other side of the car.

Raymond pointed at Dennis.

"Come on," he said, motioning with his hand.

All four doors unlocked automatically. Dennis looked at Raymond and nodded approvingly. Dennis walked around to the driver's side.

"First, can I see your driver license, sir?" the man said, looking on with anticipation.

All were seated inside the car with Dennis behind the steering wheel. Dennis searched his wallet. Raymond sat behind him in the back seat. Adjusting the rear-view mirror, he saw Raymond, winked at him and they both smiled at each other.

The interior was as clean as a new car and retained a faint new car smell. The dashboard was equipped with Alpine radio and cassette stereo. The sight obviously pleased Dennis, who couldn't conceal his enthusiasm.

"Wow!" Dennis quipped and then handed his Maryland driver's

license to the man. He turned the ignition and the car charged alive then hummed like a well-oiled machine. All dashboard and surround amber lights ignited at the same time. Quite an exciting toy for a man, Dennis thought. An impossible dream possession if you asked Raymond.

Dennis fastened his seat belt.

"Does it have air conditioning?" he said.

"Sure." the man said woodenly.

"And it works good?"

The man ignored him. The questions Dennis was asking about the car were clearly irrelevant as the car was fully equipped with all the spoilers. Raymond suspected the man was getting irritated and decided to take over fact-findings aware that if progress was to be made at all they could not afford to anger the man.

"Are you the original owner?" Raymond said.

He hesitated and looked behind his shoulders to face Raymond.

"Who is buying the car, you or him?" he said, now visibly angry.

Dennis explained the role each of them was playing in order to hunt down a good used car bargain.

Dennis engaged the gear, and they went out for the test drive.

"As smooth as it rides, I still enjoy my Mercedes Benz much better," Dennis said dryly, looking at Raymond through the rear-view mirror.

"Oh really? No kidding." Raymond caught the show-off gimmick and played along, thinking in his mind what on earth his pal was trying to accomplish. He was sure the Persian wasn't buying that strategy. He knew they drove the old Ford Mercury taxicab parked in front of his house. If Dennis had a Mercedes Benz, he wouldn't be driving a taxicab.

But contrary to Raymond's expectation, the Persian was indeed awakened the moment he realized what Dennis had just said. He must have been fooled into believing Dennis was actually rich and was probably looking for a second car. Perhaps he thought the taxicab was Raymond's to drive Dennis to his house. He looked at Dennis and then at Raymond, shifting his shoulders to the left before introducing himself.

"My name is Rafik," he said, in a formality that suggested a more congenial business attitude.

Dennis followed with the same gesture and introduced both himself and Raymond. Rafik then began to answer every silly question that Dennis threw at him regardless of vagueness. That provided Dennis with the impetus to keep up his showmanship.

In nearly twenty minutes of test driving, the BMW had taken them approximately a mile along route 29 and back to Rafik's residence, meandering through the narrow streets of his neighborhood.

While Rafik explained the details of the car's mechanism, Raymond recalled that Dennis' deficient budget of five grand for a car would offset a possible compromise and everything would boil down to a total waste of time. That was sure to infuriate anyone as impatient as Rafik. Raymond was extremely tired and had planned to play a tennis game with his tenant pal, James at six p.m.

It was already four fifteen p.m. and the sun was beginning to show signs of setting. Rafik had talked about every good quality the BMW had, except the price. Dennis had asked Raymond to handle the pricing, which would certainly be a difficult nut to crack for him. Five thousand dollars was quite a sizable margin with seven thousand, five hundred dollars, a whopping difference of twenty-five hundred dollars.

"How low can you come down on the price?" Raymond was forced to begin, studying Rafik's reaction and certain Rafik will be belligerent on the pricing issue.

Rafik closed the hood, sat on top of it, and clapped the dirt off his hands. "Mmmm... Seven thousand," he said and looked at Dennis for a reaction.

Dennis strolled toward the driver side door and pretended to be re-examining the interior. Raymond knew Dennis was trying to avoid his face.

"I suppose five grand cash would be out of the question," Raymond said as he walked toward the direction where Dennis was standing. Daring to ask that question was like swallowing a bitter pill to him. He hated it but knew it was necessary for him to ask.

Rafik laughed mockingly and came to the driver's side where Raymond was leaning back against the door. He reached for the keys in the ignition through the window and pulled it away, avoiding the curious looks on the faces of both Dennis and Raymond.

"Well, thank you for coming, gentlemen," Rafik said as he manually rolled up the window.

Dennis walked toward the taxicab, which was parked across the narrow street. He stopped, looked back at Raymond and waved him to come with him. Raymond immediately told Rafik they would be thinking about it and thanked him for showing them the car as he walked toward Dennis.

Dennis stopped in front of the taxicab and waited for Raymond to join him. As Raymond approached, Dennis waved his left hand in the air as if he had lost his voice but managed to say something that caught Raymond by surprise.

"Commissioner," he said, speaking in a low but definitive voice. "I'm the owner of that car."

"How?" Raymond asked curiously and frowned.

"Cause I'm buying it."

"At seven thousand dollars?"

"You bet," Dennis said. "I'm in love with that car. I have two thousand dollars cash to put down and we'll have to go back to my apartment to collect the balance."

Raymond stared curiously at Dennis and hoped he was only kidding. If he spent seven thousand dollars on a car, he would be nearly broke after. However, Raymond realized it was Dennis' own decision to make and he, Raymond, had to let him handle himself.

"Are you sure you want to do this?" Raymond said. He watched Rafik walk back toward his house, flicking the keys along the way.

Dennis disregarded Raymond's question and called out to Rafik, who stopped and looked back at them, unsure of what they wanted from him.

"Come here for a second," Dennis said to Rafik and started walking toward him.

"Hold on, Dennis" Raymond interrupted.

Dennis stood by the trunk of the BMW waiting to hear from Raymond while Rafik slowly paced toward Dennis. Rafik was now too close for Raymond to confide anything to Dennis without him listening.

"I'll handle this, bear with me for a moment," Raymond whispered to Dennis and bypassed him to meet with Rafik.

"I have one more final offer to make— sixty-five hundred dollars or we go pay for the Volvo we saw elsewhere," Raymond said tactically, using a technique he borrowed from one of his old customers who had used the same tactics on him during his time of automobile salesmanship.

Rafik looked down and mentally calculated while Dennis and Raymond fixed their gaze at him. Dennis walked slowly toward Rafik and Raymond, appreciative of Raymond's brilliant tactical approach and nodded approvingly.

"I'll take a loss of five hundred bucks," Rafik said to Dennis' astonishment and looked for a reaction from him.

Dennis reached in his side pocket, pulled out a stash of hundred-dollar bills and counted out the two thousand dollars down payment. Raymond looked nervously from left to right as if someone would suddenly jump out of the thin air to rob him. Rafik casually accepted the cash and invited them into his living room for the official transaction.

Recounting the money, Rafik went to a wooden desk on the far corner of the large living room to write up a receipt. Raymond admired the arts on the Persian rug they were standing on while Dennis fixed his eyes on Rafik.

Rafik came back and tore off the paper from the notebook, handed it to Dennis and waited until he read and nodded in approval. They all shook hands with Rafik and departed, Dennis rushing, keenly aware he could be driving a Beemer by dawn if they hurried.

Dennis' enthusiasm heightened as they drove off in the taxicab, and very much affected his vehicle operation. He approached a maddening 65 in a 35 mph speed zone while chancing ridiculous close calls. Raymond hated it as he never trusted Dennis' driving in the first place but managed to stay calm. What concerned him most was the lawlessness.

They arrived at Dennis' apartment at about 5:22 p.m. Dennis hurried out of the car and ran to his apartment while Raymond waited. Five minutes went by before Dennis emerged, exuberant and recklessly drove off. The rush hour traffic slowed him down for some time, resulting in an uncomfortable heat coming from the engine and blowing through the uncontrollable air duct.

Along the way, Dennis boasted about the sleekness of the car they were about to drive home and who among their friends had a BMW, who had planned to purchase one and what model.

During one of the stops behind the ever-increasing traffic, Dennis stared at Raymond.

"Commissioner," he said. "Please reconsider your no to making the trip to Lagos. The payoff is enormously gratifying. I really wish you the same great joy like I'm feeling this moment."

"I know, I know. I just can't make up my mind. I guess I'm being too much of a coward and I hate myself for that," Raymond said dryly.

They arrived in front of Rafik's house at almost 6 o'clock. Dennis parked the taxicab in front of the BMW on the wrong side of the street, abandoning grandiosity. He dashed out like a hungry child who just saw his mother. Rafik, who couldn't wait to make the sale, waited patiently by the door,

"Sorry about the delay. The traffic was too much," Dennis said.

"That's okay," Rafik mumbled and led the way inside the living room.

Raymond sat on the navy blue sofa next to a flower pot on a glass chrome plant stand. Rafik went to a different table located between the living room and the dining he used as his office, and cleared out the read letters and envelops scattered all over it.

"Why don't we use the center table?" Dennis suggested in a humbled demeanor meant to avoid upsetting Rafik.

"We have too much to write and sign, especially the temporary tags and the title," Rafik said in exhibition of professionalism.

"Are you giving us a temporary tag?" Dennis said, seemingly astonished by that revelation, but was careful not to over-react as that might cost him some extra bucks.

Raymond was also surprised at that unexpected bonus package. They intended on using Dennis' commercial tag to drive home the BMW while Raymond drove the taxicab closely behind to block the view of a possible Montgomery County Police cruiser.

Dennis looked at Raymond and winked, obviously delighted, and Raymond reciprocated but with less enthusiasm. To Raymond it was a tacit evidence that Rafik was a dealer and not the original owner of the car. An automobile dealer was more likely to sell a lemon he had purchased from an auction and therefore withhold information on defects to a buyer. A typical salesman would brag that every used car in his lot runs like a spindle just to make a sale. No wonder he reacted negatively when Raymond asked him about previous ownership.

Still, the car showed no signs of defect when they initially test drove it, erasing some doubts Raymond harbored.

Rafik pulled an extra chair from the kitchen and motioned Dennis to sit.

Dennis, while sitting, took out the bundle of cash from his side pocket and recounted it. Rafik, eyes nearly popping at the sight of the cash, began to explain a series of documents necessary for the application for a license plate, then prepared the thirty-day temporary tag. When the deal was over, Raymond observed the digital clock on the side table showed 7:30 p.m.

Dennis drove the BMW while Raymond drove the taxicab as planned. They stopped at Dennis' complex, parked the taxicab and Dennis drove Raymond back to Riverdale, where the disappointed James sat by the door entrance with Ogu sitting next to him, their tennis appointment virtually a cancelation.

Once in his white Ford LTD sedan, Raymond found himself brooding over his reluctance to accept his pal's invitation to run a drug courier. First was his tenant pal, James, who had just completed a successful second trip. Perhaps more persuasive was his high school pal, Richard, who apparently had become a millionaire engaging in the same business. Even more compelling was Denis' dramatic giant leap from a cab driver to a BMW owner.

Raymond's business activities for that Wednesday had been

successfully completed and he felt a distinct reason to enjoy a champagne evening at Dennis' apartment, at his best pal's invitation. He had had another early day, starting out at 8 a.m. He had concluded his scheduled meeting with the procurement manager for the Safeway food chain at their Landover headquarters in his effort to convince the giant retailer to consider his canned meat importation from Switzerland. He had also promptly and successfully consummated an accord with the Food and Drug Administration in Rockville, Maryland, on a means to import animal care products from a Swedish manufacturer, and subsequently branched to Commerce Department to receive forms of import licensing. All he had left to do was spend the rest of the day celebrating with Dennis over his new car, and above all, his overall success with his trip to Nigeria.

Despite his successes of the day's legitimate business endeavor, he still found himself leaning toward a shot at a clandestine operation so potentially tempestuous - something he knew could ruin his reputation and possibly his life.

"I'll have to think again," Raymond soliloquized as he pulled into a parking space at the lot belonging to Dennis' apartment complex. There were not many cars parked as most residents were still out to work. He looked around hoping to find both of Dennis' cars, but only found his taxicab isolated at the end to the lot, no BMW. It was the first disappointment of the day for him. Not only Dennis wasn't home but also he was looking forward to having the late lunch Dennis had promised to have readied, and now would be driving home to Riverdale hungry as hell. Coupled with the extreme fatigue, it was a major blow to his resistance to the hunger.

He decided to walk to Dennis' apartment anyway, hoping one of Dennis' friends was visiting and staying over. From a short distance to the door, he paused to listen to a faint sound of music coming from inside the apartment. He proceeded and gently knocked on the door. Aside from the sound of music, he also heard a ranting of a feminine voice. More encouraging than ever was the delicious smell of stock fish soup fuming out of the apartment.

The voice ceased when he knocked on the door. Moments later, he heard the sound of the door unlocking. When it was open, standing behind was Dennis' girlfriend, Annette, who let him inside as they greeted each other. Two other African-American women sat on the sofa, and the sound of dishes crackling from the kitchen revealed the presence of yet another person.

Raymond greeted everyone with only one hello and a wave of his hands and sat on a vacant chair. The two women were casually dressed in blue jeans, one wearing a reddish color T-shirt and the other, a rumpled white sleeveless shirt. They simultaneously returned Raymond's greeting with a simple hi.

Annette shut the door and formally introduced Raymond to the girls. Almost immediately, a bulky man in his late 30's appeared from the kitchen carrying two bowls, one of fufu, the other stock fish soup. He was wearing a white traditional garment and a matching white hat, exactly the same kind of Raymond's tenant, James, had given him as a gift from his journey.

He nodded to Raymond and set the bowls on the dining table before introducing himself as Ibrahim.

"Where's Dennis?" Raymond said, not directing the question to anyone of them in particular.

"He left with Kenny to pick up some guy from the airport," Annette said.

"How long has he been gone?"

"Been a while, he should be on his way back by now," she said and ran her fingers through her hair.

Ibrahim, who had gone back inside the kitchen and came out with a bigger bowl of fufu, announced the food was ready for all to join in.

As hungry as Raymond was, he resisted the temptation of joining the ladies, who quickly stood up upon Ibrahim's invitation. Besides there was no room for Raymond on the dining table that sat a maximum of four.

"May I then get you something to drink?" Annette said to Raymond, leaning on a partition.

"Thanks, but not right now," Raymond said emphatically, knowing it could ruin his monstrous appetite for a delicious fufu chow with Heineken. He shifted to the seat where one of the ladies had left for the dining table, hoping she would return after the meal to sit next to him.

The opportunity never came. The lady Raymond hoped for was Ibrahim's wife and a mother of three. Her other companion was Kenny's new girlfriend, and that left poor Raymond with nothing to do other than listen to reggae music.

The two women came back and sat on the sofa and Raymond found himself sitting in the middle, while Annette and Ibrahim, who was sweating profusely, cleared the table and washed the dishes.

Raymond hoped his stomach would remain patient while he waited for Dennis to come back.

Fortunately for Raymond, he didn't have to wait too long. Moments later, Dennis opened the door and walked inside, followed closely behind by Kenny and then a medium-built, light chocolate male with froglike cheeks. His bulging eyes looked like they were about to pop out and constantly smiled, in Raymond's opinion, a jolly character. It would be difficult to discern if he's angry.

Dennis wore a gray French suit and a collarless purple shirt, exposing the gold chain around his neck, while Kenny had on a pair of brown slacks and a blue and white striped shirt, folding the sleeves up to his elbows. He also wore his dark sunglasses, which lately had become part of his image.

Raymond stood up and shook hands with the three men as they walked in in a single file. The new guest introduced himself as Jeff and explained that he had just flown in from Buffalo. Dennis dragged a chair from the dinette and motioned Jeff to sit.

Jeff seemed shy. He avoided eye contact, fixing eyes on the barely audible program on television. He was of average height, seemingly the shortest among all the men present. The oversized light blue shirt he was wearing hid much of his paunch. It matched fairly though with a red flowered tie, a baggy brownish trousers and a pair of light brown leather shoes.

Kenny sat on one of the chairs at the dining table while Dennis went into the bedroom, where his girlfriend had been in prior to their arrival. Moments later, Dennis came out to find Kenny and Raymond discussing the explosive issue of Persian Gulf conflict.

"Have you had something to eat, Ray?" Dennis said, interrupting Raymond's conversation on his favorite topic.

"No, not yet. But I had declined the invitation to join your other guests until you got back."

"Okay. So now I'll have to prepare enough fufu for four," Dennis said to no one in particular and headed to the kitchen.

Ibrahim, who had remained silent until then, brought up the issue of the United States' rally to form a coalition within the United Nations in a bid to force Saddam Hussein's forces out of Kuwait.

Ibrahim, a devout Muslim as indicated only from his demeanor before the fufu meal, was blatant in denouncing President Bush and, later in the conversation, firmly predicted that the US President's strategy would eventually collapse with Arab nations fighting alongside their fellow Arabs.

Jeff, with his smiley face, sat still and only nodded in support for Saddam Hussein, as expressed by either Kenny or Ibrahim. He would laugh in amusement about every mouth that moved. Still, there was something about him that did not warm up to Raymond. Raymond had encountered such characters before but that one seemed strikingly familiar. He knew he did not hate Jeff but strangely enough, he did not like him either. Jeff remained silent, most probably disappointed as Raymond's pro-American views were obvious. Occasionally, he would scratch his head and grin or utter a mockery laugh that could be interpreted both ways- either laughing with you or at you.

"If stronger countries begin to take over weaker ones, few states would be in existence by the year 2000," Raymond insisted. "This is what the United States is trying to deter, and that should be the underlying factor of the whole issue."

"What right has the United States got to police the world?" Ibrahim said. Raymond knew it was a rhetorical question but chose to confront him on the subject anyway. He also knew Ibrahim had been personally offended by his defense of the American President. Amongst the group, President Bush was not popular with the African community, but no modern Republican President had been in Raymond's opinion since Richard Nixon.

Raymond paused to think of a more calculated answer to Ibrahim's rhetorical question.

"First of all," he began, "it's the United Nations, and not only the

United States, that is searching for solutions—"

"Remember, America dominates the organization, and don't tell me about UN because I know all about the use of that body to achieve their goal of world dominance," Ibrahim interjected.

"Well, someone has to assume leadership in world affairs, and that's the only means to effectively solve problems of this magnitude," Raymond said with such an argumentative voice that caused Kenny to signal Raymond with his hand to keep it cool.

Ibrahim's wife and Kenny's girlfriend remained silent but seemingly enjoying the heated debate, while Dennis, who always stayed neutral on the subject, occasionally raised his voice from the kitchen to approve or disapprove of any comment he deemed plausible.

"I'm neutral in this," Dennis said as he always did. "I'll simply listen to both sides before rendering my judgment." Dennis would ask questions like 'What do you think about what he said regarding Saddam's unprecedented aggression? Or 'don't you think America is overreacting and acting like the Sheriff of the World?'

Later in the debate, Annette reappeared from the bedroom, wearing a different outfit. She picked up a bunch of keys from the dining table, retrieved her black leather handbag that hung on the balcony's door knob, excused herself, and exited the front door.

The passionate debate continued until Dennis served dinner. The two women took to their own conversation, picking up from whatever discussions they were having prior to Raymond's arrival, while Kenny, Jeff, and Raymond joined Dennis at the dining table.

Ibrahim left to sit on the floor next to the record album rack to select his favorite tunes.

Dinner was relatively quiet. Kenny and Jeff discussed a few issues, noticeably around the main point. Nonetheless, it provided Raymond with a clue as to why Jeff came to Maryland— to be sponsored as a drug courier. Raymond also learned from their conversation that Jeff's travel expense was courtesy of Kenny the presumptive sponsor.

Halfway through dinner, Annette came back. She firmly held a brown grocery bag in her arms containing two big bags of potato chips and a medium-sized pack of mixed nuts. She had somehow managed to free one hand to knock on the door. Ibrahim had opened, and she first placed the big brown bags on the center table before proceeding into the bedroom as Dennis lustfully re-examined his sweetheart's killer rear. He turned to look at Raymond. Their eyes met simultaneously and Dennis winked and smiled. Raymond couldn't control his laughter and finger-warned Dennis he was simply going naught.

The telephone rang and Annette picked up from the bedroom. She came out to inform Dennis of who was on the line, and Dennis quickly deserted the dinner to pick up the receiver. He sat next to the two women in jeans pants.

Raymond observed as Dennis spoke with the person on the other line. "Hi! Yes. Okay…Now. Mmmm….fifteen minutes…Right."

He hung up and went directly to the bedroom.

Kenny, Jeff and Raymond all were barely eating anymore of the leftover from the dinner, and they sat lazily around the table. Ibrahim, still on the floor, disc jockeyed speechlessly.

Dennis came out of the bedroom waving a bunch of keys.

"I'll be right back, folks," he announced casually and headed for the front door.

"Wait a minute. Where are you going?" Ibrahim said and quickly stood up.

"Give me twenty minutes," Dennis said, standing by the door and facing Ibrahim, his right hand searching for the doorknob.

Ibrahim pursed his lips. "Twenty minutes, please, because we'll have to pick up our daughter from the babysitter."

"No more than that," Dennis said morosely and removed his hand from the door to unpack the contents in the brown paper bag on the center table.

"There are some drinks and snacks," he said.

Included among the wine bottles were two bottles of Andre champagne— one pink and the other white. Dennis invited everybody to help himself and to feel free during his brief absence.

Dennis returned in little over twenty minutes, his timing noticeably pleasing Ibrahim, who observed caustically when he heard the sound of unlocking the door. They had left the dining table and descended on the champagne during Dennis' brief absence. Kenny had gone to sit next to his girlfriend and they were hugging and kissing. Raymond noticed the lady was more proactive.

Dennis came in with Kenny's roommate, CJ. Raymond had met CJ several times before but never bothered to ask him to explain his initials.

CJ introduced himself to all, then pulled a vacant chair from the dining table and sat down.

Ibrahim and his wife left after a brief confidential discussion with Dennis, who escorted the departing couple outside and down the staircase and returned to the apartment.

The merrymaking get-together turned into a meeting to determine who would be interested in drug courier journey. It all began with a brief introductory speech by Dennis on financial freedom, and then a follow up by Kenny on the ultimate mechanism. Both men detailed the prerequisite for sponsorship, which was low key and ability to travel overseas.

Raymond sat still listening to much of what he had already heard from both men, but this time he was more attentive. From the passion and persuasion with which they spoke, he was beginning to suspect that Dennis had not only run a drug courier but had been deputized by the key pushers.

When Kenny began to speak, Dennis uncorked the champagne and served everyone.

For the first time Raymond caught himself subconsciously drifting in favor. Firstly, a potential courier would have to have a valid passport and secondly would be a permanent resident of the United States.

Jeff, who became a captive audience during questions and answers, contemplated his drink and sipped when Kenny disclosed the drugs had to be swallowed. After Kenny concluded with his repetitious speech, CJ was strangely calm and so was Raymond. It was an apprehensive moment of reflection for the three. None jumped to the gig right away. Raymond, in self-evaluation, just couldn't conceive himself being involved in an illegal drug deal, but the more he remembered Dennis' BMW, the more his mind tilted toward the affirmative.

CJ, although still not totally embracing the idea, but deep in his mind he felt he would make a proficient candidate to travel. However, he had to show his loyalty, and after careful thought voiced his ambivalence.

"I have all my papers complete and ready to roll— if I decide to go," he said.

Raymond thought for a moment. He carefully evaluated CJ's statement and noticed the caveat. What did he mean by if he decided to go? That was surely not a definite commitment.

The party was over at a quarter to eight, and everyone left with some pretty damn serious thinking to deal with. Could Raymond have forgotten his *Field of Oleander* dream and the warning issued to him by the soothsayer? Were his current friends turning ugly just like in that dream whereby his friends turned into poisonous Oleander plants that approached him like zombies?

Chapter 4

TOUGH CHOICE

Raymond found James alone in the kitchen preparing the evening meal, presumably for both of them. He got directly to the point. "James," he began rather impatiently. "I need to find out more on this courier journey business. I spent the entire evening at Dennis' apartment listening to what he had to say, but all I want to know from you is the safety factor."

"Ray, don't be a coward. Nothing will happen to you. After all, I'm still alive and so are Dennis and Kenneth," he said.

Raymond studied him as he was seasoning the baked chicken on a flat oven tray.

"What about the chances of being stopped for x-rays? As you know, man, I cannot afford a run in with the law. I have little or no reason to use this channel to get rich. I'd rather be patient until I make it from my legal business."

"Forget it. You're never gonna make it in this country, as long as you are black and African. You'll keep suffering until you realize what I'm telling you."

Raymond stood silent again and folding his arms he mentally reflected on the morality aspect of it all. He had steadily preached to his friends about the importance of exemplary conduct and abstinence from drug usage of any kind. If he agreed to the journey, he'd betray his conscience and become a bad ambassador to his own family, unheard of in the history of his family.

"Remember what I told you about making it in America?" Raymond said.

He decided to indulge James on this issue to remind his tenant buddy of his philosophy. He had suggested to him that to be successful in America, one must first become a good American.

James, who was always anti-America, had been outraged when Raymond further explained and said, "To become a good American meant to appreciate the enormous opportunities and human decency standards set forth by the leadership of the country." It had infuriated James and he quickly responded.

"You keep sympathizing with these people, Ray and believe me, they'll make you miserable. Wait until that happens and you'll be sorry." He angrily turned his back on Raymond.

"Do you think I should go with Dennis?"

James turned around and regarded Raymond. "I'll take you along in my next trip."

"When?"

James' face suddenly lit up as he was caught by surprise with Raymond's unexpected concession. "Don't worry, I haven't fixed the time yet, but get your passport ready and tomorrow call up Lufthansa airline to find out flight schedules for next week."

James was talking about days and weeks to sponsor Raymond in a trip to Nigeria— something Raymond had never been able to reasonably afford in a decade. Raymond suddenly began to contemplate other perks of the deal. For a long time, he had been planning to take a trip to Nigeria, the country he had left a decade earlier, but couldn't afford it. Now all he had to say would be yes and it will all be accomplished at virtually no financial cost to him.

"Okeedokee," Raymond said, but James could sense a slight note of indecisiveness in his voice.

"Don't worry. I guarantee your safety, and I'll take good care of you. Trust me," he said and patted twice on Raymond's shoulder as he began to make his way toward the kitchen.

James was noticeably pleased with Raymond's new positive attitude toward the supposed journey so far, or at least so he thought. Raymond left James alone in the kitchen and went up to his bedroom to change the blue striped suit he was wearing, and put on his pajamas. He still felt uncomfortable with his interim decision to accept the trip, but the thought of visiting his folks after so many years abroad was tempting.

Raymond went back downstairs to find James serving the macaroni and cheese with baked chicken. It suddenly occurred to him that he should've alerted James he had had dinner at Dennis' apartment. The mistake forced him to chow down some more food instead of belated admission about having had dinner.

James talked about how much fun he had had in Lagos, much the same way he had been telling it all along, while Raymond hurriedly cleared the table. Ogu was helpful in hastening Raymond's departure from the dining table, crushing some of the chicken, whole or bones, Raymond had tossed at him.

After dinner, both James and Raymond lazily retired to the living room and watched TV, occasionally discussing their itinerary for the business trip to West Africa.

Raymond finally went to lie on his bed around 11:30 and found himself almost excited about the prospect of traveling to the motherland, his very first trip in ten years. He recounted all the places he presumed would be interesting to revisit, especially Owerri, where he grew up. He'd see people who one way or the other influenced his past activities, some of whom he hadn't spoken to nor heard about since he came to America. He could see his high school sweetheart, who had lost him to the infatuations of coming to America. Most ritualistically, he could also visit the grave of his beloved late youngest brother, who was laid to rest in December of 1980, just three months after his departure to the US.

Still, on the sour note for Raymond, not only would he'd have to re-enter the United States with a controlled substance, but would have to be carrying it inside his intestines. The thought of that alone sent a chill up his spine.

Raymond restlessly rolled from one end of the bed to the other, thinking about the chances of undertaking a risk of such magnitude, and weighing his options. What would happen to his family if the substance exploded in his intestine and killed him? He thought about his mother who had been staying in America with his brother, Ed, and other times himself, but was currently with Ed some eighty miles away from Riverdale. She had had health problems lately which demanded a considerable attention, particularly high blood pressure, and her soaring medical bills were his sole responsibility. His brother, Ed, could hardly afford to support his wife and two children.

Raymond still had to consider the damage his involvement would impact on his family's reputation. In the Karr family history, no one had ever been associated with criminal activity, and for moralistic Raymond to be arrested, would disgrace every member of his family. Why become eccentric and bring a curse to his aging mother? She had stretched herself to every decent limit to be sure Raymond and his siblings received the best in education. "A good name is better than gold and silver," Raymond recalled her saying to them. Raymond had been able to raise his hopes for the future with his import business, and was managing to pay the mortgage in a beautiful home. It seemed like a dumb risk to take.

Satisfied with his decision, Raymond sank into his blanket and dozed off.

The incessantly ringing telephone provided an early unappreciated wake up call, coming as early as a quarter to 6 in the morning. Raymond usually planned ahead for an early day when necessity called for it but he just wasn't expecting one, therefore never anticipated waking up that early. James was still dead asleep, unplugging the hook to his bedroom telephone extension as he occasionally did prior to bedtime, and leaving Raymond's bedroom line as the only source of incoming calls.

Initially, Raymond was reluctant to answer the call, hoping either James would cave in and pick up or the caller would hang up and try again much later. Raymond had no choice. The phone kept ringing. Raymond cursed himself for not remembering to switch on the answering machine before turning in for the night.

Kenny expressed surprise for the long wait as soon as Raymond answered.

"How come you let the phone ring for so long?" Kenny said.

"Oh… Kenny. Good morning," Raymond said, hoping to shorten the conversation and go back to his sleep.

"You better try to answer your phone calls, man. It could have been an emergency," he said. "Anyway, you have to come and pick me up so I'll take you to the guy who'll fix everything. How soon can you get here?"

Raymond was caught off guard with Kenny's question. Raymond had decided last night against the courier deal, but he needed some time to coin up a valid excuse before breaking it.

"How about eleven o'clock?" Raymond said, trying to borrow some time.

"It's urgent that you leave immediately," Kenny said, offering no further detail.

"But—," Raymond said, trying to object, but was flat because it felt to his as though he was frustrating the effort of a friend trying to work earnestly on his behalf. "Okay. I'm on my way."

It took Raymond about twenty minutes to brush his teeth and wash the sleep off his face before changing into casual clothes— a pair of brown slacks and a white long sleeve shirt, and covered with a light spring jacket.

It was a typical fall morning, a cool but gentle breeze chilling the slightly foggy atmosphere. Raymond drove to Kenny's Adelphi high rise apartment. The traffic was light.

When Raymond drove around the circle in front of the twenty-story building, Kenny was already waiting at the lobby. Kenny stood up as Raymond approached the circle and signaled Raymond to stop and not worry about parking.

Kenny then came out from the building, sat in the front seat and greeted Raymond.

"Hi, Ray," he said. "You'd have to hurry up in order to catch the big boss at home."

The drive to big boss's residence took no more than seven minutes.

The complex, a relatively low-income community, stretched from New Hampshire Avenue across to Riggs Road, about one third of a mile, and was the prime township of Langley Park.

Four separate streets led to the burnt brick, two-story garden apartments. The boss's apartment was located on the ground floor behind a building of similar structure and second from right.

Raymond wasn't particularly impressed with the fact that the big boss, if he really was as wealthy as Kenny portrayed him, was only living in an apartment, let alone low income. Raymond guessed he overrated the boss' narcotics business status. For someone who would pay for a round trip airfare and the exorbitant Lagos hotel bill, in addition to Raymond's pocket money, Raymond expected a definition of luxury.

They parked and headed toward the apartment.

Kenny pressed the buzzer twice and then tapped gently on the door several times in a gesture that suggested they were being expected.

Raymond noticed a peep from the pinhole before the door opened. Standing behind it was a young African-American woman in a long night gown, eyes still showing fresh from sleep.

"Kenneth," she said. "Come on in." She ignored Raymond.

"Good morning," Raymond said flatly as the woman stood by to let them in.

"Good morning," she said and regarded me.

"This is Raymond," Kenny said as they both made for the chairs inside the living room.

"Nice meeting you."

"Thanks," Raymond said, not sure of the best approach to respond.

"I'll go get Clyde," she said and headed toward the bedroom.

Clyde was wearing a light blue-flowered pajama when he came out from the bedroom. His face showed no hints of being disturbed from sleep.

He looked youthful, but could have been in his early thirties. He was about five feet five. His extremely low haircut and a round smooth face gave him a conservative image, the least person to label a suspect of any crime.

"This is Raymond," Kenny said. "The guy I spoke to you about earlier."

"Hi, Raymond, good to meet you, I'm Clyde, but you can call me DC."

"Good to meet you too," Raymond said and shook his hand.

The cozy living room, although richly furnished with contemporary furniture, was still far short of what Raymond had expected from a wealthy drug lord. The single lamp at the corner was the lone source of light. The six-sitter glass chrome dinette was attractive and decorated with a brown vase of artificial roses, projecting a perfect match to the brown wall to wall rug. Raymond was still not impressed.

Raymond became a little doubtful Clyde was the big boss, speculating to see someone other than Clyde. Clyde, in Raymond's grand opinion, could have been a point man for a kingpin who wanted to remain anonymous. When Kenny told Clyde that Raymond was ready to go, prompting a series of advice from Clyde to boost Raymond's courage, Raymond knew he was sitting face to face with a Nigerian narcotics lord.

"There's absolutely nothing to panic about," Clyde said. "Nobody will stop you, since your passport and visa show you hadn't traveled too many times to Lagos. That's the catch. If your passport shows you had done that in the past, now that's when they stop to search and question you."

Clyde went on to explain in detail how the deal would work. Clyde would take Raymond right away to a travel agency to purchase Raymond's ticket, along with Jeff's at the same time. Raymond would fly to New York's JFK Airport on Saturday morning to catch a five o'clock Nigerian Airways flight to Lagos with Jeff. Once in Lagos, Clyde's brother, whom Clyde would write down his address and phone number for their use, will meet them at the airport and drive both of them to their hotel, and will then take on the operation from there.

"Do you have any question?" Kenny asked Raymond, reading the skepticism written all over Raymond's face.

"Well," Raymond said reluctantly, pausing. "Safety is still my primary concern, and I'm not talking about just making it through the customs, but having the substance stay in my stomach without complications."

"Oh, don't even worry about anything. The substance is uniquely prepared by the most qualified doctors in that country."

"What if I'm stopped?" Raymond said candidly.

"I'm telling you, nobody will question you; but let's say they stopped you. There's the money to get you the best lawyer in town. In fact, no amount of 'market' you carry in your stomach can send you to jail for more than six months. Should the lawyer fail to get you out, we'll take good care of your family until you're out, and then we'll compensate you handsomely. It'll be worth your while."

Kenny relaxed on the sofa and crossed his legs.

"He's gonna take you right away to buy the flight tickets," Kenny said, breaking the silence.

"Who did you say will go along with me?" Raymond inquired.

"Jeff," Kenny said.

"Are you coming along, Kenneth?" Clyde said then stood up ready to go back inside the bedroom.

"Two of you can go. I have to sign my lease today," Kenny said.

Raymond stared at Kenny, wondering what Kenny meant. Kenny noticed the surprise look on Raymond's face and quickly explained it to him as Clyde was heading toward his bedroom.

"You know I'm getting my own apartment, right?" Kenny said.

"What's wrong with where you live now?"

"No, that's CJ's"

"But it's a two-bedroom apartment."

"Stewart shares it with him. I was only staying there temporarily until I got mine."

Kenny uncrossed his legs and stretched his hands to grab the brownish ashtray on the far corner of the slightly tinted glass and chrome coffee table. Setting it closer to his reach on the coffee table, he searched his pockets and found a pack of cigarettes.

"Which Stewart are you talking about?" Raymond said.

"Jabari Stewart."

"I thought he had been incarcerated."

Raymond had heard from gossips that Jabari Stewart was taken in on a forcible rape charge some months ago. Raymond found that charge ludicrous. Jabari Stewart had had major problems with drug use and was heavily addicted to crack, but rape was out of character. Jabari Stewart never wanted anything but drugs.

"He was discharged for lack of evidence after nine months in jail." Kenny lit his cigarette and waved off the light on the match, exhaling smoke from his nostril.

"How did you get approved in your application?" Raymond reverted to the apartment subject.

"I'm paying five thousand dollars cash to the condo owner, so she shut up and never asked a single question on my credit. She was apparently overwhelmed when she saw the raw cash."

Kenny and Raymond talked about Kenny's new apartment for more that fifteen minutes before Clyde came out from the bedroom, dressed in a white nylon shirt and a pair of dark purple slacks that barely matched his expensive brown leather, stiletto shoes.

"Let's go," Clyde said dryly, still adjusting his well-ironed shirt.

Kenny and Raymond stood up, set to go, but Clyde once again excused himself and hurried back inside the bedroom. After a moment, he reappeared with a brown men's groom case in his hand, holding it midway up to show Kenny and Raymond.

"Can't leave home without it," Clyde joked.

They all left the apartment. Outside, Kenny and Raymond started toward the car when it occurred to Raymond, they'd have arrangements to make. Kenny would have to be dropped home first and that meant driving to Adelphi before heading to wherever they would purchase the tickets.

"How are we going to ride?" Raymond said.

Kenny stopped to think. Clyde paced faster to meet up with Kenny and Raymond. Kenny was about to respond when Clyde interrupted. He instructed Raymond to walk toward left of the parking lot where he had parked his car.

It provided Kenny with an instant solution.

"I'll drive your car to my apartment while you ride in DC's car," he said to Raymond.

Raymond wasn't satisfied with that idea, but suppressed his feeling. Kenny was well-known among their circle of friends as a car killer. Long before he disappeared, he had misused his cousin's Mercedes Benz and had rendered useless four used cars he purchased consecutively over a period of seven months. There was also an incident a few years back when Raymond accused Kenny of manhandling his car, a Volkswagen

Passat.

But Kenny now had money to fix car damages. The narcotics business had given him a new life, without the influence of crack cocaine, a drug habit he had unfairly blamed on poverty and frustration.

"Okay," Raymond said. They started walking leisurely toward Clyde's car.

Kenny stopped to talk to Clyde and Raymond, feeling it was meant to be confidential, stayed a distance. The two men talked about something Raymond just couldn't comprehend. They mentioned money and quantity in grams, but instinct hinted Raymond Kenny wanted to invest his money in Raymond's increasingly progressive trip to Africa.

When they settled their scores, Kenny warned Raymond to keep the news of his anticipated journey from his tenant friend, James.

Clyde and Raymond shook hands with Kenny, and Raymond separated his house keys and handed Kenny the car keys as they branched away toward where Clyde had parked his car.

The lot was relatively lengthy, about forty yards deep. Clyde and Raymond walked side by side along the middle, bypassing other residents hurrying into their cars. Clyde walked ahead to lead the way toward the cars parked on the right side. Raymond looked ahead to the end of the lot, trying to guess which of the cars might be Clyde's, expecting a luxury car. His residence was not exactly a penthouse, but most narcotics dealers at least drove expensive cars.

Again, that wasn't the case. All the cars in sight were either of average value or junks.

"Right this way," Clyde said, and walked to the driver side of a dirty, white 1980 Toyota Corolla.

The car, a two-door sedan, had a malfunctioning passenger entrance door, leaving Raymond with no other choice than shove his body through a narrow space between the steering wheel and the driver seat.

"I hope you don't mind," Clyde said apologetically as he sat down, trying to readjust his seat and rear-view mirror.

"That's okay. Don't worry about me, I'm fine," Raymond said, as his ambivalence grew.

Clyde turned on the ignition, and while the engine was running, began to explain again.

"You know, I'm not like most 'market' dealers you may have seen. This isn't my country, so I don't wish to spend my money here. But when you get to Lagos, ask about me. I have my share of luxury and intend to retire soon and go home to my almost completed house," Clyde said, placing his brown groom case on the console.

"That's fantastic," Raymond said.

"One thing about the 'market' business is that one shouldn't display wealth while in it. You'll easily become a target for law enforcement, and before you know it, you're busted. It's the kind of business you lay low, make your masquerade-size money, and be gone."

"Where do you live in Lagos?" Raymond asked.

"Ikeja. Don't worry, when you get to my brother's house in Lagos, you'll see my handwork."

Raymond resisted the temptation of asking Clyde what he meant by handwork.

Clyde stepped harder on the gas pedal to hasten the warmup of the rattling engine. Satisfied, he shifted the gear and backed out.

The drive to downtown Washington, DC was horrendous. They queued up on a stagnant morning traffic jam along Riggs Road, and Clyde had turned to other routes in the hopes of avoiding the bumper-to-bumper traffic. They met one of the slowest along North Capitol Street. The traffic turned a normally ten minute drive into an hour and half nightmare for them, arriving in front of the L Street building where the travel agency had a branch office, at 9:15a.m.

Clyde drove into an alley behind the large building that occupied the entire block, and veered right into a driveway, where a mini private parking was conspicuously displayed with a sign that read, 'Authorized Cars Only, Don't Even Think Of Parking Here.'

Clyde, apparently angry at the length of time they spent seating on a traffic jam, pulled in front of one of the cars parked in the lot, switched off the engine and asked Raymond to come on out through the driver side again.

"DC," Raymond said. "Your car will be towed in a minute."

"I don't give a damn," he yelled. "If that's what they want, they can have the junk. Americans claim to be the greatest in the whole world but can't even do a damn thing about their traffic."

He picked up the groom case and exited, living the door open for Raymond to come out. Raymond shut the door behind him and followed Clyde as he was walking around to the main entrance.

"Are you leaving the door unlocked?" Raymond said.

"I want to make it easier for them to go ahead and take the damn car," he said mockingly.

As they walked along the alley, Raymond thought about what Clyde had just said regarding Americans claiming to be the greatest but not being able to do a thing about their traffic. The first thing Raymond remembered was Lagos before his departure to the United States, when a traffic jam into the large city had been a traumatic experience. Again, Raymond resisted the temptation of reminding Clyde they had something worse than America's traffic in their own neck of the woods. Raymond, I didn't want to sound unpatriotic and suppressed his feeling.

They walked into the building, which at the time was busy with arriving workers. There was a uniformed security guard sitting behind a round desk where Clyde first approached to sign in before Raymond did. They took the elevator to the 12th floor. The sign on the agency door read "Central Travel Agency."

Clyde opened the door and walked inside and Raymond followed him to the desk. An African woman dressed in a red gown stood talking on the telephone, apparently the lone employee at that time of the morning. Raymond also guessed it must have been a small agency.

The woman immediately ended her conversation and hung up the receiver to warmly welcome them. Clyde called her by her first name, while she addressed Clyde by his nickname, except she pronounced the full word "District" and nothing for the "C."

Clyde introduced Raymond. They chatted a bit on the stress of American work atmosphere before settling down to business.

"Are you traveling?" she said casually to Clyde.

"No. I'm sending two," Clyde said.

She pulled an extra chair from smaller office next to hers and asked both men to sit down, and then went to another distant office and came back with new booklets of Nigerian Airways tickets. Clyde took a blank sheet of paper she gave him and scribbled a name that Raymond suspected could have been Jeff's last name, then passed the pen to Raymond. Raymond wrote his full name beginning with his last name, passed the sheet directly to her and handed her the ink pen.

She began to fill in the two booklets she had extracted from the bunch while Clyde and Raymond watched, ready to supply her with any relevant information.

It took her only five minutes to complete reservations for two to depart on Saturday's flight, and she picked up the phone and called the airline's reservations center in New York.

Clyde had already opened the groom case he carried along and took out a bundle of hundred-dollar bills. He began to count them and stopped at one thousand, two hundred dollars. He put the rest back into the groom case but left it unzipped, in case he needed to pay additional money.

The young woman hung up the phone receiver and took the money from the table where Clyde had placed it, and began to recount it.

Satisfied, she opened the top drawer of her desk for their change.

In just under five minutes, and for the first time in a decade, Raymond's name had appeared on an air ticket slated to depart for Nigeria.

Clyde stood up, ready to go, zipping close the groom case after carelessly shoving the change inside. Raymond also stood up and Clyde picked up the tickets and gave Raymond his ticket. Briefly, Raymond held it up, examined it and carefully shoved it in his breast pocket like a winning lottery ticket.

The lady stood up to escort them out. She and Clyde stood by the door and chatted for a couple of minutes before they said good-bye, and she closed the door. Raymond had already pushed the elevator button, waiting for one of the doors to open.

Raymond remembered the car Clyde parked in the lot as Clyde was signing out at the guard's desk. Raymond was standing beside Clyde, ready to sign out too, but Clyde signed for Raymond and the stone-faced guard voiced no objection.

They walked back along the same alley.

"You think the car may have been towed by now?" Raymond said, watching to see Clyde's reaction.

"As far as I'm concerned, they can have it if they want it. I've gotten what I wanted out of them and I'm ready to call it quits," Clyde said.

"But what if they—"

"Wait a minute," Clyde said abruptly. He stood still looking down as if he had left something behind. "That lady that booked the flight for us deserves a reward. She had been very helpful to me and I think I owe her some gratuity," he said and began to walk back slowly.

"But she only did her job. Why pay her for what she's being paid to do?" Raymond said. Raymond was concerned about the car, and he wanted to hurry, if it wasn't already too late. Raymond couldn't understand why he was more concerned about Clyde's car's security than Clyde was.

But Clyde insisted, so both men had to go back and sign in again to go back upstairs. However, Clyde explained to the guard it was going to be a matter of two minutes and the guard allowed them to proceed without having to sign in again.

Clyde gave the lady sixty dollars and showed no signs of endeavor as the obviously grateful lady thanked him for his generosity.

Clyde was a rare character. His attitude appeared largely indescribable, explaining Raymond's unwillingness to fully trust him, but what was there to be afraid of? Clyde talked smoothly and probably operated his illegal business the same manner, which could explain why he had been extremely successful in eluding justice. Clyde showed no signs of holding back with cash and that made Raymond believe he was a spendthrift. Clyde never grinned, yet cursed other motorists who tried to maneuver their cars in front of him, occasionally making remarks that forced Raymond to laugh. He was the type Raymond wouldn't want to jump into liking or disliking for quite a while in their initial relationship. However, Clyde had shown the ability to pay bills in totality when he afforded the expensive international flight tickets, and that was enough for Raymond to temporarily accept Clyde's supremacy.

They left the building, and this time, Raymond hoped, nothing could sway them from getting to Clyde's illegally-parked car, if it hadn't been towed away. As they approached the corner of the entrance, Raymond expected to see nothing like an old white Toyota car. He felt his heart thump a little bit. Surprisingly, it was still there and not a single soul was around it writing up tickets or towing a vehicle.

"Ah, thank God," Raymond said aloud as he sighted the car, again guessing at Clyde's reaction.

But Clyde remained expressionless. Clyde didn't even utter a word until they started driving out of the alley. Clyde told Raymond to turn around and look behind.

Raymond turned around and saw a tow truck approaching from the opposite side of the alley entrance, apparently to tow away the car. The unlucky tow truck driver had missed them by seconds.

"No kidding… we're lucky," Raymond said.

"Thieves," Clyde said and smiled for the first time.

Raymond started to be mentally pre-occupied with his itinerary as Clyde was driving back to Maryland. Clyde occasionally mentioned how safe it was to do the job of drug courier, but Raymond hardly grasped any knowledge from what Clyde was saying, only nodding and uttering an uh huh hum.

They encountered virtually little or no traffic delay, and the trip back was smooth and fast until they arrived at Kenny's Adelphi high rise resident parking lot.

Clyde pulled in front of the building and asked Raymond to have Kenny call him later. Clyde also advised that they kept in close touch quite often before he drove off.

Raymond rang up Kenny's 17th floor apartment number from the entry phone, and Kenny's roommate, CJ, came on the line to buzz him in. Raymond was waiting to board the next available elevator car when he overheard a voice that sounded like Kenny's speaking with the building receptionist at the front desk. Raymond looked back and there he was, standing alongside Jeff, and carrying a brown paper bag full of groceries.

One of the three elevator cars came down, but Raymond ignored all and decided to wait for Kenny and Jeff, Kenny's guest he inwardly was not exactly thrilled with.

Kenny's conversation with the receptionist was brief, and both men started towards the elevator to join Raymond.. Seeing Raymond from a distance of about ten yards, Kenny spoke loudly and impatiently.

"Did everything work out all right?"

"Yes sir," Raymond said, smiling and wondering in his mind why the impatience.

"How many tickets did he buy?"

"A couple."

"For Jeff?"

"Uh huh."

As Kenny approached Raymond, he changed the grocery bag he was carrying with both hands and managed to free his right hand to shake Raymond's.

Jeff remained low keyed as they boarded the elevator, only nodding at Raymond for a greeting.

Kenny pushed the fourteenth-floor button instead of the usual seventeenth, and Raymond sensed he must have signed the lease agreement he talked about and probably received the keys to his new apartment.

They came out of the elevator and walked along the hallway, with Kenny leading the way and explaining, unquestioned, how easy it would be to swallow the professionally sealed "market," He equated it to swallowing of fufu balls.

"I see you did okay, you're the masquerade," Raymond said.

"Absolutely… Wait until you see the inside of this apartment. It is lovely."

The lock was somewhat hard to open as Kenny wiggled the key left and right, but most new residents had the same initial hassle. Kenny eventually unlocked the door. He picked up the bag he supported with his legs and led the way inside the apartment.

The apartment was completely empty. There was not a single piece of furniture inside, but there were other luxury features that clearly distinguished the apartment from others like CJs on the seventeenth floor. It was a one- bedroom apartment unlike CJ's studio. The walls had been freshly painted and the tan carpet looked like it had just been installed. The kitchen floor was sparkling clean and had a brand new stove, a large refrigerator and a dishwasher. From the bathroom hallway, there was a connection with the walk-in closet, and then a second exit into the bedroom.

"This is real nice," Raymond said.

"Oh yes, buddy, what can I tell you? I'm a son-of-a-gun masquerade," Kenny said with clear enthusiasm.

Jeff and Raymond went out to the balcony via a four-foot-wide sliding glass door to glimpse at the view, which included a swimming pool and tennis and basketball courts. For some strange reason Jeff noticeably avoided his face. Raymond inwardly guessed it must have been the guest's shy nature. Still, they would soon become business colleagues, who would fly the same airline for a good twelve hours flight and, most probably, sit next to each other. The Lagos host who would be taking care of Raymond would expect to see the two of them together.

Raymond realized that if they were to become good colleagues, they'd have to start by talking candidly to each other. Raymond struck up the conversation by asking Jeff what he liked about the cold weather of Buffalo that made him choose to live there.

Engaging Jeff in a conversation with Jeff was like trying to jump-start a car with a dead battery. Jeff only responded with "yes" or "no," and when Raymond purposely asked a question that required explanation, Jeff looked frantic, his response vague.

"When was the last time you visited Nigeria?" Raymond said.

"Mmm, I'm not too sure. It's supposed to be documented in my passport. I have to look it up one of these days," Jeff said.

"Was the country as bad as they're saying it was?"

" Mmm not really."

"What about the roads and bridges, are they being reconstructed?"

"Mmm yes."

Somewhat frustrated, Raymond left Jeff and went back inside.

Kenny was hanging up an air freshener he took out of the grocery bag. He tested to see if it was properly hung and took two steps backwards to examine it. Satisfied, he went back to the grocery bag and unpacked its contents.

They were mostly the items he needed to clean the apartment. There was a pack of spearmint gum and he opened it, took one and tossed the pack to Raymond.

But there was clear assignment for Raymond in the wake of his prospective travel. Raymond had to leave for Nigerian Embassy in Washington to obtain traveler's certificate. That was necessary to expedite Raymond's re-admission into Nigeria since his passport was lost when a burglar broke into his car a while back, stealing his leather briefcase.

Raymond had been procrastinating on the replacement of the passport, but he never found an urgent need to do so. It had become necessary and Raymond had been told that it was easier to obtain a Nigerian passport from Lagos than in the United States. All Raymond needed to do was go to the Nigerian Embassy with two passport-sized photographs, and in a few minutes, a travel certificate would be issued to him. Simple, right?

Chapter 5

ERRAND

Raymond left Kenny's apartment for the Nigerian Embassy, stopping by a one-hour photo studio. He arrived at the embassy at 12:45 p.m., signed in, and the security officer showed him the general assistance section that accepted all applications. He walked in to find the secretary speaking from behind a heavily tinted glass window. The secretary could see the guests but could not be seen, only mirror image.

"Can I help you?" the voice behind the tinted glass said, with a thick Nigerian accent.

"Yes ma'am, if I could find a human face," Raymond answered.

"This way," she commanded, waving her hand through a tiny hole, just enough to slide through a fist.

"I'd like to obtain a travel certificate," Raymond said and moved toward the direction of a waving hand.

"What happened to your passport?" the woman inquired.

"I'd lost it," Raymond said, almost annoyed.

"Do you have a police report?"

"Yes, but I don't have it with me," Raymond said and instantly felt the guilt of conscience for not realizing the importance of a police report he filed a while ago.

"You have to bring it before I'll issue you with a certificate. Also two passport photographs."

Raymond saw the inevitability in what the woman was saying.

"Is that all I'll need?" Raymond needed assurance he wouldn't have to come back again.

"Yes, love, you bring them and come see me. I'll process your application and in ten minutes you'll receive it."

"Okay. Thank you, madam." Raymond said flatly and left.

The 5th District of the Metropolitan Police was located in Adams Morgan, a ten-minute drive from the Nigerian Embassy. Rather than going back all the way to Riverdale for his previously filed police report, he decided that re-filing a new report would save time. And for that, he went straight to the police precinct to re-file and obtain a new copy from the desk sergeant. It was the easiest part of the pre-travel assignment. At the precinct, he filled out a simple incident questionnaire and collected an instant report. He took it back to the Embassy. It was all done in less than a half hour.

When Raymond returned to the embassy to submit the new police report, he found a different secretary sitting behind the desk. He greeted her and asked to see the lady who was there earlier. He was not in a mood for a new-sheriff-new-order situation. She told him the lady had gone for the day. He sighed and sensed it was going to be a long day.

"What did you want done?" she asked Raymond.

"Travel certificate."

"We no longer issue that here. You have to go to the New York Consulate office to obtain that."

Jolted, Raymond could see the lady looked confused, perhaps surprised someone from her office in Washington, DC could have told him something contrary.

"Ma'am, just a little over half hour ago, a lady on duty told me how easy it would be to be issued a certificate here. She even said she'll do that herself," Raymond said.

"Well, you'd have to go back to whoever told you that then," she said. "But you are not receiving any travel certificate from this window," she said and called out for the next waiting guest.

Raymond knew his dreaded scenario was beginning to unravel.

"With all due respect, ma'am," Raymond said angrily, "I believe that such a transaction not only should be carried out as an utmost responsibility of our Embassy, but it is of paramount important that I receive it because of my urgent travel arrangements.

She ignored Raymond's plea and continued to call for the next person on line. Raymond even cited the tragic death of his father as a factor, but the lady wasn't buying that either.

Realizing how desperate and persistent he was, she wrote down a telephone number on a sheet of paper and handed it to him.

"Here. This is the telephone number for the office in New York that now issues such documents. The directives came from Lagos for us to stop issuing those so don't blame me."

Raymond reached for the piece of paper, grabbed it, and studied the numbers.

"Who do I ask for?" he asked.

"Ms. Delani."

He wrote the name on the same piece of paper. A middle-aged man walked in and stood behind him. The man was wearing a blue suit and had looked Hispanic. As Raymond was about to walk out to place the call on a pay phone, the same man asked him for directions to the visa office for a travel to Nigeria.

The lady behind the tinted glass interrupted and quickly told the man to come forward to the counter.

Raymond went on to a nearby telephone booth and dialed the number on the piece of paper. He charged the cost to his home telephone account and was put through to Ms. Delani of the New York Consulate office.

Ms. Delani, not realizing where Raymond was calling from, told Raymond to go to Washington, D.C. for a travel certificate. Raymond explained his location for the call and asked Ms. Delani if the lady at the Washington desk was right.

"Why on earth should she refer you to New York for such a minor document?" Ms. Delani asked rhetorically.

"Well, you can come to New York if you want but I'd hate to see you do all that running around just for a travel document you could easily obtain just where you are," she said.

Raymond thanked her and hung up.

The situation looked bad. Raymond had made no plans to go to

New York. It was Thursday, and his plans to travel on Saturday could be in real jeopardy.

Raymond stood by the phone booth, anxiously searching for a possible solution. He thought about a bribe. It certainly would be against his personal principle but if that avenue was to be the only option available, he knew he'd have to use it.

It suddenly occurred to him he could request to see a higher-ranking Embassy official. He could talk to someone higher in the chain of command and obtain his travel documents. Most people would be sympathetic to bereavement in a family, and Raymond planned to sound as miserable as he could.

The Spanish gentleman who came for a visa stood stranded outside the entrance of the embassy building when Raymond arrived again. He looked uneasy as Raymond greeted him.

"Any luck?" Raymond asked.

"Nope," he said. He looked worried and paced up and down, his right hand in his pocket and his left holding his black briefcase.

"I have to fly Lufthansa Airlines tomorrow to Frankfurt and then to Lagos for a business meeting and they're telling me the embassy doesn't issue visas on Thursdays," he said angrily.

Both Raymond and the Spanish gentleman shared their disappointments about the uncommon diplomatic folly, and Raymond hinted of his plan to appeal to a diplomat with a higher position in the Embassy, if necessary the ambassador himself. The man opted to join Raymond and immediately introduced himself as Gregorio Sanchez, a Mexican citizen.

After a brief discussion about his business quests in Nigeria, the two men re-entered the Embassy building and asked the receptionist to expedite their meeting with her boss. She obliged after initially objecting to Raymond and Gregorio Sanchez's request and disappeared into an inner office. She came back in a few seconds.

"Go around and come to the door that leads into this office," she said, pointing to the door.

Both men went into the office but Raymond knew the odds were heavily against them. Gregorio, as a non-citizen would probably find it almost impossible to be successful.

The same lady who spoke to Raymond waited by the door to let them in. They went into an office where a short woman in her late forties sat behind an executive desk engaged in a telephone conversation. The thick glass lenses she was wearing covered most of her forehead. Conspicuously displayed on her desk was a tag bearing only the name "MRS. UDOM.". There were guest chairs available for three, and Raymond and Gregorio Sanchez sat down, facing Mrs. Udom's tiny figure and hoping she'd get off the phone soon.

Mrs. Udom was explaining to the person on the other line why it took longer than usual to process his or her application for a passport renewal. Raymond's instincts warned him to handle his dealings with her with extreme caution.

She hung up and wrote on a piece of paper. Looking up she said, "What can I do for you, gentlemen?"

Raymond began his appeal routine, and when it was all over, the answer was a simple no.

Gregorio told his version of how urgently he needed to travel. He made no emotional appeal, only stating he had already booked a flight, same as I did.

Mrs. Udom explained to Gregorio Sanchez it was a day no visas were issued by the Embassy, but took his passport, and for the next twenty minutes, she was busy processing Gregorio's visa to Nigeria.

Mrs. Udom handed Gregorio Sanchez his passport after she had completed the documentation and cautioned,

"You know, for you, I have violated the law of our mission."

"Thank you very much, madam, for your consideration," Gregorio said, opened the passport book and smiled delightedly at the sight of a Nigerian visa stamp.

Prior to Raymond's departure from Nigeria a decade ago, some civil servants demanded bribes up front before rendering services to citizens. Raymond wondered if Mrs. Udom could have expected some kind of gratuity from him. Maybe, he thought, he didn't look rich enough and wasn't worth her time. Raymond was outraged, but decided it would be in his best interests if only he could just hold back his anger.

Gregorio had lived in Nigeria, indeed. Evidently, he grasped the knowledge of that culture. He hideously produced a fifty-dollar bill and handed it to Raymond, then motioned him to pass it to the diplomat.

Mrs. Udom was busy writing when Raymond hurriedly took the money from Gregorio Sanchez and waited for Mrs. Udom to conclude her writings.

"That's all. You may go now," Mrs. Udom said as she looked up at Raymond.

"Madam," Raymond said immediately.

Mrs. Udom stopped her writing again and looked up to face Raymond.

"Here, a little something for you. We sincerely thank you," Raymond said, immediately dropping the bill on the desk close to Mrs. Udom's reach.

"Look here, I'm not the type. Take this rubbish away from my face and get out of my office, right now," she blurted and stood up, pointing to the door, her eyes blazing. "Out! Now! Do you want me to call the security on you?"

She picked up the receiver and instantly dialed.

Raymond couldn't think of a way to save face, and for the first time in his adulthood, he was frightened by an unarmed human being.

Raymond knew one thing was certain— he had to get the hell out of there, and fast.

Gregorio watched astonishingly as Raymond picked up the money. He turned around and found Gregorio Sanchez had disappeared from the office. Raymond thought, *the least he could have done was pick up the money.*

Mrs. Udom was still cursing loudly while calling for Security. Raymond left in a hurry. He walked out the door feeling like he had just suggested a peace talk with Hezbollah to an Israeli.

Outside, he walked across busy M Street. He looked back to be sure no one was coming after him and heaved a sigh of relief for successfully making it out of the building.

An ambivalent Raymond headed for his car. As he neared the car, he remembered that Gregorio had left his fifty-dollar bill. He regretted the whole episode with the Hispanic. With Raymond's current state of mind, if he met Gregorio Sanchez again, he'd consider delivering a sucker punch.

Raymond sat in his car, staring sheepishly at passersby, still furious. He had been turned around, denied a certificate to visit his own country, witnessed injustice that favored a foreigner, and finally was persecuted for attempting to play the middleman. It was 2:40 p.m. and Raymond was still away, no hope. His hunger had vanished and all that was left was his problem. The more he thought about it, the angrier he became.

Raymond subconsciously took out the fifty and it all came back. He came awfully close to tearing the bill, but paused to think it over.

Perhaps someone from the Embassy and in a lower rank could stamp the paper for him for the fifty lousy bucks. Attempting to bribe higher officials in the country had always been risky. There was always the risk of dealing with the wrong person.

But it had always worked with lower level employees, Raymond thought, and so he'd have to go looking for an alternative. He was desperately in need of the document. However, he realized that going back into the building would require self confidence, something he knew he certainly didn't have right now.

After rethinking the idea and knowing he had to resolve the issue of his travel document, it seemed worth trying, though.

Raymond went and stood at the corner about five yards from the entrance of the Embassy building. He was looking for a younger looking staffer.

He counted six people go in or out, all of them middle aged, but he could not find the courage to approach any of them. The seventh individual, a male, looked relatively young and he quickly summed up the courage to approach him. Raymond felt the man looked less threatening and was at least mildly sure the man was approachable.

The man introduced himself as Bala Maitama after Raymond introduced himself and hinted him of his quest at the Embassy, exaggerating a little bit on the issue of why he was traveling.

"If you can find anyone who can help me out of this, I'm ready to pay half a hundred bucks for it," Raymond said.

"I think I can help you with that," Bala Maitama said. "But first, let me go in to make sure the rubber stamp will be available."

Optimism began to replace his dismal mood.

Ten minutes later, Bala Maitama came out and handed Raymond a one-page form to fill out.

"Here," Bala Maitama said. "Fill this out now and I'll take it inside with me."

There wasn't much to be filled out on the form, only Raymond's name and his lost passport number, date of birth and physical data.

Raymond handed it to Bala Maitama after completion and Bala Maitama returned to the building.

But even after Bala Maitama left, Raymond didn't really feel relieved. He was very aware of the event that took place in Mrs. Udom's office. However, if Bala was successful, it would save Raymond a lot of time, money and trouble.

Bala returned in twenty minutes to collect his reward. Bala told Raymond he was going to share the fifty dollars with the secretary, whoever she was that would stamp the form. Raymond couldn't wait to get rid of the bill and he quickly handed it to Bala.

"Give it five more minutes and I'll bring the document to you," Bala said as he pocketed the bill.

"So you're sure I'm getting the document, right?" Cause I wouldn't want to have to go to New York Consulate office before my flight."

"Sure," Bala said. "You'll see. Don't worry about it."

Raymond wasn't worried about that. Rather he was worried about how cowardly he had handled the situation with Mrs. Udom a while ago. He was feeling there might have been a more dignified way to handle the embarrassment other than cowardly marching out of her office like a zombie when she commanded.

Raymond stood by the street corner waiting for Bala to show up with his papers, while once again thinking over his decision to make the trip to Lagos. The embassy incident had soured him on the whole project. All he wanted was to drink a couple of Heineken beers and on to bed to sleep off the frustrating day.

The wait was unusually long, over forty-five minutes since Bala told Raymond to not worry. And although it seemed highly unlikely, Raymond began to wonder if he Bala had ripped him off and bolted through the back door.

A short, dark-skinned man in his late sixties came out amidst several men and women, who trouped in and out of the building. He approached Raymond, papers on hand. The man was wearing a crisply ironed cheap, gray suit.

"Are you Ronald?" he said, pointing the folded papers at Raymond.

" I'm Raymond," he said.

The man looked at the white sheet of paper and read the name on it.

"Sorry. I mean Raymond. Mr. Maitama says I should give you these." He stretched his hand from a distance of about three yards away while still walking toward Raymond.

Raymond took the papers from him.

"How come he didn't bring them himself?" Raymond said, assuming he would have like to offer Bala an additional ten dollars gratuity.

"He has gone for the day," the man said.

Raymond thanked him and he quickly returned to his office.

Raymond's mind was unsettled with what the messenger had just told him. Bala had gone for the day. Raymond started to think of how Bala had left without at least informing him. But Raymond had the papers anyway. He started going to the direction of where he parked his car without checking the contents of the pieces of papers.

Raymond drove off and it was a traffic jam along New York Avenue that provided him his first opportunity to look at the papers

Mr. Bala Maitama of the Embassy of the Federal Republic of Nigeria should go down in the Guinness Book of Records as the greatest cheat since Ferdinand Marcos, Raymond thought. The form he had delivered to Raymond was the same form Raymond had filled out with no official signatures or sealed stamps on it, only Raymond's passport photograph clipped to it. It was accompanied with a note.

RAYMOND,

I HAVE COMPLETED THE FORM FOR YOU. NOW THE ONLY THING YOU'LL HAVE TO DO IS GO TO OUR NEW YORK CONSULATE AND PRESENT IT TO THEM. THEY WILL TAKE IT FROM THERE. GOOD LUCK WITH YOUR JOURNEY AND BYE.

PS: DON'T LET ANYONE KNOW WHAT I HAVE DONE FOR YOU, BECAUSE MY BOSS MAY FIND OUT AND I WILL BE IN TROUBLE.

BALA

It was 4:30 Thursday and Raymond was supposed to be traveling to Nigeria on Saturday, just two days. Raymond decided to cancel the trip. The burden was becoming a little too much and it was something he never wanted to do anyway.

The traffic finally cleared by the city limits and Raymond was on his way home. It was a long and disappointing day, but Raymond could live with it. After all again, who wanted to be in a hurry to be nabbed by the DEA, Raymond thought. Still, he was split between working harder to make the journey and aborting it completely. He weighed the pros and cons as he sped through highway 95 North. He thought about the hassle that would involve the travel certificate if he pursued it, carrying the drugs and naturally, the scary flight for over ten straight hours.

Raymond came to the conclusion that making the journey wouldn't be in his best interest, at least for then. He decided he would simply postpone it. When he remembered that aborting the trip would also mean being able to watch the Redskins take on San Francisco 49ers on the coming Sunday's big game, his choice seemed quite clear and reassuring to him.

Raymond would telephone Clyde and Kenny when he got home. They might think he was too unappreciative, but he didn't care if that would be their assumption. After all he was his own man and made his own decisions. Why should he do business on their terms and not his? That's what was wrong with him, he thought. He always did things to please other people. It was about time for him to do things his way for goodness sake.

James had left before Raymond arrived, and except for Ogu, the house was extremely quiet. The ticking from the wall clock could be heard from every corner of the house.

Raymond loosened his necktie and sat lazily on the sofa, his legs crossed and rested on the coffee table going over the day's ugly incidents. After rethinking the folly, he told himself to wake up and move on. He didn't have to use that one stupidity as a litmus test for his manhood. he'd simply have to swallow his pride and learn how to handle those situations. He guessed he was forcing himself to forget all and it wasn't coming easy. The incident at the embassy was just too degrading to him, especially his encounter with Mrs. Udom.

Raymond almost fell asleep when he remembered to check on the phone messages. He lazily stood up and dragged himself up to his bedroom. The digital message counter showed Ramond received eight calls. That meant James had been gone for long. Raymond rewound the recorder and listened without enthusiasm as the callers took turns to let him know who they were and what they called for. Kenny and Clyde left messages too, asking Raymond to return their calls as soon as possible. Raymond had expected that. The last caller was James. He had phoned to let Raymond know there was a speed boat he wanted to purchase, and he needed Raymond's opinion on that. He also left his number.

Raymond called Kenny first, and C.J. told him Kenny had been gone all afternoon. Then he called Clyde, and coincidentally both Clyde and Kenny were there.

"How did you go, okay?" Clyde said rather impatiently.

"Problem. A big one," Raymond said.

"What is the problem?"

Raymond narrated his experience to Clyde.

"I know I blew it, man, but maybe next time it will be possible," Raymond said, trying to discourage Clyde.

Raymond was expecting Clyde to give up as much as he had done, but Clyde's reply astonished him.

"That's no problem at all. Just pack up and be ready. In the morning I'll take you to National Airport so you'll catch a flight and take care of everything in New York," he said.

"Hold on, Raymond," he said immediately, "Kenny wants to talk to you."

After pausing briefly, Kenny's voice came on the line.

"The big masquerade Karr man," Kenny announced, "don't worry. Just pack up, be ready, and tomorrow things will be better— a whole lot better, buddy."

The mood of both men seemed upbeat.

Clyde came back on the line after Raymond had finished speaking with Kenny, only to inform him they were coming to pick him up later.

"Okeedoke," Raymond said, disguising his disappointment.

"What are you doing now?"

"I'd like to prepare fufu. I'm very hungry," Raymond said.

"All right, call me whenever you're ready."

Raymond said okay and hung up.

Raymond's hunger re-surfaced with a vengeance. He had gone the whole day without food or water and now he'd have to go do some cooking on his own. Fortunately for him, James had prepared a delicious melon seed soup and all Raymond needed was to prepare fufu and warm up the soup.

Raymond still had to return James' call at the number he had left in the answering machine. Raymond replayed the tape to retrieve the numbers. When he dialed, a male voice answered and handed James the receiver.

"Ray Ray," James said. "I was just about trying again to see if you're back, and now you called. How long have you been back?"

"I'd say fifteen minutes," Raymond said.

"Be ready to join me in evaluating the boat I want to buy."

"Mmmm, okay," Raymond said. "What time?"

"I'm on my way now."

"Right on."

To be able to meet James's request, Raymond called up Clyde again while still cooking, to buy some time.

"Clyde, this is me again. I forgot I had somewhere to go with my tenant, James. So scratch coming up here."

"Oh yeah?" Clyde said. "Hold on, Raymond."

Clyde came back briefly, presumable after covering the mouthpiece and conferring with Kenny.

"Raymond, it is critical that I remind you not to tell James about your journey, right?"

Raymond said okay and hung up.

James arrived in the company of two other men, just about the time Raymond was clearing his dinner dishes. James had fixed his car and the next item on his agenda would be to purchase a boat.

The two men who accompanied James sat down on the sofa while he came into the kitchen to help Raymond clean up faster and hurry over to the boat seller's residence before dark.

When they were done, each person had a bottle of beer and Raymond took one extra bottle for the road.

As they drove along in Jame's comfortable Ford Landau, Raymond's thought switched back to his impending journey to Lagos. He felt his heart thump when he visualized a scene where he had swallowed cocaine and was about to walk past Customs officers at the check point. It became apparent in his conscience that he was not only against it, but also dreaded it.

Raymond's calmness surprised James and James was quick to ask Raymond if something was bothering him. Raymond had to pretend and faked an atmosphere of cheerfulness all through the ride and back to the house.

James and Raymond sat in the living room drinking in an impromptu celebration of James' boat purchase when Kenny and Clyde knocked on the front door.

The pricing of the boat had been as easy as pricing an apple from a local grocery store. James was determined to buy it if the price was reasonable. The Angel Gabriel couldn't have stopped him from paying the twenty-five hundred dollars the man had requested. It was the excitement of being a boat owner that gave way to the Thursday night's party which Kenny and Clyde joined.

When it was almost over at 10 p.m., Clyde, Kenny and Raymond, leaving James and company behind, went upstairs to Raymond's bedroom to confer on his itinerary. Once again, Raymond caved in to the terms of the two men. Raymond would be going to New York the following morning.

At the conclusion of their brief conference, Raymond became aware of why all the men interested in sending him to Lagos had been struggling to be sponsors. In the Lagos connection, there was a significant financial reward upon their safe arrival. Raymond had asked Kenny how Richard would fit into the ring, and Kenny explained to Raymond the whole deal. Richard had been bumped out of the transaction by Kenny and Clyde.

When Raymond spoke with Richard in Richard's hotel room prior to his departure back to Atlanta, Raymond had promised to call him first when he made up his mind, and now Raymond had been let into a different connection by the man whom Richard had paid to do a job. Kenny explained that if Raymond would be interested in going the second time, they could go with Richard as the sponsor.

Raymond thought it was inconsiderate of Kenny to suggest a second trip while the prospect of the first was still tormenting him, and Raymond wasted no time to counter Kenny's outrageous suggestion.

"Kenny, I really appreciate what you're trying to do for me, but I certainly don't intend to play a game of Russian roulette with my life and freedom in this dangerous deal," Raymond said.

Kenny quickly apologized and suggested Raymond lie to James he'd be traveling to New York and planned to spend two weeks in the Big Apple.

It wasn't enough for Raymond, so he decided to go with reality. James was his tenant and should be fully aware of where he was in case of an emergency. He felt it imperative to inform James of his real plan.

Raymond briefed James later about his intended journey, excusing his urgent need to travel sooner because of a traffic court appearance in two weeks .

It proved to be a genuine excuse, because James had previously planned that they both leave together, and that would have been within the period of Raymond's traffic court appearance. Raymond dared not be a no-show and risk a Failure to Appear arrest warrant. One thing Raymond dreaded was an FTA arrest. Raymond could see James fight back the surge of anger and disappointment, though James put on a cheerful face.

"Well, I wish you good luck, but." James cleared his throat twice and continued, "I can only wish you the best of luck."

James' anger faded away as the night progressed, or so it seemed to Raymond. Everybody was tired and Raymond needed his rest in order to function fairly in the morning. They had arranged that Kenny would drop Raymond off at the airport using Clyde's car and would therefore have to spend the night at Raymond's. It had also been arranged that Kenny dropped off Clyde and picked up the money for Raymond's hotel expenses, since Raymond would be staying in New York for the night before his flight, and the expense money until his 4 p.m. take off time on Saturday.

Clyde chose to fly to JFK airport, coming along with Jeff one hour before boarding time, all for reasons best known to Clyde alone. Clyde would be handing Raymond the directives of who to see and where to see him when he and Jeff met at the airport.

James drove his visitors home while Clyde and Kenny drove off to Clyde's apartment to implement their plans.

Raymond went back upstairs to pack his luggage, yet still determined not to fully accept, whole heartedly, the seemingly inevitable trip to Lagos. The image of crossing the gate at the customs check point, knowing that they were aware of intestinal carriage of cocaine haunted him and filled him with anxiety.

Raymond also thought of the success rate for those he knew who recently made the courier trip, including Dennis Metu, whose purchase of a BMW automobile had become the talk of Washington Metropolitan area and vicinity.

James returned and came to Raymond's bedroom while Raymond packed his luggage. They talked mostly about the fun of being in Lagos and very little of Raymond's main purpose for traveling, which was to ingest illegal drugs and courier them into the United States. The phone rang, and James returned to his room to answer.

Later, Kenny phoned from Clyde's apartment to advise he was on his way over and to remind Raymond to come down stairs and open the door when he arrived.

Raymond had finished packing and went downstairs to await Kenny's arrival. He sat on the sofa watching a detective movie and trying to weigh the consequences of the enormous risk he was about to undertake. His mind returned to the moral aspect of it, the implications of having to be associated with drugs, and dealers whom he had repeatedly castigated in the past. Raymond thought of a mayor who publicly campaigned against drugs but used crack cocaine in private. Raymond found no difference between that and what he was about to do.

He began to think again of a possible means to back out of the trip. He'd have to call Dennis and see if Dennis might have any suggestions.

Raymond shifted closer to the telephone and dialed Dennis's number. His Jamaican-born girlfriend answered in her sexy accent and put Dennis on the line.

Dennis said he would only advise Raymond to make up his mind and stopped being a coward.

"You don't have to go if you're not interested," Dennis said, "but never say I didn't let you in on the chance you needed to strike it rich."

While Dennis and Raymond were discussing over the phone, Kenny blew his horn as he drove past the front of Raymond's house, and pulled into a parking space. Raymond was about to terminate his phone conversation to open the door for Kenny, but James came quickly downstairs and beat him to it, apparently assuming it was someone he had been expecting earlier. James went outside to receive his supposed guest only to find it was Kenny.

Dennis and Raymond were still talking over the phone until both James and Kenny came inside the house.

"Commissioner, I've got to go. Someone is waiting for me," Raymond said.

"Okay, Commissioner. To tell you the truth, I'm really thinking about making the trip again, but I'm having reservations as to going the second time," Dennis said.

Raymond was surprised at Dennis's hint but chose to ignore the topic.

Raymond hung up and turned to Kenny, who had come in with James and had sat down on the sofa. James, feeling disappointed for being interrupted of his sleep, went back to his room.

"Did everything go okay?" Raymond said to Kenny.

"Oh yes!"

Kenny was about to reach into his pocket when Raymond told him to hold on until they were upstairs, where Raymond thought he might be able to better concentrate. They both talked about Kenny's own side of the experience as a drug courier and Kenny offered Raymond some advice of where to anonymously go for entertainment and sight-seeing while in Lagos.

"You'll need some sleep. Why don't we go on to get the messages straight and call it a night. I'm tired myself," Kenny said as Raymond was flipping through the channels on TV.

"Good idea," Raymond concurred and switched off the twenty-six inch screen.

Raymond led Kenny upstairs to discuss the messages from Clyde. Clyde had given Kenny three hundred dollars for Raymond and asked him to telephone him as soon as Raymond obtained the traveler certificate from the Nigerian Consulate in New York. They both retired to their sleeping positions afterwards.

Three hours later Raymond was still rolling restlessly on the bed sheet that he spread on the floor. He had yielded his bed to Kenny, who was deeply asleep and snoring loudly.

But it wasn't any discomfort that was keeping him awake. Raymond rethought the whole thing over and still didn't like it a bit. Whenever his thoughts arrived at flying into JFK airport and undergoing customs routine check, his heart pounded. Kenny had advised him to fly into Dulles International Airport on his return trip as Kenny deemed Customs more lax in their searches of arriving passengers there. That encouragement wasn't enough for Raymond's heartbeat. Raymond had never been in trouble with the law and naturally had a beginner's fear nagging him. Not to mention his moral code now behind torn asunder.

Raymond finally fell asleep, conceding he was being a coward just as Dennis had suggested. After all, he wasn't a recidivist criminal and shouldn't use this one incident as a litmus test for his personal character. For Raymond, the illicit deal was only like sampling a mask that could easily be peeled off. He would unmask right after that one trip. A recidivist criminal didn't have the self-control to quit. He did. That was enough concession for now.

Raymond woke up at dawn to find that the time was only showing 3:45 a.m., and that he had only been sleeping for a little more than two hours. That wasn't a good sign for him, as he anticipated a busy Friday in New York.

He tried to force himself back to sleep by concentrating, but encountered a new dimension of his insomnia— Kenny's loud snoring. It became so loud that Raymond couldn't concentrate enough to fall asleep. He reached out with his hand and nudged the waterbed steadily in a futile attempt to wake Kenny up without appearing to impose, but only achieved momentary silence each attempt.

Morning came gradually and the perennial sound of insects at night began to diminish as Raymond stretched from one end of the floor to the other. There was also the roaring of the 6 a.m. B&O freight train that warned Raymond it was time.

Raymond stood up and rushed to the bathroom. Later, he ironed his shirt before waking Kenny. They were set to go by 6:45, and Raymond went into James' bedroom to inform him of his early departure. James only hummed approvingly as Raymond re-emphasized that he took good care of Ogu. Raymond knew he could count on James, especially when it came to the dog, but James was too sleepy to respond more affirmatively.

"Make sure you lock the front door," James mumbled as Raymond was leaving.

Raymond knew James only meant that to convince him he was awake and comprehended what Raymond had said, but Raymond knew that James wished the hell Raymond would let him continue with his morning peace.

The morning traffic was beginning to surge, and the street lights were clouded with light fog when Kenny and Raymond headed for Washington National Airport. After a sleepless night, Raymond wondered if he would be able to sleep off the one-hour flight to New York in a bid to overcome his usual aerophobia. Thinking of the flight injected a sudden uneasiness, despite the relatively short time he'd be in the air, and he was quick to voice that concern to Kenny.

"Man, I can't tell you enough how scared I am to fly," Raymond said.

"Why?" Kenny said, looking astonished.

"It's in my blood. I just can't feel safe with the airplane."

"Well, go with AMTRAK then, but that's no use since you're still flying tomorrow for ten to twelve hours."

Amtrak sounded like a good idea to him. If aero phobic Raymond could possibly avoid a ten-minute airplane flight by using any other means of ground transportation and spending five hours, he'd go for it.

"How long does it take to get to New York by train?" Raymond asked Kenny.

"Approximately two hours."

Raymond calculated the time it would take to arrive in mid-town Manhattan, and came to a conclusion that he'd be better off going Amtrak.

"Take me to Union Station," Raymond said emphatically. He was relieved.

They headed for Union Station and veered off at East Capitol exit. Their discussion focused on tips to avoid being singled out when Raymond arrive at Dulles International Airport, and briefly on the situation in the Persian Gulf, which had received a less focus from them in the past couple of days.

Kenny and Raymond arrived at the passengers drop off at 7:30 a.m., in time enough to catch the 8 a.m. Metro Liner service. After a final briefing, Kenny drove off, and Raymond proceeded to the ticket counter. He found out that he would not only be more comfortable traveling by train, but would also save a substantial amount of cash. About eighty dollars, The Nigerian Consulate was a five minute cab ride from Madison Square Garden where the train terminated.

Raymond fell deep asleep and woke up at the terminal. Raymond grabbed his luggage, went to the cab stand, and hopped into one after a short delay standing third in line.

Nigerian Consulate had offices on the fortieth floor of the commercial building in Midtown East Manhattan. The elevator opened directly into the offices. Two service windows were open to attend the public.

Everything Raymond was told in Washington to bring along was necessary to process his application, and it took less than twenty minutes to obtain his long awaited travel certificate. It was all over at 11:20 a.m. and Raymond was set to travel the following day.

Chapter 6

Romantic Encounter

Raymond needed to find a cheap and decent hotel, and he set out walking from one hotel to another, asking and comparing prices. Kenny had suggested Hotel Wentworth on Fifth Avenue and he found none more reasonably priced.

Having checked in, he placed a call to Washington and spoke with Clyde, who was in a hurry to leave his apartment for an appointment. Clyde received his message with clear enthusiasm and reminded him of their meeting at JFK airport one hour before check in at the boarding entrance. He hung up and feeling exhausted, he laid across the bed with his feet on the floor, still wearing his shoes. His mind was preoccupied with his mission to Lagos when it dawned on him that he hadn't had breakfast. He was too lazy to hunt for food and decided to first take a nap before doing anything else.

The cozy room was clean and the queen-sized bed was comfortable as he relaxed watching CNN, hoping to doze off for good. When he finally turned on his side in his usual sleeping position, losing concentration on the TV, He still couldn't sleep. The Lagos trip had filled him with fear and kept him wide awake.

He decided to give up on napping and hunt for breakfast after all, also hoping that whatever food he was about to munch on could push him back to sleeping mood.

He stood up and changed to a casual dress, wearing only a pair of slacks and a white shirt and the same pair of shoes he had on. Reaching inside the breast pocket of his jacket, he counted out fifty dollars from the money Clyde had given him and left the room.

He wandered leisurely from one corner of the busy Big Apple street to the other, searching for a fast food restaurant and doing some looking around. He was standing by a street corner among several other pedestrians waiting for the walk signal to come on when he noticed a lady standing next to him, also waiting. She was tall, slim and attractive with straight legs.

Raymond stared at her and their eyes met, but she was quick to look the other way while he lustfully admired her gorgeous shape. She was wearing a knee-high tight crème-colored skirt with a "v" cut on each side, exposing her unblemished thighs slightly above her knees, and showing a tiny portion of her white-laced inner wear. Her blue earrings matched perfectly with the light-blue flowered blouse that only half covered her ample chest.

The walk signal came on and everyone began to walk across the street. Raymond continued to walk beside her, but cautiously to avoid a misconception, since he was aware she had already noticed him staring at her when they were standing at the street corner.

A few blocks later, other pedestrians dispersed, leaving him and her walking alone toward the same direction, her in front. Halfway down the block, she looked back and their eyes again met. It was Raymond's turn to quickly look the other way in pretense of searching for something in particular.

New York City, he said to himself, shrugged and shook his head.

He decided the next two streets would be his breaking point. Some heartbreaker like her would certainly require a Ferrari or Lamborghini to pull on the side street and invite her for a ride. Raymond wasn't in that category..

About 5 feet 8, 125 pounds, she seemed to be of Latin descent with brown eyes, a pointed and perfect nose and average-sized lips. Her curly black hair fell to the middle of her back, creating a sensational appearance from every angle of perception.

Raymond hoped the next pedestrian signal flashed the DON'T WALK signal to provide him with a final opportunity to feed his eyes on her straight legs and it did, this time with fewer pedestrians standing alongside to obstruct.

"Which direction is Broadway?" Raymond's question was vague and almost involuntary as he fixed his eyes sheepishly on her.

He knew he had just crossed Broadway. It was the street that he stood waiting to cross the intersection where he first saw her.

For a moment, he thought she was going to ignore his question. It was something he had anticipated, but surprisingly, she didn't. She turned to face him.

"You just passed it," she said. "Go back two blocks."

The friendly smile on her face and her gentle New York accent put Raymond at ease.

"Oh. I can't believe myself," he said in pretense. "Thanks a bunch."

"You're welcome."

Raymond started to walk back, but felt he had to inevitably compliment her.

"By the way," he said as he turned again to face her. "Take good care of that body."

She smiled and thanked him.

"Do you promise?"

"I promise. Take care of yours too."

"For your sake, I'll try harder," he said, hoping it provided an opportunity to strike a conversation.

He turned back again and started walking while she crossed the street. He thought of what she had just said to him and concluded she was merely returning his compliment. Their eyes met again at a half block distance, both of them simultaneously looking back, and once again she quickly faced forward. He knew he could have made a catch had he had the right stuff. He'd have to concentrate on his trip to Nigeria, which could provide him with certain instant wealth despite the awful feeling he harbored. He was feeling like a rookie airman on his first bombing mission.

He went past Broadway and continued to walk along Sixth Avenue, now seriously searching for a fast food restaurant and feeling the clumsiness of not having had breakfast. It was 3:45 p.m. and the busy streets of the Big Apple looked spectacular. Still, Raymond wouldn't settle for anything other than late lunch. Earlier on, he had come across the big hamburger places, and couldn't decide what he wanted to munch on. He had had in mind a square meal restaurant, but after his encounter with the Spanish beauty, hunger erupted, and he didn't care what he ate as long as it filled his stomach.

The Oriental Steak House claimed to have the best sushi-bar in Manhattan with Oriental menu. Curious about their ambitious claims, he headed for their restaurant and decided to give it a try. He walked into a sally-port that led inside the restaurant and was immediately greeted by two short Asian men smiling, and uniformly dressed in black suits and white tuxedo shirts with black bow ties. He was led to a seat where he barely ate the raw fish he had ordered with regrets at the recommendation of one of the waiters. When he finished, he paid the steep price and angrily walked away in an empty pocket.

He was feeling the discomfort from walking along the streets of New York without a dime in his pocket as he regretfully strolled back to his hotel room, cursing himself each time he recalled the dining ordeal. A coincidental sighting of the same Latin beauty walking along Sixth Avenue provided him with a much desired distraction. He wasn't about to miss that pretty smile in such a rare opportunity.

He immediately began to walk at a faster pace to catch up with her, and once again the "Don't Walk" signal came to his aid. However, she jaywalked. When she turned around and saw Raymond, who also decided to jaywalk toward her, she smiled at him.

"So we meet again," he said as he came closer to where she was standing.

"It's a small world, isn't it?" she said.

"What do you make of the suggestion that today could belong to us and your star and mine are magnetizing?" he said.

"Well," she said and shrugged, "Who knows. It might well be."

"My name is Karr, Ray Karr," Raymond said, hands in his pants pockets.

Raymond was reluctant to offer her a hand shake for fear of possible rejection. He relinquished that gesture entirely to her discretion.

"I'm Laura," she said. "Nice meeting you."

They chatted and walked along the sidewalk to the next traffic signal. The walk signal lit on and they walked across the street side to side.

"You're South American, correct?" Raymond asked.

"My mom is Mexican and my father is from here- Upstate New

York. I was born and raised in the city."

"So whose magnificent body did you inherit, your mother's or father's?"

She stared hard at me and grinned. "Aren't you a sweetheart," she said. "I guess my mother's."

Raymond thought for a moment he hadn't expected such a positive response.

"Where are you from? Don't tell me. I'll guess," she said and thought for a few moments. "Ghana?"

"Close. Nigeria," Raymond said. "Why did you say Ghana, ever been there?"

"My best friend in high school was from Ghana. She told me how pleasantly mannered African men can be, and your gentlemanly behavior gave a hint, I guess."

"Well I'm flattered. I knew there was something special about you."

They walked close to Raymond's hotel. He didn't want to make that known to her yet, concerned she might dismiss him prematurely by suggesting they called it a day. She was on her way back to Queens but first had wanted to stop by a Specialty Goods store. Raymond volunteered to accompany her, and to his pleasant surprise, she didn't object.

"Oh, that is so kind. Are you sure like I'm not dragging you off your way?"

"If I may ask, are you married?" he asked.

"Nope, you? Like I know African men always have wives in their home country"

"Well, my common-law recently deserted me. You know, you have a gutsy boyfriend. I'd be nervous to let my girl with such magnificent looks stroll by herself in a crowded New York City."

"What's wrong with me walking by myself? The city's safe during the day."

"I wouldn't want you to have to be opening your own doors. You deserve to have it done by me, if I was him, and I do wish I really was in his shoes to have you."

She smiled and shook her head. "What's your astrological sign?"

"Cancer," Raymond said.

"Really? It's a good sign. I'm Gemini."

"Great. What do you make of that? I mean the two stars together?"

"They're like attracted to each other."

"Is that your boyfriend's sign?"

"Nope, that's probably why we never got along very well. He sort of like kept trying to prove he was smart and I didn't like that."

"Do you live with him?"

"Of course not. We broke up like nearly seven months ago and I never wanted to see him again."

"It gives me ultimate pleasure to know there's a chance of courting a charming lady so intelligent and witty," he said.

Grimaced, she shook her head as if in disbelief.

"Like you're the kind-a guy that like make a woman think and feel good, Ray." She inserted 'like' many times in every sentence whenever she spoke.

"If being honest about women would do that, please be enchanted, for I hereby witness it in you," he said, again lustfully admiring her sexy image from head to toe.

The city rush hour traffic was at its peak. Laura and Raymond had been talking for more than thirty minutes, walking slowly and brushing by other pedestrians, some of them hurrying either to catch buses or trying desperately to hail a city cab. They walked inside the Specialty Goods store. A few people walked around, browsing. Laura had told Raymond during their conversation she wanted to buy a gift for her favorite aunt whose fourth wedding anniversary was coming up in the next week. They took their time searching for the perfect gift for Laura's aunt. She was leaning toward purchasing a gold broach but changed her mind because she thought it would be too simple. She finally zeroed in on two African-carved decorative, an elephant and a giraffe, imported from Kenya. Raymond had suggested that to Laura and she thought it was a better idea, and when it was time to ring up the cash register, she vehemently rejected Raymond's offer to have it charged on his credit card.

Occasionally, during their browsing, they'd come close to each other enough to smell the faint aroma of the shampoo she used on her dark, curly hair.

Raymond bought a small pack of heart-shaped chocolate candies when Laura was busy talking to one of the sales ladies. He intended to give it to her as a present later.

He and Laura left the store and stood outside, talking more about their lifestyle, what they liked to do and what they didn't like about the city. He told Laura he was en route to a business trip to Lagos and that he lived in a suburban town in Maryland, close to Washington, D.C. Laura said she had been to Washington once when she was nine years old and would love to be there again.

Later on, it was time to hail a taxicab for Laura, after a cherished late afternoon chat with her. Raymond took out his business card and gave it to her, writing his hotel phone number on the back, and watched as she ran her neatly manicured fingernails in her handbag to fetch a piece of paper. She found one and with the pen she borrowed from Raymond, she wrote her home phone number and handed it to him, folding it into two.

"You can call me any time after five thirty weekdays. I'm off weekends," she said.

"Really?" Raymond said. "Would I be asking too much if I request yet another round of get-acquainted talk tonight over the telephone with you?" Raymond said flirtatiously.

Raymond was becoming used to Laura's sassy smile each time he asked a question of that nature, and adored her shyness.

"Tomorrow is Saturday, so I don't mind staying up late to talk if you so choose."

She objected to his request that she called him at the hotel, but Raymond wouldn't give up easily. He used that gesture to determine how much Laura was interested in meeting him.

"Why do you insist so much that I call you first? Why can't you just call me and we'll talk, cause I kind of think you're an interesting guy to talk to, seriously."

She caved in when he explained it would be symbolic if she took time to reach him, but he didn't tell her how much pleasure he'd derive from a phone call from her. Raymond thanked her and asked her if she liked chocolate candy.

"I love it," she said.

He immediately opened the pack of heart-shaped candies he purchased unbeknownst to her in the Specialty Goods store and unwrapped one. He asked her to open her mouth and she did. He placed the candy on her tongue like a holy communion. She closed her mouth, sucked on it and thanked him.

Raymond un-wrapped his to chew but she quickly intervened.

"Let me see," she said and took it from his hand. She reciprocated his overture, and that moment became the high point so far in their first day of meeting each other.

It was time to hail a taxicab, as the evening slowly progressed and the slight chilling of early fall began to touch the flesh. Raymond could see her try to hide signs of desperation to head home, but he knew what time it was. He wouldn't ruin his chances by boring her, so he waved his hands more definitively to stop a taxicab.

No sooner had Laura left than his daring business adventure returned to his memory, escalating to a new high as he thought of the countdown to his departure. Raymond returned to his hotel room to watch CNN International Hour news for progress on the Gulf conflict.

He began again to visualize his post drug courier life and just couldn't foresee himself as a free man in the society. He knew Clyde and Kenny had spent money to get him so far, but that didn't mean he owed obligatory allegiance to them. He wasn't in such a terrible financial mess, come to think of it. If Raymond canceled the trip and hung on a little longer, his products from Switzerland would be arriving and his pre-arrangement with a local food chain would guarantee him an instant ten grand for a beginning. He'd pay taxes and live comfortably until the legitimate market grew. He'd be able to do other things in life. Above all, He'd be the super daddy he always wished for his son, one he knew his son would be proud of.

Raymond fell asleep at about 7 p.m., still wearing the same clothes he had on the whole day. The TV set stayed on. Without a concrete determination to abort the trip and return to his sense of human decency, Raymond knew he was making a head-way toward catastrophe. What a prerequisite.

He woke up to the loud sound of the telephone ringing and he picked up the receiver. The front desk clerk said he had a Miss Hazleton waiting on the line to speak with him. As she mentioned the name that Raymond had almost forgotten, Raymond's heart thumped briefly and stopped as he asked her to put the caller through.

Laura's sexy voice was unmistakable when she told him it was her. She had fulfilled her promise.

They spent over an hour and a half talking about them. They talked about African culture and how excited she was about her aunt's wedding anniversary gift, and a little about the Gulf War. Most exhilarating for Raymond was their arrangement to have brunch together Saturday morning at ten, since he would be leaving for JFK Airport at four in the afternoon to meet Clyde prior to his five o'clock departure flight.

"I'm really appreciative of your calling me. You kept to your promise, and that's classy," Raymond said.

"My pleasure," Laura said, "and I'll see you then, okay?"

At the conclusion of Their phone conversation, he would come to know as much about Laura as she did about him. At twenty-five, she had graduated with a Bachelor's degree from the Rochester College of the University of New York in 1988, and had been employed as a marketing analyst with a Manhattan based consulting firm.

He telephoned Clyde immediately after he hung up with Laura and confirmed their meeting. Raymond also called Dennis and Kenny to talk about his exciting new friend, Laura. Having concluded by checking with James to see if his common-law wife had had a change of heart, and receiving a negative answer, he hung up and set out to find a late dinner, settling on pizza by the slice. It would take care of him for the night, and he watched CNN until he fell asleep again. For the first time since he had agreed to embark on a drug courier journey, he slept uneventfully.

The hot morning coffee was refreshing as Raymond sat idly on the tail end of the hotel queen-sized bed. He had called up the room service when he woke up at seven. The excitement of his brunch date with Laura helped overshadow the stomach butterfly from his planned drug courier mission. He couldn't wait to see Laura again, imagining her charming eyes and innocent smile that exposed a faultless set of white teeth.

Raymond gulped down the last of what was left in the cup and set out to prepare for his big date. He dressed the bed, showered and groomed, hoping he wouldn't look out of place with Laura by overdressing. He dressed in his Italian dark cream, double-breasted suit and a navy blue silk shirt he left open-chest, exposing his tiny gold necklace, which matched my bracelet. He wouldn't want to be dressed sumptuously all to go out with someone dressed in a casual wear, perhaps jeans pants.

Laura called at 9:44 a.m. to let him know she was on her way. It would be a half hour before she would be arriving at the hotel. The waiting was nearly unendurable for Raymond as he sat on the bed barely watching CNN. Laura arrived much earlier than he expected, calling him from the hotel lobby in just twenty minutes. When Raymond went down to the busy lobby, Laura had gone to wait in her car, leaving him with no alternative than go ahead in what he was wearing, regardless of what outfit Laura had on.

Raymond saw Laura staring while she sat behind the steering wheel of a brown late model Nissan Stanza. He was convinced Laura looked like an angel. She was wearing light red, tight-fitted dress and a pair of gold earrings that matched perfectly with the broach pinned on her chest. She was bare legged, no pantyhose. Her legs were straight and she wore a tiny gold bracelet on her right ankle.

"You arrived earlier than I expected," he said as he took a seat next to Laura. He buckled up with the passenger seat belt while simultaneously checking out and admiring Laura.

"I overestimated the Saturday morning traffic," Laura said.

"Your outfit is fantastic," he said.

"Thank you, and so are yours."

He thanked her as Laura engaged the automatic gear, and they drove off for their first date.

Laura drove to a French restaurant in Greenwich Village, south of Manhattan, where they had planned to go. Raymond noticed, as they entered the lavishly furnished restaurant, that most patrons in the restaurant were as well dressed as Laura and him.

When the brunch was over, Laura maneuvered her way to settle the bill behind him. Raymond had called up the waitress, a middle aged white woman with a European accent, to demand the tab and she told him Laura had taken care of the sixty-one dollars bill. He was ticked and a little disappointed.

"Is this supposed to be a date or just a lunch treat by you? I'm not impressed at all, Laura," he said with a frown.

"I'm sorry, George, if I offended you, but I thought it would only be the right thing to do if I'd treat in New York. If I come to Washington, you'd take care of that," Laura said apologetically.

"That'll mean going Dutch, isn't it?" he said.

Laura did not understand Raymond's statement, at least so Raymond thought, and Laura kept on apologizing.

Raymond paused to think for a moment.

He felt his disappointment evaporate after mentally processing the impact of what Laura had just said- Laura coming to visit him in Washington, DC, and becoming his guest. It could only happen in a dream. He was speechless for a few moments.

"Do you forgive me?" Laura said with a friendly smile.

"Only if you accept these thirty-five dollars from me," Raymond said, holding the money for her to receive.

"Oh, c'mon, Raymond," Laura said, "Do I have to?"

"Accepting the money can only go halfway in repairing the disappointment. Laura you shouldn't have done it."

"All right all right. Anything to make up for this," she said jokingly in a low voice while receiving the money. "Now do you forgive me?"

Raymond nodded affirmatively.

"Still friends?" Laura followed and extended her hand to shake Raymond's. The minor feud drew attention from the two African-American women sitting next to their table. Raymond's thought was that one day instead of shaking hands they would kiss each other. However, he had a strong feeling it could take a while for that to occur, or maybe never, for he knew his intended journey to Lagos amounted to a reckless gamble with his freedom.

Laura and Raymond left the restaurant and drove to Hotel Wentworth, hiss layover hotel. Raymond suggested they spent the rest of the afternoon at the hotel's bar for drinks. Laura told him she never was a drinker, but could handle a glass of wine just so we could talk further.

The front desk clerk told him they didn't have a bar service. Their disappointment showed on both of their faces, sending Raymond's mind racing for an alternative. He desperately wanted for both of them to spend his last afternoon in New York together before his departure at 5 p.m., and he felt it would be ungentlemanly to suggest going up to his hotel room on their very first date. On the other hand, going to another hotel would jeopardize his meeting Clyde at the airport on time.

"Other than having one of the hotel maids go buy drinks for us to kill the time upstairs, I can't think of anything else to do," Raymond said.

"Why don't we buy it ourselves while we're here before going up?"

"Good idea," he said, carefully hiding the surprise feeling and the excitement to Laura's suggestion in him.

Raymond and Laura walked side-to-side two blocks down Sixth Avenue to a beer and wine store, attracting as much attention from people walking by the streets as a celebrity couple. Some passing guys openly commented, congratulating Raymond for walking and talking with a beautiful lady. Others merely whistled, perhaps just to loud their approval.

Raymond selected his favorite, a six-pack of Heineken beer. Laura left her choice of wine at his discretion and he chose a large bottle of chilled Martini and Rossi Asti Spumanti, paid the bill, and they walked back to his hotel room. The fourth floor hallway was quiet and free from intrusion. Raymond nervously unlocked the door and opened with caution, leading the way just in case he had left a mess uncovered before his hurried departure. The hotel maid had cleared the coffee tray and whatever mess he had left.

Setting the drinks on top of the chest of drawers while Laura stood and looked around the room, Raymond lifted his suit-jacket from the lone upholstered chair in the hotel suite.

"Please have a seat and make yourself comfortable," he said as he walked to the closet to hang the suit jacket.

Raymond dialed room service and requested two drinking glasses and a bowl of ice cubes. Laura sat down on the chair, placing her hand bag on top of the chest of drawers. He turned on the TV set again and they briefly discussed the Persian Gulf conflict.

Moments later, the hotel maid knocked on the door. She came in as Raymond opened, holding a tray containing his order. The maid walked straight to the small wooden coffee table to set the tray down.

"Thank you, miss," Raymond said as the maid was about to walk out the door.

"That's okay," the maid said in a thick Spanish accent. She left, almost slamming the door behind her.

If the maid had grievances, she had a terrible way of hiding it from guests. Raymond hoped Laura didn't notice, although he didn't care if the hotel maid's problem had stemmed from his room service request. It could have been that she received nothing from him in the form of gratuity.

He served the ice in her cup and opened the sparkling wine, filling her cup before his. He picked up both cups and carefully handed Laura hers. They both followed with cheers and sipped the drink before he switched over to drinking his Heineken beer.

Raymond had hardly consumed half of his first beer and Laura's glass of wine was still close to the rim when their friendship began to unfold into romance. A knock on the door disrupted their conversation on political life in Washington, DC. Raymond stood up from the bed and went to open the door. An elderly Irish woman wearing a purple dress and a set of eyeglasses stood in front of the door, her purple handbag hooked on her left arm, and a flyer on her right hand.

"Sorry to disturb you, sir, but I'm looking for a Dr. Fessenden. I have an appointment to meet him at one o'clock here," the woman said in a weak tired voice.

"What room number did he tell you to go to?" Raymond said.

Laura came behind him as he held the door half open, and Laura leaned slightly against him trying to listen in to what the senior citizen was saying.

"The clerk at the desk told me he's in room six-o-four."

"Oh!" Raymond said almost with a sigh of relief. "This is fourth floor. You need to go two more flights up. This is four-o-four."

"Oops," the woman said. "I'm sorry. I think I'd pushed the wrong button in the elevator."

"That's all right, ma'am. Take care and good luck to you."

The lady apologized her way back toward the elevator and Raymond and shot the door behind him and silently heaved another sigh of relief. As they were about to retire back to their previous positions, Raymond held Laura's hand and she gently squeezed his. Raymond led Laura to her chair with his left arm around her waist and her right arm downward almost across his back.

"I'd like to re-emphasize that you're a knockout. Of course, you must have heard that so many times you must be sick of hearing it," he said.

They stood closely, now facing each other.

"I think you're handsome, too," Laura mumbled, but Raymond ignored her knowing she was merely reciprocating his candor. He had other thoughts.

Raymond could only wonder how a beautiful and highly intelligent lady like Laura allowed a mediocre like him get so close to her. He knew he had never scored a chick that elegant in his lifetime and the mere thought of prospective first sex with a new girl always made him feel like he'd piss in his pants. However, this time, the prospect of imminent sex with Laura there and then triggered a signal in his buttocks for number two. He hurried downstairs for the toilet on the hotel's lobby for fear of letting out an embarrassing fire cracker in his own bathroom. Moreover, he worried it might repel Laura and bust his chance to achieve a new and significant milestone.

In a record time, he was done with the toilet and raced the stairs back to his suite. His urine steamed and the heat from his shit could burn a grass. He apologized to Laura for having left so long and again boldly orchestrated their previous romantic posture.

Laura responded to Raymond's gentle pull on her waist and he wrapped his arms around her. Laura placed hers on Raymond's shoulders and crisscrossed them behind his neck, pressing her large and firm breasts hard against his chest. Raymond started to kiss her on the side of her lips, but she slowly opened her mouth and gently sucked twice on his lower lip. They paused briefly to lustfully stare at each other, and then began again with more gentle kisses, before exploding into a deeply passionate and lengthy kiss.

The prolonged kiss catapulted Raymond into seventh heaven, and he could imagine She felt the same. Laura started to caress Raymond's chest and unbuttoned his double-breasted jacket. She seemed to be having a little difficulty with the large buttons, but Raymond was enjoying watching her sexy fingers struggle tenderly for them, so he let her struggle on. There were only two to unbutton.

When Laura accomplished her task and began caressing Raymond's chest and biceps, it was his turn to unzip Laura's dress. Raymond extended both of his hands behind her neck, pretended to be having difficulty of his own unbuttoning Laura in order to ensure her full consent of what he was intending to do. Laura withdrew her hands from his chest and Raymond anxiously watched Laura unzip her dress to his pleasure.

She immediately kicked off her shoes and they resumed their tight hugging. Laura ran her fingers through to feel his chest, while Raymond's hands traced the lines of her tiny panties as he rubbed through her nylon dress.

"Let's take off our clothes," he suggested, and lustfully watched her reaction.

She stopped momentarily to stare at him and smiled, then slowly backed away from Raymond. Raymond quickly removed his jacket and began to unbutton his shirt. Raymond went to the closet to hang his clothes, wearing only his briefs, while Laura faced the half-sized mirror on top of the chest of drawers and plucked her earrings.

He came out of the closet to find her placing her bra on the chest of drawers, wearing only her tiny light-green panties. Laura turned around and walked toward him, exposing her ample breasts to him.

The tiny panties she was wearing barely concealed the upper portion of her soft pubic hair. Raymond cherished her defined curves and thought she was perfection personified.

They stood by the side of the bed and hugged each other, kissed once before Raymond buried his face between Laura's breasts, his pelvis curving out extensively to hint of the readiness for sex. He thought what could happen if Laura suddenly changed her mind on having sex with him. It would certainly devastate his emotion, so he'd have to start something immediately. She reached inside Raymond's briefs to feel his stiffened penis then pulled him gently toward the bed as if she had suddenly grown impatient. Raymond knew there was no going back, and in his mind thanked God with his whole heart for creating women.

The tense moment came as Raymond and Laura arrived in front of Nigerian Airways pier at exactly 4:55 p.m., fifty-five minutes late from the time he was supposed to meet Clyde, and five minutes before boarding. Laura had sped as fast as possible to get him there in a manageable time, since his lateness was inevitable. Laura had been everything he had ever wanted in his sex life, and Laura had expressed the same feeling toward Raymond and he was flattered by her candor. Sex with Laura left him insatiable. After every climax, one titillating glimpse of Laura's heavenly body would ignite a new and sudden urge to go at it again. They'd slept together after prolonged love making session and when Laura gently shook him awake, they had hurried into the shower and then out to dress up. Raymond managed to grab his luggage and they hurried downstairs to pay his hotel bill before speeding off to the airport.

Locating Clyde was the last step before boarding the flight, since he had the name and address of whoever would take care of the supply side of the drug deal in Lagos. Laura and Raymond arranged that she wait in the car for him to run inside to locate him. If he didn't find Clyde, they'd have to drive back to the hotel and the journey would be cancelled.

As soon as Raymond entered the departure terminal, he spotted Clyde nervously pacing up and down the large waiting area, looking around to see if he would emerge. Raymond quickly ran back to where Laura was parked waiting, grabbed his suit jacket from the rear passenger seat and bent over to kiss Laura through the window after shutting the rear door.

"I'll call you from Lagos, okay?" he said as he slowly backed away from Laura's car.

"I expect to hear from you, darling," Laura said.

Laura watched him step inside the door and Raymond turned around to wave his final good-bye. Laura waved back, marking the last of their sight of each other.

Clyde was frustrated about Raymond's tardiness when both men came face to face in front of the departure gate, but nonetheless he was relieved to see Raymond finally show up in time enough to board the flight.

"Jeff didn't show up," Clyde said in a wrinkled face that depicted a combination of shock, disappointed and betrayal. "But there's one Bryan Jason, a Jamaican already aboard the mobile lounge, who is also headed for the same mission. You'll recognize him through his foreign facial features and his slight Jamaican accent if you ask him questions. Meet with him and both of you should get along."

"What happened to Jeff?" Raymond asked.

"He's a playboy but don't worry about that right now. I'll take care of him later."

Briefly, the two men discussed Raymond's Lagos connection as the ticket agent processed his boarding pass. Clyde handed Raymond a white piece of paper with an address and a Lagos telephone number written on it.

"This is the guy who should be waiting for you and Bryan at Murtala Mohammed Airport. He's my brother. If he's not there to pick you up, catch a cab to his house. He'll take care of your expenses in Lagos and expedite that side of the market deal."

The ticket agent handed Raymond his boarding pass. Clyde immediately handed Raymond a puffy sealed white envelope and asked him to hide it inside briefs.

"There's ten thousand dollars in it. Give it to my brother. The other guy also has the same amount with him, and should also do the same thing. Please be sure to find him. He knows nothing about Lagos. In fact, he's never been to Africa before," Clyde said as Raymond was struggling to adjust the envelope he was stuffing inside his underwear.

Clyde then handed him two additional hundred dollar bills and told him it was for his initial use in Lagos. When Raymond started toward the Mobile Lounge, Clyde held out his hand for a handshake. Raymond ignored in pretense but Clyde reached out and grabbed his hand to force the handshake. Raymond then hastily proceeded to the mobile lounge for the long awaited and contemplated journey.

Chapter 7

TRAVEL

It was a hectic nine and one half hour flight that mostly quivered from JFK International Airport, New York to Lagos, Nigeria. The cabin, scarcely filled with passengers, had provided Raymond with enough room to stretch out, and he seized the opportunity. Enthusiasm ran high among some of the passengers, mostly Nigerian nationals, as the mobile jetway approached the DC-10 that had captured Raymond's imagination. He began to immensely admire the art of aircraft engineering as the jetway finally docked by the front side door of the big jet. As the flight attendant motioned Raymond to the coach section, he adjusted his neck tie, brushing by First Class passengers. Some of them were barely reading the books in their hands, half staring to see if they were being noticed by other passengers.

Raymond's shyness emerged at odd times. He was determined to walk with confidence but was betrayed by guilt of low morale. He walked faster, paying a great deal of attention to his uneven steps. He suddenly lost count, bumping into a First Class passenger rearranging the luggage in her carry-on luggage compartment.

"Excuse me, ma'am, I'm very sorry," he said to the woman.

Irritated, she glared at Raymond and immediately concentrated back to her luggage, ignoring his apology. He paused for acknowledgment, but looked every bit of a nuisance.

He proceeded toward the Business Class, feeling disappointed and embarrassed, a feeling that held in his mind until he got to his designated seat. Cursing silently at the lady, he took off his suit jacket and shoved it into the carry-on luggage compartment, locked the compartment and sat down to observe events. He immediately noticed a familiar face in the smoking section – the father of a close friend back in Washington, DC. The man wasn't someone he wanted to meet on such a clandestine mission as he was certain the man would intrude. Raymond, who was wishing he met no one he knew or who knew him, had always disliked smoking anyway so he ducked his friend's dad to avoid risking invitation to sit next to him for the long flight.

In a while the DC-10 rumbled along the tarmac, proceeding to the runway. Stationed at each seating section were flight attendants demonstrating on safety measures. Raymond was preoccupied with figuring how to fasten his seat belt.

Raymond was chronically aero phobic and the jet's movement scared the heck out of him, sowing some seed of doubt in him the Nigerian Airways jet could make it off the ground. He felt he would be hard pressed to bet ten dollars that the jet could. The worn out seat and the chipped off paint reminded him of an aerospace museum.

Right from take off until landing, Raymond observed every movement in the cabin, and his heartbeat pounded while the airplane maneuvered through turbulence. His eyes dilated all through the night flight. He had been thinking about the purpose of his infamous journey. It was his dream, when he arrived in America ten years before, to strive to become the best African in America. Being American, Raymond thought, required a certain measurable personal code of conduct among family members, friends, co-workers, and neighbors. There were those who owned America, and if at any time one made a move in the right direction, one was included, and asked what one could do for the country. There were Americans who brought out the best of their ability to maintain changes, and didn't ask what their country could do for them. There were people who lived in America, spending most of their lifetime seeking financial recovery, and therefore asked what their country could do for them. Finally, there were those who set America backward. They asked what they could do to America. All these myriad thoughts filled Raymond's brain.

Raymond had always been dissatisfied with his own category of living in America. Those in the more positive category, he'd admired and their feisty patriotism he'd aspired. Fighting to move up had been his goal since his arrival in the United States. Still fighting his fiercest battle only to maintain status quo, and fitting himself at the bottom of being American, left him feeling hopeless. He knew it would invariably result in failure. He couldn't eat the late dinner or early breakfast, thanks to aerophobia, only coming back to life when the airplane finally touched the ground with a thump, a chirp of rubber and the roar of reverse thrusting engines.

Passing toward a crowded hallway that led to the Nigerian Immigration check-point, Raymond began to wonder if he landed at Murtala Mohammed International Airport. Ten years earlier, the airport had been an architectural work of art. Now the dirty walls and non-functioning luggage conveyor belts put a significant dent in his memory of Murtala Mohammed Airport. The moment the arriving passengers approached the immigration officials who demanded their passports for screening, Raymond encountered a shock he had lost track of in his decade of absence. A man in his early thirties hissed from the side, waving, and as Raymond looked in his direction, he made a gesture that caught Raymond's attention. He singled out Raymond and asked the passenger behind him to move along the long line.

He offered to help expedite Raymond's screening process. Raymond carefully studied him and became apprehensive, but seeing the man on that official side of the gate relaxed him.

"I can help you do your paper quick-quick," the man said to Raymond.

From his observation, the man was being too careful in avoiding the use of "sir" in addressing Raymond, as that might betray the man's disguise as an authorized senior Immigration official. But Raymond wasn't fooled. The man was slim and pale. He was wearing a light-brown trousers and a matching jump suit, with a silver pen tucked in his breast pocket, possibly to give him the look of an airport official. Raymond noticed his worn out pair of black shoes but was willing to play along and gently handed the strange man his emergency travel certificate, which substituted his lost passport.

Carefully, the man took the paper. Raymond noticed that the man avoided his face and passed the white sheet of paper to the Immigration official in the booth. The official, a medium built man, about forty years old with a heavy Yoruba accent studied the papers and shook his head, raising his bushy eyebrows while looking at the man he called Raymond's helper.

"Go talk to him," the Immigration officer said, implying that Raymond's helper lead him aside for briefing.

As the Immigration officer only motioned with his head, Raymond noticed his slightly trembling hands that held his documents. Raymond searched his mind and couldn't remember a possible flaw with the papers, and he knew he wasn't subject to deportation back to the United States, although he almost welcomed that outcome. Speaking in broken English, the Immigration officer warned Raymond that his emergency travel certificate wasn't enough to re-admit him back into Nigeria. When Raymond asked what that meant, the Immigration officer explained it was a matter of unnecessary delay, but would cost a little gratuity to expedite a much faster entry.

"It will cost you one hundred American dollars," the officer said with a smile.

One hundred U.S. dollars was equivalent to one thousand Naira, and Raymond thought his so-called helper was well aware that mentioning the amount 'thousand' for bribery would sound outlandish.

Determined not to fuel the bribery scheme, Raymond asked to see the big boss.

"Sir, I'd like to know what problem the Nigerian Consulate in New York could not have detected," Raymond said with an angry look.

Though disgusted, Raymond managed a little smile. Both he and the officer were being noticed by other passengers behind him. Sensing possible trouble, the officer asked his accomplice to quickly return Raymond's document. He must have felt stranded at a crossroads. Raymond supposed he figured a little more pressure could have persuaded him to give in.

"No problem. I beg, find me something now," the man said, stretching out both hands with Raymond's travel certificate on one hand and the other to beg for a bribe.

"I don't have Naira bills sir, and if you don't mind, can I have my bag?" Raymond said with anger that sent the man a distinct back-off message.

Sensing Raymond's growing anger, he gently handed him the bag and looked at his wrist watch. He shrugged and pretended to have been late for some appointment, walked away, hopefully with shame and obvious disappointment. Raymond watched him as he turned his sharp pointed face for one last glance at him. His image reminded the young American of a malnourished Doberman.

Raymond proceeded toward the taxicab stand where he was greeted by a mob of cabbies who crowded the exit, each trying to grab Raymond's suit jacket to board their taxicab. Raymond began the inevitable struggle to retain his right to choose since the airport taxi was so disorderly. Raymond was mobbed by about twenty men in their forties and fifties whose underarms were evidently devoid of deodorant. The aroma that fumed from their clothes and sweaty bodies was largely due to a combination of hot African climate and malfunctioned air conditioning. The trip itself was hectic enough, and even to speak was more energy demanding to him than the struggle to secure his own luggage. He felt a sense of resignation as the struggle narrowed down to a two-party duel, each party siding with their apparent leader.

The pushing and shoving continued for about ten minutes when suddenly a well dressed young man in his early thirties approached. He was wearing a pair of light-brown pants and a tan silk shirt with tiny gold stripes. His gold necklace was a dynamite match around his neck and his muscled chest.

"Hey!" the stranger yelled. "Stay away from him. Do you understand that?" He was addressing the feuding cabbies in an authoritative voice.

The cabbies, unsure of the authority of who may have approached them with such audacity, suddenly stood calm while the young man motioned Raymond to come with him.

"You all should be ashamed of yourselves," he said, snatching Raymond's bag from the leader of one group.

For the first time Raymond felt relieved, and followed him down the hallway leading to ground transport exit door. What a difference ten years in the United States made.

"My name is Ike. You're from the Ibo tribe, aren't you?" he said in a calm and friendly voice.

"You bet," Raymond said. "I'm Raymond, and if I'm not mistaken, you're Ibo too."

The Ibos have a distinctive accent, even when they attempted to conceal it. Raymond shook his hand and they both proceeded to the terminal exit. Raymond's curiosity began to distract him from fully paying attention to their conversation about the Nigerian International

Airport woes. Raymond tried to think of a logical reason why Ike would have taken such initiative toward a complete stranger. For a moment, Raymond pretended he wasn't looking Ike's way, but with every slight opportunity, Raymond looked at Ike, his mind struggling to make sense of the unsolicited kindness. Raymond simply concluded Ike probably just wanted to get him out of that horrible situation and perhaps in a random act of kindness, would only escort him to a more organized taxicab stand.

With Ike leading the way, they both walked outside via a set of malfunctioned double doors and as they brushed past two groups of uniformed policemen, the high humidity and the constant horn-blowing by motorists were a distinct reminder of good old Nigeria. The sentiment trickled in a sudden urge for Raymond to see old friends and relatives.

There were faces with tribal marks and men dressed in large traditional garments, sights that eluded Raymond in the span of a decade. The country had undergone a period of hardship, no doubt, and corruption had plunged the economy into chaos. Widespread news about the dismay steadily poured in to the States. Hit hardest, according to friends who had visited earlier, was the lower to middle class. Many of the people Raymond saw looked unhealthy, and there was no second-guessing the severity of malaise. Indeed a specter of economic anarchy. Nonetheless, it was still regarded as the pride of black Africa since citizens of other African states yearned to emigrate there.

Ike and Raymond strolled along the busy sidewalk while discussing the down turn in both the economy and infrastructure. Raymond glanced at his wrist watch only to discover that he needed to set it to local time. Ike told Raymond it was 8:44 a.m., six hours ahead of Eastern Standard Time, and Raymond reset the time accordingly.

Approaching a parking lot, where there were more taxicabs painted bright-yellow, Raymond decided it was time to go on his own. The men fighting for his luggage had long gone and he could finally hail a taxicab of his choosing.

"I think I can do it on my own now. Thank you so much," Raymond said, trying to reach for his suit jacket.

"Oh no," Ike said, "I'll take you to wherever in Lagos you want to go, if you don't mind."

Raymond knew the offer was the kind that never comes without financial cost. He quickly rejected it, but with an excuse that proved to have fallen far short of conviction.

"I'd have to call on too many of my friends before proceeding to my home state of Imo. So, don't worry. But thanks a lot, though," Raymond said.

"No that's okay. I have nothing to do but drive around today. I was only at the airport to drop off a cousin on a trip to Madrid," Ike said.

Raymond simply gave up and thanked Ike for his generosity.

They carried on with their discussion on the dismal economic status of the nation as they walked past a clamoring group of taxi drivers vying, probably illegally, for patronage. They arrived at Ike's car, a brown 1990 Jeep Cherokee. Ike hastened ahead of Raymond to unlock the passenger door. Raymond was sure he could handle whatever surprises that would spring out. Ike carefully placed Raymond's bag on the rear seat, and Raymond climbed into the plush front seat to a pleasant aroma of a brand new automobile. The minty interior reminded Raymond of the cockpit of a helicopter. Ike shut the rear door and went around through the back of the car to unlock the driver's side. Raymond shook his head in disbelief, wondering how such a young man could afford an automobile that luxurious in a country like Nigeria..

Ike switched on the ignition and reversed.

"How much will this cost me?" Raymond said, just to get the money object out the way if need be.

"Oh come on, Raymond. Do I look like a taxi driver to you?" Ike said wryly.

Raymond apologized and sharply diverted Ike's attention to an issue he thought was more genuine. "Now let me see, I need to proceed to Owerri. Can you take me to a good transportation service?"

"I thought you said you wanted to see some friends," Ike said.

"Never mind, I'll do that when I come back to Lagos."

It was Raymond's ploy to emancipate.

Ike and Raymond made an exit onto the busy highway. Raymond

only knew they were at Ikeja but didn't have an inkling of where he was headed. He wasn't worried about that either. Raymond had never stayed in Lagos for any longer than a week or two at a stretch. In fact, he had only visited the capital city two times and stayed a total of eighteen days throughout his life.

The currency Raymond had was all in American dollars, and it occurred to him he needed a currency transaction. He asked Ike if Ike knew where he could change dollar bills into local Naira, but Ike busied himself sifting through his music albums. Holding his hands upright, Ike signaled Raymond to hold on. When Ike finally selected his choice of music, he told Raymond the only place he knew was the local banks. When Raymond suggested they asked around, it was as difficult to change lane as it was merging into the highway. Because Lagos drivers weren't so kind to let them through, Ike had to risk an accident.

Having been gone for a decade Raymond was somewhat disoriented. He realized he hadn't witnessed flagrant public nuisance within that period. But certain characteristics such as defacing public sideways and area parks didn't come as a surprise to him, and Ike showed no iota of interest when Raymond brought up the subject. Ike simply dismissed the acute problem as a result of homelessness for which the government was responsible. Raymond was convinced, but astonished by what he thought was Ike's gross insensitivity toward the issue of homelessness.

Ike finally pulled to the right lane after weaving through traffic and the drivers cursing him loudly, shouting through their windows. They drove to the next exit heading toward Maryland section of the city of Lagos. Traffic became even more congested as they were held in a middle of the ramp. Ike cursed and looked at the time on the dashboard. It was 9:40 a.m.

"I knew I should have gone to the bank in Yaba. I always make this same mistake, and now we could be stuck here forever," Ike mumbled, his voice sounding a note of disgust and anger. "Are you in a hurry?"

"Not at all," Raymond said.

"If I may ask, what do you do for a living?" Ike said.

"Well, my last job was taxicab, but I have now completed a negotiation to import food products from a company in Switzerland."

The traffic moved slowly but steadily for a few yards and stopped abruptly. Ike cursed again and then looked back at the clock on the dashboard before assuring Raymond it will decongest from two intersections ahead.

"You could become a very rich man if you engage in an import business in America," Ike said.

Raymond chuckled. "Well, I hope to become one, but I'd have to work as hard as anyone else before achieving it. Hard work always pays off the good old fashion way"

"Which state in America do you live in?"

Raymond was about to tell Ike he lived in Maryland when the motorists behind, outraged by an apparent two-car length gap that existed between Ike's car and the one in front of them, began to honk their horns in protest. Ike quickly moved a few yards ahead. The super-slow traffic was now beginning to irritate Ike so much that he decided to search desperately for any available alternative route. Ike wheeled to the right in a desperate attempt to drive along the shoulder lane when they moved past the ramp.

"What state did you say? I'm sorry, I'm still upset about the wrong exit I followed," Ike said.

"Maryland. I live in a little sub-urban town called Riverdale, close to Washington, D.C. How about you, Ike, what part of Lagos do you live in?"

Ike told Raymond he lived in Ikeja where the international airport was located.

As the traffic moved slowly, Ike wheeled the Jeep Cherokee toward the shoulder lane and unlawfully stayed on that course until second intersection where he intended to exit. Other motorists followed behind to form a new lane. Some drivers in front wheeled in when they saw the Cherokee through their rear view mirrors. The traffic on the freeway was moving freely, and Ike was nothing short of delighted by the now steady flow. As they moved faster, Ike raised the volume of the reggae music. Raymond was still tense and wary of Ike's hidden intention and he sensed Ike read it in him.

"Do you have a choice of music?" Ike said. "I have, as you can see, so many choices."

"All kinds," Raymond said. "Play anyone of them."

Raymond felt Ike was only attempting to portray a calm personality to make Raymond feel more comfortable around him.

Raymond was beginning to feel the impact of an all night sleepless flight. He yawned repeatedly as the music lulled him. He felt his eyes closing involuntarily while struggling to stay awake, but the comfort of the Jeep Cherokee's seat compounded to make sleep irresistible.

Ike shook Raymond awake and told him where they were—at the commercial bank in Yaba, Lagos. They got out and Ike led the way through a narrow path leading to the side entrance of the bank building. Ike asked a uniformed security guard, who stopped them just before the main entrance to conduct a routine check, if a Ms. Bonner had shown up for work. The security guard, a stout middle-aged man with a big nose and abnormally large lips, humbly asked to be excused, apparently to check on Ms. Bonner. He hurried inside and in three or four minutes, came out to tell Ike Ms. Bonner wasn't in her office.

Facially wrinkled in a show of frustration, Ike looked at his watch, stroked his nose with the tip of his index finger and thanked the guard. He then left through the main entrance and walked to the corner of the olive green painted two-story building. Ike searched his pocket and produced a bundle of money, then selected a five Naira bill.

"I know that stupid guard. Each time I come here for a transaction, he always wants a bribe before I can meet whoever I want to see."

Raymond was a disappointed with the bribery issue but remained expressionless. He was under the impression that he'd eventually pick up the tab since the purpose of their coming to the bank was solely on his behalf. He wasn't sure if he could afford it.

"Ike, what's all this about offering bribe just to see a bank official? We're not here for a loan, are we?" Raymond asked Ike in disgust.

Picking up the tab wasn't only the issue for Raymond. Bribery was a bitter issue when he was struggling to expedite his bid to travel abroad for further studies. At that time, there was nothing Raymond could attain from the government without spending extra money he did not have much of on an official, even when he was absolutely entitled to it. Raymond could recall on one instance when he went to the city of Owerri to obtain a waiver from Student Advisory Board. He had forty

Naira to his name but was forced to relinquish all just to get past the secretary. To his dismay, the Foreign Students Adviser himself wanted a bribe of a hundred Naira. And so Raymond left town without a waiver and out all his money. He hitchhiked home to his village, hungry, tired, and frustrated.

This time around, Raymond had become used to parastatal fairness thanks to a decade in America, and Ike could detect the irritable attitude from his facial expression. Ike tried to convince Raymond they would only be wasting their time if they decided to leave only because they couldn't offer the security guard at least something. Ike also further explained the essence of dealing with Miss Bonner.

"She has a better rate for us in currency exchange, and I also would be receiving a very important message from her," Ike said.

Raymond walked behind Ike through the main entrance door that led to where the security guard was sitting. Ike handed him the five Naira bill and explained to him how urgently they really needed to see Miss Bonner.

The security guard eagerly stretched out his short hands and collected the bribe. "Thank you very much sir," he said in a deep cracked voice.

His face had greed written all over it, and Ike's face registered contempt.

The guard excused himself again, ran in just like he did the first time, and this time around came back with a lady following behind.

What Raymond couldn't comprehend was how the bank was such an empty place. Normally, a bank would be a much busier environment. But Raymond was too tired from the flight to ask, and only concentrated on the money transaction and impending six hundred-mile journey east of Lagos. It would be a direct violation of the drug courier profile professed by Clyde.

"Oh, Ike, how are you?" the woman said. Her voice was reassuring. Her initial rapport with Ike gave Raymond an impression of two ex-lovers waiting for an opportunity to meet again, perhaps rekindle an old flame.

"I'd like you to meet my friend from America," Ike proudly said.

The woman regarded Raymond. "You're the ones on top of the world," she said, readjusting her gold necklace, the brown skirt and light pink blouse she was wearing. Her sexy smile exposed a set of white teeth that had an out of place right canine, her unblemished face fixed directly on him.

"What's the sense of being on top of the world while my country is suffering?" Raymond said in an attempt to sound patriotic.

"What's your name?" she said, chastising Ike with her demeanor.

"I'm Raymond, and Ike told me you're Miss Bonner."

"You can call me Tracy," she said.

Raymond immediately obliged and Ike, who was almost acting flamboyantly, revealed something Raymond wished he knew.

"She's single," Ike jokingly and loudly said to Raymond.

Tracy laughed. "Listen to you," she said and gently slapped Ike's fore arm.

"You are pretty," Raymond said.

Tracy looked flattered by Raymond's compliment.

She invited Ike and Raymond to follow her to her office. On the way, Raymond asked Tracy why the bank was so empty. Tracy reminded Raymond it was Sunday and that she was just in on overtime. Raymond then realized why the traffic was not flowing freely, except for the exit. Ike freely guessed it was due to an accident somewhere ahead.

They proceeded to the staircase but Tracy had to have a word with the security guard. Raymond guessed it was to put any other visitors on hold.

"How do you like her?" Ike turned to Raymond and said confidentially.

"She is one of the sexiest ladies I'd ever seen in Lagos," Raymond said.

Raymond knew she was okay, but sexiest would be an obvious exaggeration, considering her slight overweight. Her complexion, though fair, appeared to have been artificially toned with bleaching cream.

"You know, she's available for you and she appears interested too,"

Ike said, again in a low voice.

"I know, but when I come back from Owerri, I may talk to you about her," Raymond said, pretending he was interested in her.

Raymond wanted to stick with Laura. He finally cited his marriage as an excuse to close the subject and succeeded in it.

Miss Bonner came back in a while and led the way to her office.

Her office was fairly Spartan.She pulled an extra chair from the adjacent vacant office and both men were seated.

After a twenty-minute discussion, dominated by political and economic malaise of the nation, Ike and Tracy got down to the money exchange business. In the end, Ike told Raymond to give Tracy two hundred American dollars, and he did without delay. Surprisingly, she didn't go to a safe drawer or the bank counter. Rather she immediately reached her handbag, opened it, and carelessly dumped the two hundred dollars, and then took out a stash of Naira bills from the same bag. She placed it on top of her desk and replaced her handbag. Counting out one thousand, eight hundred of the Naira in bills of twenties, she shoved the rest back in her handbag and asked Raymond to re-count the money. Turning to face Ike, she warned him the next transaction would cost him more than the nine Naira to a dollar bill she usually agreed to.

Raymond's hands trembled as he counted the delicately worn out naira bills. The fresh smell of bank money always gave Raymond a sense of wealth fulfillment and Raymond expected a bank transacting such large sum of money to hand him fresh bills. But the bills Raymond was counting were dirty and completely softened. Raymond needed to be wary of what was acceptable out there. However, with Tracy's official capacity in the bank and dire consequence if such scam were exposed Raymond was relaxed. Raymond felt he could always come back to exchange the worn out bills if needed.

It was all over in half hour and Ike thanked Tracy for her gesture. Ike led the way out of Tracy's office. Ike was about to reintroduce the topic on Tracy Bonner's availability as a single lady as they walked along the narrow path, back to the Jeep Cherokee, but was interrupted when the security guard hissed at them. They stopped, turned around and the security guard waved his short hands to signal them to come back. Ike took out a bunch of keys from his pocket and handed them to Raymond, singling out one he explained unlocked the vehicle's doors, and asked Raymond to proceed and wait inside the car. Ike then hurried back to the side entrance with the guard. Raymond proceeded to wait inside the comfy wagon.

A few minutes after Raymond waited, it was becoming extremely humid inside the SUV and Raymond had difficulty figuring out the mechanism to roll down the automatic windows. If Ike could trust Raymond, a stranger, with the keys to such an expensive automobile in a large and vulnerable city like Lagos, he had to be a one-of-a-kind Lagosian. Raymond concluded Ike's trust in him must have been because of the high regard Ike had for him. The American's thought shifted to his impromptu plan to travel out of Lagos, a decision that was just not sitting well with his conscience. Of particular concern was carrying with him a large sum of money, to the tune of ten thousand dollars that was not his. One hold up by an armed highway robber and Raymond would be in debt for that much money – to the bad guys.

Moments later, Ike walked leisurely out of the building, with Tracy walking beside him. Halfway toward Raymond, they stood and chatted for a few moments. Tracy walked back to the bank and Ike hurried toward the Jeep. Raymond unlocked the driver's side door and Ike climbed in, holding on to the steering wheel.

"I'm sorry for spending a long time," Ike said as Raymond was handing him the bunch of keys.

"No problem at all, as long as I can get to hometown by dinner," Raymond said.

Ike looked at the clock on the dashboard and again reassured Raymond there was absolutely no problem time wise.

As they pulled out of the parking lot and drove away from the bank compound, Ike suggested that Raymond hire a car-and-driver from Lagos to Owerri and back to Lagos, since Raymond was only going away for three days. Ike's suggestion came across as a brilliant idea to Raymond, except for the financial aspect of it. It would cost a fortune and Raymond will be in need of all the money he could save for hometown folks. Raymond wanted to portray an image of success and achievement. He had only scored at the minimum academic level with a Bachelors degree, and to his folks, mediocrity didn't earn respect. Flashing Naira bills to relatives would be his only way out, and Raymond knew it would all be possible due to the country's dismal nine to one foreign currency exchange rate with the American dollar.

When Raymond finally gave Ike's idea a good second thought, it appeared to him that arriving hometown in a chauffeured car could earn him the dignity he wanted. The more Raymond thought about it, the more he liked his idea, but the cost kept interrupting that fantasy. Raymond decided if it was somewhat affordable, he'd go for it.

"About how much money do you think this car thing will run me?" Raymond asked, trying to sound casual.

"I don't know exactly. It really depends on the kind of car and how many days you'll spend," Ike said as he re-inserted the reggae tape into the cassette player.

Raymond felt inadequately informed by Ike's vague answer so he decided to adopt a wait and see attitude.

"Let's go find a car," Raymond said.

It immediately occurred to Raymond he'd have to be sure whichever vehicle it would be, it would have to be no more than two years old. There were too many junky cars roaming the streets of Lagos, and it seemed like very few purchased late model cars since Raymond left the country. Most people pretty much maintained what they had within the past ten years. Considering the dangerous prospect of highway robbers, having to travel in an unreliable vehicle could turn out to be a catastrophe. Raymond implored Ike to see if that arrangement could be feasible.

Chapter 8

SCRATCHED AGENDA

Ike drove for about twenty-five minutes in almost no traffic and finally arrived at a commercial car park opposite a local market place. Raymond followed Ike as they proceeded to an area Ike called a "motor-park". They were solicited by commercial vehicle operators, who stood by their yellow painted cars to show off their late model cars. It appeared to Raymond they were used to passengers who drive in on classy late model cars like Ike's. However, Ike concentrated in soliciting vehicles that would be inconspicuous to commercial identification, and to Raymond's delightful surprise, found a fairly decent late model white Peugeot. Ike quickly got down to business discussions with the owner-operator.

Price negotiation was more intense than Raymond anticipated. However, Ike was familiar with the current inflation in the country, which placed Raymond at an advantage, embarking on a phenomenal bargaining. When it was all over, Raymond was hungry. His estimation before getting to the motor-park was two thousand Naira, an equivalent of roughly two hundred American dollars, but the outcome of Ike's intense bargaining resulted in a substantial savings.

The owner-operator of the luxury sedan interviewed Ike and Raymond. First, he asked to know how many passengers were going to be involved. He looked disappointed when Ike told him Raymond was the lone passenger. Ike insisted the deal would have to be on a flat rate basis. The driver, who introduced himself as Rasaki, made an initial request for one thousand five hundred Naira for Raymond's two-day stay. It was roughly a hundred and forty American dollars, already sixty dollars less than the two hundred dollars Raymond had estimated the chauffeur budget may cost. Raymond almost misinterpreted him, thinking he had mentioned a figure much higher. As he repeated the price, Ike grimaced and shook his head, then told the man to be serious or lose their patronage.

Upon Ike's verbal threat, Rasaki, a Yoruba tribesman who spoke only broken English became apprehensive. Medium built and peach dark complexion, with tribal marks of four parallel strokes on each side of his cheeks, his ability to articulate his reason why it would cost Raymond that much money enhanced the equilibrium in the pricing duel. Ike warned Raymond in Ibo tribal language to stay out of it and leave it between the two. Raymond had no choice. In fact, Raymond found himself enjoying watching the skirmishing. The asking price was well within his budget. He knew all along that he already had his car and chauffeur and therefore could care less.

"We can only pay six hundred Naira," Ike insisted.

Rasaki quickly objected strongly, advising Ike to try someone else, turning his back on him. However, both men needed the services of each other, and both damn well knew it. So Raymond hoped Ike wouldn't call the bluff.

"Well, you must hurry up and give us your last offer, otherwise we'll have no choice than do just that," Ike said, obviously ready to throw in the towel.

The outcome of the deal was astonishing to Raymond. Both agreed on a meager one thousand, one hundred Naira. Raymond felt it was a remarkable bargain, and he enthusiastically accepted the deal. Raymond began to realize how invaluably meeting Ike had proven to be.

Rasaki, now Raymond's chauffeur, after being congratulated by his business associates for pulling a big one, asked Ike for a twenty minutes preparation before taking off for the long journey. In his own explanation, he needed a change of clothing, but Raymond would have urged him to do just that anyway. Ike took Raymond aside to tell him the driver must change his smelly clothes and they saw the chance for a quick lunch.

Rasaki, excited over his sweetheart deal, drove off, and Ike and Raymond went into the market square in quest of a restaurant. They walked past a row of small, filthy looking restaurants on the right side of a narrow walkway. The thought of sitting and dining in such deplorable environment nearly subdued Raymond's appetite. However, Raymond recalled his years in high school when he visited "Mama-put," as was popularly known to be for such miniature places of eatery, and enjoyed the delicious spicy soup served by young beautiful African girls. It used to be part of the fun.

Halfway down the third row of the muddy walk, Raymond spotted a seemingly decent looking restaurant with a cleaner environment and suggested to Ike that they try the Inn that had no business name posted. Ike observed it further and noticed the slight improvement and seconded Raymond's opinion. They went in.

The seats were long, wooden benches and there were three tables in the narrow room. All three tables were decorated with faded red and white striped plastic table cloth, all stained with spots of food. Irritated by the gross eating environment, Raymond whispered to Ike that they tried another restaurant, but Ike told Raymond the inevitable.

"This, believe me, is the best we can find along the neighborhood. We have none better."

Both men were debating on the choice of staying or further searching when a heavy set, middle-aged woman waved her way in through a split curtain entrance that led to the kitchen.

"Excuse the dirty table, I will clean it. I'm available to take your order now," she said.

Ike initially ignored her gesture, and the sight of the woman Raymond supposed was the waitress, shabbily dressed in traditional blouse and wrapper almost entirely killed his appetite. Raymond felt there was no way he could have eaten there. Ike, although still speechless, seemed more relaxed. The woman appeared to be doubling as the waitress and the cook, since Raymond didn't see anyone else in her restaurant. She wiped off the spots in one of the adjacent tables and asked them to transfer to a cleaner table.

Raymond inquired what kind of soup she served. Surprising because Raymond thought they definitely would be leaving the dirty environment to search for a much cleaner one.

"I get any kind you want," she said, in broken English.

Raymond knew then he'd have to close his eyes and swallow the cold food. They sat down, discussing the old fashioned restaurant menu, while "Madam," as Ike referred her, waited impatiently for them. Raymond ordered a plate of rice and stew with goat meat. Ike ordered fufu with egusi (melon seed) soup.

Ike and Raymond resumed their discussion on the homeland's economic woes before their lunch dishes arrived about five minutes later. Madam was carrying a large tray when she returned from the kitchen. She placed the fufu dish closer to Ike, and the rice dish before Raymond. She then hurried back to the kitchen and immediately returned with a bowl of water for Ike to wash his hands. Traditionally, it was best to eat fufu with clean bare hands. Surprisingly for Raymond, the delicious aroma from the food unlocked his appetite.

While descending on their meal, Ike and Raymond discussed politics, economy, and the drugs epidemic. They talked about the upcoming transition of government from the military to civilian rule and the chances of a free and fair election. Raymond lashed out at his homeland's leadership for a non-concrete program in place to eradicate unemployment and looming economic problems. Once again, Ike couldn't agree with Raymond more on one of the many governmental issues. While they discussed drug problems, Raymond was a little surprised when Ike told him that drug dealership, as opposed to its dependency, had engulfed the nation.

"How does American government deal with the dealers?" Ike said.

"Believe me, Ike, they're extremely tough on dealers."

"I can't believe that people in their right mind will do that in America," Ike said. "They're enemies of progress, who would do anything to enrich themselves and have unfortunate drug dependents kill themselves with the substance."

Ike and Raymond unanimously castigated all drug dealings, Raymond hypocritically, denouncing the notion that drugs be legalized and treated as a medical problem.

"How do dealers get the stuff into America?" Ike said

"Frankly speaking, I know little about it, but according to the news media, people who had been arrested include boats and ship operators and pilots of commercial airlines and private aircraft." Raymond's hypocrisy was beginning to annoy even himself and he began to search for an exit strategy on the entire subject.

Raymond requested an orange soda, preferring it over regular water to be on a safe side. He hoped to avoid the use of a dirty cup to drink water. It was served immediately.

"I've heard of Nigerians, who continuously shipped drugs to America," Ike continued, "how do they do it successfully? They must be super-duper masquerades. The government of the United States has a very tight security around their borders."

"Again, as far as I know, that Nigerians import most drugs into the United States is an innuendo." Raymond explained to Ike about some Nigerian nationals that had engaged in usage and sales, but were brought to justice. "They obtained drugs locally and probably imported from countries like Colombia. Nigeria does not grow coca leaves."

Ike and Raymond were concluding their nearly half hour lunch at about one o'clock when Raymond spotted Rasaki wandering across, apparently searching for them. Raymond told Ike, who immediately dropped the other half of the piece of meat he was chewing, quickly washed his hands, and dashed out of the restaurant to stop Rasaki. Ike shouted at Rasaki twice and disappeared from Raymond's sight. Raymond was just about finishing the remnants of the orange soda when both Rasaki and Ike walked in. Ike told Raymond it was time to go and ordered Rasaki to proceed to the car and allow him and Raymond a few more minutes to finish lunch. Rasaki nodded and Ike came back to resume his fufu lunch.

"In your little knowledge, now, what are the kinds of drugs Nigerians get involved with?" Ike said.

Raymond explained that cocaine was the only narcotic and that all other mixes originated from it.

"You mean the white powder?"

"Yes. I always see it on the television news, and that's the closest I'd ever come to it. To be honest with you, Ike, that's one subject I'm very naive about, but I know very well how dangerous it can be to the user," Raymond said.

Raymond also explained and detailed the examples of athletes who died of cocaine overdose like Lionel Bower of the University of Maryland.

"I also know it is a crime of high magnitude if caught selling it."

Raymond chewed down a piece of meat and washed his hands.

Could have been that inwardly he was becoming guilt tripped for the same hypocrisy.

The lunch was delicious, and despite the flawed sanitation, Raymond still enjoyed every bit of it. Surprisingly, no other customers came in to dine all the over half hour they spent there.

Madam was dozing off on a chair in the kitchen when Raymond came inside and woke her up to pay her. When Raymond reached his hand inside his jacket, Ike came in and quickly handed Madam the fifteen Naira he had drawn from his pocket and told Raymond it was his treat.

They both hurried out of the small restaurant for the car park, where Rasaki was waiting rather impatiently in the car. Raymond thought about the journey as they hurried along. It was an exciting prospect, especially having been absent this long. A two-day only visit would certainly disappoint several friends and relatives, but Raymond did have commitments in Washington too. He intended to return to the country in December for his father's memorial service and a friend's wedding. That would be more than enough to offset anyone's disappointment.

Rasaki looked a little worried. They hadn't yet made a deposit to secure his interest and he openly communicated that to Raymond.

"You know you haven't paid me yet," he said, "and you're aware that in our business money on hand wraps up the deal."

Ike arrived and immediately responded. "No, no. You get your money after the service."

Raymond empathetically understood the chauffeur's concerns and he simply obliged. Having settled the money issue, Raymond shook hands with Ike, who asked to know where he, Raymond, would be staying when he came back to Lagos. Raymond told him there was a good chance he would be staying at Federal Palace Hotel, close to Bar Beach. Ike then went to his Jeep Cherokee to fetch Raymond's luggage. Rasaki opened the trunk and waited for Ike to bring the luggage. Secured, they said good bye and Rasaki drove off, headed for the car park exit that would begin a long exhausting journey.

"Owerri here I come," Raymond said to himself.

The prospect of visiting his hometown ended as abruptly as it was planned. They were driving along the outskirts of Lagos when Raymond noticed a red light on the dashboard, signaling a malfunction of some sort with the engine. Rasaki, who was well aware of whatever could have been faltering, glanced twice at Raymond through the rear view mirror and, finding Raymond staring precariously at the signal, pulled over to the side of the highway, cursing in his Yoruba language.

"Sir, I want check the car, I beg," he said, pulling toward the shoulder lane.

Rasaki stopped in front of a parked tanker-trailer and came out of the car, then walked back toward the seemingly abandoned tanker-trailer, leaving Raymond confused and nervous about what he was trying to do. Raymond watched him steadily and cautiously as Rasaki was leaving, only to find him standing astride, urinating on the middle wheel of the unattended vehicle. Raymond eased back inside the car and left the door open to have a better observation of what else Rasaki might have been trying to do. Raymond wouldn't want to be abandoned along an isolate highway.

Moments later, Rasaki reappeared and went directly to the hood and lifted it open. Having fidgeted on some spark plug wires, he came to the driver side, pulled the keys from the ignition, and went behind to the trunk. He came back with an orange-colored rubber can filled with water and emptied it inside the radiator. On his way to return the can, Raymond followed and retrieved one of the magazines he had packed inside the suit jacket. Hopefully, Raymond thought, he'd be in Owerri City by 8 p.m. in order to have a full day, and perhaps an extra half day before driving back to Lagos to meet Clyde's brother. Clyde's brother would panic, but Raymond hoped to explain. The man was sure to understand Raymond's reasoning. Bryan Jason, whoever he was that boarded the airplane with Raymond for the same mission, should have been able to handle the hassles of the Lagos taxi drivers.

Fifteen minutes later, Rasaki shut the hood and cleaned his hands with a rag he took from underneath the driver's seat. He inserted the key into the ignition and turned it to start. Nothing happened. There were no lights and no sound of engine starter.

Initially, the helpless driver appeared confident and went under the steering wheel several times, trying the ignition starter each time he fidgeted on the electrical wires. He went back to reopen the hood.

Both men spent the next hour trying unsuccessfully to get something positive happen to the car, perhaps a miracle of some sort. Rasaki labored feverishly to sustain his rewarding contract while Raymond stood by helplessly and offered sometimes senseless suggestions. Rasaki became so disappointed and disgusted that he began to curse more frequently in the Yoruba language, and Raymond could see the little hope Rasaki had fading away.

"Master," Rasaki said to Raymond in a final concession. "I go try stop another car for you. This one done break down, and I can't repair it."

Raymond wasn't surprised by Rasaki's revelation. The disappointing news had sunk gradually to Raymond, and he could hardly blame Rasaki for such an uncontrollable circumstance. Raymond had been having second thoughts about undertaking the impromptu journey anyway. That was sure to turn out to be the opportunity he had hoped for to cancel it. For someone who had left his hometown a decade ago, Raymond wanted to resurface in a much more dignified fashion and, although Raymond was being chauffeured with little money to spread, he had his doubts.

"Well, how can we get back to the city?" Raymond said.

Rasaki appeared surprised at Raymond's calmness. Poor Rasaki must have known all along his car was perhaps in hopeless condition, but he had held back that expression, thinking Raymond would be mad as hell and scold him should he reveal the bad news. Rasaki kept studying Raymond's face as they stood in front of the useless car, and Rasaki appeared more concerned with Raymond's local journey than his loss of potential income opportunity.

"I go find you another good one," he said empathetically to Raymond.

The first taxicab both men waved at pulled over after several trucks and other non-commercial vehicles sped by the highway. The taxicab had two grudging female passengers occupying the back seat. Raymond later came to learn the taxi was driven by a young Ibo tribesman in his thirties, who also spoke fluent Yoruba.

The taxi pulled over a few yards ahead and Rasaki ran up to discuss his car problem with the driver. Raymond watched as the taxi backed up the fairly maintained Peugeot closer to enable a transfer of luggage. Rasaki grabbed the small bag he had packed his clothes in. The cabbie angrily came out from the driver's seat, cursing as he exchanged harsh words with his two female passengers. Raymond noticed his indigenous Ibo tribal features, his broad nose and thick lips. Raymond knew immediately he'd met a home boy.

"Are you Ibo?" Raymond said.

"Yes," the driver said and went on to explain why his passengers were scolding him - because he'd interrupted their ride home to attend to Rasaki and Raymond. The driver had humbly tried to explain and apologize to the passengers, but they wouldn't listen, voicing outrage and causing him to lose his cool.

Raymond was explaining the unfortunate circumstance surrounding his disappointing transportation as the driver transferred his luggage from trunk to trunk, while Rasaki cleared his documents from the glove compartment of the disabled vehicle. The two grudging middle-aged women in the taxicab were immediately silenced, perhaps by Raymond's seemingly imposing presence as Raymond sat in the front seat and adjusted his seat. Raymond flamboyantly removed his jacket as if the taxicab was one of his fleet of taxicabs. The two women didn't even attempt to voice their own objection, only stayed quiet and carefully avoided eye contact with Raymond whenever he looked in their general direction.

Raymond broke the silence and greeted the women in a gentlemanly voice. They responded humbly in broken English, and Raymond could read the flattering expression on their faces. Raymond needlessly apologized for the inconvenience.

Rasaki and the driver, after arranging the route, took their seats and were all set to first drop off the women and then go back to the city. Rasaki took a seat as one of the two women shifted to the middle seat.

The thought of canceling his journey to Owerri hovered in Raymond's mind during their short ride back to the city after dropping off the women. Raymond had gone to seat next to Rasaki at the back where he calculated the pros and cons of the canceled trip, but a final change of heart came when Raymond further recounted his financial status. It was mid September, and if Raymond was successful in his illicit mission, he'd visit them when he returned in December. That was only if he successfully dodged the bullet at the port of entry.

"I think I'd have to postpone the journey," Raymond whispered to Rasaki.

"Why now? I say I go get you another better car, I promise," Rasaki said.

Rasaki persuaded Raymond further, insisting Raymond carry on. When it became obvious to Rasaki Raymond had taken a final stance, Rasaki handed Raymond a complete refund of his deposit.

Raymond redirected the taxicab toward Ikeja, producing the piece of paper that had Clyde's address and gave it to the driver.

Chapter 9

DEBRIEFING

A six-foot iron gate blocked the taxicab from entering a narrow compound of the address Clyde had directed Raymond to. The façade was elegant and had a palatial hint. A civilian security guard, dressed in a white Hausa tribal garment walked lazily out of a small guard-post and pushed open a pedestrian entrance gate separated from the main gate by a concrete pillar. He came to the driver's side of the windows, looking from one passenger to the other, a toothpick tucked in his mouth.

The driver produced the piece of paper Raymond had given him and asked the guard in the Hausa dialect if they were at the residence of a Mr. Ben Njoku.

The guard grinned his tobacco stained dentures, opened the gate after a brief rapport with Rasaki and the taxicab driver. Inside the compound, they were greeted by a teenage boy, who came out from the front door of the one-story building, apparently to help with Raymond's luggage. It was Raymond's first hint that he was expected. The cabbie came out of the car simultaneously with Raymond to unload Raymond's suit jacket.

"Are you Raymond or Jeff?" he asked.

"Raymond," he quickly responded.

The boy began assisting Raymond with the suit jacket from the opened trunk, almost struggling as he climbed the front steps. Rasaki came out and whispered to Raymond,

"The fare should be fifteen Naira. No pay more than that," Rasaki said.

Raymond nodded in approval despite a dissention he felt from his intuition. The Ibo tribe native taxi driver had gone an extra mile to transport Raymond, accepting a pay cut from his previous grudging passengers. Raymond didn't foresee a cash settlement of less than thirty Naira, considering the cabbie's troubles.

The cabbie put Raymond on the spot when Raymond asked him how much the fare was.

"We're both Ibos," the cabbie said, speaking in broken English. "I'll take anything you give, if it's not for the hard times, I should've transported you free of charge as brotherhood is concerned."

Raymond decided to offer him the thirty Naira he had guessed it would cost. It amounted to only three U.S. dollars.

"Is thirty Naira enough?" Raymond said, observing the cabbie's facial expression.

"Anything, brother, anything," he said, avoiding eye contact with Raymond.

The cabbie proceeded to the back of the car, noticeably pretending to be double-checking if Raymond's belongings had all been extracted from the trunk.

Rasaki looked disappointed, but nonetheless Raymond felt he should have understood the fact that Raymond was in a difficult spot. Rasaki tried to hand signal Raymond to suggest Raymond had volunteered an excessive offer, but was cut short by the quick reappearance of the driver, who must have sensed it coming.

The teenage boy stood at the opened entrance door of the house, waiting. After discharging the cabbie, Raymond entered the house and the boy shut the door.

Ben Njoku was leaning against the door frame that led to his bedroom when Raymond entered the large, lavishly decorated living room. Ben was shirtless and wore only a pair of jeans and was barefooted. He slowly walked toward Raymond and casually said hello. They shook hands and Raymond introduced himself and asked him if he was Ben.

"Yes. What about Jeff?" he said in a thick Ibo tribal accent. "Clyde told me he was coming along."

"He was supposed to meet me at JFK, but when I got there he was a no-show. Clyde probably knows where he is," Raymond said quickly in an effort to brush aside the issue.

"What took you so long? I waited at the airport from the moment the airplane flew in and I stayed until everyone cleared Customs."

Raymond felt glad Ben missed finding him anyway. Raymond had wanted to first visit his home town, which certainly would have constituted an operational risk based on a typical drug courier profile.

After a brief discussion about the disappointments Ben had been encountering lately on who was to be flying in and how the person had been scratched at the very last minute, Raymond told Ben about Jason, who supposedly flew with him on the same airplane. Raymond revealed how he was instructed by Clyde to get together with the stranger before the plane touched the ground.

"I had seen a face that looked foreign and stranded at the airport, certainly not the look of a typical African. I have a feeling that was Bryan Jason," Ben said.

Ben and Raymond immediately set out to look for Bryan Jason, but first Raymond gave Ben the ten thousand dollars Clyde had asked him to deliver to Ben. Raymond was surprised by Ben's indifference as he received the huge stack of raw cash. It was as if Raymond had repaid him a one dollar loan. He simply collected the bundle, went to his bedroom and came back out in less than a minute. To Raymond, ten grand was a staggering amount of money.

"Let's go," Ben said. He shoved his large feet into a pair of unbuckled sandals that he kicked out from underneath a brass and chrome coffee table.

As Raymond stood up and readied to go, Ben went back into the bedroom and in a moment came out again, buttoning up a red flowered shirt. Ben led the way downstairs to his garage where a gray late model Peugeot. In front of the car was also parked a blue Mercedes Benz sedan with an elegant white interior. Ben chose to drive the Peugeot.

The security guard opened the gate and bowed to them as Ben drove past him. Raymond returned by waving his hand but Ben ignored it all as if the guard was non-existent.

The airport looked nearly deserted, with few passengers coming out from a late Sunday evening flight and only greeted by ever present, overly aggressive taxicab drivers. Ben and Raymond had retrieved a valet parking ticket from a computerized machine installed at the gate, and pulled into a diagonal parking space.

"We will split locations to find Bryan Jason," Ben said. "Perhaps you should go to the information desk to have him paged to meet you there, while I look around the other end to see if I can find anyone that looks stranded."

"Okay," Raymond said.

The information desk located at the center of a large waiting area inside the main terminal also had identical luggage conveyor belts installed for the use of other airlines. Two young Nigerians, perhaps in their mid twenties, one a chubby-looking man and the other, a petite woman, sat behind a semi-circular counter, chatting leisurely when Raymond approached the counter.

"Yes, can I help you?" the man said, seeming slightly irritated for being interrupted.

"Yes sir, I'd like to have someone paged for me, please," Raymond said.

"Is he a passenger—? Because we can only page passengers, or if you're a passenger, we can page your host. You have to show us your air ticket, though."

Raymond explained how he had missed Bryan Jason. But the woman, not fully satisfied with the explanation, interjected.

"Well, we'll give you the benefit of the doubt. But don't come up here again unless you meet the airport passenger requirement."

Just as she lifted the telephone receiver to dial a page, Ben's voice came loud. "Raymond! I found him!" Ben said as he excitedly ran toward Raymond.

Raymond thanked the two employees anyway and walked toward Ben.

Bryan Jason had no single piece of luggage only the clothes he wore. All three men walked to Ben's car, while enthusiastically talked about the miracle of successfully locating Bryan Jason. Ben and Bryan Jason did most of the talking. Raymond was so exhausted from a day of traveling disappointment and was in sore need of a pillow and a bed.

Raymond sat on the back seat and Ben was preparing to drive back to his residence. He asked Bryan Jason why he had remained at the airport all day instead of catching a cab, and Bryan Jason explained.

Bryan Jason was dressed casually in a pair of ash-colored trousers and a white, long sleeve shirt. The black pair of leather shoes he took off had no fashion identity to its style. He looked Jamaican when Raymond met him, quite contrary to the description Clyde had given to him. Raymond had seen his face several times when he was searching for him at JFK airport's mobile lounge. But with a dark complexion, thick facial features, and low-cut hairstyle, and with his five foot, seven inch height, he didn't fit Raymond's impression of a brother of Dennis's girlfriend, Annette, who possessed a significant size body for a female. Looking at him, Raymond remembered Clyde had told him he was her brother, and it was then that his face began to look to him like one who would be the Bryan Jason. Raymond couldn't have linked the two relatives without being introduced or seeing him together with Annette.

"I had seen you in the airplane, and I kind of suspected you'd be Raymond, but was reluctant to approach you. I was expecting you to come to me. Once I started to approach you, but changed my mind because— you know," Bryan Jason said.

Bryan Jason had lost much of his Jamaican accent and spoke more refined English.

Another problem erupted. Ben's Peugeot wouldn't start. Moreover, it was almost evening, and the temperature was rapidly falling. If they had to wait outside for the car to be either repaired or towed away, Raymond wasn't dressed for the chilling evening weather, wearing only a silk shirt and a pair of slacks.

However, everyone stepped out of the car. After securing the locks, Ben hailed a taxicab to take all back to his home. He explained he had a personal automobile mechanic that he had contracted to come to rescue his car.

At the home they all sat around in Ben's living room, discussing confidential issues strictly relating to their mission. Ben either wasn't interested in other issues, or he was the shrewd type in business. He was simply a boring personality. He only talked when Raymond or Bryan Jason asked him questions. Illiteracy could have been to blame. Bryan Jason had also given Ben the ten thousand dollars cash as directed by Clyde, and he had asked Raymond and Bryan to choose their favorite hotels, if they had any. Bryan Jason said he had no choice and would be staying in a hotel close to Ben's residence, while Raymond chose Federal Palace Hotel in Lagos Island, which he had told Ike prior to his aborted journey that he would be staying in.

Ben was adamantly opposed to Raymond's idea of checking into Federal Palace Hotel but sensed he couldn't talk Raymond out of it. Ben contended it would be more convenient for him to keep track of both Raymond and Bryan Jason if they stayed in a hotel close by his house.

"This business is a masquerade game. Only divined masquerades play it and it must be played with absolute caution," Ben said.

When the debate was over, it was agreed that Bryan Jason would remain in Ikeja while Raymond caught a taxicab to Federal Palace Hotel in Eko.

Enthusiasm seemed farfetched between Raymond and Bryan Jason. The fear that had been ravaging Raymond about their illicit mission in Lagos had left him at a substantial distance from excitement. They sat in the living room trying to share each other's experience with misfortune. Bryan Jason explained his wife of four years had fled with his long time savings of nearly ten thousand dollars, essentially leaving him bankrupt. He wanted to run a quick drug courier and use portion of the pay-off to save his home in Maryland from foreclosure. He spoke with slight composure and had an American passport which, in general, was a safe bet for drug couriers to make it through customs - free of questioning.

Another intensely debated issue was Raymond's precipitous intent to honor his court appearance in Maryland for driving with a suspended license, scheduled for September 28th, less than two weeks ahead. Ben argued that a twenty-one-day minimum stay in Lagos would be necessary to provide a bona fide purpose of journey as true vacationers during screening by Customs agents back in the United States.

Ben's contention was idealistic to their overall endeavor, but Raymond was determined to honor the summons and avoid being issued arrest warrant for FTA (Failure to Appear). It had been a constant problem, which had plagued Raymond over the years, reneging in payment of his traffic violation fines that subsequently led to suspension of his drivers license. Raymond, in the last New Year day, had made a resolution to change that costly habit for good.

The same argument was heightened by Lufthansa Airline's flight schedule.

"It departs Murtala Mohammed Airport Monday evening," Raymond said, measuring Ben's reaction, "two days shy of my court date, and that means an even earlier departure than you would at least be a little comfortable with."

Ben was obviously dissatisfied with the situation.

"I'd pay whatever fines you will have incurred if you'd skipped the court appearance, just so your alibi can be smoothened at port of entry," Ben said with a mock smile that Raymond interpreted as a sign of frustration.

Ben's pressing appeal for Raymond to stay for the two weeks was ominous, his reasons plausible as he lectured both men on the full details of successfully running his clandestine drug courier operation.

"Firstly, Raymond," Ben further explained, "you have established a genuine reason for coming home after a considerably long absence abroad. But that being a plus, you shouldn't negate it all with an eyebrow-raising short stay. It surely appears phony and ridiculous if, for one who had not been to his country in a long period, you can only spend less than ten days."

Ben's explanation aptly exposed that possessing a passport that hadn't been excessively used in a Lagos-New York and New York-Lagos trips would most likely alarm Customs agents to suspect the pattern of a drug courier.

Raymond's passport couldn't manifest that. It would be a brand new passport and, according to Kenny and Clyde, obtaining a new passport would only be a minor problem in Lagos. Raymond just couldn't risk an FTA in a U.S. court that was certain to earn him at least a night in jail, plus fines and accumulated arrest record. It was yet another irony considering the enormous risk Raymond was about to undertake in his new role as a drug courier.

It was almost 7 p.m. when they concluded the plan. Raymond would be departing Lagos on a Lufthansa flight on Tuesday, nine days later, and travel through Frankfurt, Germany, and then connect a flight from there to Dulles International airport near Washington, DC.

Bryan would remain in Lagos for three weeks to ascertain his mandate, and would fly Nigerian Airways directly to JFK airport where Clyde would be waiting.

Ben dropped off Bryan Jason at a nearby low profile hotel and handed him a thousand Naira cash. He then drove to the airport freeway toward the airport in order to find a taxicab that would take Raymond to Federal Palace Hotel in Eko.

From inside the car, Ben waved down a cab, and Raymond transferred his luggage with the help of the driver. Ben also handed Raymond a thousand Naira cash and told Raymond he would be in touch with him in two days before the taxi drove off.

Chapter 10

LATE DIGRESSION

Federal Palace Hotel was out of suites in their new complex building. However their old adjacent building was scarcely occupied, and at substantially low two hundred and eighty Naira a night rate. Raymond wondered why at such a bargain price it was not equally booked out. The building's outer walls itself, although big and its compound excellently manicured with live plants and blossoming flowers, showed clear wear and tear as Raymond stepped out of the cab in front of the main entrance. He was exhausted and therefore more than willing to spend his lay-over anywhere. Moreover, he had told Ike he'd be staying there, and if he was to see Ike again, he had to keep to their mutual plans.

He had no delay checking in. He simply walked up to the concierge, the doorman leading the way with his luggage, registered with a five hundred Naira deposit, and was led to his suite by the extremely polite doorman.

He was too tired to even unpack his clothes when he sank in one of the two twin beds joined together. It had been a long day and he could finally relax and think over his assignment. He began to recall again his discussions with Ben, who had vehemently dissented on his plan to leave his neighborhood for the Federal Palace. Ben had carefully explained the importance of keeping to his idea but he just didn't consider a short stay in Lagos a more substantial risk than the mission itself. Why Ben laid much emphasis on him spending at least two whole weeks in Lagos was in his opinion simply much ado about nothing. Ben had advised both him and Bryan Jason to keep a low profile and not make their presence known to friends and relatives. He had to avoid any and all contact with his sister and cousins in Lagos. Ben practically forbade them from doing much of anything except stay in their hotels, and twenty-one days of that could bore an overfed python to death. In fact, right after Ben concluded with his instructions, Raymond began to feel bored already and focused his attention on the fun he had with Laura in New York.

Raymond woke up Monday morning tired and hungry, just lazily stretched on his bed and deeply thinking and dreading on the day he would be quizzed by the U.S. Customs agents at Dulles International airport. It would also be the day that, from every perspective, he knew he would be going to heaven or to hell. He also knew if he succeeded he'd have ten thousand dollars in raw cash to pay his bills up to date, and he will have Laura. What a great feeling it would be to have her in Washington as his guest, just as she had suggested. He fantasized he'd take her to the myriad museums and parks of Washington, DC. They would walk side-by-side along the Washington mall, from Lincoln Memorial through Washington Monument and to the colossal architecture of the United States Capitol. Later at night, they'd attend a party given by any of his friends or acquaintances as there was sure to be one. They might even host one. It would provide him with the golden opportunity to introduce Laura to his colleagues and show off with her. There had been a widespread rumor among friends and the neighbors that his common-law had dumped him to move in with another man, and circumstance had made it a stinging calamity. He was badly in need of confidence booster and Laura's presence in his house would make up a lot of grounds.

Still, Raymond had a lot to go through before he could get there. His daydream went on until interrupted by a slight knock on the door. He struggled to get up and slowly walked to open, but first peeped through the pinhole. It was a hotel maid holding supplies in his hands, a neatly folded white towel hanging on his left arm.

Raymond opened the door and waved him in. The maid, a dark-skin young man with one bold stroke of Yoruba tribal mark on each side of his round cheek, politely greeted and apologetically explained as he steadily made his way toward the bathroom that he was unaware of Raymond's occupation of the room the previous night. It was then that Raymond first had the opportunity to examine his room. He carefully looked around. Although the room was spacious, he could see that the walls were splattered with patches of compound waiting to be painted and the ceiling had seen its glorious days. The double glass windows on one end of the wall had cracks and on the opposite side the window was permanently shut as the sash had long caved in. He opened the door, leaned his head forward and looked from left to right. He sighed in disgust. The entire second floor was under renovation as evidenced by dusty hallway, scattered buckets of compound, paint-soiled ladders, broken cinder blocks and sheets of wallpapers. The bathroom looked like it was abandoned with a greasy bath tub that lacked shower curtain. If he had wanted to take a midnight shower as he sometimes desired, it would have been nearly impossible without having to go downstairs to request bathing supplies. The room service telephone was cut off line, the wires stripped off the wall.

He stood hands on hips decrying the hotel's deplorable living condition, while the maid uttered words of apology on behalf of the management - or lack thereof.

"I will certainly try to do something to make sure I get you a room in our new hotel by the end of today, "he said warily, his left wrist held behind with his right hand.

Raymond looked at the maid and grimaced. He suspected the maid would be gone by the end of the day and he wasn't buying such obvious empty promise. He thought to himself that if the maid was looking for a tip, he was in for a big disappointment.

After the maid walked out of the room in obvious disappointment, Raymond decided he'd check out of the hotel and find a more decent one. He took a half-measured shower, went down to the hotel's restaurant for a breakfast of toasted bread and egg omelet, drank a cup of tea, before going to a pay-per- call telephone office on the ground level and placed a call to Clyde, his sponsor back in the States. Clyde wasn't in and he left a message with Clyde's wife, who had picked up that he called. She informed him that Clyde's brother had telephoned earlier to confirm his successful arrival in Lagos with Bryan Jason.

After the phone call, he began to seek advice from just about anyone he came across on checking into a better hotel. Luckily, he met a helpful young man in his early twenties who told him about some supposedly luxurious Eko Hotel a mile away, and he decided he'd explore it.

"Let's go," Raymond said and the man followed him toward the front exit.

The bell-man immediately signaled for the next up taxi and they were on their way to Eko Hotels.

The young man, light chocolate complexioned and average height, told Raymond he was unemployed and hailed from Cross River State, and introduced himself as Tim. He was born and raised in the city of Calabar in the southeastern region. They both sat in the back seat of the Peugeot taxicab discussing the inconveniences Raymond had encountered from his hotel suite. Not that it mattered for the young man to know, but Raymond was striking a conversation, trying to dig out the stranger's true intentions for his unsolicited service. According to him, there had been a disappointment with a scheduled meeting with his colleagues and no one except him showed up, leaving him with virtually nothing to do all morning. Raymond knew it was a gimmick.

Although Tim's story had nothing to do with Raymond's accommodation problem, and Raymond detected some holes in those stories, he pretended to believe them and thanked him anyway for the help he was offering.

Eko Meridian Hotel, also known as Eko Holiday Inn, had an ultramodern building complex approximately one mile away from Federal Palace Hotel, just as accurately as Tim had described it. The twelve-story building stood by the sea shore, and most of the guest suites had a panoramic view of the Atlantic Ocean. The main entrance gate into the hotel's large and excellently manicured compound was manned by uniformed security guards, who stopped and checked every vehicle that approached the entrance. They seemed to have been screening taxicabs more intensely than non-commercial vehicles.

After signaling the Mercedes Benz ahead of Raymond's taxicab to move on, one of about five guards at the narrow gate came to the driver's window, bent over and spoke in broken English.

"Where you de go?"

Tim leaned over and responded pompously, "We're going to book in here."

The guard, beleaguered, reluctantly waved the driver to proceed then walked down toward the next vehicle.

The taxi driver pulled around a big circular driveway and stopped in front of the busy entrance. Raymond paid the obviously inflated fare of ten Naira and asked the cabbie to hang around for a few more minutes, just in case they'd be in need of his services again.

The ground level entrance of the hotel building had no partitioning, with their offices located down a large hallway. Four receptionists, three uniformed females and a male, stood behind a large marble stone counter. The left side of the building, also the ground level, was used as a casino and had an exclusive entrance constructed to separate the gambling customers from the hotel's guests. Raymond later learned the entrance's seclusion was geared toward preventing prostitutes from soliciting business from guests.

Raymond's inquiry was brief since visibly he was pretty impressed by its opulence. By looking at the building alone, he knew that nothing would deter him from staying there, unless of course there was no available room. The answer to that was yes and the price was within budget— five hundred Naira a night for city view suites and eighty Naira extra for the single ocean view suites. He settled for the city view and paid the deposit of two thousand Naira. Collecting his card-entry key, he, along with Tim, went directly back to the waiting taxicab driver. The taxicab took them back to Federal Place Hotel where Raymond retrieved his luggage and the money he had deposited for checking into their shabby hotel.

Raymond was booked to a sixth floor suite that had a malfunctioning television cable box, a minor problem he knew was solvable. The cable privilege, as explained in the hotel's brochure Tim had picked up from the counter, bolstered Raymond's already made up mind to stay there. It had him focused on watching CNN to keep abreast of the Persian Gulf conflict. The suite was exactly what he had hoped for, with small-sized refrigerator fully stocked with assorted drinks. He placed a call to room service and complained about the malfunctioned cable box. A female voice came on the line. She claimed to be the assistant manager and apologized, promising to act upon it right away, which she did to his much appreciation. She moved him to a larger suite on the eighth floor for the same price.

Raymond and Tim descended on the cold bottles of locally brewed beer in the refrigerator. He found Tim too young and inexperienced about world affairs, prompting his narrowing of their discussions only to places in Lagos where tourists mostly liked to visit. He knew he'd need some entertainment to keep his mind away from temptations of visiting his sister and her family. He remembered Ike, who would be meeting him at Federal Palace Hotel, supposedly when he came back from Owerri. He had completely forgotten their arrangement. He had to do something to catch up with Ike. He believed Ike would definitely be a more exciting companion than the relatively youthful and inexperienced Tim. He'd have to go back to the Federal Palace Hotel where they were supposed to meet and leave a message for Ike before the end of the day. They had arranged for Ike to call him at the hotel by dusk that day.

Raymond, having taken a taxi back to his previous hotel to leave a message for Ike, chose to return to his executive suite rather than hang out late as he had planned prior to his room switch. First, he had to discharge Tim for the day. He felt that Tim was beginning to attach himself to his programs, and he rather dismissed that notion quickly before it became an impossible task. He gave Tim ten US dollars and dismissed him. Few people in the country made that much money in one month.

He returned to Eko Meridian and went directly to the hotel's large and expensive restaurant for an early dinner. It was four-thirty, and since he skipped lunch, he couldn't wait until six o'clock for supper.

The magnificent restaurant, a class of its own, was located by the south side of the hotel building, and faced a large marble swimming pool surrounded with a beautiful garden. Inside the dining area, there were two sections; one with contemporary furnishing, and the other with African designed chairs crafted from bamboo. It displayed a classy touch in African art, re-invigorating his pride as an African.

It was easy for him to choose which side to sit. Like other guests, mostly Europeans, he sat and admired the wealth of African culture.

The dinner of pounded yam and Egusi soup cooked with goat meat, Raymond's very favorite, was everything he expected from the ninety-five Naira a plate chow. Sitting idly to let the heavy meal settle, he placed an order for a bottle of local Gulda beer from the busy waitress, who earlier cheerfully handed him his bill even before he finished his meal. He had the feeling she distrusted him. Probably because he just didn't look like he could afford to dine there. He didn't blame her for such perception of him. He had maintained his usual stoic composure as she studied his face, and he placed his order of beer anyway.

As the waitress came back with his order, he informed her of his preference to sit by the large balcony, which had an unobstructed view of the packed swimming pool. She placed the beer on a table outside, then came back to escort him to the table amidst foreign nationals, all guests of the hotel either on vacation or resident Lagosians on an evening refreshing hour.

The high humidity was hellish, but refreshingly balanced by the criminally cold beer, as Raymond sat cross-legged, thinking deeply once again about his secret and dangerous mission in Africa. His thought constantly focused mainly on ingesting the drugs. Dennis had repeatedly cautioned him during several of their briefings, that enduring the pain of swallowing the hard-coated substance that will contain the drugs would require tremendous amount of effort and courage. He was feeling heavily obligated to carrying on with the mission, and in retrospect blamed himself for being cajoled into accepting a task so risky in every sense of human decency. An accidental burst in his intestine would render him history and unsavory headlines in the evening news. The airplane, which he had always ultimately considered a danger of its own, could go down in the middle of the ocean, making it three major risks all at once.

Raw heroin exploding in his stomach was his most dreaded focal point. He could see himself sitting inside the airplane, naturally hysterical about being airborne and all of a sudden there'd be a feeling of chemical substance rattling inside his stomach and spreading all over his weakened intestine. His brain was clouded with the thought of the horror if such tragic moment occurred. Would he call in one of the flight attendants and tell her that he had swallowed illegal drugs and that he was feeling an explosion inside his intestine? What could she do when there'd be no doctor around and the airplane was in midair across the Atlantic Ocean?

Assuming there'd be a doctor aboard the flight, a hazardous occurrence like a drug burst in the intestine would definitely require a major surgery to save his life, and of course that wouldn't be available on a commercial flight. The flight attendant would panic and perhaps hurry to the cockpit to notify the captain. The other passengers would surround him to witness his despairing last moments, some of them terrified at the sight of a dying man. The captain would come, pleading for tranquility among passengers while he laid in pain, slowly but steadily losing vision and breath. There would be no remedy and he'd be dead upon landing. The press would be invited and his name released to be printed all over the news media. Friends, family members and all would read about the tragic end of a Raymond Karr. His darkened corpse would be covered with a black plastic bag, loaded into a waiting meat wagon and carried to a local coroner's office for autopsy.

If such a thing was to happen, how would his mother handle the grief of losing her first son and in such a disgraceful manner? She had lost her last born child, Charlie, at the age of nineteen, and now her first son just for a lousy ten thousand bucks. His eight months old son would grow up without his father and become a child whose hope for the future would depend on mere luck. He had planned on a bright future for him. He would have him trained as a conditioned athlete as well as a scholar. He would prefer football, his favorite sport. Who knows? He might be drafted to play for the Washington Redskins. He had chosen his name after his favorite player of the team— Charles Mann. The name had sounded so genuine especially for the fact that his late beloved brother's name was Charles.

The funeral. There'd be grief and heartache all over their compound in Owerri, his hometown. His lifeless body would lie face-up.

Raymond's mind snapped, causing him to shrug almost spontaneously before he realized he was in a public arena. He foresaw the entire evening ruined by his imagination. It trigger an instant resentment from his conscience, and all of a sudden he hated himself, Kenny, Clyde, Dennis, James, and everyone else whose activity directly or indirectly impacted his being in a Lagos restaurant that evening. His appetite for beer or anything else evaporated. He abandoned the nearly half full bottle of beer he was drinking, went into the restaurant and stopped by the counter to sign a guest slip for his bill to be garnished off his deposit with the hotel reservation. He went up to his suite, carrying a heavy burden of portent.

Raymond sat on the plush queen-sized bed in his suite pondering over his clouded future and hardly listening to the news program featured on CNN channel. Why did he ever listen to Dennis? How come he didn't simply reject Dennis' invitation to talk about it and just remained as resolutely opposed to drug as he had done in the past? He felt he had been such a lame duck accepting to run a drug courier for some out-law. When Dennis initially revealed his intention to visit Lagos for an exploratory business venture, he retrospectively felt he should've realized drug was the deal, fully aware Dennis naturally lacked business instinct, and should have stayed the hell away. He realized that even if he did not die of intestinal drug bust, there was still another big obstacle to overcome – the US Customs. He was fully conscious of the fact that were he to be apprehended, he'd be well on his way to hell in a hand basket. Dennis' BMW had flashed his eyes, but shouldn't have lured him into a dangerous deal. It was a tremendous error attending the night-of-euphoria gathering at Dennis' apartment. It looked like the world was crashing down on him.

Suddenly, it occurred to him that he could easily pick up the telephone and call Ben to tell him he had changed his mind. He tossed the idea around in his mind for a few minutes. The seemingly good idea eased the tension in his mind. He felt relieved of the moment of sadness, enabling him to again see the comfort of his suite and settle down to plan a careful method by which he would approach his new opposition. It would cause eyebrow-raising, but since his life was on the line, he didn't give a damn what impact it would make on his relationship with anybody. We're talking Raymond Karr's precious life here. In the past he had always found it difficult to disappoint anyone, especially friends, but what was one disappointment in a lifetime?

He lifted the telephone and dialed Ben's number. He noticed his heartbeat pounding while the other line rang, and the longer the delay in picking up, the more timid he became. It was finally picked up by someone who claimed to be Ben's business associate, and who also told him that Ben had instructed him to receive his telephone call. Apparently, Ben had been waiting to talk to him, and may even have tried to reach him at Federal Palace Hotel. He probably had run out of time and had to leave the house, but asked someone to receive his message.

Raymond left a message with the man about his change of hotel and why he hadn't phoned earlier. He also gave him the telephone number of the Eko Meridian Hotel, where Ben could come and see him should there become any need to do so. Most importantly, he expressed his urgent desire to speak with Ben as soon as possible, and then hung up.

He sat still on his bed deeply thinking of a diplomatic approach to Ben when he returned his call, as he was sure he would be doing soon. A sudden change of heart would not only ruin Ben's hope for a new source of wealth, but Ben would also lose some of the money they had already spent for his expenses so far, and he wasn't in a position to refund any of that— the flight ticket, his hotel expenses both in New York and in Lagos. Now that he had checked into an expensive hotel, a deeper indebtedness for that too. He'd need an air ticket back to Washington, D.C. where he'd return home with empty pockets.

Minutes ticked by and Raymond still had no come up with viable solution. If he were to avoid the drug courier deal, he'd have to come up with some plausible explanation. He thought he might flatly tell Ben that he had changed his mind and just didn't give a damn how Ben felt about it. After all, he was his own man and should do only what he wanted to do and running a drug courier wasn't one of it. Certainly there'd be a downside. Certainly Ben would be furious at him. What if Ben decided not to pay his air fare back to the States, and why should he? Sabotage this magnitude could prove more disastrous than one could imagine. Ben may even decide to instantly terminate his hotel accommodation, leaving him helplessly stranded in Lagos. He had undertaken the task of providing him a new passport, and if he decided to disembark on that project, he'd be sunk.

Ben might also try to harm him but he just couldn't get himself to believe that Ben resorting to such extreme measure to even up the score was at all possible. It certainly would be an overkill. If he had meant to dupe Ben, he wouldn't have delivered the ten thousand dollars Clyde had given him before his departure from JFK.

A little more than an hour later, Raymond decided on one approach to the troubling issue. He'd simply pretend, when the time to swallow the substance came, to be unable to perform. He'd fake vomiting and stay on that course until Ben would give up the quest and declared him incapable. Ben would hardly blame him for it although he'd be a little angry, and certainly disappointed. He would try several times more and fake as much, occasionally cursing himself for not being man enough.

When Ben would finally give up on him, he'd pretend to be so angry at himself that Ben may even begin to sympathize with him, convinced he'd be feeling like he was the big loser from the disappointment.

Raymond's flattened spirit was rekindled, enabling him to feel once more like he'd survive after all. His mind had struck off any idea of becoming ten thousand dollars rich when he arrived in Washington, and quite frankly, he cared less about the dismal nature of his financial situation. He'd rather preserve his life and freedom, to hell with the money. He had good prospects in his import business. It didn't make sense to risk a seemingly bright future for a lousy ten thousand bucks.

That solution, although tentative, was enough encouragement for Raymond to sound off an evening snore. For the first time in more than two weeks, Raymond Karr slept like a baby.

The loud noise of the telephone ringing interrupted Raymond's evening snooze. He had no doubt in his mind who could be the person trying to reach him – Ben.

Perhaps not much surprising after all, it wasn't Ben. It was Tim calling to thank him for the ten dollars he had given him and for his generosity. He was so anxious to continue with his peaceful sleep on the comfortable bed that he concurred with everything Tim said, including, as he later regretfully realized, coming back the following morning as early as ten o'clock. He would have vigorously objected to that but was so eager to get Tim to hang up the phone so he could continue with his sleep.

Less than five minutes after Tim had hung up and he was just about sounding off the sleep again, another ringing of the phone disrupted him. He picked up the receiver and there was no mistaking of Ben's voice asking to speak to him.

He was somewhat relieved that Ben called because Ben had information for him. He had his passport and the money to use around town. He had carefully planned to receive the allowance and save in case Ben overreacted to his decision to railroad the deal. He could use it to bail out his ass. Ben began questioning him on how he was faring, speaking in Ibo dialect.

Their conversation was brief. Ben only expressed how glad he was to learn Raymond had settled in a better hotel, and informed Raymond that someone named Emeka would be in touch with him as early as the following day. From Ben's pre-introduction of the Emeka, there was no second-guessing that Ben was speaking of one of his lieutenants. They concluded and Raymond hung up.

The sleep in Raymond's eyes vanished and his thoughts went back to business. He began to memorize how he would conduct his vomiting drama, come curtain-raising. He envisaged himself sitting by the table, Emeka, and possibly Ben, sitting by his sides, watching excitedly and guessing how much of their "market" he could take in. He also foresaw them looking worried at each other after his second or third vomiting noise.

His mind eventually slipped from putting the finishing touches on his act into the guilt of betraying Ben and Clyde. Clyde had been good to him and now Ben, who a short while ago telephoned to express his own happiness that he was comfortable at one of the most expensive hotels in the world, had indicated his determination to foot the bill and take good care of him. Ben said Emeka would be bringing some cash the next day when he'd come to meet him. Clyde had mentioned also that they not only wanted to make money, but also would be offering him the opportunity to do the same. He felt he shouldn't pull an eleventh-hour sabotage on them since they had recruited him in good faith.

The other side of the coin looked even more troubling after weighing the pros and cons of the deadly gamble. There was still the danger of drug exploding inside his stomach, and also a better than average chance of being stopped by the U.S. Customs agents. The phobia from the flight itself was no less a factor either. He wouldn't change his mind to abort the mission. His precious life was involved, and that would also affect his family, especially his eight-month-old son. His demise could ultimately lead to the innocent child's demise all through his lifetime.

A further contemplation would invigorate Raymond to go ahead with the pull out.

Now that he had decided against the mission and his hope for the future was bright once again, he'd have to find something that he'll occupy his mind with for the duration. It was Monday night, and he didn't know what could possibly be happening on the first night of the week in Lagos. Back in the States, it would have been a hell of an exciting night watching Monday Night Football. Still, he was on a different continent and a different time clock. Then he remembered the casino in the hotel building. Although he never developed enthusiasm for gambling, there could be other fascinating events that might provide a solution for a lonely night. A bingo game or slot machine should be enough fun until he got tired and would want to go to sleep again.

Chapter 11

REALITY CHECK

A solid knock on the door awoke Raymond at 9:30 Tuesday morning. Walking gingerly to the door and feeling disrupted, he opened to find one of the hotel maids, a fat middle-aged woman in a white apron, standing a distant away from the door, a log book and pen in hand. She had come to take stock of the items in the refrigerator. Without closing the door, Raymond lazily walked up to the bed and sat upright, wishing like hell the maid would hasten up in her stock-taking routine.

Tim walked in as the stock clerk was busy filling in zeroes in his inventory sheet since Raymond hadn't even had time to explore the refrigerator. Tim's presence at that time of the morning was particularly not a welcomed one for tired Raymond who was out at the casino until its closing at 4:30 a.m. It had been an expensive night for him, but nonetheless an exciting one. When he was done, he was five hundred Naira poorer, nearly all of the money he had when he first went inside. He spent most of it on the slot machines. He had played and lost two bingo drawings of fifty Naira each, and, at the slot machines, he had won a series of jackpots that paid one hundred naira per hit. At a certain juncture, his luck had him on the positive column in cash, as high as eight hundred and fifty Naira. Then it fluctuated downwardly to the minus column.

Tim's presence irritably kept Raymond awake for some indecipherable reason. They had nothing important to discuss, and certainly no in-house chores was necessary as the seemingly efficient hotel services had been more than adequate. He really wanted to ask Tim to leave and perhaps come back later but the same modesty that had had him indebted to friends and acquaintances took a sudden control of him.

He pretentiously exchanged cheerful greetings with Tim, inviting him to have a seat and make himself comfortable. He then labored to get up and, at the same lazy composure, walked to the bathroom to shower up. He knew he definitely wasn't going back to bed with Tim present, and the man Ben told him would be coming would be due to knock on the door soon.

A warm shower in a richly furnished bathroom provided him with sound refreshment. He came out of the bathroom to find that the clerk had gone and Tim was sipping on a beer from the bottle, sitting crossed-legged and watching television. He reached on top of the refrigerator, grabbed and glanced at the pink slip the stock clerk had left then replaced it.

"Ooh! I see you're going right at it, Tim. I think I'll do the same," he said.

Tim giggled. "Do you want me to get one for you?"

"Please do. I'd appreciate it."

Tim quickly stood up and went directly to the refrigerator to fetch Raymond a bottle of beer. "What kind do you like?"

"Guinness stout would be perfect."

Raymond proceeded to the wardrobe to dress up while Tim fetched his beer.

As had been the case since he met Tim at the lobby of Federal Palace Hotel's old building, Tim had shown no sign of experience in anything except hardship, which unmistakably could be read from his face and his dress. He just sat and drank his beer, talking back only when Raymond initiated a topic. When he made suggestions often they were childish and clearly illogical, making it more difficult for him to get his mind off finding alternatives to staying out of sight as Ben had suggested. Ike, whom he met upon arrival at the airport, and who could have made an ideal associate for him, was not available and there seemed to be only a remote chance of the two hooking up again.

However, Tim had proven to be particularly a good errand boy. He dusted Raymond's shoes unsolicited, hung his night-robe and dressed his bed, and so he had some value in him. Raymond invited Tim to join him and sit in the balcony to glance at the ocean and the big ships sailing to and from the shore. Tim first carried one of the two folding chairs inside the room outside then returned to clean up and reorganize everything. Satisfied, he picked up his beer and walked outside to the balcony to join Raymond, who was looking fixedly at a big cruise ship as I slowly sailed away.

Feeling hungry, he remembered he had no more than a few Naira bills left in his wallet after spending like a drunken sailor the previous night at the casino. He mentally calculated, as he stared blankly at the sea, that to sign another signature for an expensive lunch at the luxury hotel would undoubtedly put him to an additional one hundred Naira short of the deposit he hoped to be refunded at the end of his stay. He was hoping that Emeka, whoever he may be, brought along the money Ben promised he would be delivering to him that morning. He left the balcony, went inside and searched his pocket. He counted eight dollars in all and decided he would go chip. He added it to the forty-two Naira he took out of his travel bag and sent his errand boy, Tim, off to buy a roadside food.

Tim returned with several bowls of food, including rice, beans and chicken stew, all budgeting within the fifty Naira Raymond had given him to manage in the food buy. He even made a cash deposit of twenty Naira on the fragile bowls, and still returned with almost fifteen Naira in change, leaving the breakfast for two to a minimal cost of just fifteen Naira. The Eko Hotel charged eighty-five Naira a plate.

Raymond sat on one end of the large balcony Tim on the other, both eating and drinking quite merrily, when Raymond heard the telephone ring. As Tim started toward the double sliding doors in an apparent move to answer, Raymond commanded him to sit still. Although Raymond had expected Emeka to telephone or show up at the front door, he wasn't taking any chances and had to pick up the telephone receiver himself.

It was Ben calling to ask Raymond if Emeka had shown up yet. Ben most probably would have gone crazy if Tim, a stranger, had answered the phone.

Ben sounded a little upbeat as he spoke, and that was something Raymond least expected from him. "I just called him a while ago, and he told me he was about to head toward your hotel,"

"How long would it take him to get here?" Raymond said nonchalantly. He cared less about how long it was going to take Emeka to get to the hotel. He had decided to call off the deal that brought him to Lagos and that was what mattered to him. Of course he will have to play it cool and pretend to be going along until time to display his concert. He needed to pretend he's deeply involved and not sound too pacifying as that might tip Ben off that he was up to something strangely unsettling. For now, Emeka had money for him and he needed every penny of it if he was going to be stranded in Lagos.

"Give him a few more minutes. He should be there. Give him ten or fifteen minutes."

"Okay, I'll be waiting."

He hung up and went back to the remnants of his breakfast, and found Tim comfortably relaxed in his chair and picking his dentures with his fingernails. But he knew he definitely would have to excuse Tim whenever Emeka arrived, and this time he wouldn't be hesitant. He would simply ask Tim to return the bowls and come back the following day, and to keep the deposit on the bowls as gratuity.

Twenty minutes went by before Emeka called Raymond from the courtesy telephone at the lobby before coming up to his suite. Emeka was wearing a blue-striped suit over a white shirt and a brown-flowered neck tie, the same color of the pocket kerchief tucked inside his breast pocket. His clean-shaved face and flat nose reminded him of Clyde in the United States, and instantly warned him to be wary of such smooth operators. He stood aside, holding the door open to let him in after both men exchanged greetings with a firm hand shake. The smell from Emeka's cologne blew hard into his nostrils and spread rapidly all over the cozy suite.

"Did master call this morning?" Emeka said in Ibo dialect. He was about to sit on the Futon sofa bed vertically placed at the other end of the wall from the queen-size bed. Referring to Ben as "master" reassured Raymond his speculation about Emeka as Ben's lieutenant was accurate. That also meant that Ben himself was someone bigger in the underworld crime hierarchy than his appearance revealed.

"He phoned not too long ago, about ten to fifteen minutes," Raymond said, looking studiously at Emeka.

"Was he angry at me?"

"Oh no, just asked if you had arrived, that's all."

Emeka noticed Tim through the sliding glass door and lowered his voice considerably.

"Who's that on the balcony?"

"Oh! A friend. He'll be leaving shortly. Don't worry about him."

"How soon?"

"Very, very soon. As a matter of fact, let me discharge him right away," Raymond said, and went to the balcony where Tim was sitting, still drinking his beer. Tim behaved like a loyal servant when Raymond told him he'd been excused for the day, gathering the bowls to put them back in the same brown paper bag he brought them in. Raymond simply explained that he, Raymond, was about to hold a confidential business meeting with Emeka and some other people who were coming, and Tim obliged and gulped down the remnant of his beer. He was leaving with almost thirty Naira in his pocket, an amount of money only few privileged employed Africans could take home for an all-day hard labor.

No sooner had Tim left, promising to return the following day, than Emeka delved right into the subject matter. "I'd like to describe this whole bargain as far as your end is concerned," he said with a threatening note in his voice.

Before the bad news will follow, Emeka firstly informed Raymond that his passport was approved and ready, which brightened his face. Then it soured when Emeka told him that they'd hold on to passport until his boarding time at the airport. He grimaced as he knew immediately what that meant.

"Raymond, I'm sure you have a question or two but I just want you to listen."

A question or two? I have a thousand questions, Raymond said in his mind but of course he knew he'd have to swallow them all. "There shall be no betrayal in this agreement," Emeka said and paused to scratch his nose. "The deal is simple. You have to agree to be sponsored for a 'market' that will pay you ten thousand dollars cash."

He studied Raymond as if anticipating a certain definite reaction, then continued. "To make this possible, we had paid your transportation and all your hotel expenses both here and in America. You know, as businessmen, we have already invested a lot in you."

He paused to adjust his neck tie. Raymond remained silent and stared blankly at the wall. "You're at a point of no return now, but don't worry about anything. We'll do everything possible to make your 'market' endeavors as comfortable and trouble-free as even you will appreciate. There's going to be a little rough side, but you're a man. I guarantee you will handle it just fine. Others, including your friends, had done it successfully, and I don't expect otherwise from you.

"We operate our market business as a network. There's our Bangkok connection, mainly through our point man over there, and the American connection charged to Clyde, whom you contacted in America. Each operation is as efficient as can be, and that's the reason why our couriers have had remarkably little trouble with safe passage and intestinal explosion. As for here in Nigeria, there is absolutely zero risk. Around here we're supreme masquerades, we have people—and I mean people who control the power—looking out for us. You're a Nigerian, you know what I mean. I don't have to explain that in details to you. Money talks around here." He became pedantic in his admonition. "Anyway, simply obey my instructions, and there'll be absolutely nothing to worry about." He paused, yawned, and this time adjusted his bracelet, before continuing. "Let me not forget to also inform you that there's a heavy penalty for anyone who backs out on us, or tries to cheat us. As a matter of fact, we have well paid people who efficiently take care of those on our black list, and believe me, those men can be real mean."

Again, Emeka paused and tried to observe Raymond's reaction. But Raymond avoided his direct stare.

"I'm quite sure that I shouldn't go into deep detail on this with you. You don't have to worry about that, because I see you as an intelligent man, and you look gentlemanly. I don't expect you to do anything stupid."

At this juncture, Raymond really began to feel permanently trapped.

"Now, here's where we are," he continued. "You're on a secret errand. Beginning from now, you should not make contact with any of your relatives or old friends. Keep away from that guy that was here a while ago, although that may not necessarily matter, as I see he's too young to be considered dangerous, but you should know better. You'll have anything that you might need to limit your outside engagements. You will have women, drinks, good food—you name it. If you need women, just telephone me and I'll have them here within half hour for your pleasure. I'm not talking prostitutes. I'm talking, of course, exotic undergrads just looking for handsome rich men to have fun with. You can have as many as a dozen of them shower you up at the same time—all of them at your discretion. If you like is bimbos, you can have that too"

Emeka paused to reach his hand inside his inner breast pocket, took out a stash of money bundled together, and placed it beside Raymond.

"Here…. This is two thousand, five hundred Naira. It's for your spending pleasure. Fortunately, there's a casino here, making this hotel a much more fun place to be. If you run out, pick up a telephone and call me up."

He reached for the pen on the TV stand and wrote his number on the back of a maintenance receipt slip that was meant for service request. He began again as he sat back on the Futon.

"Come Thursday, I will personally take you to our juju priest. He is the strongest medicine man of all, and one of the most feared in this country. But I'll let you see it to believe it. After you see him, you'll realize how strongly you'll perform, and how, without obstruction, you will breeze through the Customs Agents gates like a masquerade. We'll be visiting him Thursday evening."

Raymond sat still, now staring at Emeka and looking hypnotized, and digesting the instruction. Everything Emeka had just told Raymond began to sink in and Emeka's promises of safety somehow breezed in some reassurance. Still, Raymond refused to believe that Emeka was making a vile threat at him when he hinted that their secret organization had a hit squad to handle anyone who backed out on them. His mind raced as Emeka resumed speaking.

"Now do you have any question?" Emeka said dryly, raising his eyebrows, his forehead wrinkled.

Raymond paused for a moment in a voided mind until it struck him that a question had been directed at him. The thousand questions he had in his mind had vanished.

"Oh no! I understand everything," He said, struggling to overcome

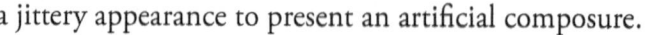

a jittery appearance to present an artificial composure.

"Okay then. I'll have to be going."

"All right!" Raymond said and stood up before Emeka in a move to hasten his departure.

Emeka followed him to the door where they loosely shook hands. But before discharging each other, Emeka paused.

"Remember, if there's anything you may need, be in touch. And, oh, just so you know… between now and Thursday, a guy by the name of Goddy will come chat with you. Don't worry about him, for he is only interested in our enemies and not our friends. Just answer his few questions and let him go, that's all," Emeka said as he waved his index finger as a sign of warning, this while walking toward the elevator.

"Okay," Raymond said and walked back inside the suite, closing the door securely behind him.

He sat back on the wooden chair in the balcony, thinking deeply about Emeka's admonition, and trying to dissect it all. He hoped that he could be so convincing with his vomiting act that it would not constitute a "back out," and not done unduly and deliberately. If he couldn't swallow the drugs, he should hardly be blamed for such natural ineptitude and shouldn't be regarded as backing out.

However, whether Emeka's faked vomiting ploy would be sufficient enough to convince Ben and Emeka he wasn't deliberately backing out remained the key. He saw no alternative than clinging to pessimism.

It was almost noon and the meeting with Emeka had been on Raymond's mind ever since the man left. Now that he had digested Emeka's threat, a little walk downstairs, or even to the casino, which resumed daily operation at 10 a.m., wouldn't be too much to ask for from himself. He felt he shouldn't be such a timid man as to deny himself a little fun. Dennis and Kenny, and many others, had done the same thing, and they all survived it. Why shouldn't he?

He remembered the two thousand, five hundred Naira Emeka dropped beside him on the bed. It was a lot of money to be sitting there. He figured he'd go to the casino to free his mind for then. He'd have to pass on the women Emeka had promised him. Laura was very much in his mind. Better yet, he would've liked to go outside the hotel to look for fun, but with Tim gone and Ike not yet in touch with him, that chance was remote.

His plan to look for some excitement at the casino was pre emptied by a beer-induced sleep, and he sank into his comfy bed immediately. He slept all afternoon, waking up occasionally to go to the bathroom and finally woke up at 4 o'clock to answer the phone. The caller introduced himself as the Federal Palace Hotel employee, whom he had asked to forward Ike's telephone call.

The hotel employee told him that Ike had telephoned and had scheduled him for a meeting at six o'clock. The venue was to be at the lobby of the same hotel. He wondered in his mind why Ike couldn't simply call Eko Meridian Hotel to ask to speak with him directly. He suspected the employee had purposely arranged it to be sure he collects his reward money.

Raymond arrived at the Federal Palace Hotel in a taxicab exactly 2 minutes before 6 p.m. As he walked inside the lobby, there were fewer than ten men and women scattered around the entire first floor, mostly Yoruba tribeswomen taking a time out from an on-going meeting somewhere inside the hotel building.

He found a vacant table and sat before ordering a beer with the eager waitress.

A few minutes later, Raymond recognized a familiar face approaching the section he was sitting. As the man greeted him in a heavy Yoruba accent, he immediately recollected the day the man was making promises to track Ike's telephone call following his offer of a substantial monetary reward.

"Have you seen him yet?" Raymond said.

"I want to call him now. I'll be right back," the man said and quickly went back to the cashier's desk. He came back moments later to invite Raymond to speak with Ike on the telephone in the office.

"So how was your journey to your hometown?" Ike asked him over the phone.

"Guess what? I never made it."

"What do you mean?" Ike said with astonishment, lowering his voice as if Raymond had revealed a secret.

Raymond briefly narrated how the Peugeot had broken down on the outskirts of Lagos, how he managed to cope with the disappointment, and his decision to switch hotels, carefully side-stepping his involvement with crime underworld's Ben.

He got off the phone with Ike, mutually agreeing that Ike would pick him up at his hotel at 8 p.m. for a night out. Ike would be coming along with his girlfriend, and presumably with another girl for them to double-date. He accepted without questions. He didn't give a damn about any kind of fun stuff as long as it was something to help occupy his mind. His crime mission in Africa was too daunting.

The employee who re-united Ike and he timed his arrival perfectly as he hung up the receiver. "You see, sir, I told you I could do it for you," the employee said with a broad smile.

"Oh yes," Raymond said and faked a smile. "Now how much do you think this is worth for you?"

"Anything you give me sir, is okay."

The employee looked at the male cashier, who was about to discharge a paying customer.

"Like how much?" Raymond said.

"You know that I did it because of you, so anything you give me is fine for me."

Raymond could make no sense out of what the employee said. The employee chatted with the cashier in Yoruba language, then became silent.

"So is it one Naira or one million Naira, or something in-between?" Raymond said, breaking the silence.

They both giggled without saying anything.

"Okay," Raymond said, "is twenty Naira enough or too much?"

"Oh! That's good sir," he said as his smile broadened.

Raymond's initial offer appeared to be too much. The cashier, sitting on a stool, stared at Raymond with a surprise look. The generous offer also seemed to have surprised him too.

Raymond dipped his hand inside his side pocket, took out two twenty Naira bills and one ten naira bill, and held his hand out for the hotel employee to collect.

"Here, this is fifty. You take it and thank you." He left the office as the obviously delighted man repeatedly thanked him as he walked outside to catch a taxicab back to his hotel, where he planned to meet Ike for their double-date.

Ike was dressed formally in a brown suit and a matching bow tie, very unusual attire for a Tuesday night out, considering Raymond's perception of a Nigerian bachelor in a sporty Jeep Cherokee. The two young ladies waited inside the car while he went upstairs to fetch Raymond. He cautioned Raymond immediately he stepped inside the hotel suite that the ladies were eager to meet the man who lived in Washington, DC, the center of world politics. The classy exposure in the opulent Eko Meridian hotel added to the grandeur.

Raymond, satisfied in front of the mirror that he was ready to meet a new chick, came out of the bathroom and motioned Ike he was ready to go and they both left. Inside the elevator they were riding alone, Ike looked up at Raymond. "Remember, her name is Ayisha and she's dead gorgeous," he said and giggled. Raymond gestured with an OK sign. When they arrived at the Jeep, Raymond, eagerly anticipating, opened the door behind the driver seat and immediately smelled the heavy feminine perfume coming from inside. Now seated next to Ayisha, he examined her and was satisfied that she was as gorgeous as Ike had described her- average height and an excellent shape, dark complexioned and a perfect nose with a sassy smile.

A Foreign Relations student at the University of Lagos, she wore a grayish gown with ruffles around her shoulders. It matched perfectly with her high heel shoes, white earrings, and a white handbag.

They went to the Sheraton Hotel at Ikeja. It was a place to go to show off; dining in their plush restaurant, and later joining the on-going dancing on the first floor of the building's east wing.

Raymond saw clearly the excitement on Ayisha's beautiful face, but his mind was still constantly disrupted by the secret errand that brought him to Africa, of which he was the errand boy. If he had to spend the money that Emeka had given him and accept all the fun they promised to pay for, his plan to avoid the drug carriage would be hampered by a guilt of conscience.

However, he portrayed a gentlemanly charisma and, although Ike had expected him to be more enthusiastic than that, he was able to keep Aysha on the dance floor and chatted with her all along. They even kissed and he promised her they'd spend some time together before his flight back to the United States—a promise that he sincerely believed he would keep. But it wasn't an ideal night for him to carouse with women, especially still fresh from his romantic fling with Laura in New York. Laura had hinted how jealous she could become, and although she joked about it, she did say she'd want him to keep his eyes off of other women, which he had promised to do. Moreover, he was beginning to doubt if he could successfully back out of his drug courier assignment.

After a long night of mixed emotion, Raymond was the first to be dropped off at his hotel. Ayisha had stepped out and he had briefly kissed her before helping her climb back inside the Jeep. Before Ike drove off, he promised to keep in touch with her through Ike.

He unwound and sat on his bed and in deep thought about everything, from his idea of avoiding his obligation to the daunting task of making it through JFK airport. He finally fell asleep at approximately 4 a.m. and when he woke up, the clock on the night stand showed 12:25 p.m. Wednesday. He had made no plans for that day because it was the eve of the day when Emeka would be picking him up for the visit to the juju priest's shrine.

Chapter 12

A PRIESTLY VISIT

Thursday at 9 a.m., shortly before Emeka's arrival, Raymond heard an unusually solid knock on the door. When he peeped through the pinhole thinking it was Emeka arriving much too early for the visit to the Juju priest, he saw a strange man standing arms folded. When he inquired, the stranger responded with a bellowing voice.

"Goddy!"

Instantly, Raymond recalled the name from Emeka's last visit. He unlocked the door, unhooked the chain and stood aside to let in his sudden guest. As Goddy strolled in, Raymond curiously observed him. Bulky, bloodshot dull eyes that gave him the look of a cold-blooded killer, and six feet two with a protruded stomach, he was dark-chocolate complexioned and sported a walrus mustache that had one noticeable gray hair close to the middle. His receding short and nappy hair circled around a distinct bulge just above the back of his neck. Hippopotamus would be a perfect nickname for him.

He was accompanied by a younger looking man holding a brown briefcase. The youngster stood about six inches shorter than Goddy. Raymond noticed that the younger man was built by stature as though he was Goddy's younger sibling but he could not detect any facial resemblance. Although the younger man's general physique looked like Goddy downsized proportionately in every physical category, his m-shaped nose was much too tiny compared to Goddy's distinctly larger flat nose. He was also much darker, full shabby dark hair and sported a scanty short beard that looked like they were carefully sewed on to his square jaw. Both men were casually dressed in slacks and collar shirts.

Raymond smelled a body odor but wasn't sure whose among them. But the odor was sickening him to his stomach as both men stood side-by-side close to the TV stand. He avoided Goddy's steady stare and noticed the younger man carefully avoided his.

"Have a seat, gentlemen," he said casually as he was ridding the chair of his dirty clothes.

Goddy declined on behalf of both men.

"We're in a hurry so let's get to the matter right away," Goddy said. Raymond could care less that he did not introduce his associate.

Raymond placed back his dirty clothes and positioned himself by his bed. Folding his arms signaled Goddy that he was ready to listen to them. Goddy motioned his hand and the younger man quickly lifted the briefcase, placed it on his right thigh and opened. From inside the briefcase, he took out a medium sized brown envelope and handed it to Goddy, who immediately began to speak.

"You see, Raymond, we are the good guys. That is good guys for you but bad guys for anyone who dared to disrespect us. You see, good guys for good guys and bad guys for bad guys, dig it?" he said, simultaneously demonstrating with his hands and then chuckled, briefly looking at his young colleague and quickly turning back to face Raymond.

Raymond saw through the thin-veiled mockery. The young man faked a smile with repeated head nod in approval. Raymond was inwardly beginning to develop pure hatred for the young man. It seemed to him that every time he looked at the young man's direction, the man would quickly face down. Especially irritating to Raymond was that the young man wasn't reciprocating his concerted efforts to create a friendly atmosphere. It was all making him uncomfortable and quite frankly afraid.

"I want to show you what happens to the bad guys," Goddy continue and from the brown envelope took out a bunch of photographs.

Raymond watched with intense curiosity as Goddy began to adjust his position to better exhibit the characters in the photographs to him. As he glanced at the first of the colored photographs even before Goddy was poised to begin the expose, he was visibly frightened by what he saw, much to the satisfaction of the constantly observing young man. The lead photograph showed a dead man lying in a pool of blood at what looked like a half-opened door of either a house or an apartment.

"These are some of the faces of our enemies. Enemies meaning those who tried to swing our markets in one way or the other to their own benefit…or to their own demise, I should say," Goddy continued and chuckled again, trying to blend meanness with sense of humor, while holding the stack for Raymond to see clearly.

"The reason why I'm showing you these pictures is for you to know that bad things happen to our bad guys. I don't have to go into details. You're a smart man, a fellow Ibo man, so you know exactly what I'm trying to tell you. I don't have to explain that to you, do I?"

Raymond wasn't sure if that was a rhetorical question but timidly answered anyway.

"I guess not," he said in a somber voice, unsure if that was enough to satisfy his guests. He was eager to give those guests whatever they wanted so they could get the hell out of his hotel suite.

Goddy shoved the first photograph to the back of the stack to expose the second. Again it showed a close range shot of another dead man on the roadside. Raymond, unlike in the first photograph, guessed in his mind the dead man was a Nigerian. Goddy kept holding the photos at a distance as though Raymond was about to snatch them off his hands but in reality Raymond wanted nothing to do with any of that. He was well aware of Goddy's uneasiness and went to an extra length to be still. He knew he wouldn't want to provoke these guys or confront them in any way.

Goddy shuffled to the next, but this time fear had so captivated Raymond to the point of incomprehension that his face was then only staring while his mind was deep in thought about what his journey was rapidly evolving into. He was certain the third photograph was no less shocking and so must have been the fourth, fifth and sixth. Despite his growing lack of interest in looking at those photos as Goddy kept showing and stacking them at the back, he lit up and was completely aghast of the content of the ninth photograph. It was a close range camera capture of the corpse of Isaac Dillum, III. slain son of the Mayor of Washington, DC. Fortunately for him, neither Goddy nor his young associate noticed the shock that irresistibly forced out of him. He quickly noticed that the photo only captured the corpse of Isaac Dillum, III but not his daughter's. He managed to stay calm. The photograph was exactly the same position released by the Washington, DC press - legs inside the car and back on the ground, only this time not covered with the white sheet and captured from a real close up range.

That Goddy held the ninth photograph no longer than he held the previous eight was a hint to Raymond that the two men knew absolutely nothing about the Dillums murder mystery sensation in the United States. Goddy's last ten photographs were virtually eclipsed by the combination of shock and terror besieging Raymond. He was well aware that he had stumbled into a knowledge that could potentially end his life as he knew it. In fact, he was so far removed from the last of the photographs that followed the ninth photograph that they could have contained the corpse of any of his closest buddies and he wouldn't have noticed. That was the extent of the shock from seeing the uncovered corpse of Isaac Dillum, III. For then, all he wanted was for the two men to get the hell out of his hotel suite.

After the last of the twenty-one photographs, Goddy concluded admonishing him with one statement.

"A word is enough for the wise," he said and shoved the stack of photographs back inside the brown envelop and handed it back to the young man. The young man quickly placed the brown envelope back inside the briefcase and closed it, firmly gripping it as if it contained a million dollars.

As the two men slowly made their move toward the door, Raymond wiped the cold sweat off his forehead with his hand.

"It was really nice meeting you guys," he lied to the men as he stood still and watched them exit. They ignored him and continued their way to the elevator. Raymond's full attention focused on the distinct bulge at the back of Goddy's neck and in his mind wished it was a malignant cancerous tumor.

No sooner had Goddy and his assistant left than his mind delved right into the trauma of the ninth photograph. Questions began to fill his brain. Could Goddy have possibly realized the dangerous significance of technically confessing to the double murder of Isaac Dillum, III and his young daughter and disclosed it by way of photographic evidence to someone who would be heading back to the States in just a few days? Did they not know that the ninth photograph was such a damning evidence that would surely draw in the FBI in shutting down their entire operation and bringing all to a swift justice? What was really going on here? Whatever it was, the genie had been let out of the bottle.

Other equally troubling questions kept recurring in his mind, such as where Clyde, a sub-urban District of Columbia resident, fit in all of that. He had to have known about the highly publicized double murder of Isaac Dillum, III and his daughter. If he didn't, he would be the only one in the region who was devoid of such knowledge. Also if Dennis, Kenny and James all knew about such a high profile murder mystery, and remained mum on it. Sure they were well aware of the two million dollars reward that went along with whoever tipped the information that would help solve the murder mystery. The mere thought that Dennis, and Kenny for that matter, underwent the same threat and failed to inform him before he undertook the journey felt like blatant betrayal to him.

He climbed onto his bed and faced the ceiling in deep thought. If there was any illusion that horrific trouble loomed for him, Goddy's visit had set it all straight and in focus. He knew that not only was he squarely in the dragnet of a vicious drug smuggling ring, but also had acquired a knowledge that could spell the end of his life, thanks to the revelation of the ninth photograph.

After careful thought and processing of all possible scenarios, shaken and confused, he concluded that he was simply going to oblige in his current drug courier mission, make that his last and quietly disappear from everybody, his best pal Dennis included. It was just too much for him to deal with and too dangerous to even discuss what he had witnessed to anyone else. But the weight of what he had just learned dominated his thoughts until he fell back asleep.

When Raymond awoke, his thought re-focused on Emeka, who was to pick him up for the scheduled visit to one of the most powerful and renowned juju priests in Yorubaland. He could only assume it had to do with his ability to swallow the drug, and probably his safe passage through U.S. Customs as well.

Juju was an African version of voodooism, which had been a ritual of cult practices since the history of the Dark Continent, and was still very much in practice. The men and women, who presided over the cult, otherwise known as priests and priestesses or juju doctors, commanded significant respect from a good majority of the population. Even the government heads of most African states had been rumored to have had direct or indirect access to the vaunted powers of this supernatural being.

The entire populace of Africa, once in the ancient times, worshipped juju as a religious god before the introduction of Christianity by the Europeans, which subsequently led to the abolition of most of its inhumane practices, such as the killing of twin babies. History has it that at a certain period in West Africa, giving birth to twin babies was considered an immense abomination. Recently, juju practices, as Raymond had come to witness after his decade absence from Africa, still enjoyed a significant number of followers amongst indigenes, including members of dignified social status. In fact, the institutional powers of some chiefs in a typical African tribe were deemed unprecedented if the chief consulted a supposedly more powerful juju priest. Some employers consult juju priests for enhancing judgmental ability to hire ideal and competent workers, a handful of employees consult juju priests for potency in promotions. Even some college students resort to juju inclination for ability to study more ferociously.

Beside the goal of personal success as a premium reason for consulting juju priests, other ominous motives stand characteristically behind this visit with the celebrated cult leaders. Some vicious members of the society, when trying to destroy the life of a personal or family enemy, had often resorted to juju to either render their enemy's life useless by bringing insanity to them.

During Raymond's childhood growing up in Eastern Nigeria, he had occasionally paid visits to the juju priests' shrines, and had, in most cases, witnessed strange events. As a child born of devout Christian parents, he was taught to believe juju practice as the devil's workshop by Catholic priests, as well as preachers, who taught religious lessons. He was still naïve about the institution and curious to reach a new perspective toward its mastery.

At 6:15 p.m., Emeka finally showed up and both men drove off in his white Mercedes Benz. The drive took over an hour and a half before they arrived at a large concrete-fenced compound in a remote neighborhood, almost a hundred miles from the city limits of Lagos.

Raymond's heart thumped over uncertainty and he made no attempt to ask questions about where they were or how he should conduct himself in the presence of the juju priest. His mind, on two occasions, had contemplated the idea of discussing Goddy's visit but he wisely realized the potential danger. He simply went along with whatever Emeka said until he noticed him pull into a narrow path leading to a house off the dirt road.

They walked inside a gate with a missing door, after parking the car beside two other small cars, an old and dusty Volkswagen Bug devoid of license plates and a late model Subaru saloon. As they started toward the front door, Raymond noticed a face peeping out from one of the slightly opened wooden-carved windows on the right side of the house's front entrance. A dog barked three times from inside the house.

Emeka knocked slightly on the door, setting off a frenzy barking of the dog and an elderly Yoruba woman opened. A teenage boy wearing only a pair of khaki shorts and no shirts, struggled to force the sharp-mouthed Doberman inside one of the adjacent bedrooms. Emeka, who apparently was a fairly known client, greeted the elderly woman in Yoruba language, and they briefly chatted with each other before she asked the two men to come in and be seated inside a cozy but scarcely furnished living room. Only four wooden chairs and a large stool placed in the center occupied the large living room. The blue painted walls exhibited scattered filth of greases from edible palm oil. There was one dimly lit, forty-watt light bulb hanging from the ceiling, providing the only source of light.

The teenage boy came out from the room where he had cornered the dog into, and greeted them. He then passed through an obscured hallway entrance where the elderly lady had proceeded after ushering the guests to their seats.

There was silence in the house, except the occasional barking of the dog coming faintly from inside the bedroom.

Emeka began to explain to Raymond why he credited the priest as one of the best in western Nigeria. It was also the first time he discussed the issue in detail since he hinted Tuesday morning that they would be making such a visit. Emeka also explained briefly how his other couriers maneuvered the U.S. Custom's intense check at JFK airport, all six men crossing unquestioned while others, who were sponsored by different organizations, were apprehended after interrogation, thanks to the wonderful performance by the priest they were about to consult.

Both men sat alone for about twenty minutes before an elderly man in his mid-seventies, wearing a white Yoruba tribal garment, appeared from the same obscured, narrow hallway. Emeka stood up and Raymond casually followed. The elderly man regarded both men as he greeted in the same Yoruba language, and seemed to be guessing at his sudden guests. He stared inquiringly left and right at Emeka and then Raymond, and back at Emeka. Still guessing, he approached to shake Raymond's hand while he chewed on a cola nut. Emeka spoke to him in Yoruba language, prompting him to immediately hug him with much more enthusiasm and a broader smile that exposed his scanty upper denture and camel brown gum. Raymond assumed in his mind that Emeka must have been refreshed his memory of who they were, and perhaps the purpose of their visit. Moments into their discussion, Emeka turned to Raymond.

"Do you want to drink palm wine?" he said as he turned to face Raymond.

"No, not really," Raymond said in a very low voice but with visible humility.

Emeka turned again to face the elderly man, said something to him while pointing at his own wrist watch. They chatted a little further before the priest invited them to follow him through the dark hallway.

The priest led Emeka and Raymond to the back of the brick building and across a patchy cemented yard, which was corrugated and where three children interrupted their game of tossing a worn out tennis ball to guess at the visitors. Three women in traditional dresses and in their forties and fifties chatted with each other end of the fence. On the opposite end of the yard where the priest led Emeka and Raymond were three other smaller brick huts, two attached and the third standing alone. Emeka and Raymond followed the priest inside the stand-alone hut, which housed his shrine.

The house had no electricity and was divided into three sections. The first outer section was the main entrance, and the two windows on both sides of the entrance door were the only sources of light. There were a few makeshift armchairs. Hanging on the wall behind the larger chair was a twenty by twenty-inch painted portrait of Oduduwa, a charismatic ancient African leader and the founder of the Yoruba tribe. It hung on the unpainted cinderblock wall. The cemented floor was bare, the windows without blind. The same first room served as a consulting chamber where he also discussed his fee before proceeding to the next stage, which was the middle room.

The priest sat in the lone wooden chair by the right side and offered both Emeka and Raymond the makeshift armchairs on the left.

Again the priest, who had no knowledge of English language, began to chat with Emeka in Yoruba dialect. Raymond sat with his arms folded and watched the two, guessing as they supposedly discussed his drug courier mission, and how to avoid being fished out by the US Customs. Emeka mostly listened and occasionally answered the priest's questions.

When the priest and Emeka concluded their consultation, the priest stood up and Emeka followed him as he opened the center door. There was near total darkness in the middle room, and Emeka and Raymond stood by the lone entrance door until the priest lit up two candles.

The smoke and aroma of burning incense filled the room, which was equally as large as the first room. Hanging on the four walls were mostly animal skins of several kinds. Among them, and more conspicuously displayed due to its larger size, was the skin of an alligator, from its intact skull down to its long tail. There was a monkey's skull, tiger's tail, a bunch of coral beads and a handful of white snail shells, each stuffed with brown chick feathers.

A wooden stool was placed beside a larger than life carved human skull. Emeka, who was translating the priest's commands in Ibo, told Raymond to sit on the wooden stool. The priest then went to the left corner and retrieved a similar chair and ordered Emeka to sit on it, before he exited.

Emeka and Raymond were surrounded with items on the floor, which ranged from tortoise shell to chunks of dried tree roots. Emeka broke the silence that began immediately after the priest exited his chamber.

"I hope you qualify easily," he whispered to Raymond, looking as if he needed a response.

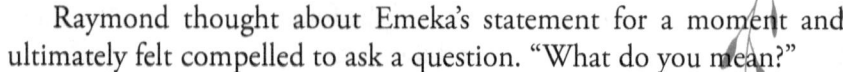
Raymond thought about Emeka's statement for a moment and ultimately felt compelled to ask a question. "What do you mean?"

"Well, he will determine if you can perform."

"You mean—."

"Swallow the 'market'."

Raymond started to think again. That could be his golden opportunity to avoid swallowing cocaine. He hoped and silently prayed he wouldn't 'qualify'.

"I see," Raymond said aloud and kept quiet from then on, guessing at all kinds of strange objects in the dim candle lights.

After about seven minutes the priest came back out with a live rooster. He gripped the rooster by its two legs and head down. A rooster was traditionally symbolic of the appeasement of imaginary gods. He carefully handed Emeka the rooster by its legs and began to take off his brown striped garment and his uniformed tribal hat. He also ceremoniously took off his animal skin pair of slippers, leaving him wearing only his loose pair of shin high drawers.

Opening one of the wooden carved bowls by the right corner of the wall, he picked up a piece of chalk-like material and stroked it on his forehead, and then drew a circle around each of his breasts, his navel and finally on the metatarsal of each of his ten toes.

As he replaced the wooden bowl in its previous position, he reached to the wall, unhooked the string of coral beads that hung next to the alligator skin and wore it like a necklace. He took out a string of brass-made objects, about the sizes of cherries, with smaller objects caged inside each one of them, which bounced around to produce a bell-like sound. He tied it around his right ankle.

He continued his preparation, wearing several other materials, and when he was finally ready to approach his oracle, looked like a feisty ghost in the dim light of only two burning candles. The white powdered material he applied around his eyes and the white stroke of chalk on his forehead, highlighted from the darkness, which almost muted his cobra dark complexion.

He then turned around and spoke to Raymond in Yoruba. Emeka translated. "Follow him."

Raymond's heart skipped a beat. He nervously followed the priest to the inner room. There was only a black door blind separating the priest and Raymond from whoever lived on the other side that the priest was about to consult. The priest held Raymond by his shoulders and positioned him to face the black curtain, then began to unbutton his shirt, following with a command that Emeka translated, asking him to pull off his shirt, shoes and socks.

The priest took out what looked like a horse's tail, and gathered other unidentifiable materials, and waited for Raymond to completely undress. There was a sudden feeling of fatigue in Raymond followed by sheer nervousness, causing a cold sweat to drip down his forehead. Nonetheless, he managed to maintain a sense of composure, partially confident there was no danger. However, he wasn't exactly thrilled with the prospect of being asked to proceed into the shrine alone.

Raymond was now wearing only his underpants. The priest rubbed ashes on Raymond's nose, and then gently lashed the horse's tail all over his body. The priest soliloquized as he was performing this segment of the ritual, and finally took a piece of the root that was lying on the floor, the size of a match stick, tucked it between Raymond's lips, then asked Emeka to instruct him that he chewed it to crumbs and swallow.

The priest stepped up his chanting as Raymond began to chew on the stick.

About two minutes later, the priest took an unlabeled, greenish bottle half filled with liquid and held it up to Raymond's mouth. Raymond obeyed his command to gargle and swallow as interpreted by Emeka, who evidently was quite familiar with all the pre-sacred procedure. The priest set the bottle down on the bare earth-coated floor, held Raymond by his left shoulder and pulled him back a step away from the door.

Each time the priest moved his legs, the brass metals rubbed against each other on his ankles and jingled. He reached for a pair of medium-sized, handheld gongs adjoined at the top, and reached for a ten-inch long stick. Holding both the stick and the pair of gongs in his left hand, he stood in front of Raymond, about two feet away, facing the black curtain. With his right hand, he picked up a small bell that was placed realm-side on the floor and gently jingled it twice, then replaced it, before switching the small stick over to his right hand.

The two gongs produced separate tones, one high and the other low, as the priest repeatedly struck on them, chanting a song that Raymond couldn't understand its wordings. He kept up the chanting and gong beating for almost ten minutes, and then stopped abruptly. He dropped both the instrument and the stick on the floor, called on Emeka to bring in the rooster, before resuming his incantations.

Emeka stood up from his bench, walked up to where Raymond was standing and waited behind him, his hands on a tight grip of the giant rooster's strapped legs.

Moments later, the priest stopped his chanting again, and this time turned around to receive the rooster from Emeka. He waved it around Raymond's head four times, while he murmured as if in a trance, then stopped. He turned around to hold the rooster upright, stretching his arms forward to the black curtain.

Another minute went by before the priest brought down his arms and drew a machete from its animal-skin scabbard. He placed the ill-fated rooster on the floor, and with a heavy piece of wood, trapped both of its legs to the floor. He grabbed the helpless rooster by the head and stretched its neck by pulling it cautiously away from the wood, machete in his right hand and ready to strike.

The sight of the beheaded rooster struggling futilely filled Raymond with a remote sense of outrage. Raymond was chilled witnessing the cold-blooded action. Didn't the rooster deserved some kind of reprieve? He observed as the priest spilled the blood from the rooster's profusely bleeding neck on the floor, from one end of the door where the black curtain hung, to the other, chanting his incantations.

Raymond managed to steer his conscience to reality. After all, he ate chicken almost daily. He shrugged it off and focused his attention on the priest and his fascinating spiritual consultation process.

The priest stopped, after series of ritualistic performances, and tossed the now lifeless rooster beside the door. He turned around and commanded Emeka and Raymond to continue to stand and listen carefully to him as he alone entered inside the deep shrine. He also urged Emeka to promptly and accurately interpret. Emeka and Raymond heard his voice yell and praise for almost fifteen minutes from the time he entered the innermost chamber. At the conclusion of his incantations, and still from behind the black curtain, he began to speak to Emeka, who quickly turned his left ears toward the direction of the deep shrine and interpreted the words to Raymond in Ibo language.

"There's a conflict about you," Emeka began to interpret. "You have appeared in a double image, both images facing forward. One image stands behind the other. Your image standing behind has your arms stretched forward, your face trembling as if you're struggling to get out of some hardship. Your image in front stands dignified and contented with the joy of life. Between both images is a barrier that consists of a thick cloud of smoke, which follows your every move. It just can't get out of your way when your distressed image behind tries to meet up or touch your happy front image."

The priest paused for a few seconds and continued, this time to interpret his vision.

"Your image behind the thick cloud represents your present condition, while your front image reveals a happier one in the future. The thick cloud of smoke means a pestilential encounter you will have to conquer before achieving success. You will finally achieve your goals, and life will become exuberantly savored with self-fulfillment. But you'll have to go through difficult troubles first."

The priest's revelation was to Raymond a direct interpretation of the mission that brought him to Africa and ultimately before the shrine. The young American inferred that all the troubles would begin from his swallowing the deadly heroin thru crossing the U.S. Customs gate. It sounded okay as long as he made it safely through.

"You're a very difficult person to accurately predict. The problem I'm having now is that I only see your mission here today as just a fragment of this vision. I cannot fully understand this, and neither do I understand why it's occurring the way it has. There's also a scene where you have appeared through a mirror. In the scene, you're uncharacteristically placing your left foot on the tail of a little newly hatched cobra snake, with the full knowledge that it will bite. You've respected it in the past and kept your distance, but now feel you had been respecting it out of cowardice and now trying to prove otherwise. You're thinking that this little cobra couldn't be that harmful.

The priest continued. "I don't see the little cobra actually biting you, but I'm seeing you quickly withdrawing your foot and hopping on your right leg, cupping your two hands over your bent left knee in an obvious reaction to the pain inflicted by the little cobra."

The priest paused for a moment to think and then turned to face Raymond and Emeka.

"In addition to the three hundred Naira that you will be billed for this service, I will require additional three hundred to neutralize this turbulence for this young man. Is that a go ahead, my son?"

Emeka gently tapped Raymond's shoulder and answered. "Yes Pa."

For what felt like twenty minutes, the priest spoke from inside his shrine, and in the end, instructed Emeka and Raymond on what to do as deterrence to all these potential problems.

"I'll give you a medal that you will keep all through your mission," the priest said. The jingling of the metals he tied around his ankle revealed he was on his way out of his deep shrine. He came out, pulling aside the black curtain, wondering with his eyes as if he was searching through a cloud of smoke. He approached both men and commanded them to go out and wait in the outer room.

Emeka and Raymond sat quietly and Raymond folded his arms. The priest came out and handed Raymond an egg-shaped black object, the size of a walnut. He spoke in Yoruba as he handed it to him, while Emeka interpreted accordingly.

"Here is a replica of what you will swallow on your way back to America. When we go back to the house, I'll give you something that will make it easy for you to swallow. It will boost your ability to perform, both in ingesting and in excreting. You must search for it whenever you take a shit. If by Tuesday you don't have it out, you must come back to see me. If you do, please wash thoroughly and give it to Emeka so he will return it back to me."

The sun was almost setting, and the room grew even dimmer. Raymond took the object and tightly clenched his fist as if it might escape.

The priest continued with his instructions.

"Everything is fine now. The road is clear and you should expect no problems in America. You shall go in peace, my son."

He paused to hand Raymond a brown leather medal the size of a half dollar. The medal was manually sewn around with visible white thread. "This you have to be handy with when you're about to leave the airplane. Touch it twice on your forehead and put it back inside your pocket as you approach the checkpoint. Don't leave it in a room where there's a naked woman. If you do, it will lose its potency. You must secure it at all times. You young men are prone to promiscuity, and Lagos has lots of attractive women. Having married four wives myself, I can report to you that the woman can become a hot water that will burn you upon contact. I advise you to keep away from girls until your mission is fully accomplished. My father says business before pleasure." He chuckled and continued. 'I implore you to remember what my father had said to me," he concluded and busted out laughing. Emeka laughed along while Raymond managed a smile.

The priest stood up and went back inside the middle room. Moments later, he came out fully dressed in his original garment, and holding Raymond's shirt and pair of shoes. He handed them to Raymond before retaking his seat.

After Raymond buttoned up, the priest stood up and led both men out of the sacred house and back to the residential quarters. On the way and inside the cemented yard, the priest interrupted the conversation among two of his four wives who stood facing each other by the entrance. Meanwhile, Emeka and Raymond sat down in their chairs. One of the priest's wives walked in and Raymond recognize her as the same woman who had opened the front door for the two when they initially arrived. She was carrying a small bowl half filled with soup, richly made out of okra seed. Emeka explained to Raymond it was for swallowing the sample.

To say the least, it was a terrible experience for Raymond fighting to force it down his throat. He felt its presence in his stomach all through the night, right from the time they left the juju priest's domicile to their return to Lagos City, and in Raymond's hotel suite.

Friday morning began with emotional uncertainty over Raymond's options. Although his visit with Emeka to the juju priest obviously introduced a renewed confidence in him, he felt there was still potential danger. One image that continuously bugged him was the priest's revelation of his foot on a cobra. To his personal understanding of the priest's vision, the black venomous snake represented the dangers of drugs, and stepping on it meant swallowing the drugs. Raymond saw it as a possible sign that if he hadn't visited the juju priest, he would have been a dead man by Wednesday had he not decided to go along with Emeka's plans.

The first vision was nonetheless an encouraging one. Raymond would finally achieve success, but first had to undergo substantial troubles. If the priest was speaking of Raymond's mission, then Raymond would have nothing to worry about so much since he would ultimately end up happy and ten thousand dollars richer.

Raymond felt a sudden urge to be around Laura, and the more he visualized her in the luxury suite with him, the stronger he desired to hurry back to the United States. He mentally recreated the alluring image of her perfect shape, a face like an angel's, and her seductive smile.

Raymond looked around the suite, imagining what it would look like in Laura's magnificent presence. She would light up the entire suite. They'd make love with intense passion until they were both exhausted, and then they'd sit side-by-side on the balcony, watching the waves of the Atlantic. Later when the heat of the sun intensified, they'd go down to the swimming pool to cool it all down and further advertise their newly found romance.

Raymond wished vehemently that a miracle happen, and there would be a knock on the front door, and he'd open, and behold it would be Laura.

A knock came from the door all right, but standing there was the ever nagging Tim. Raymond would have preferred to be alone with his fantasies, although he recognized the impossibility of his day dreams.

Raymond opened the door, and faked a smile at Tim. Raymond decided he would be calling Laura later on during the day.

Tim had his teenage sister bring over a lunch of pounded yam and vegetable soup stuffed with cooked snail. They ate and drank beer as usual on the balcony until Raymond felt the urge to go to town for sight-seeing.

Tim made a few alternative suggestions, but Raymond wanted to go to the shopping mall for a mini spending spree. He still had most of the money Emeka gave him, and all of a sudden his mind had drifted into a spending mood. The thought of Laura, coupled with the assurance by the juju priest that he would ultimately succeed in his mission, had given him a new hope, and he was up for anything fun.

Raymond and Tim left in a taxicab, while Tim's sister stayed on in the suite for treats of malt, orange soda and Coca Cola drinks, plus cable television. It was the first time Raymond had the opportunity to enjoy Lagos scenery aside from mission related engagements.

Their initial stop was at Leventis supermarket stores in Lagos Marina, where Raymond purchased a shirt for Tim and a pinkish blouse for Tim's sister. He also purchased swimming trunks for himself.

When Raymond was satisfied and tired, he went back to the hotel.

The pressure in his bowels reminded him of the sample still inside his stomach. It had been more than twelve hours since he had swallowed it, and if he successfully passed it out just as the juju priest had instructed, it would be a positive sign for him, at least in reassurance of his ability to excrete the cocaine through his system without grave consequence.

Raymond proceeded directly to the bathroom the moment they walked inside the suite, and closed the door. He stood for a little while thinking of a means of searching out the sample, and finally came up with a plastic bag to block the toilet bowl.

The object was among the first segment out of Raymond's waste product. Raymond searched it out to clean and wrap it with paper towel, secured it inside the bathroom closet for Emeka whenever they'd meet again.

Leaving the bathroom, Raymond came out to find both Tim and his sister snoring, Tim on the mini sofa-bed, his sister on the queen-sized bed. The teenage girl had cleaned the mess Raymond had left when they ate breakfast, and the entire place was then nice and quiet, and again suggestive of a romantic scenario. So far Raymond's mission had been put back on a positive track since he had seen the juju priest and blessed with its vaunted sacred powers. Now that Raymond had successfully passed out the replica the priest gave him, further suggesting that his vision, which revealed he'd succeed eventually after a cloudy encounter, was shaping up. Although the priest had said it didn't seem to be directly linked with Raymond's mission in Lagos, the priest had made sacrifice, charging additional three hundred Naira, supposedly to cleanse his body for immunity against potential problems.

It was almost one p.m. and Raymond was feeling bored again, and sick of the snoring from both Tim and his sister. Raymond felt it was time to have fun, and there was plenty of it waiting for him to call the shots. Emeka had promised to flood his suite with college girls should he desire such an aura of romance. Ayisha, whom he had met through Ike, could provide him with any channel of fun he would want.

Raymond realized he'd have to make a choice between Emeka's promise of college girls and Ayisha.

Raymond gave a careful thought to Emeka's, and finally concluded that such an erotic environment wouldn't be in the best interest of his religious faith, although he was on the verge of breaking it by coming to Lagos on an illicit venture. He felt it was better to limit his sin to just his drug courier mission. He also felt he wouldn't want his life to typify Sodom and Gomorrah.

Picking up the telephone, Raymond called Ike, but was told by a male voice that Ike was out. Feeling a little disappointed, he hung up and decided to try phoning Laura in New York. Laura picked up and sounded excited at the sound of Raymond's voice. Raymond had promised her, when they kissed good-bye at JFK airport she would be hearing from him when he came back, but now that he called much earlier than she expected, it was a surprising thrill. It was nearly seven o'clock in the morning, New York time, two hours shy of Laura's time to be at work, and she made it clear she would need a full half hour with Raymond on the phone, even if it meant sharing the telephone bill from the long distance call with him.

"I tell you what," Laura said. "You give me the number where you're calling from and I'll hang up after fifteen minutes and call you."

"Don't worry, Laura. We can talk as long as we want," Raymond said.

Indeed they could have spoken for the whole day, and given Raymond's potential value in the drug smuggling world, Emeka would gladly pay the bill. Still, Raymond wasn't about to disclose that to Laura when she insisted that she share the bill, citing her concern that as a tourist, he'd probably need all the money he could lay his hands on.

"I want you to be safe and sound when you come back. No reason to stay away from me any longer than you had promised me," she said.

After talking much about their new and exciting encounter and how much they missed each other, Laura tried to convince Raymond to fly back through JFK airport. Raymond tried unsuccessfully to convince Laura he'd have too many business stops to make in Virginia.

Laura made Raymond an offer almost impossible for him to pass. She would follow Raymond to Washington, D.C., if he'd consider flying through New York.

"We'll spend the weekend together, how about that?" Laura said.

"Hold on for a moment," Raymond said.

Raymond lowered the receiver from his ear and covered the mouthpiece to think over the suggestion. JFK airport was as deadly as a viper for importing narcotics. Both Dennis and Kenny had sternly warned Raymond against such avenue, and Raymond's tenant buddy, James, had explained the airport was well equipped to search out couriers, regardless of their expertise in concealing the goods. With the suggestion Laura had tabled, Raymond's resistance significantly softened.

Raymond placed back the receiver to his ear and asked Laura one question.

"How are we gonna work it out? I'll be traveling with Nigerian Airways, which departs on a Tuesday. You'll be working during weekdays."

"Can't you come back like Friday?"

"It's not possible, Laura, the flight is only twice a week—Tuesdays and Thursdays at night. I have to be in a traffic court Friday at nine o'clock, and can't travel on Thursday."

"So it'll have to be Tuesday?"

"Uh huh."

"Oh, come on now, Raymond. Okay, I'll tell you what. How about if I take Friday off. Can we leave Thursday evening when I get off from work?"

"That means I'll have to spend Wednesday night in New York."

"Can you do that?" Laura hesitated briefly, "if I pay your hotel bill?"

Raymond quickly thought it over. Although the danger of flying into JFK airport had been stressed to him several times, he would be willing to take the chance for Laura. After all, the juju priest had assured him of imminent success. That happier image of him that the priest envisioned could be his romance in Washington with Laura.

"You got it Laura," Raymond said. He had a strong conviction that everything would be all right. "But only on the grounds that I pay my own hotel bill without debate, right?"

"It's a deal, if that's the only objection," Laura quipped and giggled.

They spoke for a few more minutes before hanging up, concluding that Raymond call her when he got to the hotel he'd be staying in, which they both agreed to be the same Hotel Wentworth. Laura also emphasized that Raymond promptly inform her of any change of plans should that occur.

Chapter 13

CONTRADICTION

Raymond sat on the bed in his hotel suite, carefully planning his trip back to the US. Since he'd ingest narcotics inside his intestine and endure for only ten hours, instead of the dreadful twenty-two hours it would have taken from Lagos to Frankfurt, and finally to Dulles International airport in Virginia, he felt a heavy burden lifted from him.

However, it also meant that he would be excreting the drugs from his rectum in a hotel bathroom instead of the privacy of his own home, but he foresaw nothing so complicating with that. He could do that easily and then simply stuff the excreted drugs inside his luggage then fly from the local LaGuardia airport to Washington National airport. No search was required on local flights, and for a well-dressed gentleman walking along with a gorgeous lady like Laura, passersby would only stare at them with nothing but sheer admiration.

He picked up the telephone again and dialed Emeka's number. Emeka was still away and once again he left another message to call him back as soon as possible. He then searched out the piece of paper he had written Ben's telephone number and dialed. Ben was just arriving at his house and was to leave immediately when the phone rang. Upon recognizing it was Raymond, he answered and said he had an urgent need to go back out and apologetically promised he would be returning his phone call the moment he got to his destination.

Raymond sneaked in a warning statement. "I just want to let you know that following my visit with the juju priest, I now feel comfortable with myself and would like to fly in through JFK airport," he said with a note of caution in his voice.

Ben almost dropped the receiver as if it had all of a sudden turned ice cold but managed to compose himself. "Oh! Okay. No problem. I go get your ticket for Nigerian Airways," he said, his calmness surprising Raymond, who anticipated a strong and immediate objection.

After bidding each other goodbye, Ben slammed the receiver and cursed.

Moments after hanging up the telephone, Raymond stood up from his chair to switch on the television for a CNN Headline news update on the Persian Gulf conflict, but was distracted by yet another ringing telephone. It was Emeka returning his call. After a brief chat on social issues, he informed Emeka of his intent to change his flight route, and lied that his choice of the new travel plan was intended to minimize flight time.

"Well," Emeka said. "I must warn you that most of our couriers make it safely through Dulles. Anyway, I don't expect you to have any problem. You should be safe but I only want you to realize that Dulles airport is a lot safer."

"I know I'm gonna be safe. I have confidence in myself, thanks to you know who," Raymond jokingly said.

"You mean the...

"Juju man, now."

"Yup, he's wonderful, the best," Emeka said dryly.

"Anyway, that's all I wanted to tell you," Raymond said.

"Okay. Do you need anything? Money?"

"Oh no, I still have about fifteen hundred Naira with me."

"What about the thing, did you see it?" Emeka said in reference to the replica of a wrapped drug Raymond had excreted.

"Oh yes! I almost forgot that too. Yes, it was out with ease. No problem at all."

"Very good. All set then."

"I'll call you again on Sunday just to be in touch."

"Okay. Let me know if you need anything."

"You bet," Raymond concluded and hung up. He then sat on his chair imagining his friends' jealousy if he arrived in Washington, D.C. with Laura. They would want to know where and how he met her.

Dennis would try to find out from her if she had a sister that looked like her, or girlfriend who might want to meet someone – him.

He stood up once again to switch on the television. Tim and his sister were both awake, each facing the ceiling and silent. Tuning to CNN, he went to the refrigerator and retrieved a bottle of Gulda beer. Tim sat up and requested one for himself. Raymond obliged and as he walked to hand Tim the big bottle, he noticed Tim handing his sister the blouse Raymond had bought her at the supermarket.

"Wow," she said childishly, seemingly surprised as if it was her first ever, her cute eyes expanded. She examined the blouse, front and back, and sized it against her chest in sheer admiration.

"Thank you, sir," she said.

"You're certainly welcome," Raymond acknowledged absentmindedly.

Tim showed her his new shirt as he also thanked Raymond. From the look on their faces, the American could sense the depth of their appreciation.

Tim's sister left shortly after but Tim himself showed absolutely no desire to leave the high-class hotel suite. Raymond's guess was that Tim would rather the gift of staying at the luxury hotel than the gift of a shirt. At the moment though, Tim was a welcomed guest, and for his sake Raymond had dined cheaper plus he had a choice of variety. Tim's presence would keep his mind away from the possibility of re-examining the whole issue of his obligation in Africa. He wouldn't want to find himself in the same state of mind as his first day in the hotel's restaurant. He was now confident and ready to go.

It was three o'clock in the afternoon when Raymond sent Tim to the same carryout restaurant Tim had previously bought their meals from. Ike had telephoned again, and they were discussing what activities to engage in on Sunday afternoon when Ike had arranged to drive Ayisha over for an extended visit.

Tim came back with the usual set of bowls containing a little bit of everything—rice, blackeye peas, plantain, yam, stew, and goat meat. The smell of everything had Raymond almost drooling. He drew the phone conversation to an abrupt conclusion, deciding they'd simply go to the casino and spend a couple of hours, and then Ike would leave both Ayisha and Raymond alone for good. Raymond and Ayisha would return to the suite to get comfortable with each other. Of course, sex was the ultimate goal in everyone's mind.

The lunch was delicious as usual, but about half was still left over since both men had had breakfast that hadn't completely digested.

Within the next hour, Raymond was feeling bored again. Tim had left to return the empty bowls and there was nothing else left for him to do except go to the casino, which was no interest to him at that moment. He sensed a boring Friday and Saturday ahead but a hopeful Sunday when Ike would drive Ayisha over. He'd have to look for something to kill two empty days, and by the time Ayisha and him would be concluding their date, it would be only two days left to see Laura. He could handle those two idle days.

When Tim walked back inside the suite, Raymond asked him if he could suggest any other fun activity in Lagos. None sounded interesting enough and so they settled on going out for a swim at the hotel's pool.

Raymond was ready in few minutes. Tim, with no trunks and no desire to swim, waited by the deck, while Raymond joined other guests inside the pool.

The employees of the Eko Meridian Hotel had a flair in distinguishing their international guests from domestic customers. For one thing, they tipped more generously. For that, white foreign guests were being served to the point of near worship. The hotel itself was mostly filled with white guests, some of whom the government of Nigeria sponsored to reside in the country. The few African guests weren't the swimming pool types.

Tim, looking like he did not belong there, sat and drank his beer on a chaise lounge that Raymond had secured upon arrival. Noticeably, they were the only non-white guests present, but Raymond was clearly unmoved by this minority predicament. He felt it was his home country despite his suspicion that he and Tim being of domestic grown looked a little awkward in an environment only foreign nationals paraded.

Raymond was in the pool having a conversation about America's National Football League with a middle aged Canadian couple, when he noticed that Tim was been ordered to surrender the chaise lounge. Ordering the event was a waiter who stood next to Tim. Raymond saw the waiter offer the chaise lounge to a Caucasian group of a male and two females, who had just arrived at the pool. He hoped what he was witnessing happening with his chaise lounge was only his imagination.

The uniformed waiter, slim and in his mid-thirties with dark skin and a mild Yoruba accent, walked to where there were some old and rugged chaise lounge, drew it halfway and motioned Tim to take it before walking away. Raymond abruptly ended his conversation with the Canadians. The waiter had indeed offered his chaise lounge to one of the Europeans—a mid-twenties brunette.

Raymond was infuriated when Tim confirmed the obscenity. The three watched as Raymond beckoned the waiter.

"Come up here, right now," Raymond shouted angrily, drawing the attention of almost everyone around the pool. He folded his arms and waited impatiently as the waiter was on his way, and half way toward Raymond, began to explain why he had done it.

"Master, I think say you are swimming, and by the time you come out, I go bring you another one."

"That's not my question, sir, my question is, why did you give away my chaise lounge?"

"Make I go bring another one, sir."

"To hell with another one, I need you to show me the exact one I had before, and I mean the exact one. Did you hear me?" Raymond angrily shouted.

The waiter attempted once more to explain as everyone inside and around the pool focused on them. Raymond, who lost his cool, shut him up immediately by barking again.

"Look here, son-of-a-bitch," he continued, pointing his right index finger closely right at the waiter's face, "you have five seconds to pull that fucking lounge and bring it here or you'll face a severe consequence, right now. And I don't give a goddamn who they are, I'll still have my damn lounge any mother fucking ways."

The scare in the waiter's face was obvious, and Raymond felt good about it. The waiter stood humbly and was about to plead again, obviously embarrassed and battling a horrifying dilemma.

"Please, Master—."

"You have four seconds," Raymond continued. He counted down to three when he saw the man with the two girls signal the waiter to take his, seemingly to avoid trouble. But the gesture wasn't enough for angry Raymond.

"Look, I'm not interested in that one. I want this one," Raymond said and pointed to the exact lounge that one of the ladies was sitting on. Once again, the male guest spoke to the brunette in their language and she stood up. The waiter, looking embarrassed, reluctantly took the chaise lounge and returned it to where he had initially picked it up.

Raymond now had his chaise lounge back, feeling his dignity restored, although he didn't give a damn if it may have been eroded in the eyes and minds of other guests at the pool. He just didn't care.

After the incident, Raymond rejoined the Canadians in the pool to resume their discussions on the NFL games, noticing their attitude toward him had shifted from that of benign to outright admiration.

Raymond and Tim left the swimming pool around six-thirty p.m., when most of the guests were retiring back to their suites. Raymond decided he was simply going to call it a day and watch the evening news and perhaps a late movie, then sleep off the empty night.

Raymond took a quick shower and put on a pair of jeans and an "I-LOVE-NY" T-shirt. He and Tim left to board the elevator. When one of the four elevator car doors opened, they met four other people riding inside. One of them was a middle age man of Arab descent, but the other three were the same East Europeans he had encountered at the swimming pool earlier. The male was dressed in a pair of brown pants and a well-polished pair of black shoes, while the two women were both dressed in gowns that hinted party atmoslphere.

The moment Raymond noticed them, he purposely initiated a conversation with Tim. The three were chatting among themselves in their native language but when Raymond and Tim entered the elevator car, they went totally radio silent. Tim, noticing, confided to Raymond in broken English that one of the girls had rolled her eyes at him. He responded loudly and arrogantly in plain English, "I don't give a fuck who feels how about me. If anyone doesn't like me, he or she can jump ship, buddy." He chose to avoid looking directly at their faces but was sure they were very much aware that his arrogant comment was directed at them.

As the elevator opened to the ground floor, the three waited for Raymond and Tim to leave before they did, and Raymond walked out with Tim following behind. "That's right," Raymond said openly, "I should have some priority for a damn change around here."

Raymond and Tim walked toward the main exit. The doorman opened and Raymond casually asked him if there was any social event close by the hotel on the Friday night.

"Yes sir," the doorman said. "There's disco on the rooftop."

"Where?" Raymond said with astonishment.

"The last floor of this building, sir; the thirteenth floor."

"What time does it start?"

The man paused to think. "I believe eight o'clock."

"Thank you very much, sir," Raymond said and walked away with Tim, who quickly asked to tag along to the disco nightclub at the rooftop. Raymond, not wanting his company any longer, at least for the day, played a deaf ear. But Tim repeated and Raymond couldn't help but say okay. He felt that after all Tim had served him well and he was only looking for a means to kill a boring evening. For that reason, both men returned to Raymond's suite and he changed to his party outfit.

He paid the eighty naira gate fee for two and walked in with Tim. A handful of patrons were already seated and drinking. The disco club was designed fabulously to suit the dignity of the building that housed it. It was the size of two big conference rooms joined together and dimly lit in blue and purple light. Two spotlight bulbs hung on top of the ceiling and their amber neon lights hovered and highlighted the wooden dance floor in the middle, cascading on two boogying white couples. The bar shaped like the figure S was located at the left end of the clubhouse and wrapped around in rich black leather. The stools were silver metal with black cushioned seats, and the tables were chrome glass, the room heavily air conditioned.

One of the waiters, a man in his thirties dressed in white tux half jacket, approached Raymond's table.

"Welcome, sir. Can I serve you?" he said humbly, shouting to be heard amidst the loud house mix jam that blasted.

"You sure can," Raymond said, "and a cold Star beer, and my buddy here with whatever he would want to drink."

The waiter ushered them to a vacant table and Tim requested a bottle of Gulda beer and then leaned over to talk to Raymond.

"You know, those idiots are here?" Tim said.

"Who are they?" Raymond said.

"You know… from the pool."

Raymond looked behind him to notice he was once again sharing a common social interest with the chaise lounge trio they had encountered at the swimming pool and later in the elevator. The three Europeans were seated, chatting and drinking from their glass cups. One of the two girls bent over to kiss the male while the other fixed her eyes at the direction of Raymond's table in the dim lights of a nightclub. Her eyes met with Raymond's and the American noticed her lean over to speak to her colleagues. They all turned their heads around at once to look in his direction. As Raymond stood guessing at what was happening, he positioned his chair to face their direction and they quickly looked away. He felt he wouldn't want to look or act cowardly, or for that matter, attempt to disguise his hatred and frustration toward the unfair treatment of black guests compared to white ones. He was still mad about the disrespectful chaise lounge incident at the pool that bounced in their favor. So he stood up to walk confidently to the bathroom, just to pass through their table and try to prove he was in no way remorseful, and that he wasn't going to be intimidated either.

He returned from the restroom shortly afterward to resume drinking. The dance floor had now increased by another three dancing couples. Tim concentrated on his drinking while he visually searched around for any possible single female dance partner. Everyone in the club seemed to have been paired, except for one of the ladies in the infamous chaise lounge three's company. He now deemed them his enemies. There were a few other tables where it looked like one or two girls were unpaired, but they were older and busy talking to each other, making it difficult for him to approach them.

Tim was quick to remark on that. "It looks like this place is only for white people," He said.

"Yup," Raymond concurred. "But I can turn it into a place for everyone if I want to."

Tim regarded him. "I know these people. They're not going to dance with you if you're Nigerian."

Tim's remark, although plausible, generated a mood of flamboyance in Raymond, causing him to buy drinks like a filthy rich brat. He also, without concern for anything, talked to anyone around him about anything, mainly what brought them to the country.

Moments later, he tapped Tim by his shoulder. "I want to ask that lady for a dance," he said.

Tim stared at Raymond as if he had threatened to swallow a poison pill. "Don't do it," he said quickly. "They may accuse you of trying to interfere with them."

"So?" Raymond said and stood up ready to swing into action.

Tim's attempt to dissuade him fell on deaf ears as he was already on his way. He wasn't anticipating a positive outcome anyway but simply wanted to prove he could do whatever he wanted, including approaching the chaise lounge three. After all it's his country.

His chest out forward, he stood tall before the three and made his mock request.

"I wanna dance with her," Raymond said loudly and pointedly to avoid their uttering annoying phrase like "huh?" or "pardon?"

The odd girl, the same one whom Raymond forced to give back the chaise lounge, hair tied in a French braid, looked the other way, while the two lovers stared astonishingly at him, looking confused.

"Pardon me?" the man asked.

"I said I'd like to dance with her, if you don't mind."

"Sure," he said, with his hand gestured as if he was introducing Raymond to her.

"Ma'am, do you mind stepping up to the dance floor with me, please?" he rhetorically asked the confused girl.

Raymond was certain she was obviously going to be negative and he wanted her to do just that. She turned and looked at him, pretending to be ignorant of what he had just said to her.

"Huh?" she muttered and spoke to the two in their native language.

She sat her glass on the table and stood up. For a moment, Raymond thought she may have been trying to free her hand to slap him. Instead she began to walk toward the dance floor. He cautiously followed behind her, wondering why on earth she had agreed to a dance with him, a total stranger who had been so arrogant to her and her colleagues. He began to feel somewhat appreciative of her honoring his request to dance with him, but for some reason, he frankly wouldn't have given a damn if she hadn't.

Raymond and the girl danced to four different disco songs and he still saw no signs of desire in her to leave the dance floor. Now he was beginning to fully appreciate the situation. He thought he'd have to leave the termination of the dance session up to her.

Two more songs later, Raymond, too tired and thirsty, badly needed to drink his beer while it was still cold. He decided at the end of that song he would end the dance himself. He was still wondering why she had agreed to step to the dance floor with him in the first place, and now she wouldn't quit. He didn't know what she could have been thinking as she danced and avoided eye contact with him.

Toward the end of the song, he and the girl were about to exit from the dance stage when the disc jockey immediately switched to a slow song. The decision to re-invite her to slow dance with him while they were halfway toward her table came spontaneously. He simply asked her if she would like to try a slow dance, falsely claiming it was one of his favorite songs, and she succumbed without objection, turning around to lead the way back to the dance floor.

As they were walking away he wondered if she really understood it meant his arms around her, but she knew it. She was the first to raise her arms, and he fitted his body into her five foot six shape and pressed his chest hard against her full firm breasts.

Shortly after, her colleagues joined them on the dance floor, and their presence inflicted him with the guilt of conscience. Somehow, he felt like apologizing, but he wasn't quite sure if that was appropriate, how to take the initiative. Whichever he'd choose, he'd have to start by introducing himself to the woman he was dancing with, whose cheeks were tightly rested on his shoulder, his mouth brushing slightly on her right ear.

"What's your name?" Raymond said.

The girl raised her head so her mouth would be close to his ear.

"Manuella," she said with a very romantic accent, her mouth also brushing on his ear as she spoke.

He introduced himself and they took turns asking about each other, obviously relishing the closeness. With her deep East European accent and little knowledge of English language, all Raymond could comprehend was her name and nationality. She was Romanian. Raymond invited her to talk outside after the song, which was the third slow song back to back, and she immediately accepted.

The song the couple chose to be their last apparently became the last slow song for then, and the disc jockey changed to a fast beat. Manuella went over to her colleagues and excused herself. They were also about to walk out from the dance floor when Manuella approached them. She then came to where Raymond was waiting at the end of the bar before the exit door.

"Let's go, yes?" Manuella said and ran her fingers through her hair to fix a portion that pulled off the braid.

Raymond extended his hand to Manuella, and she firmly held it and followed him to the noiseless hallway where they formally became friends and found out a little bit about each other. Manuella and her friends were apparently vacationing in Lagos, where parents of both girls had lived in the seventies as family friends. They had decided, as her colleagues were now engaged to be married, to revisit the country.

The thought of Laura hampered much of Raymond's zeal to speed up cuddling activities with Manuella. He felt he wouldn't want to disappoint Laura when they met again in New York, especially after he had specifically promised her he wasn't going to fool around with other women. The excitement Laura's beauty and feminine personality had generated in Raymond's heart was frankly unqualified.

Raymond and Manuella spent about forty-five minutes alone in the hallway, discussing whatever they could, despite Manuella's severe handicap in English language. He even tried a few words in Romanian which Manuella jokingly promised to teach him some time in the future, and he in turn gave her a brief lecture on Ibo customs and traditions.

Raymond noticed Manuella willfully avoided the unpleasant chaise lounge encounter that first linked them together, as much as he did. The two also pretty much parted each other, thanks to his reserved composure that stemmed from his reminiscence of Laura.

With nothing else left to discuss, he led Manuella back inside the night club to find that her colleagues were ready to go and were waiting for her to return. Manuella introduced her colleagues to him and he introduced himself and shook hands with the lovers, before walking along with them to the elevator. Raymond first gave Manuella his suite number then invited her to either visit or call whenever she pleased, and Manuella gracefully accepted.

As one of the elevator cars opened, Manuella stared at Raymond and smiled, while her friends bid him good-bye. Raymond put his right arm around Manuella and pulled her closer to him, intending to kiss her by her cheek. Instead Manuella positioned her lips and as he rose to the occasion of kissing her, she playfully snaked her tongue into his mouth, hugging him tightly before smiling and saying goodnight. She joined her waiting colleagues inside the elevator car.

Raymond went back to find that Tim was barely keeping his eyes awake and hurriedly paid his bill before leaving for his hotel suite. Tim left alone to catch a taxi home, while Raymond exited at the eighth floor, and into his suite to relax and think over the strange affair of daytime enemies and nighttime lovers.

He spent most of Saturday inside his hotel suite. He slept on and off until 3 in the afternoon. He was feeling too tired and lazy to do anything, just thinking and telling himself he was satisfied with Laura alone, and the prospect of seeing her again in less than five days was titillating. If anything, he wanted to keep his relationship with the Romanian dame strictly platonic. He highly appreciated her opening up to him, though, especially after his ungentlemanly behavior.

Later in the evening, he went down to the casino where he killed the rest of the day and returned to his suite at around two a.m. Sunday morning.

He woke up at 8 a.m., unusually early considering his late hours at the casino, and his mind was probing the extraordinary romantic ecstasy he had found himself enjoying since he had left Washington for his drug courier mission. First it was Laura, and then Ayisha, who, by the way, would be visiting later on that day. Perhaps the strangest of all, there was a Romanian woman he least expected to be close to. What a mesmerizing romantic escapade.

Soon after trying to figure out why lately he had been so unusually lucky with beautiful women, Raymond's mind slipped to thoughts of football - the NFL. He contemplated the chances of his beloved Washington Redskins making it to the Super Bowl.

He was too weak and tired, and to get up from his bed to turn on the manually controlled television was a hassle. There was still enough sleep in his eyes, but for some reason, his thoughts of new luck with women kept him away from dozing off. When he finally summoned enough strength to stand up, he turned on the TV, and then went directly to the bathroom, where he decided a shower might help him overcome the currently nagging sleeplessness.

It was almost 11 o'clock sunny Sunday morning, after Raymond had showered and made his own bed. He sat pondering what to do about usual late breakfast. Tim, who had always arranged it, also had a late night, and must have been still sleeping.

A slight knock on the front door, which hinted like Tim's knock, and Raymond had the same mixed feeling he usually had whenever Tim came over. Tim was a useful errand boy but at the moment he preferred doing most things on his own. He took his time before going to open the door, calling out loudly at supposedly Tim to hold on for a moment. But first he went to the television set and selected a CNN Headline News channel to prevent Tim from tuning to the local cartoon channel, something Tim constantly did since when they first arrived at the hotel.

Satisfied with the picture adjustment, He went to the door and opened it carelessly without looking at Tim. He started to walk back when a startling feminine voice caused him to turn around immediately.

It was Manuella—alone.

Raymond froze. "Well hello," he managed to say, surprised and aware that if his skin was white he'd be blushing at that moment. "Come on in. How are you?"

"Fine, thank you," she said in her feminine east European accent, sounding like she had just learned how to say that in English language.

She walked inside and looked around the suite, seemingly impressed by the plushness of Raymond's suite. She was wearing a pair of blue jean shorts, sensationalizing her blameless straight legs, and a white muscle T-shirt that exposed her flat lower abdomen and around her waist area, and a pair of white Converse snickers. Her shoulder length, dark hair was banded at the back with a pink ribbon. She looked like a high school girl.

"Please have a seat, Manuella," Raymond said cordially. "Make yourself comfortable."

Just yesterday, Raymond Karr had contemplated how he would limit their eyebrow-raising friendship, and concluded it would have to be virtually platonic. Still, he wasn't sure if he could resist a temptation of the magnitude he was encountering.

He found out how little Manuella's knowledge of English language was. They spent over an hour over beer interpreting and re-interpreting each other. It seemed like she was fed up with her non-romantic Lagos vacation, unlike her colleagues, who were partners in love. He wondered what had brought her to him, and decided on a wait-and-see approach.

Tim came by at noon and brought lunch for himself and Manuella. In the next hour, Tim returned the bowls as usual, and left for good. Raymond took Manuella outside to the balcony, and to the splendid and panoramic view of the Atlantic Ocean. After a while, they both silently and mutually consented to continue from where they left off the previous night. They followed with series of passionate kisses, pressing their bodies hard against each other. The temptation became so irresistible that Raymond began to rub his hands on her loose-fitted bra. His conscience weighed heavily against proceeding further, drawing his mind to his promise to Laura, but he was having hot pants for his surprise guest. He knew that despite the promise, as well as the juju priest's admonition to refrain from women until mission was completed, there was no way he was letting such gratuitous opportunity go. Yes the juju priest had cautioned that the woman can be a hot water that will burn upon contact, but it doesn't mean it cannot be used to put out a burning fire.

Yielding to the compelling temptation, Raymond placed his palm around to Manuella's sexy flat and bare abdomen while they stood with her back against his front, looking without interest ships sail by. His fingers were caressing hers just less than an inch shy of her pubis, and the fantasizing prospect was driving him wild crazy. She occasionally sent her arms backwards to grab him around his neck and gently pulled, turning her head around to tap a kiss at him. In one of their intermittent kisses, she had held so long that Raymond began to gently probe his fingers a little lower than her navel. Eventually, he slipped his fingers slightly inside her shorts, and then panties, and stroked along the upper line of her pubic hair. She brought down her hands from around his neck to slightly resist, then guided his right hand to her breasts, before unbuttoning her jeans shorts to pull the zipper halfway down.

The incessant ringing of the telephone forced Raymond to lead Manuella inside the suite. He held her hand while he talked to Ike, who was calling to remind him of his date with Ayisha that afternoon. According to Ike, they would be on their way shortly, and be arriving in twenty minutes. When the jolt from Ike's information ran through Raymond, he dropped her hand. She went straight to the bed and laid face-up across, her shorts still unbuttoned, her white nylon panties partly exposed through her half unzipped flap. The sight of her in that position instantly injected Raymond with the courage to go ahead and disappoint Ike and Ayisha.

Raymond told Ike to cancel the date immediately, and lied that there had been an urgent need for him to meet his sister at the airport, and that he would telephone Ike as soon as he was finished attending to the emergency. The excuse may have sounded phony, but he could care less. He intended to fully seize the rare opportunity for a serendipitous moment.

He hung up the receiver after discharging Ike, dashed onto the bed to lie beside Manuella. She had noticed the usual masculine curve by Raymond's pelvis, and moved closer to him. He was just about to climb on top of her when an instant remembrance caused him to immediately jump off from the bed like a love-making teen would react if his parents were unlocking the door. He had just remembered the juju priest's instructions on the sacred medal.

He quickly rushed to put on his clothes, simultaneously asking her to excuse him for a few minutes. She looked astounded. "There's problem?" she said.

"Oh no," Raymond said immediately. "I just want to meet a deadline downstairs, and I'll be right back. Okay?"

It wasn't okay with her as she fixed her eyes on him, guessing with disappointment while he was hurrying his dressing. He didn't care. All he wanted to do was to quickly remove the medal from the room, lest it be abrogated, but had no plan in place on where to safely hide it. He reached for the jacket inside the closet and took it out of the pocket, and hurried into the bathroom, carefully handling it as if it could disappear on contact with light.

While inside the bathroom, his mind raced rapidly for a solution. But when it dawned on him his hands, which were clenching the medal, possibly may have been infested with sexual fluid, he instantly dropped it on the floor as if it had bitten him.

"Oops, excuse me," he uttered stupidly.

While still nervous and confused, caught in the dilemma of sanctifying his hands first or picking up the medal as it may appear desecrating to leave it on the floor for long, he bent down and stopped short of picking it up, thought for a moment then immediately stood upright. He finally decided to first wash his hands in a desperate bid to achieve purity before he could pick up the sacred medal.

He dried his hands and felt somewhat confident enough to pick up the medal He put it in his breast pocket and left, taking along his passport. He took the elevator downstairs and walked to the receptionist's counter where he met with one on duty, a skinny man in his late thirties, dark-chocolate complexioned.

"Do you know where the assistant manager is?" Raymond said. He felt that if he could find the man, he would slide the medal inside the cover of the front leaf of his passport and have him secure the passport in their safe deposit.

"He does not work on Sundays—only Monday to Saturday," the receptionist said.

It felt like a major blow to Raymond's plan. He began to think again. He stood staring at the floor, while resting his right arm on the counter. It was bad luck, he thought. It may have already been too late. Once again he had been stupid, and couldn't remember a simple instruction as crucial as the juju priest's. He cursed himself and looked up to face the receptionist.

"Can you do me a favor?" he said. "Would you be able to secure this passport for me till tomorrow?" He held up the passport and flashed it before the receptionist. The baffled receptionist visually inspected it before responding to him.

"I can do that, but why can't you put it in a safe here?"

"Do you have a safe?"

"Yes, for our guests."

"How much does it cost?"

"Nothing… All you'll have to do is deposit five hundred Naira, and when you return the key, you get a refund."

"But I already have two thousand Naira deposited with you guys."

"I will check your name before. What is your room number?"

Raymond dictated his full name. The receptionist picked up a large book numbered by pages with the hotel rooms, and opened the page that had his room number on it. After moments of calculation, he began to fill out a pink form he took out from one of the drawers. He then handed him the ink pen.

"Sign here," he said.

Raymond obliged and handed back the ink pen. The receptionist then tore out the lower portion of the slip that was boldly printed with serial numbers, same as the one printed on top of the form, and handed it to him. He placed the upper portion back inside the big book and closed it.

"Come around," he said and pointed to the door that led inside the office.

When it was over, Raymond had a key and the receptionist was holding another key. To open the safe, two people had to be there—himself and an authorized employee.

Raymond came back to the suite to find Manuella zipped up and sitting on the bed, in a look of awe. He tried to think of how to make it up to her, but just couldn't find a solution. Yet another show of ungentlemanly behavior toward her could resurrect the past ugly chaise lounge events, and certainly could trigger a permanent hatred toward him.

In spite of the inexcusable but implicit bad behavior against Manuella, Raymond was bothered mostly by what could be the serious consequence of his forgetfulness. All along he had been confident, since the priest handed the medal to him. Since he had gone contrary to the priest's instruction, the confidence would vanish, leaving him with a horrific task on a mere human strength devoid of spiritual guidance. He figured he'd have to find a way to bring Manuella and himself to some kind of understanding.

"What's the matter?" he said, pretending as he sat next to her, putting his left arm around her shoulders.

"I want to go," she said in a low voice, looking down in a frowned face.

"But why….because I went downstairs?"

She remained silent despite his inquiry. He wanted her to believe it was no biggie, but with her face showing dissatisfaction like a disgruntled teenager, he knew he would have to do more than just ask questions.

He took Manuella by her arm.

"Come here, babe," he said in an apologetic voice.

Manuella slowly stood up and wiped the tears rolling down her cheeks. Raymond knew Manuella wasn't going to take it lightly anymore.

"Good Lord," he began again, and with his arms around Manuella's bare waist, squeezed her tightly against him.

"Darling, if it's something I did wrong please forgive me, would you? You may be thinking I'd done something wrong, but believe me, I know of nothing, absolutely nothing that I'd done as far as you're concerned."

Watching Manuella wipe her tears, he thought she looked as beautiful as ever, and the sensitivity brought his emotion to a brink of shedding tears of his own.

"However whatever it may have been, do you forgive me?" Raymond continued.

He felt her nod on his shoulder, and that feeling made him heave a sigh of relief.

"Can I have a kiss?" Raymond followed, and slightly pulled his chest away from her to watch her reaction.

Manuella slowly raised her head for her lips to meet his. For over ten minutes they stood kissing, and once again onto the bed for yet another intense sex Raymond ever had since Laura.

Raymond walked Manuella, at her request, to her sixth floor single suite, where they held a brief conversation on their possible chances of meeting again somewhere else, either in Washington or Bucharest, where she lived in. Without conclusion, but promising to get serious on the issue over the telephone later, they kissed goodnight, and he returned to his suite to shower and think of what to do following his afternoon mischief.

The one thing that heavily troubled Raymond's mind was whether to notify Emeka of the medal infamous incident, and for that matter, seek Emeka's own take on the snafu. But such idea sounded counterintuitive to him. What if Emeka got very angry at him and decide to do something unpleasant? Maybe his conduct unbecoming didn't neutralize the sacred powers of the medal, after all. The medal wasn't there when Manuella was undressed.

Raymond decided he'd have to carefully weigh the whole incident and see if he had actually broken the laws of the sacred medal's sanctity, before deciding to notify Emeka. Raymond was becoming sick and tired of the entire courier affair, and if he didn't like it by the time he had been scheduled to swallow the drugs, he still reserved his right to call it off. Emeka's indirect threat of what could happen to Raymond if he backed out may have been only a means to inject fear into him to secure his loyalty. Emeka looked harmless and spoke too gently to be a killer. He could still put up his show of vomiting noise, should that becomes necessary, in order to smoothly sail away from the burden of swallowing balloons of drugs.

He changed to his jeans and "Washington, DC" T-shirt and headed for the casino.

At the steps of the hotel's large open entrance, Raymond ran into the friendly Canadian couple he met at the swimming pool. They greeted each other and briefly touched on the chaise lounge issue, when he impulsively shouted at the person who had just come out from a taxicab.

For God's sake, it was Dennis "the green bottle" Metu. Dennis had decided to make the trip for the second time.

Raymond quickly discharged the Canadians and dashed to Dennis, who was accompanied by a male associate. Both men flew in from the United States. They had arrived on the Sunday morning flight, and had checked into Federal Palace hotel, but had decided, after a well rested morning and afternoon, to kill the evening at the casino.

Dennis's presence in Lagos for a second trip was an ultimate confidence booster to Raymond. During one of their many discussions back in the U.S., Raymond had contemplated on coming along with him for Dennis's second trip, but contemplated he wouldn't want to do something that he would live to regret, and that the mission so daring, should be a once-in-a-lifetime experience.

In retrospect, he wished he had gone along with Dennis during Dennis's first trip, which would have been over by now, and Raymond wouldn't be facing the nightmare anymore.

They all spent the evening together at the casino playing bingo and jackpot slot machines, retreating at 1 o'clock after discussing their itinerary from henceforth. Dennis had been sponsored by someone other than Clyde, and had brought along a new courier following a promise from Richard, his previous sponsor, for a handsome bonus.

"Dennis," Raymond said. "I have intention to depart with the Tuesday night's Nigerian Airways flight to New York."

"Commissioner, I adamantly oppose such idea but it's up to you," Dennis said. "If you feel comfortable doing that, go right ahead. It's at your discretion. Good luck at JFK."

Raymond went to bed with little concern over both the courier mission and the sacred medal incident, dismissing the priest's gift as a mere superstition. Instead he felt the uneasiness of guilty conscience for forgetting he had promised Manuella a bedtime telephone call. He also thought about Ayisha, who was supposed to have visited with him.

Emeka, as they had previously arranged, would be picking up Raymond on Monday at 1 p.m., and would drive him to his house where he would spend the night, and stay until 3 p.m. Tuesday, the day Raymond was scheduled to swallow the drugs. It was also three hours from Nigerian Airways departure time to JFK Airport in New York.

Waking up at eight o'clock, Raymond showered and dressed casually in his slacks and white and light blue checkered shirt. he sat on the bed watching CNN.

The telephone rang, and it was Manuella. He quickly apologized for the previous night's delinquency, and this time truthfully confessed.

"My business associate came in from the United States and we had spent the entire evening at the casino," he said. "Remember my departure is this afternoon."

"Yes. I'm not happy," she said.

Raymond and Manuella spoke on the phone for a few minutes. Although some of what he was telling Manuella certainly made little or no sense at all to her due to her limited English, Raymond tried to be precise, and Manuella understood the bottom line—that Raymond would be headed back to the U.S. soon.

He invited Manuella to come by for the discussion, and Manuella gladly accepted. In just about eight minutes later, Manuella slightly tapped once on the door, and when Raymond opened. She was dressed in a summer outfit—a slight, see-through yellow dress and a pair of hand-made animal skin slippers.

"Good morning," Manuella greeted in a mellowed voice and a sexy smile.

"How are you doing? Please come right in," he said and held the door open, then closed as soon as Manuella stepped inside.

Manuella stood staring lustfully at Raymond, instead of proceeding to the sitting area. He spread his arms and Manuella impatiently attached her body on his like a magnet. He sank his tongue into her mouth and she sucked like and infant.

Raymond and Manuella had a tremendously romantic morning. Tim had returned at a quarter to seven, and Raymond had sent him to buy breakfast, but instructed him to spend about an hour at the casino before going to the carryout. Manuella and Raymond desired their last privacy before his departure. They had also exchanged telephone numbers and addresses for a possible reunion next summer, most likely in the United States.

Emeka failed the 1 o'clock pickup time as planned, and that gave Raymond the opportunity to telephone Ike. Someone else picked up the phone and told Raymond Ike hadn't come back. He left a message for Ike to call him in the United States.

Emeka finally sent his younger brother, a twenty-five-year old slender look alike of him, who drove over with a white Mercedes Benz sedan. The younng man paid Raymond's hotel bill with cash, and drove Raymond to their large plush house in Ikeja, where Raymond would be staying until the time to swallow drugs and departure to the U.S.

He was led to a luxury bedroom, one among several, perhaps exclusively for guests of his drug courier status. The king-sized bed, upholstered with brown leather, was placed in the middle of the cozy room, with a mirrored headboard against the white painted wall. On the opposite side of the wall was a large glass window, covered with brown flowered curtains.

The building, a class by itself, was concrete fenced, and the living room was large enough to host a union rally.

Raymond set his luggage on the floor, took off his shoes, and sat on the bed, admiring the symbols of wealth that surrounded him. He had had a shortened sleep last night and was feeling too tired following the late morning hot sex with Manuella, and badly needed some rest to counter the enormous exhaustion.

The much needed sleep never came as he rolled from one end of the bed to the other. His mind involuntarily focused on the entire itinerary, from the trauma of swallowing drugs and the growing fear of attempting to evade a tight security manned by JFK airport custom agents, to the airplane trip that would last more than ten straight hours. Even when he managed to erase the fears in his mind he still couldn't fall asleep. He stayed awake until Emeka came back from work around eight o'clock in the evening.

The youngest of Emeka's brothers slightly tapped three times on the door and swung it open. He peeped in, and ascertaining that Raymond was decent, emerged to tell him dinner was served.

"Okay," Raymond said and stood up as the boy left.

Raymond had had a loss of appetite at late breakfast when he dined with Manuella, probably because of the intoxication that Manuella's presence brought to his imagination. Now he should have been hungry, but the loss of appetite still loomed. He leisurely walked downstairs to the family's royal-style dining room, and on one end of the long China oak table, experimented unsuccessfully with the rice and plantain dinner, scooping only a few spoons and chewing down only a piece of goat meat.

He joined Emeka and his two late evening guests in the living room, where he spent much of his time moping unenthusiastically at the local programs on television. A half hour later, Raymond went back to his bedroom to kill the rest of the night.

Raymond's eyes fixed on the white painted squares of the ceiling board, creating imaginary images from minor chip off on certain areas of the roof. At some point during the night, his thoughts and silent prayers went to his sickly mother and his son, and wished he was home with all of them. But he quickly diverted his attention to his fear of flying in an airplane.

Raymond looked at his wrist watch, which he had placed inside his shoe. It was only a dismal 2:15 a.m.

The sleeplessness persisted and when he finally fell asleep, he woke up and again at almost 4 o'clock. It felt like a night of holocaust. During the short sleep, Raymond had dreamt of a mountain where everyone easily climbed to the top without effort. But with a terrifying fear he managed to climb a few steps and gave up. He suddenly realized it was the only way to home, and as he was so ravaged with the fear that backing down looked even more terrifying and that he was trapped in the middle, he woke up and recited "The Lord is my shepherd," which lately he had been rehearsing more often.

Early in the morning, he began to intensely focus on the awesome task ahead. Just in a matter of twenty-four hours, the airplane that he would be boarding would be about to touch down at Kennedy airport. He wondered, if he didn't die of an explosion inside his stomach, what would happen if he was apprehended. How could he deal with adversity in case that materialized, especially since the odd was so mountainous with an existential threat of losing his freedom?

After a few thoughts, he realized he wasn't in any way ready for failure. He thought about the juju priest's supposedly sacred medal. If he had indeed compromised the integrity of the medal's sacred powers, and if he would be too nervous when the custom agents approached him for questioning at JFK. All thoughts compounded, he knew he was in for a hellish time ahead.

Disingenuously, although he just couldn't imagine himself in legal trouble of that magnitude, he still couldn't picture himself successfully making it through the highly efficient U.S. Customs.

Raymond took his morning shower at 8 and flatly rejected the cook's invitation for breakfast. His appetite was completely gone. Emeka, who was about to set out for the day's business, walked in to his bed room for the final arrangement before Raymond's departure to the airport.

Firstly, Emeka's teenage brother would lead him to the local market center for purchases of a variety of items, enough to fill a large suitcase. It would serve, according to the boy, as a decoy for evading the U.S. custom agents, and also legitimize his claim to be coming back from a well-deserved vacation.

Secondly, the teenager instructed that Raymond avoid drinking such stomach upsetting beverages as orange juice and milk, which might result in prematurely forcing out the ingested drugs while Raymond was aboard the airplane. That restriction would last until Raymond's heroin swallowing time, scheduled for 3 o'clock that afternoon, and subsequently his departure from the house at five, exactly one hour before boarding time.

Emeka drove Raymond and the teenager in his Toyota Pathfinder SUV to a big shopping center and dropped them off, then proceeded to his destination. Raymond and the teenager spent over three thousand Naira in a shopping spree, collecting anything they deemed tactically manipulative for distraction, from African clothing and art work, including a fifteen hundred Naira large replica of the Oba Akenzue of the Benin tribe, to Nigerian raw food items. They even purchased the large, expensive suitcase needed to efficiently pack all goods.

Surprisingly to Raymond, Emeka's twenty-something younger brother demanded his passport and U.S. alien resident card, which he immediately surrendered to him without objection. The young man voluntarily explained it would be for Raymond's ticket confirmation, and he left immediately after their return from the shopping center, taking along the large suitcase. Their teenage brother returned in the same taxicab.

At about 1:15 p.m, the cook, a heavy set young man who spoke only in broken English, came upstairs to Raymond's bedroom and invited him to lunch. Raymond weighed his appetite and it wasn't enough, and once again, he turned it down. His only wish was to be able to sleep, even if for only one hour.

Raymond went to the shower for a cold splash. When he was done, he came back to bed to try again for a nap, but to no avail. Only deep troubling thoughts. Lots of thoughts until show time.

Chapter 14

PERILOUS DINNER

On one corner of the floor, inside the bedroom, sat two large identical rubber-made bowls, one next to the other, and each three-quarter filled with lukewarm water. Next to the bowl on the right side was a smaller fragile bowl topped with a matching brown cover, and containing hot fresh fish soup enriched with pureed okra.

Raymond sat, elbows on knees, on the heavily rugged floor with his back leaning against the wall. The teenage boy sat upright the same position face to face with him. The sight of a brown groom case set on the floor beside the teenager scared him like a bunny rabbit and sent a chill up his spine. He was sure it contained the deadly heroin he was about to send inside his intestine. The teenager was well aware of his fears. He had fed the same to many others before and knew that all first timers he had encountered experienced the same petrifying moment. They were waiting for Emeka to come by and receive the replica that Raymond had swallowed at the priest's residence. Emeka also would be giving him further procedural instruction.

"You'll be amazed at how easy this will shoot down your throat," the teenager said in order to break the surreal silence.

"Oh I know," Raymond quipped, heart pounding like a train engine. He briefly turned his eyes to face the teenager and then back to the groom case. So this is it, he thought. The bag that contained death, something he had never seen live, except in the news on television. His mind flashed back to the day President Bush held a bag of crack cocaine during a televised address to the nation. In his speech, the president castigated the use of narcotics while urging the nation to adhere to the 'Just Say No' slogan coined by a former first lady. Raymond had hailed the President's endeavor in undertaking a monumental task to eradicate drug use, but now heroin was sitting right in front of him and he was about to swallow it to import to the United States. He felt he had fundamentally betrayed his own principles all to help fund his quest to go to George Washington medical school and to be with Laura.

For all he knew, he could have been patient enough until his legal import business yielded profit within a few months. Instead, at any moment from then, he would be sending deadly and illigal drugs down his intestine.

The thought induced enormous fear in Raymond whenever he heard footfalls coming from anywhere inside the big house. It might be Emeka, and that would mean the ever dreaded show time.

The world seemed to have converged on him as his heart thumped. He constantly told himself catastrophe loomed ahead and involuntarily uttered the word, "damn," which seemed to have confused the teenage boy. The youngster, hearing the American curse, stood up and left the room, carefully carrying with him the groom case. In a few minutes, he returned, accompanied by his big brother.

The boy sat down the same way as before he left, while Emeka carelessly took the replica he had given him, and sat on the bed.

"Are you ready?" Emeka said, not looking at either Raymond or the teenager.

They both answered simultaneously, "yes."

"Briefly," Emeka began in Ibo language, "there are only a few facts I think you ought to know before we proceed with swallowing of the market. Firstly, the stuff you are about to swallow was coated to perfection by well paid professionals whose duty it is to ensure proficiency in terms of safety. The equipment used is designed in Germany exclusively for this, and cost as much money as it would to set up a small industry. Of course, you should know that the 'market' itself is very expensive, and that explains further why we went the distance to be sure your life is protected, and the 'market' preserved."

Emeka cleared his throat and continued. "Secondly, the medical doctors who approved the safety are the best in their field, and would be quick to reject any suspected ball that had bust potentiality. As a matter of fact, most of our couriers usually do this in the doctor's presence, but he wasn't available when I telephoned his house. However, he did leave a prescription for your use. It's supposed to deter any forcible bowel movement during flight."

"Finally, as I had articulated the first day I met you, our boss doesn't condone dishonesty. He hates it more than anything else, and just as I told you that very day, will go to every length to punish any duping individual. By this, I mean one who would not deliver the market wholly to Clyde. I'm sure Goddy addressed this issue more specifically. That's it. Peace unto us all." He searched his jacket pocket and brought out a small plastic wrap containing two pills he said the medical doctor had given him for Raymond, a pink and green capsule, and a white tablet. He handed them to his teenage brother. "Only after performance," he instructed as he was leaving.

Raymond's memory instantly captured a vision of the ninth photograph. But the scare from that had deflated. He got it. Just don't try to swindle them of their drugs or money and he'd be okay. Dishonesty was something he just never practiced. It was not in his DNA to cheat anyone… good or bad. After all, he knew no one in a criminal enterprise and so even if he were to attempt a double-cross, he wouldn't know what next to do in terms of cashing in. He'd simply hand them their drugs, collect his money and skip town for good.

The young man nodded and took over operation.

Before the teenager began to produce the shells of walnut-sized black objects, he made a few remarks to Raymond.

"You know," he said, "there's nothing strange about this thing. They are as big and as shaped as the balls of fufu that you've been eating all your life, and if you bear in your mind that you're swallowing fufu, you'll have no real problem performing."

Somehow, Raymond was feeling the dread in him easing a little bit. He had anticipated a much more ceremonial atmosphere, but contrary to his expectation, even Emeka wouldn't be present. There was only a teenage boy and himself in an elegantly furnished bedroom. Ben wasn't present either, and there were no mean-looking faces to force him into doing anything. If he could take it in, he would, and resign his fate to luck, while bearing the drugs inside his intestine. If he ever made it to the Hotel Wentworth in Manhattan, he'd be in heaven, with Laura by his side. Ten thousand dollars was nothing to sneeze at. Why shouldn't he close his eyes and do what Dennis and Kenny, and others had done, and in twenty-four hours, he'd be sitting—pretty.

He watched with nervousness, despite his little encouraging thought, as the boy unzipped the brown groom case, and took out five small size balls. He put them inside the first bowl on the far left side.

"Take it from this bowl and wash it in the second bowl before dipping it in the soup," he said. "Take your time. Don't rush it."

Raymond dipped his hand inside the warm water and took out one of the five balls. It felt as stiff as a nutshell. He washed it from the second bowl, and then dipped it inside the slippery okra soup, supposedly to aid the balls in passing along the throat with ease. The boy noticed his shaky hands.

"Don't be afraid," he said. "A lot of people do it. You'll see how easy it actually is when you swallow the first five."

Here we go, Raymond thought. That was it, the highest risk imaginable. He retrieved the ball from the soup and immediately opened his mouth to reluctantly dump it in. With his tongue, he positioned the egg-shaped ball as quickly as possible so the posterior end would lead the sail through his throat. He swallowed. It was hard, but not as bad as he thought either. He felt confident he could do it. The shell looked safe. He didn't have to be worried about it busting inside his stomach.

He then swallowed another, and another, and another, seven, eight, nine, ten, and on and on. Each time he finished with a bunch of five, the boy dumped another five or so. Somewhere down the line, he lost count of how many he had swallowed, but he cared less because it was beginning to be more and more difficult for him to swallow.

He must have swallowed about twenty-five or so when it began to force him into a vomiting noise. The youngster, in a bid to have him take in as many as possible, kept up the pressure on him, each time telling him how disappointing it would be for him to quit so early and not even earn half the ten thousand dollars he was looking forward to.

He kept forcing them in, despite the vomiting threats, and soon the problem of swallowing escalated when he began to feel his throat tightening and hurting badly. He had been swallowing balls of fufu since his childhood all right, but quite frankly, he wouldn't have been able to swallow more than thirty balls in one meal, even if he was hungry to a point of starvation. The froward spirit of his that told him to be a man and face it like a challenging task enhanced more intake than he would have ordinarily swallowed.

The youngster, who kept producing the balls, kept on voicing dissatisfaction as Raymond vomited and re-swallowed again six balls in a row. When it got to the eighth, it was a no go—period. After four tries, he was still unsuccessful.

Emeka casually strolled in and again sat on the bed.

"How many has he taken so far?" he said wearily.

The youngster looked back and gestured with a hand signal. Emeka looked up, made a mental calculation, and nodded his head in what appeared to be an approval signal.

"Are you sure you can't take anymore? It's money," the youngster said.

"I'm positive," he said. His voice had cracked, and because of the severe soreness in his throat, was slightly angered by the youngster's question.

"Congratulations," he said and extended his right hand to shake Raymond's. "You've made it."

Raymond reluctantly shook his hand.

"Did I swallow enough to earn the ten thousand dollars?" he inquired.

The youngster first looked at his big brother, then turned and answered. "Yes."

The youngster handed him the pills, and with the water in a glass cup, Raymond swallowed them and washed his hands for good. He stood up, feeling like he was carrying his neck. It was excruciatingly sore even when he spoke or spat. He couldn't even swallow his saliva, or move his tongue as freely as usual. The experience was almost unimaginable for him. To say the least, it was horror at its height. He thought that if Dennis had undergone the same process and still had the guts to repeat, he must have had a super human being for a friend.

Now that phase one had been successfully taken care of, Raymond's fear switched to the danger of the balloons exploding in his stomach.

Emeka went out to fetch his car keys, while Raymond hurriedly gathered his clothes in the closet. Soon Emeka returned and handed him his passport and alien resident card, with a confirmed one-way ticket to JFK airport.

"We must leave now because the flight departs in about forty minutes," Emeka said, glancing at his wrist watch.

Both men hurried to Emeka's Toyota Pathfinder, and drove off to the airport.

En route, Emeka gave him his last instructions on what to do to avoid appearing suspicious at Kennedy airport, and advised him to be strong and simply follow the priest's instructions on placing the sacred medal on his forehead before the aircraft touched down, and before approaching the Customs checking area.

Emeka also instructed Raymond to go directly to Clyde, who would ultimately inform him of how many balloons he had swallowed, and who also would pay him the ten thousand dollars cash instantly.

"Do you have money for your local transportation from Kennedy airport?" Emeka asked.

"I only have about two hundred and seventy-something," Raymond said.

Emeka reached into his side pant pocket and produced a hundred dollar bill, and handed it to him.

"Here, take this just in case."

Raymond was delighted at Emeka's gesture. He'd need it to help his expenses in New York City, where he'd be staying overnight before flying to Washington with Laura. There was no need informing Emeka of his intended detour. He'd telephone Clyde to let him know after he had arrived in his hotel in New York. He was sure Clyde would object to that, although it would be meaningless to me if Clyde did. Nothing could stop Raymond from abiding by his promise to fly to Washington with Laura.

The excitement from the prospect of taking Laura to Washington, DC never sank into him as he was aboard the airborne jumbo jet, at least not as the aircraft had taken off. Raymond tried unsuccessfully to retrace that excitement, much as he had felt when Laura and he reached the agreement over the telephone. He tried to visualize Laura's gorgeous shape, the splendor in her dress, and her charming, sexy smile. Then he imagined how great it would be to be romancing such a beautiful woman, especially after it was rumored that his common-law had left him to stay with another man.

The whole fantasy wasn't clicking at that moment, and in fact, it began to seem somewhat unrealistic to him. He searched his memory to be sure their earlier affair hadn't occurred in a mere dream. Each time he thought about that, he kept telling himself to wake up and not be ridiculous.

The phobia of being airborne was very much alive in Raymond, but another fear more dreadful was beginning to trickle into his conscience—the fear of his sexual encounter with Manuella. He started thinking about the priest's medal. He remembered quite well what the juju priest had said about Lagos being flooded with exotic women, and for him to stay away from them.

He carefully thought over everything, and came to conclude that he was only searching for a justification of his misdeed, which could potentially ruin his faith.

Just over two hours into the night flight, Raymond was feeling tired and stomach heavy, and the pain from his throat intensified, triggering severe headache, which dismally added to his overall discomfort. Some of the passengers aboard the half-filled Business Class section of the jet's seats were either asleep or positioned to doze off. So was the gentleman two seats away and separated from him by an empty middle seat. The gentleman had earlier told Raymond he was on his first visit to America, and had humbly requested his assistance to negotiate transportation once they arrived at JFK airport.

Raymond wanted so much to sleep off the flight, but his nervousness compounded with the fear of an air crash, a cocaine explosion inside his stomach, and the Customs agents at Kennedy airport. Even when he came close to feeling drowsy, a certain aircraft maneuvering which led to the seat belt fastening signal lighting up, brought him back to alertness. That problem persisted until nearly halfway into the movie when he finally found himself totally subdued by sleep.

But not for long, for he was jolted awake by a sudden violent jerk inside his stomach that felt like an explosion of the balloons. His heart thumped, and his body trembled as he managed to sit up. He nearly started to yell for the flight attendants, who were also watching the in-flight movie. He stopped to think first of how best to approach the situation. He was almost certain the die was cast. The scare from the reaction he was feeling inside his stomach heated up his mouth, and threw him into stumbling confusion. He grabbed the pillow that was supplied earlier by a stewardess and pressed it hard against his stiffened belly. But the jerk persisted at a faster pace.

Raymond began to look at the hopeless options at his disposal, fully aware that it was to be the very end of his life. To notify the obviously helpless flight crew would earn him less sympathy. They might even refuse to help, even if they could do something that might alleviate the dreadful situation. He was a criminal.

If he attempted to vomit or move his bowels, and in the process die with disgusting feces all over him, he'd be creating a scene no one would ever want to see. Besides, it would be too long before anyone realized the toilet had been occupied for a prolonged period.

The jerk intensified, and soon came a feverish feeling on his body. He really panicked. He had brought a shameful and bitter disappointment to his entire family. He had no will, and no relative knew where to find the deeds to his house.

Raymond decided to awake the man two seats away to confide in the stranger about his unfortunate situation. He began to review his past conversation with the stranger to see if he had been friendly enough to him. There had been no element of animosity, or anything that could be misconstrued. He felt it was very important and urgent to pass his message to his family via the crew captain.

Raymond managed to tap gently on the stranger's shoulder. The gentleman woke up and stared warily at him with exasperation. For some reason, Raymond became dumbfounded and simply grinned at the man, pointing foolishly toward the now folded movie screen as if he wanted to show the man a spectacular scene. But there was no movie and no screen either. The gentleman sat up, and with the freshness from the sleep in his eyes, stared at him.

"I'm sorry," Raymond said. "I wanted you to see something, but that's okay."

The gentleman said nothing. Raymond was sure the gentleman must have felt disturbed as he slowly rested back his head and turned to face the window. He had changed his mind in a split second to talk to the gentleman about his ordeal. He decided he just might as well go ahead and pass away right there and let the will of the Lord prevail.

Raymond was dying as a sinner, and there was no clergy around to administer a last sacrament. He started going through all the prayers he knew, and initiated some new ones of his own.

"Oh God of Abraham, Isaac and Jacob," Raymond began to pray, "please spare me from dying in this airplane." He kept trembling and praying, while the reaction inside his stomach continued. Fear engulfed his entire mind, body, and soul while he called on the Almighty in his mind, closing his palms together in a praying position. He made his confessions. He had been such a fornicator since he assumed the deadly task of stomach drug carriage, engaging in sex with Laura, and Manuella. He was a Catholic and born of a staunch Christian mother and father, both of who had preached all his life that it was morally unacceptable to fornicate. Furthermore, he had visited the devil's shrine, and had been bestowed with an evil medal associated with Satan—something his mother would choke on if told, and also which would undoubtedly add to the woe of his premature death.

The trauma continued for several hours, and astonishingly, Raymond wasn't in critical condition, as he considered himself to have been, and certainly not dead. He imagined that someone who was about to die couldn't be thinking as alertly as he was thinking. He pinched himself hard on his right cheek to check if he would feel the pain. It was reasonably felt although he was thinking he would have felt the pinch sharper under normal circumstances.

Raymond continued with his prayers for forgiveness, while he tried constantly to find a proper, and perhaps more dignifying, position to die in, looking silly trying out each position.

Lord Jesus Christ, Raymond thought, if I ever make it to Kennedy airport alive, I wouldn't mind surrendering to the authority. If I can pay for my mistake any other way than disgraceful death, I will never go contrary to the law for the rest of my life, and I'll never visit a shrine other than your holy places of worship, my God.

Raymond reached inside his breast pocket, took out the now

seemingly satanic medal and angrily flipped it away toward the mostly empty middle seat section of the cabin, and it was gone. He felt somewhat relieved he had done away with the devilish symbol.

Soon after, Raymond fell deep asleep, only regained sanity when the in-flight service woke him up for breakfast. The reaction inside his stomach was gone and the fever had evaporated, but still he wasn't hungry. He unsuccessfully tried to force some bite of bread, but his throat was too sore to swallow. What ran through his mind was that he would be surviving after all, and thanks to his prayer for forgiveness of the aberration, and of course his rejection and ultimate disposal of the satanic medal. He had overcome what looked like imminent death with his faith, and would continue to pray until the airplane touched the ground.

The captain had just made the announcement of an imminent landing at JFK, the seat belt signal on. The traumatizing expectation of death, and the relief Raymond had had from realizing he might live again, gave way to nervousness about what might await him at JFK airport. The sudden shift to uneasiness somehow angered him. He had asked God in his prayer to spare his life, and to punish him instead with a run in to the airport Custom agents. He was sure he was on the brink of death during the flight incident of confusion, and that his being alive was most probably as a result of his apology to the Almighty. He wondered if he was headed to prison. He knew Clyde had promised to come firmly to his defense with the fee for a credible attorney, but for a possession charge so indubitable, what kind of sympathetic jury would exonerate him?

Raymond visualized what the consequence would be if he were to go to jail in the United States, the shame it would bring to his family, his son's faith in him, his mother, his house, and his friends. Knowing the future would be decided in just a few minutes, he came close to pissing in his pants. He would have traded that dreadful moment for a weekend in hell.

The nervousness in Raymond grew worse as he felt the jerk from the release of the aircraft's landing gear. The airport was in sight on a clear, sunny morning in New York. He stiffened his resolve and decided to simply go to the luggage conveyor belt immediately upon arrival, pick up his heavily packed luggage, and walk confidently to present it to the Customs agents for search. There was a good chance they would allow him to pass through along with other passengers. After all, they weren't particularly targeting him.

All the encouragement Raymond tried to grasp in his conscience did absolutely nothing to help his nervous situation as the aircraft made its way to touchdown. The only positive thing coming his way was that the whole issue would be decided within the next five minutes. The captain had just announced the plane would be on the ground in one minute. But something unusual happened. The pilot, just about to glide the plane to the runway, aborted his first landing attempt, and had to climb up again. According to the captain, who immediately announced through the intercom, another aircraft was about to take off at the same time, prompting the air traffic controller to order their airplane to circle one more time. That activity nearly forced out a bowel movement from him.

Finally, the plane carrying Raymond Karr landed.

The gentleman, who sat next to him, had slept almost all through the flight. Now that everyone was coming out of the plane, and walking toward the immigration gate, he had become talkative and was asking questions that Raymond quite frankly didn't pay much attention to. All Raymond could remember was his request that he help him find ground transportation, and Raymond simply assured the gentleman to count on him—the only way to get him off his back so he could get busy with his heavily troubled mind.

Raymond, so sickened with a stomach butterfly, just couldn't handle the ravaging fear that loomed, and subconsciously he found himself again reciting Psalm Twenty-three – The Lord Is My Shepherd.

"I have faith in you, Almighty God," Raymond murmured. "You have rescued me from imminent death from the cocaine that I'm bearing in my stomach. Please give me a new lease of life, and take control of my future from here on. I know I have sinned through my acts, but deliver me from this one last trouble, and I'll sin no more."

He then repeated psalm twenty-three two more times and concluded with, "May Thy will be done oh Lord."

Chapter 15

CHECK MADE

Raymond was fifth in line at one of the immigration check booths, behind four women and a man. Behind him were about 7 other people. They were all waiting for documentation. When it was Raymond's turn, the attending officer, a slim sixtyish white man, golden blond and trimmed white mustache with a friendly attitude, smiled at him and requested to see his passport. He managed to smile back and searched through his small folder. He took out his resident alien card and handed it to the officer.

"Now we're talking," the officer said and smiled broadly, exposing only his lower set of white teeth that Raymond thought looked too perfect to be real. "There's the beef," he said as he turned to engage the computer. Moments later, he handed Raymond the resident alien card. "That's all she wrote, Mr. Karr, you may proceed. Welcome back, I've gotta tell ya that much" he said and then called out for the next in line. But with the state of mind Raymond was in, the officer's friendly gesture stopped far short of his full appreciation. Emotionally, he was sinking fast, nonetheless, played along, forcing himself to reciprocate with a smile before proceeding to the Customs check point. He knew it was where the game would be played.

The baggage conveyor at the international arrival section was located between the immigration gates and Customs check points, all in one large open area in the airport terminal. Once cleared by immigration, passengers who wished to claim their baggage would then proceed to the conveyor belt on the left side near the wall, while others would line up at any of several narrow gates for Customs clearance.

It was at the baggage conveyor that Raymond stood, along with several other passengers, waiting rather impatiently, to identify his decoy - the big brown suitcase he and Emeka had stuffed with variety of items. He stared nervously at the Customs officers, mostly women conducting mere pat down searches, and signing the slips that were handed to passengers by the flight crew shortly before arrival. The sight of a calm atmosphere at the check area, though ominous, calmed him a little bit.

He became impatient when his suitcase failed to make the first and second tier. If only his luggage would show up soon enough, in time enough to hurry over and simply be frisked by one of the women officers, he'd be walking away a free man. He briefly took his eyes off from the conveyor belt to watch as the first passengers, who had received their luggage, were headed toward the taxicab exit.

But what he didn't realize was that the real tough guys were on their way and were a little behind schedule. To contain nerve wreck, he began to pace left and right, impatiently hoping his luggage would be the next to roll out.

Several bags slowly rolled out in a single file, and immediately were claimed by their owners. Still there was no sign of his big brown suitcase. He sensed a smothering disaster well underway for him. His initial instinct was that he may have already been marked for doom and that to track him, agents wanted to resort to a delay tactics with his luggage. Despite the horrifying prospect, he still remotely harbored some hope that his luggage would eventually arrive, although the uncertainty still loomed in his mind. Cold sweat ran down his forehead.

He waited and waited and waited. There was still no big brown suitcase in sight, and the conveyor belt, which had been crowded with baggage, now was scantly sending out one bag every ten seconds, and then twenty seconds, and thirty, and fifty, a sign that nearly all the luggage from his flight had been discharged. This notion simply escalated the fear in him to terror. His mind raced with sheer panic. There was no doubt in him the scenario spelled trouble any way he looked at it.

The worse of spellbound chaos began to manifest. He looked around to see if anyone was watching him, and sure enough there was. The Customs officers, who had emerged mysteriously, kept looking suspiciously at him, and he noticed a group of white men in civilian clothes turning their faces away from him when he looked their way. There was still a short line of passengers yet to be attended to, and on the other side of the small gates, were many casually dressed men of different nationalities, who busied themselves pacing authoritatively up and down the area. From his own initial perspective, they were cab drivers soliciting fares. His vehement wish, as he stood still waiting and hoping for his luggage, was that if only he could make it to where the men were standing, he would be a free man. Strangely enough, those men too were looking at him practically the same way. He approached the conveyor belt and visually inspected other bags nearly identical to his to see if somehow he had been confused with the actual color or size.

Nearly all the luggage in that category were being claimed at once by their owners, erasing any doubt he was mistaking his own suitcase for someone else's. Another minute went by with no sign of his suitcase, and to end any hopes, the conveyor belt stopped rolling. His blood raced in panic and stars clouded his vision. This stinks to high hell, he thought, and it doesn't have to take a Nostradamus to predict the impending doom either. Once again, he tried three times to recite psalm twenty-three in his mind, but each time couldn't go beyond the phrase, *The Lord Is My Shepherd*. A white American, formally dressed in a black suit and blue-striped tie, was making his way toward him. He saw the man approach and decided to end his prayer with a simple sign of cross. Even that became difficult as his judgment was impaired because while trying to hurry it up, he was so nerve wrecked that in place of "In the name of the Father, and of the Son, and of the Holy Ghost," he said "In the name of the Holy Ghost." When it dawned on him that he couldn't make any sense under enormous pressure and panic, he decided to abandon any further attempt to pray.

He stood like a helpless hostage contemplating what his captors' next move on him could be. One million possibilities must have run through his mind. He even contemplated for a moment that Emeka may have snuck in dope in his suitcase, anticipating him to breeze through Customs. Even worse, he thought it might have all been an elaborate set up by the Drug Enforcement Agency.

His tensed mind eased slightly when he saw that the formally dressed white American was only an airport official aiming to clear the few unclaimed luggage off the conveyor belt. He pulled himself together and approached the official, who bent over to retrieve an unclaimed green duffel bag.

"Are there any more unclaimed luggage left behind? He said, his voice cracked and shaky.

"No sir," the man said dryly without looking at him.

"Well, can you tell me where to file a missing luggage report?"

"Down the hallway to the right."

He picked up his suit-jacket and went to stand in the now shortened line, where he was immediately approached by a forty-five year old man of Spanish descent. He was wearing a pair of blue jeans and an untucked blue checkered shirt.

"Sir, come with me," he said in a slight Spanish accent, and began to walk slowly toward the first exit booth.

Raymond followed him and immediately noticed that the idling men he thought were taxicab drivers soliciting fares, were actually the nightmarish obstacle he had been dreading since accepting the courier deal—the U.S. Customs. He noticed their conspicuous barges, which some of them wore around their necks and others on their front waistbands. If they had a gun, they were well hidden since Raymond saw none.

"Alex Jacobo, U.S. Customs special agent," the man said and lifted his barge for Raymond to see.

Raymond was thrown into confusion and completely disoriented.

"Put your bag down on that corner," he said authoritatively, pointing to the floor base of the Customs search table.

Raymond, in total panic, dropped his heavily packed suit-jacket as the agent directed. He now began to sweat profusely. With his trembling hands inside his pockets, he approached the agent face to face, trying unsuccessfully to conceal cowardice in its most festive exhibition.

At about five feet seven, pale-faced, and a flamboyant attitude, the agent looked up directly at Raymond and asked him a question that instantly jolted him. "What do you have in here?" His voice was so low and close to whisper that only Raymond could hear him.

It was a deer-in-the-headlight moment for timid Raymond. He somehow managed to snap out of it. "What do you mean, sir?" he said in a bid to escape total dumbfoundedness. Somehow, it dawned on him that he needn't submit himself entirely to doom. He had to put up some kind of resistance. If there was to be any luck, hanging on would provide the opportunity for that to happen, and who knows, he just might pull this one off.

"How many balloons did you swallow?" the agent said, this time a little louder.

The mentioning of balloon further threw Raymond into confusion. How the hell did this guy know what he had inside his stomach? The enormous fear that had him in critical check wouldn't yield to any reasonable thought from him. *My God, this could be D-day*, he thought. He had to say something because silence would otherwise signal check made.

"You mean fufu inside my stomach?" he managed to say.

Not quite understanding what Raymond had just said, the agent studied Raymond's face. From the opening between two buttons, he slipped his fingers inside to the left side of Raymond's chest to feel his heavily thumping heart.

"Be honest with me, how many balloons of heroin did you swallow inside your stomach?" the agent said again.

"I didn't swallow heroin."

The Customs agent repeated the heartbeat examination before saying, "Bullshit. I'm taking you along for an x-ray. Stand right here and I'll be right with you."

Raymond turned cold then hot as sweat kept stringing down his forehead. He nervously watched the agent walk quietly away to confer with another of his colleagues, a grey-haired white man wearing a dark brown suit, who nodded approvingly as he was being briefed. Raymond looked around to find that the man he had sat next to during the flight was also being interrogated by another agent, and there were several other passengers, all men, who were gathered for the same x-ray examination.

Agent Jacobo, who was the first to approach Raymond, came back to him, holding a sheet of paper and a black pen. He placed the paper on the baggage search counter, next to where Raymond's suit-jacket was placed.

"Come here sir," he said. "This form is for you to sign a consent to an x-ray examination. Sign where the check mark is. You may consider reading it first before you sign."

It read in plain English and in three lines that the passenger would consent to an x-ray by U.S. Customs agents. That was all.

"Sir, if I must be x-rayed, why do I have to sign for it?" Raymond said, almost aimlessly.

"'Cause that's the procedure."

"I don't think I want to do this. I'm submitting to the x-ray because you're forcing me to, but for me to sanction that is out of the question."

The agent simply collected the paper and went back to the gentleman he had talked to earlier when he left Raymond by himself. In his mind, he couldn't stop cursing himself. He seemed to be losing total control. When the agent left with the form, he was at a loss as to what card to play next. He couldn't even comprehend that all his demons were alighting on him. In the emotional commotion, his predicament seemed like he had planned it that way, as if he had been preparing for a long time to meet his doomsday. It was total chaos.

The agent came back to Raymond, this time along with another man dressed in brown pants and a dark-blue jacket. He immediately introduced himself to Raymond.

"Mr. Karr," the gentleman called out. As Raymond turned to face him, he continued. "Bob Deaver here, U.S. Customs Narcotic specialist. I'm in charge of the Kennedy airport operations."

Looking straight in Raymond's eyes, the man began to advise Raymond on the procedure. "There are two ways you will have to sign this Consent Form," he said. "Whichever way you choose, you'll end up signing the consent form. The best way is to sign it right now, and we take the x-ray. If you're negative, you'll be on your way home within minutes. The other way is to detain you for as long as it takes to get you sign it."

"Even for days?" Raymond asked.

"Days, weeks, even months or years," he said. "So my advice to you, sir, is to simply cooperate and we'll be as fast as we possibly can to get you outta here."

Raymond was dumbfounded for a moment as the men waited for his response. Meanwhile, other agents had begun to surround him, and one of them, also a thirty-something male, approached him and checked his heartbeat.. He spoke excitedly in French to one of his colleagues, who enthusiastically looked on.

"I don't know why I'm being forced to signing this form. Have the rest of these guys signed yet?" Raymond said, looking at a group of about six Nigerian passengers gathered for the same purpose.

"You're the only one left, sir," Mr. Deaver said, took off his eye glasses, rubbed the lenses against his shirt and put it back on.

Raymond looked around and found he was the center of attention. He knew then he had no choice other than cooperate. "Okay. Let's do it," he said and knew it was really check made against him.

All the passengers from the Nigerian Airways flight were led to a corner inside the same Custom area, including the man who sat next to Raymond during the flight. One of the agents emerged with a bunch of handcuffs, and in ten minutes everyone was cuffed. Another of the agents pulled out a card from his breast pocket and read them their Miranda rights.

The first question came from an elderly man demanding why they were being treated like criminals when nothing had been found yet. Other passengers followed with verbal protests, and one of them put another question forward to an agent standing next to him.

"I demand an explanation," he said, "for allowing all white passengers who flew on other airlines to pass, free of harassment, through Customs, while having Nigerians, regardless of age, go through the belittling hassle."

"Because Nigeria is a drug country," the agent replied arrogantly.

Raymond remained silent but thoughtful while they were all driven, two in the back of each official sedan, across the tarmac to a trailer hospital unit installed by the United States Customs for drug screening. Raymond regretted changing his flight arrangements. He thought he could have still seen Laura and stayed with her for as long as he wanted to, had he taken the trouble to fly Lufthansa to Virginia, discharge the devil inside his stomach, and flown back to New York to pick her up. He had been struck by his impatience. With cocaine inside him, and an x-ray in a few minutes, he was virtually a dead man. Agent Jacobo had asked Raymond if he had heroin in his stomach at the customs search area. Raymond wondered if the agent was referring to something else, or if he simply used the word "heroin" instead of cocaine. Raymond wondered why they used that word, heroin. An agent had charged Nigeria to be a drug country, and Raymond thought that to be a ludicrous statement, for in his narrow minded view, Nigerians didn't possess the scientific capability to manufacture such complex chemicals. If the agents were looking for heroin, and he had cocaine, then there may be a chance he'd be a free man because the x-ray might show negative for the presence of heroine.

Raymond was grasping at straws with this thinking.

At the makeshift hospital, they were ordered to sit on a long waiting-bench inside the large trailer, while the medics readied the x-ray machines. Again, the same man who sat next to Raymond during the flight was sitting next to him, and was to be the first to be x-rayed, their hands still handcuffed behind their backs.

"You're clean, right?" he said to Raymond in broken English.

"I don't know, man, I'll have to wait and see," Raymond said with extreme uneasiness.

All the rest of the passengers were clean. When it was Raymond's turn to face the camera, all five of the customs officers couldn't wait to see his x-ray result, and were gathered around the technician in a suspenseful mood. In the forefront was Agent Jacobo, who had followed the technician into the adjacent room to have a firsthand view. He had come out to place the negative against a brightly lit x-ray reader, and had made a joke out of it.

"You see all these objects around this area," he said, circling his pointer finger around the stomach area. "They're called ballooooons," he said wise cracking.

The other officers laughed. One of them produced a shackle and Raymond was shackled aside until the rest of the passengers were exonerated and driven back to the airport main terminal, free of handcuffs. The two officers—Alex Jacobo himself and one other white American male in his forties—stayed behind to guard Raymond closely, while their boss, Mr. Deaver, handled the paperwork. The entire hospital staff started to get busy and Raymond watched, in dismay, other custom officials come in and out to the small bench he was shackled against, to witness a big criminal cornered into the caging hands of the law.

The scenario was to Raymond a reminiscence of his early teens when thieves were caught and brought to a police station nearby his childhood residence. They used to watch, crossed arm, and with the wildest imagination, the faces, clothes and everything associated with those extraordinarily strange human beings.

Childishly, somehow Raymond had believed that thieves, who usually operated in the shadows of the night, were not born of human being. Rumors of thieves being caught miles away used to spread like wild fire, and Raymond had made numerous unsuccessful attempts to catch a glimpse of someone labeled a thief. Raymond's first successful sight on an alleged thief had come at the age of fifteen, after the Nigerian civil war, when soldiers paraded the suspect across to be handed over to the police department. It was an intriguing sight to see, and Raymond couldn't stop thinking or telling stories about it—how the thief was dressed, how he had screamed during an intense flogging. Children of Raymond's age group and adults listened with full enthusiasm no matter how many times he repeated the story. They spread the story along, sometimes exaggerating a little bit. Now he himself was the one in a spotlight of infamy.

Agent Jacobo lectured Raymond, in the same mocking attitude, of the difference between what Raymond had in his stomach, which was heroin, and what Raymond thought he had, which was cocaine. To Raymond's greatest fright, he bitterly broke down when the agent disclosed the magnitude of his offense, and the imminent and severe jail time that awaited him, not if but when he is convicted.

Angry at Clyde's deceit and crying like a stranded child, Raymond made his first request to the agents surrounding him. "Is there any chance you guys can covertly follow me to Washington where someone I only know by his first name would come to pick up the objects I have inside my stomach, and that would prove me innocent of the full knowledge of the drug?" Raymond proffered.

But it only led to more ridicule.

"Tell that to the jury," Agent Jacobo said, chuckling.

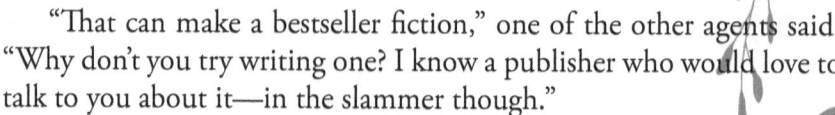

"That can make a bestseller fiction," one of the other agents said. "Why don't you try writing one? I know a publisher who would love to talk to you about it—in the slammer though."

Everyone laughed hard.

"I have no knowledge of the drug at all and that's the truth," Raymond said, trying unsuccessfully to convince them, as well as avoid incriminating himself any further.

In attempting to shape his possible line of defense, Raymond told them briefly what happened when a man named Emeka, in Nigeria, took him to a juju priest. But Raymond twisted his story a little bit.

"Sirs, off the record, it was the juju priest who convinced me the balloons were only to improve my manhood, and after swallowing them, I was told to reproduce it to Clyde, who is his associate, and who is supposed to be in charge of his U.S. operations. Clyde is supposed to guide me from there as part of the ritual," Raymond said. "If I had known what I swallowed was drugs, I would have flown Lufthansa airline through a less suspecting Dulles airport entry."

Raymond was hoping they would be fascinated enough by his story and heed to his request to go to Washington to see Clyde come up to receive the drugs, but to no avail.

"Boy, you sure can write a fiction," Jacobo said giggled.

Raymond paused to think. He remembered there could be an attorney who could push further for his plea.

"Is there any chance I could speak with an attorney?" Raymond said.

"What do you need attorney for?" one of the men said. "You're gonna plead guilty, and your African ass will be put away and forgotten about."

His statement led Raymond to another round of bitter weeping, one that came intermittently all through the day.

It was around noon, and time to account for Raymond's personal effects. Agent Jacobo was assigned the task. Sitting on a chair, opposite an office desk, he went piece by piece to account for everything he owned inside his suit-jacket, from his ring to his clothes and money. He handed Agent Jacobo a total of three hundred and seventy-seven dollars, informing the agent that Emeka had given him the one hundred dollar bill to subsidize his local transportation, and that the rest was his own money. He also surrendered to Agent Jacobo the Nigerian currency of nearly a hundred Naira. The agent wrote Raymond a receipt for the amount and all his belongings, before finally sending him further inside the trailer where about six-hospital style beds were installed. Raymond was the lone patient in the entire unit.

He spent all Wednesday afternoon and evening shackled arms and legs against the metal bed, and continued until Thursday evening. In his mind, it was the most miserable time of his life. Agent Jacobo and the rest of the officers had left Wednesday afternoon, after handing Raymond over to customs police. Three were assigned in each shift, and one uniformed U.S. Army reservist accompanied them, also replaced at the end of each eight hours shift. The guards observed all of his twelve bowel movements that shot out of his anus like an automatic weapon. That was after being forced to drink a nastily tasting liquid he couldn't identify, which triggered a stomach purge.

Meanwhile, all his miserable thoughts focused on the consequences of his life behind bars, and never for a second did he relent in cursing himself for ever accepting an unlawful task he knew so little about. Most excruciating of his thoughs was his son and stepdaughter, whom he had so much wanted to raise to perfection. His son was only nine months old, and his daughter eight years old with bright academic promise. They'd have to be separated, probably for life. That thought always led Raymond to weep uncontrollably like a child. He could read the irritation from his open and loud weeping in the faces of the armed guards.

Raymond's thoughts went to his mother. He didn't know how she could handle the message of her first son being arrested on a drug charge, and facing a lengthy prison stay. She would most probably be devastated more by Raymond's activity than his being incarcerated. She had told Raymond, when he was growing up, she would disown anyone in the family who committed any crime. His brothers and sisters had worked hard to maintain a status of excellence in their family tradition, and they had had no problems this big. Becoming the first outcast would propagate a flurry of condemnations from the family.

Raymond had just assumed a mortgage on his four bedroom home, and it was certain to be foreclosed, his down payment and improvement expenses totaling almost fifty thousand dollars, gone down the drain. The house had been the pride and fruit of his ten years of labor. Losing it all in such a mischief would put a lasting dent in his heart. His life had boiled down to futility.

He also stood to lose the import business he had worked so hard to create, and there wouldn't be a product imported that would bear his company's name on it, something he had been fantasizing about over the past month.

Raymond also thought about Laura, whom he was supposed to call earlier that Wednesday from his hotel room. She must have been wondering why he hadn't shown up, and could be glued to a seat watching the telephone, guessing impatiently, and waiting for his call. All his expectations about an idyllic romantic fling in Washington were shattered. He was in a situation so irreversibly chaotic that even to call up Laura to cancel their arrangement would be virtually impossible. The agents had been so strict that even when he told them his wife and children were still waiting at National airport for his arrival, and that he would want to call his brother to have him inform them of his ordeal, they refused.

"Where do you think you are, Holiday Inn?" one agent said sarcastically.

"I really feel sorry for you," another of the agents said with a smirk..

One of the most excruciating pains, both mentally and physically, was to be handcuffed and leg shackled at the same time against a bed for nearly two days. Right after the x-ray on Wednesday morning, Raymond was attached to his bed, only released for his bowel movements. Raymond realized that the world could turn to such an ugly place with one stupid mistake, and he saw himself living the monstrous side of it. The world turned upside down, and to say he was in agony was an understatement.

Chapter 16

MUG SHOT

Nicholas DiGiovanni, an Italian American, was the DEA special agent assigned to handle the government's case against Raymond Karr. Forty-two, five feet eight, medium-built with a military-style haircut, he maintained the persona which, even in a civilian attire, stood out as a law enforcer. He was wearing a pair of worn out jeans, a light blue Polo shirt, and a new pair of beige Nike sneakers. A tiny silver earring glittered in his right ear.

"We're gonna do your fingerprint, dude," he said in a slightly cracked but macho voice.

Mr. DiGiovanni stood next to Raymond, running his fingers through an ink pad, then carefully pressing them hard on a recording card. Finger by finger, he nodded in approval to every successful imprint.

Raymond was extremely exhausted from days of being shackled on top of the hospital bed, where he cried his eyes out most of the time. He had managed only one meal of scrambled eggs, which he reluctantly accepted to eat out of the two meals offered him from Wednesday morning until Thursday evening. He felt very weak and nauseated, following the past tumultuous forty-eight hours. He had been driven across the airfield to the main terminal and offices of the narcotics division of the DEA. Waiting to receive him at the door was agent DiGiovanni himself, who led him immediately to a holding cell.

After administering series of Raymond's fingerprints, it was time to take his mugshot photographs, yet another incident he had never envisaged would happen to him. He had always seen the FBI's photos of their most wanted criminals posted on the bulletin boards and Post Office walls, and had always wondered why anyone would harm himself in such a shameful manner. Manuel Noriega, the former Panama head of state's widely publicized prison mugshot had been one of the most shocking to Raymond, and the astonishment made him thank God he was stern in being crime free all his life.

"How would you want your picture to appear in your country's newspapers?" DiGiovanni said as he handed Raymond a flat metal sign inscribed with an eight-digit prisoner identification number, then walked back to ready the camera.

Raymond, in a nervous reaction to what he just heard the agent say, involuntarily discharged a loud gas. The agent, distant away, paused to think of the fart sound that came from the direction of his prisoner. Unsure he heard right, he resumed dusting off the camera lenses, knowing that a smell will confirm his suspicion, and hoping he was wrong. Raymond knew that if his mugshot would be publicized, with his name on it, in a national newspaper, it would be the equivalent of a death sentence. Tears began to well his eyes. Agent DiGiovanni, noticing, was stoic still unhappy about his suspicion that his prisoner may have farted on him.

Luckily for Raymond, it was an odorless fart. He had worriedly sniffed the air around him and was relieved there were no foul smell. He didn't want to further infuriate his jailers. Who knew how they might react to an offensive discharge from a prisoner at their mercy, accidental or not? Earlier, during one of the times he had been left alone at the makeshift hospital, he had let one go in a test-fart and the damn thing smelled so badly it nearly pissed him off. But that was before he was allowed all the bathroom breaks for the number twos that yielded the balloons of heroin.

After wiping off his tears, it was time to face another reality. The mugshot. Raymond said a silent prayer, and told himself he would try to face the camera with such a facially innocent composure, so when people would looked at his picture, they wouldn't find the slightest trace of a criminal. Cameras don't lie, he thought. He knew he'd violated the law, but he was far from being a criminal, and he intended to, at the very least, portray that impression on the photographs.

The agent took six sets of photographs of Raymond's face, each set consisting of one front and two sides, and he did everything he could to look innocent. Smiling, avoiding wrinkles on his forehead and all that stuff – everything Raymond could think of. After DiGiovanni was done, he handed him one of the three sets of the mugshot.

"Here," DiGiovanni said. "What you'd look like in the newspaper headlines of your country."

Again, unfortunately, Raymond wasn't successful in concealing the face of a criminal. He sat still examining them and all of a sudden chuckled, blowing out air from his closed lips in a failed bid to conceal the silly laugh that forced out. In the mugshot, he looked every bit like a maniacal villain.

After the session, DiGiovanni led him to his office desk and motioned him to sit on the guest chair by the side, while he gathered a notebook and an ink pen.

"Okay," DiGiovanni said after he had everything set to write. "Now tell me all about it, who you really are, who you work for, who gave you the heroin, and everybody involved in it."

Raymond wondered why he should talk about his case without the presence of a lawyer who, at least, would be sure to protect his statements from gratuitous exploitation. He had read in the past about coerced testimony and misinterpreted statements that had often plagued defendants in court proceedings, and he was determined not to commit himself as of then. Already consumed by a horrifying beast of criminal indictment, his instinct warned him to be wary of tripping off as he navigated the legal minefields. He felt if only they would follow him to Washington, DC and see for themselves that he indeed was not really acutely aware the evidence was heroin and he didn't own it, everything would look good for him. Other than that, he would have to hold on to the facts until he saw a lawyer who then could expedite his proffer that they had already declined. Meanwhile he chose to stay his initial untruthful story about the balloons being given to him by the priest, and DiGiovanni took notes of everything. When Raymond concluded, DiGiovanni gave him a piece of advice.

"Just play it cool, man, and plead guilty in court."

Mr. DiGiovanni set the pen aside and paired his fingers. "That's it," After a brief pause, he began filing the yellow sheet he had written on. "Now let's re-account for your money."

DiGiovanni took out a white envelop and opened it. Bill by bill, he separated the currencies and began to count out loud, placing the counted bills directly in front of him, beginning with the fifty dollar bill. Raymond noticed the hundred dollar bill was missing but lacked interest in whatever the agent was doing.

Concluding his count, instead of the three hundred and seventy-seven dollars of which the receipt was initially issued to him, DiGiovanni gave Raymond a receipt for two hundred and seventy-seven dollars. Raymond stared at the agent after studying the receipt, and could only utter a few words.

"It should've been three hundred and seventy-seven, but that's okay."

"Why did you say that?" DiGiovanni said.

"Well, a hundred dollar bill is missing," Raymond said. To prove it further, Raymond explained the circumstance surrounding the bill, just as he had explained it to agent Jacobo, and how it was given to him by Emeka for his local transportation. He also produced and showed DiGiovanni the receipt that agent Jacobo had given him for the correct amount, all at DiGiovanni's request. Raymond asked DiGiovanni if there could have been a policy that required bills of such amount to be kept separate.

"There shouldn't be, not unless if it's more than two thousand dollars, which would then be forfeited entirely," DiGiovanni said, looking somewhat embarrassed as he combed his short hair with his five finger. "I don't know, man. That's the only money I see. I don't know what to tell you." He began to put back the bills inside the white envelope.

Raymond recalled there was a time, during the initial hours when he was officially arrested at the hospital, when Agent Jacobo and some of his colleagues were discussing an apparent impending furlough program facing the agency. From their discussion, the furlough program heavily affected their department. Raymond had heard one of the agents make a comment, stating they worked hard and weren't appreciated, and that they're not deemed important. One of the agents, particularly angered by the prospect, lashed the government, using words as "fucking" and "assholes" in addressing the politicians in Washington.

It dawned on Raymond he was headed to prison and wouldn't be needing the money, so he told Nick DiGiovanni to donate the rest of the money to any charity organization, preferably the American Cancer Society, which he had once been an active volunteer.

"Oh no," DiGiovanni said. "We'll credit it to your prison commissary account for your use in purchasing items like deodorants, soap powders, cigarettes, and all that kind of stuff."

Raymond remained silent while DiGiovanni concluded his paperwork, and then dragged Raymond's suit-jacket from under his desk.

"Let's go," DiGiovanni said, producing a set of handcuffs from his belt.

The agent handcuffed Raymond and led him to another office, two doors from his, where a middle aged Pakistani bespectacled with a pair of thick lenses, sat writing on a document. Both DiGiovanni and Raymond stood quietly for a few minutes, apparently waiting for the Pakistani to conclude with whatever he was writing. When he was done, he put down his pen, then folded the file and set it aside on his desk, before removing his glasses to rub his eyes, while turning to Agent DiGiovanni.

"Are you ready?" he said.

"All set," DiGiovanni said.

The agent held Raymond by his arm and pulled him forward to sit on the lone vacant chair in the narrow office, and then handed the Pakistani a file he had brought along from his office.

As soon as Agent DiGiovanni handed over the file, the Pakistani stared at Raymond and joked. "Are you ready to go home?" he asked in a thick Indian accent.

"I may not have the right answer to that question again for the rest of my life," Raymond said flatly.

"Well," he countered. "Let's hope you will."

Raymond was becoming too embittered and irritable from the teasing, but there was clearly nothing he could do to stop it. He knew the slim chance he may have had in winning sympathy or empathy from anyone definitely wouldn't come from showing any signs of arrogance. So he would have to stay humble.

Yet again, tears began to roll down Raymond's cheeks. Agent

DiGiovanni pulled a chair from the next office and sat down close to the entrance while the Pakistani wrote on the file DiGiovanni handed him.

Raymond kept thinking. He still intended to try to convince them he didn't know the balloons in his stomach were heroin, and technically, that was the case, since he had thought all along it was cocaine which, according to custom agent Jacobo, would have been a much less serious offense.

Soon after the question-and-answer session about Raymond's identity, which lasted over forty minutes, his hands were free from the cuffs only so he could sign the papers, and he was immediately handcuffed again. After a minute or so, he was led by Agent DiGiovanni back to his office, where another agent was waiting. Raymond felt like a manhandled war prisoner, completely worn out from being chained to the bed for nearly two days, and managing only two light meals between. It was almost nothing, considering the loss of appetite he had from the day he left his hotel to Emeka's house, and also the fact that he had stooled more than ten times overnight during the process of ejecting the balloons in his stomach. He also was feeling the impact of little sleep and the discomfort from wearing the same cloths without a shower.

The waiting agent, a slim built young, white American male in his late twenties, produced his own set of handcuffs while Agent DiGiovanni uncuffed Raymond, and the young agent took over Raymond Karr's custody.

"Good luck, Raymond," Agent DiGiovanni said as the young agent marched him toward the exit door.

Raymond ignored DiGiovanni, although he detected a note in DiGiovanni's voice and demeanor that struck him that the man wasn't trying to be sarcastic on that one. He meant what he said, and boy did Raymond feel he needed a lot of luck.

The new custodian cared less about the tightly fitted handcuffs on the prisoner's wrist, despite Raymond's emotional plea for the custodian to loosen and ease the excruciating pain they were inflicting.

"Don't worry," he said. "It ain't gonna be a long ride, only a few minutes."

The slow traffic made it a long ride, almost half hour drive to the Metropolitan Correctional Center in lower Manhattan. Soon after the custodian drove off, he sternly warned his prisoner as Raymond sat in front of the custodian's late model Ford Mustang, hands chained behind him, that any attempt to escape would cost Raymond as much as Raymond's life. Raymond noticed the custodian's uneasiness, and it was enough to strictly heed, realizing that as nervous as the custodian appeared to have been, he could pull his pistol and shoot at Raymond if he provide him with a probable cause. The custodian looked too young and too eager to live, and appeared to be insecure around criminals.

There came an incident Raymond felt was a close call later. He had tried to scratch the nagging itch on his right thigh against the inside door handle of the car, and the custodian became nervously suspicious of Raymond's movement and responded immediately.

"What do you think you're doing?" he snarled. He started to pull the car over to the shoulder lane.

Raymond quickly told the custodian he was merely trying to scratch an itch, but it didn't convince him, and he nervously put his right hand on his gun holster while he steered with his left hand.

"Look, man," the custodian said, shifting his face repeatedly between Raymond and the road ahead. "You're not supposed to move at all. I'm warning you to stay cool until we get to MCC. We should be there in a few minutes. Is that understood?"

"Sir, I'm not trying to escape. I don't know how I can do that with my hands tightly handcuffed behind my back. Besides, I have never been in such a predicament before, so I wouldn't know how to escape even if I'd wanted to." He tried to sound as convincing as possible.

Still not satisfied, the custodian pulled over and re-inspected the cuffs, and then drove off again without adjusting the tight grip. Only to ascertain it was still intact.

The Metropolitan Correctional Center was a high-rise maximum security prison located at one hundred block of Park Row Drive in lower Manhattan, and adjacent to the New York City Police Department Headquarters, popularly known as One Police Plaza. The jail also served as inmate housing for New York jurisdiction, a holdover for prisoners still undergoing litigation in the federal courts.

The custodian parked his car in front of the prison's iron gated entrance. He hurriedly stepped out and came around to open the passenger door. Gently, he helped Raymond out, holding Raymond's arm, and shut the door immediately, then led Raymond to the pedestrian prisoner entrance by the side of the large and heavily fortified garage door.

With the telephone hanging on the wall, the custodian called in and identified himself, and moments later there came a loud buzzer that signaled the iron door had been unlocked. The custodian led Raymond as they went inside a narrow hallway with multiple surveillance cameras mounted above every corner. There was a small window at the right corner of the hallway where the custodian surrendered his pistol. The custodian came back to resume the lead to the elevator. On the third floor, they were at offices for inmate Receiving and Discharge, or "R & D."

Raymond was deeply bitter as the custodian was officially handing him over to the jail authority. Every entrance had highly secured steel door. He heard the voices of uniformed correctional officers coming from walkie-talkie radios. He was embracing the height of misery, knowing he'd have to spend years enduring such an awful environment.

Soon after the handover, Raymond was led into a cell, where he sat alone on a metal bench awaiting his fate. He folded his arms to shield off the cold air that was viciously blowing out from the vent. He studied the high ceiling and the dirty walls that surrounded him, and sat upright to avoid contact with the walls. There were pools of saliva on the floor, left by previous prisoners.

Hungry, tired, and extremely depressed, he was left alone in the bullpen for two hours before a guard opened the steel door to escort him to an office, where he was subjected to a new round of fingerprinting and identification photos, which lasted over an hour. He then gave up personal information, which also took a painfully long time. He thought he was going to starve to death. He couldn't wait to eat, and hopefully there would be a meal soon. However, he was too embarrassed and mentally exhausted to ask for a meal, and he was also under the impression that a prisoner had no right to be fed or comforted, and that every negative treatment he received was legitimate.

Then came the time for Raymond to change his clothes and put on his inmate uniform. A dark-brown jumpsuit gave him an image of a hardened criminal. He was observing the female correctional officer standing by an entrance door, looking visibly empathetic, but she quickly turned to face the other way when Raymond looked steadily at her. his first thought was how he would be perceived by Laura or Manuella in his new attire. His thoughts spread to other people as he was being led back to the bullpen—his family members, friends, and business associates. Once again he bowed his head, buried his face in his hands, and broke down bitterly, feeling the agony from becoming a symbol of utter disgrace.

The prison identification number he was assigned was the same number from the mug shots at the airport. Raymond was told by the officer, who processed him, to always memorize the number because he would be required to recite them from time to time. Just as he was escorted to the seventh floor cells, and supplied with a brown blanket, a white towel, and a set of white bed sheets, the unit's correction officer unlocked the big iron door, demanded that he recite his identification number. The officer held up a two-by-two inch card, which his head shot picture was attached to, and also his personal data. The officer listened as Raymond struggled to recite the 8-digit prison number.

The officer waved him inside the noisy arena where a zoo of other hold over inmates made the most out of their little world, and where he would first learn to cope with his life as criminal.

Raymond was assigned to the top bunk bed in a narrow cell, approximately six by six feet. There was a toilet and a sink in front of the bunk. Raymond's Spanish cell mate was asleep when he arrived, leaving him with no choice but to quietly spread his bed sheet on the bed with a thin mattress and climb up to think about his heavily clouded future.

The correctional officer, who had left after showing Raymond his cell, returned shortly to hand him a tiny tablet of soap and a tooth brush and toothpaste, and showed him the direction to the bathroom— information Raymond assumed was a hint - he hadn't showered in three days.

Misery kept reaching new height for Raymond Karr. All the misery of life compounded in Raymond as he struggled to climb on top of his bunk bed—the increasing agony of confinement, the thought of his family and friends, how he will handle breaking the news to his brother, and ultimately to his mother, the knee sagging hunger that was almost hindering his ability to speak or breathe, the cold air that blew out of the vent. Every damn subject was bad news.

From the tinted thick glass window, the lights of New York City shined brightly while Raymond fixed his eyes on the star light on top of the Empire State building, thinking of his ruined world. So this is it, he thought. This is where his life will be spent looking at freedom, just out of reach. He looked at cars moving up and down the streets, and childishly touched the thick glass window to feel the object that separated him from the free world, and in his demoralized state of mind, came to a distinct conclusion that life was indeed worth living, and freedom was second to nothing.

Soon after, Raymond's thoughts of facing a doomed life gave way to the need for him to make himself at home, and that he badly needed a shower. He immediately jumped down from the bed and walked gingerly to the bathroom, picking up his towel from the metal locker that was provided to every inmate. That night was only the beginning of the most distressful years of Raymond Karr's life.

Chapter 17

NEW PROFILE

Raymond, now inmate Karr, woke up late the next morning, his first as an inmate, and also the Friday morning he should have been in a traffic courtroom in Maryland. Hungry and having missed the prison's 5:30 a.m. breakfast because of his worn out state of body and mind, he climbed down from his top bunk bed and staggered to the sink for a morning wash up. The night had been infinite and dreadful. When he was finally able to sleep, an unusual dream kept him guessing if it was indeed a reality that he was headed to prison. In the dream, he had found himself a free man in the company of acquaintances, whose freedom, unlike his, had not been eclipsed. He woke up to realize it was a mere dream, and the nightmare just began.

Tormented by the whole affair, Raymond walked dejectedly to the noisy common area, where a bunch of other inmates gathered to tell tales, perhaps of their ordeal, while others noisily cheered at a Spanish program that played on television. He sat on one side of the first of four steps leading to sunken common area and watched timidly, supporting his elbows with his knees to rest his chin with his hands. Those whom he had once wondered about their hellish lives would now become his neighbors and roommates. He also kept reliving the events of the past two days, wishing like hell he had chosen a different course and spewing vitriol at himself.

Once again, wonders never ceased to happen, even in such a predicament for Raymond. He fixed his stared at a face across the common area, and vaguely identified him as a neighbor in Maryland—a thirty-three year old Nigerian male, also wearing the prison's brown jumpsuit. He too had become a victim of a drug dealer's business mechanism.

Raymond stood up and strolled toward him. He appeared to have been inevitably re-calculating in his mind his woeful missteps as he stood dejectedly, arms folded, perhaps recreating the incidents that had led him to where he was sitting.

"Look at this guy," the man said, seemingly surprised and smiling while staring hard at Raymond.

"Charlie, what in the world are you doing here?" Raymond said as both men firmly shook hands.

"Let me guess why you're here… game of the masquerades, right?" Charlie said.

Raymond nodded in agreement and genuinely laughed hard. While they discussed their ordeal, another inmate, also a Nigerian, fifty-one, slim and disheveled, joined them at Charlie's introduction.

"Ray, meet Nathaniel and Nat, this is Raymond. And boy what a place to meet, Ray, isn't it?" Charlie said. Raymond and Nathaniel exchanged a loose handshake.

"I wonder if there other Nigerians beside us," Raymond said.

"Oh, in this cell block alone, there are as many as seven other Nigerians arrested for the same offense. Believe it or not, some of them have spent nearly a year here," Charlie said. Raymond felt a butterfly squirm in his belly. Instantly, he lost his appetite despite the enormous hunger that had him almost shivering.

Just as he was digesting the bad news he had just heard, Charlie revealed another shocker.

"Ray, I'm in a hell of a jam. My wife, along with my younger brother and his girlfriend, are all in custody right this moment for the same reason."

Raymond's jaw sagged. The jaw-dropper had just overshadowed his mood of the proverbial belly butterfly. He folded his arms in sheer wonder.

"To make matters worse, our dad, who flew in with our sick mom for medical treatment of a severe heart problem, are all waiting right now for our return from our visit to homeland. Undertaking this trip was our only hope to pay for her treatment."

Raymond's eyes almost popped out of their sockets, wondering how dejected Charlie must be feeling. The sympathy he was having for himself now shifted to Charlie. Nathaniel sighed and shrugged simultaneously. Although he had been around a few times when Charlie told friends his tragic story, it never seized to be awestruck.

Charlie's parents would later leave the US without his mom receiving the much needed medical treatment. Few months later, and following their lengthy prison sentences of four years each, his mom died of heart failure, and his father would die a year after of heartbreak.

After they ended their discussion, Raymond returned to his cell, and for the first time, met his cell mate, a twenty-two year old Cuban national, who spoke little English. The young man, short and light skinned with a stocky boxer image, told Raymond, during their get-acquainted chat, that he was recently slapped with twenty years imprisonment for brokering in a sting operation by the DEA to purchase several kilos of cocaine. All the news he heard both from Charlie and the Cuban inmate about the lengthy prison sentences being dished out to drug offenders plunged him into a new depth of depressing mood, prompting him to climb back into his top bunk bed to quietly lament over everything.

The on-again-off-again hunger kept Raymond awake, and after rolling around the bed several times, he jumped down from his top bunk bed feeling like he was about to die of starvation.. He knew he had to find something to eat as soon as possible. He had never been that hungry before, and had no idea when the jail would be serving lunch, never mind what was to be served in the menu. Because of the dire hunger he began to think he might not survive until lunchtime.

He walked outside of his cell room to the common area to glance at the wall clock. It struck at 11:30 a.m., and according to another inmate he had spoken to earlier, ten minutes before lunch. Strangely enough, a craving for rice and fresh fish stew made him yawned repeatedly, but that was wishful thinking in the confines of a jailhouse. He had heard that jail food tasted like it sounded, and to daydream for anything other than cold cuts would be ridiculous. Somehow, the hope of surprisingly eating a fairly decent meal hung in his mind, but he chose to adopt a wait and see attitude. Whatever he found in the menu, he'd surely devour. He was so hungry he could eat a raw elephant.

Fifteen minutes later, the long awaited meal came. Outrageous was the word he felt closest to the description of what was in the disposable plate he was holding in his hands. He loathed the chow as if it was worth being investigated for human rights violation. There was barely cooked, tasteless potato salad, a slice of cold bologna, and a slice of wheat bread. He lifted the meal to his nose to find that none of the food items smelled like an edible commodity.

Although the sight of the food erased some of his appetite, he didn't care at that moment what he ate as long as he ate something. He managed to chew and swallow the entire contents of the dish. After all, he was in jail, and he'd have to get used to it if he were to survive.

Over the weekend, he learned a lot about the crime he was involved in, courtesy of other Nigerians in the holdover jail. He learned that there were other classifications of the controlled substance called drugs, and studied their respective penalties. One of the harshest penalties was for an LSD substance or crack, followed by heroin, one that he was unwittingly involved in. Thirdly, and less severe than the former, was the most popular, cocaine, which he previously thought he was carrying. Then came marijuana, with relatively minor penalty, depending on the quantity involved.

He also learned about the sentencing guidelines for first-time offenders, second-time offenders, and the rest of the penal hierarchy. There were other separate categories of non-violent and violent offenders and the difference of severity of punishment under the less harsh old law, and the unpopular new law. The new law also included mandatory minimum sentences, which had had some Judges outraged because of the enormous power it accorded to prosecutors.

Other inmates hinted on the nonchalant attitude of public defenders toward drug offenders, especially black men and foreign nationals, who stood at the most disadvantageous. Perhaps more importantly, Raymond learned the essence of keeping his case to himself alone and not share it with another inmate. There was the egregious act of stealing information and feeding them to government prosecutors in return for lower prison time.

Despite the enormous odds against him in returning to a life of freedom anytime soon, he summed up courage to plan a strategy for defending himself. Damn all the talk about doom and gloom. He'd put up a fight and fight like hell before he'd concede. After all, some people who had been in more serious legal trouble had, one way or the other, successfully escaped incarceration. He was a first timer and it was reasonable to ask for a second chance to prove his involvement was a one-time deal. Moreover, he had offered to assist Customs officers in tracking down the man who sent him to Africa, but was given a cold shoulder. The more he thought about freedom the more eager he became in speaking to a lawyer.

It was Monday morning and the duty correctional officer had opened Raymond's cell door at 5 o'clock a.m. to instruct him to prepare for a court appearance. He was told that he should be ready to have his breakfast immediately, an unusual unwelcome priority afforded to inmates on the morning of their dreadful day in court. Raymond anticipated it though. It was the date fixed for his arraignment before a federal Judge in the Eastern District Court of New York in downtown, Brooklyn. He had also looked forward to it because he knew he would be meeting face to face with a lawyer, whom he expected to relieve his tension and outline defense strategy. There would be a lot to talk about, including possible bail arrangements. He owned a property, and therefore could afford to post a collateral bond up to twenty thousand dollars, and he anticipated a bail bond in the neighborhood of ten thousand dollars. If that could be expedited, he would be flying to Washington, where he planned to make concrete arrangement to raise attorney fee and handle the rest from there on.

The big electronic iron-gate for the seventh floor cell block was unlocked, and coming inside, documents on hand, was an officer from the Receiving and Discharge office. He came to escort the group of inmates from Raymond's seventh floor jail cells to the court bound bullpen. They had all washed their faces and, for those with monster appetite, had the cold breakfast. Early morning cold weather was felt along the hallways as they were marched down to the R & D on the third floor, wearing only prison jumpsuits.

The bullpen they were ordered to go into was already filled body to body with noisy inmates, so close Raymond could feel the breadth of inmates around him. He squeezed in to stand in the middle of the crowd and the correction officer slammed the iron door, locking it with a large metal key. Cold wind blew from the air duct, and it kept every inmate shivering and desperately elbowing their way to find a possible warm spot in any corner of the sardine packed holding cell. Some openly insulted the officers, wherever they may have been, shouting abusively at the top of their voices. The misery from standing in a cold pen lasted until 8 o'clock when the protocol began. One by one, they were marched from the pen to the dressing room, ten yards away, and back after they had changed from their brown jumpsuits into the same stinking clothes they were wearing at the time of their arrests.

With every move the prisoners were ordered to make, their mug shots and prison identification numbers were pulled. Each prisoner, once called out, would be required to loudly say his name and prison identification number, before he would be cleared to be led out of a cell.

At 9:30 a.m., the U.S. Marshals came in to escort them to the district court in Brooklyn, about ten minutes or so hassle across the Brooklyn bridge traffic. The security detail was the same during handover. Inmates were called and required to recite their full inmate identities, before being handcuffed hands behind. Every detainee was ordered to face the wall and closely monitored by six U.S. Marshals.

Raymond found encouragement brewing inside him over the prospect of fighting for his freedom. He was about to see a lawyer and with a little luck, would arrange bail. The freaking nightmare could be winding down in just a few hours. He'd fly to Washington right away and rid himself of the smelly clothes. He'd shower up and eat a real food in a glass bowl. A nicely chilled bottle of Heineken would wash down with utmost satiation. He'd go kiss his mother and then hold his son. Laura could wait a little. When he gets to her, he'll ask her to forgive him for overstaying in his trip to Africa, a little lie, however, a very necessary one. In a situation like that, even Honest Abe would do no differently. With the little he knew about her, she'd forgive and forget with a passionate kiss, then an intense love making. All could be happening real soon with a lawyer and a reasonable bail setting. For a responsible man without a prior criminal record, it wasn't too much to ask for. He hadn't committed a crime in the past that went undetected or unpunished, and the crime he was charged with wasn't one of immoral conduct. Nonetheless, he was extremely remorseful.

The tinted glass of the Ford van was heavily fortified with solid gauze. The vehicle sped across Brooklyn Bridge and veered off to a service road and into a tunnel, and proceeded to the basement of the courthouse building, where several other marshals were waiting to safely expedite their transfer from the van to several unheated bullpen, to await their court appearances.

A couple of hours later, Raymond got called up from the freezing bullpen to be handcuffed and escorted by a U.S. marshal. The marshal marched him through a large hallway and into an electronically controlled, narrow elevator exclusively used to lift prisoners to the courtrooms. Inside the elevator car stood a partition which Raymond was ordered to step behind and to face the opposite direction. Raymond was then led inside a large office where a lady introduced herself to him, and asked that his handcuffs be removed. Raymond sat on a wooden chair to face her, and she began by issuing Raymond a stern warning about what would happen if he gave her any false information about his background.

They went through Raymond's entire life up to that minute—what properties he owned and what he planned to have, his academic records, and so on. When it was over half an hour later, a seventyish white man with a silver blond hair walked in and immediately introduced himself.

"Mr. Karr," he said. "I'm Patrick Cunningham of the Public Defender's office, your court appointed lawyer." He was wearing a black suit and a red striped tie. His grey eyebrows gave him the look of a no-nonsense Irish businessman. The exposed portion of his neck, around the edges of his necktie, reminded Raymond of a crocodile's skin.

He was the man Raymond had been wishing desperately to meet with. The man who could lift his hopes and fight for his rights and privileges in all of the mess. The lawyer would be demanding from the judge that his client be released on bail at an affordable collateral, and then strategize with him in a secluded office to tell him he had been mistreated by the Customs agents. He could even demand that Raymond be compensated. That was what defense attorneys did for their clients. Freedom could be moments away.

Raymond instantly loved him.

"Why don't you have a seat right there, and make yourself comfortable," Mr. Cunningham said as they arrived at another desk.

They were in the same large office, where other employees of the court sat behind their desks carrying out administrative duties. It pleasantly surprised Raymond that they were not suspenseful or hatefully staring at him, the menacing villain around. He sat down and watched Mr. Cunningham pull a chair from the desk sat before placing his briefcase on his lap.

Speaking in a low hissing voice, he gave Raymond the first knockout punch that clearly defined the young man's future. He leaned over to whisper in his ear.

"No matter what happens, you're gonna go to jail."

Raymond's heart skipped a beat. "I'm sorry, can you run about me again?" he said in a somber voice.

"The number of years will spending in prison will depend on what kind of judge is assigned to your case. But yes you definitely will spend some time in prison," the lawyer, avoiding eye contact with his client.

Raymond, in total dumbfound, could feel the hot air from his breath. That was certainly not what he had anticipated from his own defense attorney. Stupidity set in and his mind raced to assess the situation as he wondered if the man speaking to him was actually working for the prosecution. What if Mr. Cunningham was pretending to be his lawyer in order to solicit damaging information that would assist the government in winning an easy conviction? That could not be happening to him, he reasoned in his mind.

"You are my lawyer, right?" he said to Mr. Cunningham.

"Yes, I believe I made that clear to you, otherwise I wouldn't be here speaking with you."

"I'd like to explain to you in detail what..." Raymond started to explain but Mr. Cunningham quickly interrupted him.

"Look," he snapped. "I don't want to hear your bullshit. If you think I'm here to waste my time, you're making a big mistake. You can hold on to your big lie, and if you want to go along with it, you're damned sure spending ten, fifteen years in jail."

Raymond was instantly heartbroken. He made no further comment, only listened while the public defender outlined his unwelcomed defense strategy. The meeting lasted for only three minutes before the same two marshals hurried in.

It was time for the dreaded court appearance.

He was handcuffed again and led along a dimly lit hallway, while his court appointed attorney took a different route. Approaching a door, where two armed marshals stood guard, the escort freed him from his handcuffs and motioned him to take a short walk to the defense stand, right next to Mr. Cunningham, whom he now hated with a passion.

The courtroom atmosphere was calm, by far the cleanest environment he had been in since his arrest. He could breathe the refreshing air from the spacious courtroom. Surprisingly also, he saw no audience sitting and stretching their heads to catch a glimpse of his face – the image of a hardened criminal. There was the already seated judge, two clerks, a court stenographer, two bailiffs, and three members of the prosecution team. All eyes were on him as he walked nervously to take his stand, facing a bulky and mean-looking, white judge. He locked his ten fingers in front of him in a humble posture.

Cold sweat ran down his forehead and an uncontrollable tremble began to plague his legs in a nervous breakdown. For a moment, he thought his knee joints were beginning to fail him. He felt he was looking at the man who would, in all likelihood, send him to hell and celebrate it with a champagne toast. He was a man Raymond never wildly dreamed of confronting—a judge in a criminal case, and Raymond Karr the criminal. When he had read about other criminal offenders during his years as a non-criminal, the situation had never sunk into his thoughts as a reality, only as half believable fairy tale. Moreover, it had always seemed inconceivable to him that he would one day find himself facing a judge and being charged with a priority criminal offense. Raymond was too sure and too proud that would never happen.

He was too nervous to pay attention to the procedure that would determine his fate. He was wrestling with his trembling legs, trying to manage the gut-wrenching fear to obscurity, shuffling his feet nervously. The entire proceeding probably lasted about five minutes, but it felt like a whole hour. When it was over, the only thing Raymond was able to comprehend was the stunning response of Mr. Cunningham when the judge asked him if a motion for bail had been filed.

"Your honor, the defense will ask for no bail in this case," Mr. Cunningham said, folding a document the court clerk had handed him.

The next move came from the bailiff who walked up to escort Raymond back to the waiting two marshals standing by the prisoner special entrance door. The cold steel of handcuffs rubbed against each other, quickly reminding Raymond of the slums of the bullpen, and the loss of round one—the most important round in his battle to regain his freedom. It provided him with a glimpse of what the future held for him. He felt betrayed by Mr. Cunningham as he stood alone inside the small cell inside the electronically controlled elevator. His hope to be free on bond had been shattered.

Raymond woke up to the usual 5:30 a.m. breakfast call and lined up behind Charlie, waiting for his turn to receive a paper plate of potato salad and a tea bag. It had been a restless night, and for the first time, Raymond had reminisced the wonderful moments he had with Laura Hazleton before his travel to Lagos. Silly, he thought. The thought of what he had missed had been especially depressing. He imagined all the fun he would have been having only if he had successfully made it to Washington. Now he will never see her or the nation's capital for the rest of his life.

Soon after breakfast, he and Charlie joined a group of other Nigerians sitting at the far corner of one of the four tiers, where they were contemplating their own situations. Everyone seemed to have had a similar experience of being apprehended just when he was about to reach an incredible new height in his romantic life. Raymond hardly contributed to the discussion, only listened as they all took turns telling tales of their ruined lives.

One thing seemed obvious to him. There would be absolutely no opportunity for a second chance, regardless of one's criminal background, something he had refused to believe.

The constantly busy three telephones provided for inmates on the seventh floor finally were available for Raymond's use. He had planned to telephone his brother, Ed, in Lexington Park, Maryland, to break the terrible news of his arrest and incarceration. He had tried a couple of times the day before, upon his arrival from the court, but each time the operator put him on hold in order to first confirm the acceptance of his collect call. He would hang up because momentarily, from such a distance, he lacked the ability to control the alarm that would inevitable set off when his brother, Ed and his mother would learn about his ordeal. The previous night he had decided that since it had to happen sooner or later, he might as well get it done in the morning and get it over with.

Raymond's heartbeat thumped as he stood fast this time around, waiting for the long distance operator to put him through. He was wishing, as the line was still on hold, it wouldn't be mother who would pick up the call. If only he could quietly speak with Ed and let him handle the rest as carefully as he could or saw fit, he would be spared with the agony of re-living endlessly his mother's scream and bitter cry, feeling of sheer disgrace and utter disappointment. He wouldn't be there to console her.

Finally, the operator's voice came on the line, asking Raymond to go ahead.

Raymond's mother's hello voice was unmistakable, throwing him off guard.

"Mom, it's Ray," he began, trying to sound as casual as he could.

"Oh! Ray, my dear son, God, I'm so glad you called. Where have you been? I've had six straight days of terrifying dreams about you, nightmare I should say, and I kept dialing your phone number and no pickups; not even your answering machine."

"Mom, remember I told you I was going out of town for a few days? Well, I'm just about to conclude the business, and should be coming back soon." He didn't specify the day he intended to be back, not realizing how much he had committed himself to explaining further. His mother was quick to ask him when exactly, and what the business was all about, and how successful.

"Mom, don't you think it's better to discuss this in detail when I come back? For now, let me talk to Ed real quick 'cause I only have the line for a few minutes."

"All right, my dear. Just hearing from you and knowing you're fine relieves the enormous fear I'd been having recently. Do I hope to see you in another day or two, dear?"

Raymond choked before replying. "Yes Ma."

"Great." She handed the receiver to Raymond's brother, Ed.

"Eddy," Raymond said casually, still unsure of how to begin.

"Oh! Ray, thank God you telephoned. Mom has been giving me hell, night and day, complaining about you being gone. You know how troublesome she can be when you're gone for long. Why put me through this?" Ed asked exuberantly.

"Eddy, I know how badly you feel about this, and I'm sorry. I guess I'll have to start by reminding you that what I'm about to reveal to you demands your courage as a man, and I know how old you are. You are man enough to handle difficult situations like the one you're about to hear."

Raymond paused a while before continuing, slightly impressed with the way he'd handled the introduction so far. "Eddy, tragedy, the likes of never before, has struck."

Ed immediately followed. "Oh no…. What now? Who died?"

He cautioned Ed to avoid audible emotional expression for the sake of their mother, and then continued. "No death is involved. Someone set a trap and I walked right into it."

Raymond went on to explain how the law had had him, and that he probably would be spending the rest of the century behind bars. He withheld from his brother the details of his journey, only promised he shall be writing to explain soon. He asked Ed to take over all his entitlements and responsibilities as the first son of the family in their homeland. For his mortgage, he told Ed he'd be talking to his court appointed public defender to have the lawyer explore the possibilities of handing over of the mortgage titles. They also spoke briefly about Raymond's common-law and his son. He will be calling to find out if they were back to the house, which didn't seem like a possibility.

"I'll keep you updated, and please handle Mom properly," Raymond said.

Raymond overheard his mother pressing Ed to hand her the receiver while Ed tried unsuccessfully to dissuade her from coming back on the line.

"Raymond, Mother says she really has to speak with you. What should I tell her?" Ed said with a subtle note of disappointment and despair in his voice. Raymond knew very well that, growing up whenever they had a brotherly quarrel, his name became Raymond instead of the affectionately pronounced Ray.

He was hoping Ed would win the verbal struggle, but again Raymond was unlucky. However, he quickly gained his composure.

"Put her on the line," Raymond said dryly.

"Ray, dear, about Rebecca, Is she back yet?" Mom asked.

"I tried to telephone James to find out, but there was no answer. I guess she's still away. Don't worry, Mom, she'll be back. I know she will," Raymond said.

"You know she has your son, who is also my grandson, so be sure to make it your first priority when you come back, okay?"

"Okay Ma."

"And I'll see you in a day or two. Do you want to speak with Eddy?"

"No, Ma, I'll have to run."

"All right, dear, take care."

Raymond hung up the receiver and stood still to think. Deep in his thoughts he knew how impossible it would be to be with his mother in days. He also looked beyond that, realizing Mr. Cunningham had told him, during their initial consultation that if the judge was lenient enough, the minimum sentence he could receive would be forty-one months and only if he pled guilty to save the government from the troubles of trial proceedings. The public defender had also guaranteed him a conviction and stiffer penalty should he dared take the case to trial.

Raymond contemplated for a moment and knew the odds were heavily stack that his mother would be seeing him in two days or in two years, perhaps many more. Realizing he had once again lied to his mother, something he had vowed never to do four years after he felt he was a born again Christian, his conscience irked him into a sudden discomfort. His inhibitive Catholic values quickly reminded him he must confess to his God. He immediately looked up and asked for forgiveness and followed with a sign of the cross and a silent recitation of Penitential Rite.

"Boy am I in trouble," Raymond quipped as tears began to run down his cheek.

Before walking to the telephone, Raymond had promised his Nigerian colleagues that he would rejoin them in a few minutes. Instead, he walked directly and dejectedly to his cell and climbed unto his bunk bed, broke down and further cursed himself.

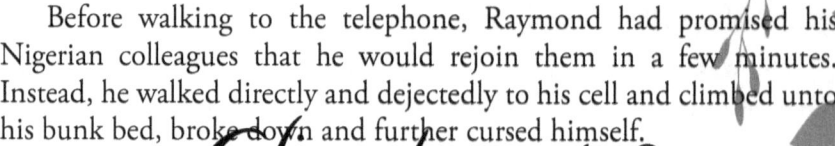

Chapter 18

AWE

The confined life of a prisoner didn't simply end in being locked up in a cell, especially in the New York district. Prisoners were infinitely subjected to a tormented life beyond imagination, and endured absolute and indiscriminate dehumanizing treatment. In other words, regardless of one's criminal status, violent and career criminal or nonviolent first-time offender, one was still labeled a criminal and didn't deserve any sympathy from anyone.

Life following Raymond's first court appearance was so dreadful that he, on two occasions, seriously contemplated suicide. In the last contemplation, he actually sought any instrument that could effectively enhance a speedy exodus to end the mental torture he felt was simply too agonizing to bear. It was, and always remained hard to imagine how anyone who went through the experience, or heard about it, would even think of committing any more crime. In fact he clung more to religion because he feared hell might be as torturous as jail.

It was nine o'clock Wednesday night, two days after his court appearance, and he was beginning to get somewhat acquainted with some of his inmate colleagues, who encouraged him to take heart and not consider himself a criminal, contrary to his status with the U.S. Department of Justice.

"We only made a mistake," one of them had said. "As long as we stay away from such temptations in the future, and ask Almighty God to forgive us our sins, we needn't think much about it."

His humble message would have sunk in with time, but only if situation didn't get worse.

The situation did get worse. Raymond's name had just been blasted over the loudspeaker to pack up and be ready for a jail transfer. Destination was the federal prison in Otisville, a harrowing three-hour prison bus ride. The high level security prison was located in a remote countryside northeast of the state of New York. Several other inmates were called for the transfer, but none of Raymond's new friends was among them.

Charlie, out of curiosity, came out of his cell to listen in, wiping his sleep-disrupted eyes. When he heard Raymond's name, he waited until all names were called before setting out in search of his jail buddy. Seeing how worried Raymond was, he assured him that it wasn't actually that bad. He hinted to him that he would be meeting many other Nigerians, and that there was a good chance he would be seeing someone he'd known out in the free world. He also assured him of a much better food quality service.

Raymond quite frankly cared less about anything. He did not expect a situation in the prison confinement where he would be served a decent meal, at least from what he knew about jail, it is so farfetched. Nonetheless, he was leaving. Staying anywhere wasn't at his discretion any longer, and neither was anything else.

After speaking with Charlie, Raymond dejectedly walked back to his cell and tears welled up his eyes. He reached under his pillow to collect his only belonging—the receipt of his seized properties at the airport.

Seven inmates of various nationalities were marched out from the seventh floor cell block, escorted by a Correction Officer, from the R & D to the third floor offices. The C.O. had had all assembled inmates state their first names and prison numbers before they stepped through the iron-gate. The inmates then proceeded to the elevators for a ride downstairs to the third floor.

It was 9:30 p.m., and the bullpen Raymond and the other inmates were locked inside was as usual freezing and packed body-to-body with prisoners from other units, who had arrived earlier. The cold steel bench was fully occupied, and so was the cold floor, which had absolutely no space for them to sit. They had no alternative than to stand and attempt to shiver off the attacking cold air that never stopped blowing from the vent. There were four other empty cells similar to the one the prisoners were packed in, but according to a sarcastic correctional officer, whom he pleaded with to help ease their agony and transfer some of them there. Inmates had no right to choose how prisoners should be handled or classified. An inmate who overheard their conversation then explained to Raymond the painful treatment was called "Bullpen Therapy," whereby as a criminal, one was reminded he was no longer a complete human being.

Raymond concluded what he had always thought about criminals. He had all my life considered anyone who committed crime to be less than average human being, not realizing he would one day become subjected to the same standard.

The prisoners stood miserably until 1 a.m., when the hard steel gate opened and a stone-faced Correction Officer stood by with a bunch of ID cards. Reading from the cards, the C.O. called out five inmates who responded by the usual stating of their first and last names and assigned prison numbers. The African American C.O. strained his ears to comprehend two non-English speaking Spanish inmates.

The officer again slammed shut the steel gate and was gone. Raymond couldn't help but notice the dispiriting sound of the heavy steel gate and hated everything.

That process continued at a frustrating slow pace, and when it was his turn, he came to realize it was a process whereby inmates were escorted to a dressing room to put on their orange color prisoner transfer jumpsuits. These colorful costumes were designed to make a potential escapee an easy target, both night and day. The next step was to escort the group of five to a different bullpen to await completion of the process.

The horrible condition remained the same in the final stage holding cell, until two o'clock a.m. when the highly secured prison bus arrived. The two bus lieutenants, with the help of other Correctional Officers on duty, shackled him and his fellow inmates' arms and legs with chains that extended around the waist. They were finally set to begin a journey they were called out for at 9 p.m. the previous night.

Raymond hopped along behind almost half of the inmates, and the other half behind me, as they were escorted by four heavily armed guards, and marched into the unmarked fifty-two-sitter bus idling in the basement garage. The three-hour journey would then begin with

Special Forces riding in a U.S. marshal cruiser in front, automatic weapons on hand.

Three hours into their journey, the road sign on the right side of the road showed they were almost at the conclusion. The time, according to an African-American inmate sitting next to Raymond, was 5:15 a.m., and the bus veered off to the left. Raymond saw the sign that read, BUREAU OF PRISONS, FEDERAL CORRECTIONAL INSTITUTION, OTISVILLE, NEW YORK.

Astonishingly, he could also see the relief showing in the faces of other inmates, most of whom had made the nightmarish journey several times before.

As the bus slowly approached the security gate, Raymond surveyed the fenced facility that had been, until that day, a legendary house, providing its residents with a lifestyle that was unimaginable to him. Not only would he witness that unthinkable lifestyle, he certainly was just about to live it.

The armed guards took their places, semi-circular form, holding their weapons in at the ready, while the inmates hopped down from the bus. He was greeted by a sudden surge of early morning cold wind that gusted through the surrounding forest. Unprotected against the cold temperature in their ordinary cotton clothes, they were marched in a single file to a small front security pass office, and paraded through a narrow metal detector gate. They exited to the rear of the office, walking a distance of a hundred yards in freezing temperatures, to the institution's R & D office.

Raymond's dispirited mind was busy trying to cope with the cold steel of shackles and chains rubbing against each other, and his ankles were sore from the friction. He had tried to hasten forward to shorten his exposure to the wintry temperature, but that worsened the pain from the friction. The holding bullpen in Otisville prison was much smaller and sloppier, with pools of spit on the floor and stains on the walls. They waited, rather impatiently, to be released from their bondage within confinement, while the two Correctional Officers assigned to unlock their handcuffs took their precious time. Raymond rested the back of his head against the wall, occasionally holding his breath to fend off the fart discharged loudly by some of the most inconsiderate human beings in existence – his new colleagues.

Slowly but steadily, the prisoners were all free from the chains and in another cell. When the time was up, they were called, one at a time, to three narrow cubicles where they were extensively inspected, everywhere from deep inside their throats to a fraction of an inch inside their anuses. Once through with physical inspection, they were each handed a pair of dyed-green briefs, a white T-shirt, and a dark green jumpsuit, all already used by other inmates, and then ordered to proceed inside an adjacent bullpen to dress up and await the conclusion of the current process.

What followed was the Bureau's most essential process—the prison mug shots. It was certainly the slowest of all. One after the other, he and his fellow inmates took two photographs each, holding upright on their chests a numbered plate showing their prison numbers. Raymond still couldn't overcome the embarrassment from the process, for it represented to him the most damning criminal posture of all. Every holder of the mug shot plate, regardless of how innocent he looked, would instantly turn into a menacing character.

They would remain in that holding cell until all inmates were categorically interviewed by one of three Counselors, whose responsibilities included quizzing new prisoners about the nature of their crimes and the condition of their health. They were then returned to the holding cell to kill the time slowly until 7:30 a.m. when, according to the institution's intake policy, they would be marched into the prison compound.

For the first time since his arrest at JFK airport, Raymond felt like a freed eagle, walking outside in an open air without shackles and chains. In the prison, he could see, and for that matter, cherish the sight of the morning blue sky. He didn't mind the extreme tiredness he felt in his body, nor did he care about the cold morning wind. He was staring somewhat with amazement at the other inmates, who were walking freely from one building to the other, instead of a confinement in a single building like the Metropolitan Correctional Center in Manhattan.

However, he and his fellow inmates would encounter one more slow protocol. They lined up outside the laundry office in order to receive their bedding and basic hygiene supplies—a process that consumed another hour. Raymond would miserably undergo that process, back and forth, fifteen times for his future court appearances.

He was assigned to his cell, again occupying the top bunk bed, and was handed the prison's regulation handbook by the unit officer. He took a few moments of his relaxation to flash through the more essential Code of Conduct from the forty-five-page book. The first thing Raymond realized astonishingly, and to his further dismay, was the pass system which prohibited all inmates from staying within sight of compound officers, or anywhere around the compound, ten minutes after every hour, from six o'clock a.m. wake-up call until eleven p.m. lockdown. Movement from prisoners' cells to either the recreation center or work assigned area was only to take place within ten minutes at the top of every hour. Nonetheless, just as Raymond's fellow inmates had hinted him at MCC, it was much better than the strictly confining Manhattan jail.

Chapter 19

A STUNNING RE-UNION

At 11:30 a.m., it was announced through the institution's loud speaker that Raymond's cell unit was to proceed to the cafeteria for lunch. Raymond was just about to doze off when the information blasted, instantly awaking him. Extremely tired from the journey, he slowly walked outside his cell to join the rest of the inmates from his unit, and they all walked tiredly to the chow hall. Inmates were also prohibited from several other activities. One inmate among their group, a skinny twenty years old Ethiopian cheat, half ran toward the front. He had earned an unsavory reputation for cheating in everything, including simple card games. A compound officer immediately yelled.

"Walk!" he bellowed and then warned, "Inmates are not allowed to run inside the compound."

"What does he mean by that?" Raymond whispered to an inmate standing next to him.

"You can't run in here, man. The law is established to alert officers when an inmate attempts to escape. It carries a significant penalty," the inmate explained.

Food service was decent and in an orderly fashion. Inmates used real silverware, and they sat on chairs genuinely designed for dining. Lunch was ham and fried potatoes, and there was a buffet-style salad bar and slices of bread. Raymond felt like a member of the Olympics team, staring, with tremendous satiation, at the spread he had greedily packed on his tray. There were several choices that he had difficulty deciding what first he would sink his denture on.

In the middle of lunch, he was joined by a homeboy, who claimed he knew him from Maryland. He began by describing the night party where he first met Raymond. He also cited several other encounters that Raymond barely remembered. However, they talked about friends they both knew in common, and there were several. Another Nigerian with a boyish face, six feet and slim built, with a noticeable scar just to the left side of his lower lip, wadded in, smiling. He hesitated before he called him by his full name.

"Do you recognize me, Raymond Nnamdi Karr?" he said.

"I sure don't," Raymond said, staring hard at his face.

"Come up when you're done with lunch and I'll be waiting at that corner, where a group of Africans are sitting," he said, pointing to a crowded table yards away.

"Okay," Raymond said enthusiastically and turned to look at the direction the man was pointing.

The homeboy he was chatting with, who had introduced himself as Andrew, immediately remarked on the man as he was walked away.

"That guy's real funny," Andrew said.

Raymond couldn't wait to find out who the guy was. Calling him by his middle name pretty much evidenced a deep knowledge of each other way back. When he had devoured the contents of his plate, he spotted the same man standing and looking at his direction, eagerly awaiting. He was under the impression the boyish-looking man was really desperate to meet with him, and with the resounding accuracy, which he had pronounced Raymond's full name, especially his middle name, he knew the man must be someone he would really be astonished to see again.

Raymond stood up and walked to where the man and his colleagues were sitting. They were all looking at him as if he were an unsuspecting celebrant about to be exposed to his surprise party.

"Take a careful look at me. Are you definitely sure you don't recognize me?" the man said, pausing and lifting his face for Raymond to examine.

After a brief and careful examination, Raymond, still clueless, gave up. "I'm quite sure I don't."

"Okay, do you remember this?" the man said, pointing to the scar across the left side of his lower lip.

The tip was exactly what Raymond needed to recall their old

friendship. He screamed his name and heartily embrace him.

"Oh my God, Uzoma Amadi!" Raymond yelled, attracting the attention of almost everyone in the large cafeteria.

Reunion with Uzoma Amadi remained by far the greatest surprise Raymond would encounter during his entire ordeal. His story with Uzoma Amadi, who would later tell him he was seriously considering changing his first name from Uzoma to Dave, dated back to their freshman years in high school. Government Secondary School in Owerri, Nigeria was where the young and naïve duo became buddies. They hung out together and became neighbors in their dormitory, until separated months later by an inter-house system, where students were housed in separate dorms.

Uzoma was the most significant freshman in their year. He possessed an unparalleled ability to ridicule others and making funny and embarrassing mockery out of anyone's missteps. Uzoma would ridicule you at leisure, regardless of how careful your word or action was. He was as skinny as a flamingo, so skinny his adversaries called him Stockfishbone. He never did appreciate his nickname, but it never bothered him as much as his mockery would bother anyone who dared to refer his as that.

It was this ability to tell jokes and ridicule others that kept Uzoma and Raymond, who never seized to be entertained, as close friends. Ironically, it was the same that brought their friendship to an abrupt end.

Raymond's severance with Uzoma began one cool evening, when the school's traditional dance group, the Atila-ogwu, had accepted Raymond for a try-out to join the coveted entertainment group. Uzoma and Raymond had had a minor friends' quarrel earlier, and for some mysterious reason, Raymond's ridicule had unusually stuck to Uzoma more than his did to Raymond, a rare occurrence by any stretch of the imagination. Their colleagues had laughed hard at Raymond's jibe, badly depressing Uzoma. In the embarrassing ridicule, Uzoma had joked that Raymond had grown butt hair, hence now to be nicknamed as such. During those days, it was a nickname associated with someone who was no longer fit to play as a child. Raymond, ostensibly humiliated, had fired back by telling a joke about how poor and wretched Uzoma's parents were, and how he had bought his first new bathing towel and showered eleven times a day, just to show off and savor his first ever luxurious possession. Raymond also followed with another stinger. He told that Uzoma bought his first tooth brush ever, and brushed his teeth eleven times a day, and then smiled unusually broadly at every single person he had encountered to show off his bright teeth.

Raymond's joke had drawn an endless laughter among colleagues and spectators that continued long after and Uzoma never had the opportunity to counter, for the recess bell rang everyone into their classrooms.

Uzoma, who apparently was still reeling from the joke, had scored a perfect timing when he ran into a shy Raymond trying to learn new traditional dance steps in the very presence of many.

He didn't say much. He didn't have to. All he had to do was laugh, mock and ridicule Raymond, who was awkwardly attempting to simulate the dance instructor. "Hairy Butt," he shouted repeatedly.

Utterly embarrassed, Raymond lost his cool. He quietly dropped out of the twelve-man dancing group to rough up Uzoma. A fist fight broke out. Uzoma withdrew back about five yards and flew toward Raymond, stretching his right leg for a kung fu kick. Raymond simply grabbed Uzoma's foot, and hung on for about two seconds. Uzoma tried an unsuccessful safe-landing by twisting and falling front-to-ground, He successfully used his hands to break the fall, but landed his mouth on one of several cinder blocks that wedged the flower garden. Blood profusely gushed out, setting the school's paramedics in motion.

The injury had left a significant scar just below the left side of Uzoma's lower lip. Most students, and even some teachers, aptly observed that it couldn't have picked a better spot to occur on dirty-mouthed Uzoma. Their friendship ended from then on and they never spoke or ridicule each other for the next two years they spent together in the high school before moving on. Raymond had transferred to the neighboring Emmanuel High while Uzoma had flunked out to pursue other career opportunity

It was that very scar that Uzoma pointed at to remind Raymond of who he was, nineteen years later. Their re-union would begin a new friendship in hard times. Time had consumed animosity.

The momentary happiness from meeting Uzoma again subsided

when Raymond woke up from the deepest sleep he had ever had since his incarceration. He no longer had dreams about freedom or thoughts about his mother and his son, and no reminiscence of the wonderful times he had with Laura. Of course, the hopes of attending medical school at George Washington U had all but vanished. He just went to bed and slept soundly and uneventfully.

He was awakened by the loud speaker for the prison's routine 4 o'clock stand-up count. His cellmate, a thirty-year old Israeli, who told him he was in on espionage rap, had just returned from his kitchen pots and pans job, and briefly lectured him on the compulsory standing during the prison's three count times weekdays and four during weekends. The world kept on seeming like it was just about ending.

Raymond sat on his bed wondering if his brother, Ed, had told his mother what had happened. He also wondered, if Ed had fed her the bitter news, how devastated she must have been feeling. Once again he thought about everything, from the fate of his son to his house and its mortgage payments, including the enormous responsibilities that he was faced with in his home country.

After the standup count, inmates marched to the cafeteria for dinner in the same lunchtime disciplined order, and then to the recreation center. There, Uzoma introduced him to several other Nigerians, most of who admitted they either knew him or knew someone from his famous family. Everywhere he went his outside world memory went along, often captivating him to a noticeable trance. While the other inmates played shuffleboard and shot pool, he sat on one corner to think and regret, and finally, that Thursday evening, he decided it was time to look at other options available to him.

His thoughts began to be even more irrational. Since there would be almost no chance of being let out on bail, he decided he would place his case in the hands of a formidable lawyer. First, he would contact Kenny and Clyde in Maryland to detail them on his ill-fated trip. Then he would ask Clyde to follow through in his promise to provide him with the best attorney in town. If that could be arranged, he could live again and learn his bitter lessons. Then he'd settle down and concentrate on his import business, and if half of his original plans went his way, he would be rich in another year or two. He would solidify his romance with Laura and ask her to marry him. With financial security, she would be all his and wouldn't object to his proposing her. He imagined what it would be like watching he match to the Alter to wed him. What an exciting moment that would be. It could only be possible if he could pull off his one humongous problem. It would be difficult, but with all his effort, and a little luck, his dreams could come true in just another year or two. He would do everything he could to work it all out.

It was ten o'clock Friday morning when Raymond placed a collect call to Kenny. He had chosen Kenny because of the obvious risk if he spoke with Clyde over the phone. He was warned by his inmate colleagues to be extremely careful who he spoke with, and what to say over the monitored telephone. The caution of being monitored was conspicuously placed above each telephone, and he had been tipped off on its use to mount evidence against defendants in court. To speak with Clyde would undoubtedly provide them with strong evidence against him, and also contradict the statement he had made to DiGiovanni.

The phone was picked up by CJ, who placed on on hold and went to Kenny's new apartment to fetch him. Forty-five seconds later, Kenny's voice came on the line.

"Kenny, I've been derailed. I couldn't make it through JFK," He said to him.

"Oh Lord! What happened?" Kenny said, obviously shocked.

"Listen, I can't tell you anything over the phone right now 'cause it's being monitored. The only thing I want you guys to do is have a good lawyer come see me, and we'll take it from there. He will be our medium of communication."

"Okay, but be real careful how you telephone. I mean, just don't call too often. Then we'd all be in trouble and no one can work on our behalf. It's good that at least one of us remain free to be able to help you out."

"All right," Raymond said. "In that case, I'll call Monday to see how you've done."

"Don't call Monday. Make it Tuesday."

"Fine, Tuesday then."

Raymond's name appeared on the institution's call-out sheet for orientation on Tuesday morning. It reminded him of the stereotype he was faced for being a lower class personality. The instructor stressed the mandatory G.E.D. class for everyone who didn't attend high school in the U.S. He preached that because the government realized inmates would eventually be integrated back into the society, they were introducing the system to help them begin a better life.

Raymond had found this preaching incredibly ridiculous, and had asked him provoking questions, but received passive answers.

"What would be the logic behind keeping me out of reach with my business, house and other engagements, and by denying me bail, which would have enabled me to arrange my investments, before serving my time in jail? Therefore if and when I would be released back into the society, I wouldn't need to start from G.E.D," Raymond said.

"You certainly have a point there. But I think it has more to do with the penal structure," he said.

Another inmate quickly jumped in. "Someone in a higher social status would have certainly made the bail, and would have the opportunity to arrange his investments before going to prison if he had to."

The instructor, who himself came across as though he bore some grudges against the American government, seemed quite convinced Raymond had raised an interesting and indefensible issue.

Nonetheless, at the conclusion of the orientation class, Raymond dashed to the housing unit to place his phone call to Kenny, and to find out from his brother, Ed, how he had handled breaking the sad news to their mother.

He was waiting for the operator's voice to come on the line when a shocking AT&T recorded message shot back to announce the number he had dialed was no longer accepting collect calls. Raymond tried again to be sure he had dialed the right numbers, but received the same recorded message. Then, more desperately, another and another, to no avail. Panic replaced his courage, and once again, events turned for the worse.

Nervously he dialed Clyde's number to find it was no longer in service. He would find out months later he had dialed the wrong number. For the first time, he decided to telephone James at his house in Maryland. But James had apparently heard of Raymond's ordeal, and the news was rapidly spreading across Washington, DC like a wild fire with tornado effect. James told Raymond he was afraid, unsure if he might be sought after by the authorities.

James' only advice for Raymond was to keep cool, and that he would be contacting Kenny and Clyde himself to persuade them to fulfill their promise of coming to his rescue. James also gave him a surprising hint;

"Your wife's back in the house, along with the kids," he said.

"Did she come to pick up her stuff?" Raymond said, seemingly surprised.

"Nope…. To stay."

Raymond couldn't figure what to make of James' revelation, and simply remained stoic on the topic.

"James, please, I can't talk about her in a time like this. I just want you to help me contact Kenny to either get me an attorney, or pay one that I'll consult myself," the frustrated young man said.

James attempted to persuade him to speak on the phone with his common-law but he wouldn't budge.

Raymond hung up with James and immediately called Ed at his office in Lexington Park, fortunately reaching him immediately. Ed hadn't told mother about his plight yet. He was so worried to death about what mother's reaction might be. He just didn't know how to approach the problem, so he simply advised Ed to handle it in any way he saw fit and at the time of his own choosing. Raymond only wanted to talk about trying to secure his mortgage and keep up with the payments. They agreed that Ed should rent it out.

However, if his common-law had been back with his son, she would be occupying the rooms intended for rent.

Raymond's conscience was unsettled at the thought of asking a woman who had his own son, to vacate the house and very likely become homeless. If he allowed her to stay, the house required a mortgage payment of up to one thousand dollars a month. She had no job. The house would certainly be foreclosed in another month or two if payments weren't made, and she would still be homeless with his son.

"Eddy," Raymond said. "I have no idea how this situation can be

addressed."

He went on to discuss the dilemma with Ed, and they came up with no workable solution. It would become the one issue that will principally motivate his spirited effort to dig out whatever he could to drive for his freedom. His family badly needed him.

Ed promised he would try to resolve that after he had discussed it with Raymond's common-law, to find out her intentions. It could be that she only came back to say a final goodbye. They also agreed to speak again Wednesday, the next week, the same day he had planned to telephone James.

Chapter 20

AGONY

The first week of November was a dreadful one for Raymond because of his inability to contact either Kenny or Clyde. He sat on the steps, head on hands, in one corner of the common area, and stared blankly across the hall, wondering why all of a suddenly they were avoiding him. They were his only hope to raise money to hire a lawyer, and he needed to if he had any chance of beating the rap. Of course he suspected they may have decided to abandon him, perhaps afraid he might pose a potential danger to their own freedom. Whatever caused them to put him out of line with them; whatever they may have been doing at the moment, he knew it wasn't at all looking good for his plans. Could it be that he was staring oblivion right in its face?

The prison didn't supply inmates with deodorants and lotion, and he had to live through the wintry cold weather looking and smelling like a homeless man. He had been planning to use some of the cash they'd send him to buy personal hygiene needs at the commissary. He had been staying away from other inmates at the indoor games because he thought he stunk so badly he could smell himself. Inmates also relied on their commissary accounts to purchase detergents to wash and maintain their briefs, otherwise they would continue to use the population undergarments washed in the general laundry. They were mostly worn out and had visible feces lines. He had no money and hadn't yet established a commissary account.

But he was less concerned about all that at the moment. He had to concentrate on trying to save himself from drowning, as he looked forward to Wednesday to find out what James had learned of Kenny and Clyde.

The only highpoint of the weekend a Washington Redskins' victory in a game that he couldn't watch. The State of New York was blacked out for all the other games, except for the New York Giants in the afternoon, and Buffalo Bills in the evening.

There was also the war of words being exchanged in the United Nations, the U.S. Congress, and in the Persian Gulf. The few inmates enlightened enough to care about global events, weren't particularly impressed by President Bush's policy in the region. In fact, they so much resented their own government that they could have sided with Adolph Hitler. Raymond suspected it must have had something to do with their bitterness over being incarcerated. His mind often drifted to what must have brought each individual to the federal prison and mind-guessed the unthinkable… murder, armed robbery, bank heists, narcotics dealing, etc. And just like in his case, criminals did not appreciate being stopped cold from their dreams of easy and instant wealth.

Once again, Raymond had been surrounded by those who angrily opposed every opinion he voiced in support of America, and he loved to analyze global issues, something that kept him feeling alive and involved. Astonishingly, the most offended were the African-Americans, who bitterly complained that black folks in the U.S. military were disproportionately deployed to war zones that were most vulnerable to enemy attack. Whenever he was in a gathering that discussed such hot-button issues, attempting to dispel the narrative made him look like he was a sellout on African-American interests. Sometimes, though, he successfully got his messages across to silence critics, especially when he raised the undisputed fact that the entire United States Armed Forces was commanded by an African-American, who himself had achieved success through valor, unhindered by the race factor. Still few belligerent inmates believed the African American head of the Joint Chiefs was himself a sellout.

Wednesday finally dragged by.

Raymond went straight to the telephone immediately after the unit officer had cleared the four p.m. standup count. He first dialed Ed but was told by the secretary that he was busy at the moment with a customer on their showroom floor. He hung up and dialed James' number. It went directly to voicemail, unusual given that it was his phone and he had never set it to answering machine without a ring. He waited five minutes and then dialed again. He desperately needed to speak with him for obvious reason. Among all, he'd want to know if

James had been in touch with either Kenny or Clyde, or both, and if they had arranged for him to meet with a lawyer, or come up with the money for him to retain one himself.

He couldn't believe his own ears when he heard the telephone company's recorded message that his line was disconnected. There was no doubt in his mind that James had done it and it was meant to avoid contact with him. He had essentially been abandoned by all his so-called friends.

He aimlessly dialed Ed's number at work again, not minding whether or not he could speak to him. The day's hope of freedom faded fast as he began to mentally dissect the situation. He never really had friends, he thought, only fair weather friends. It began to dawn on him that his fate would now rest in the hands of an unsympathetic Public Defender, who earlier had assured him he would be going to prison, no matter what.

Ed came on the line. He still hadn't heard from James nor did he hear from Francine, Raymond's departed common-law. He complained that his load of duties at his job were too demanding, and that he had little or no chance at all to drive the ninety miles or so from Lexington Park to Riverdale. However, he promised to drive over to Riverdale that weekend.

"Have you hinted mom on this problem yet?" Raymond said, afraid of whatever answer he'd hear. Ed said he hadn't and Raymond felt a little relieved.

"I just haven't determined the right approach nor have I summed up enough courage, Ray," he said and sighed in frustration.

"I perfectly understand," Raymond said in a rattled solemn voice. After a few discussion on how Raymond was coping with jail, they hung up and arranged to speak again the next Monday, following Ed's trip to Riverdale.

Raymond hoped that somehow, miraculously, Ed would hear from James.

Raymond was on the phone Monday afternoon, waiting nervously and impatiently for Ed to pick up. Again he had to be placed on a long hold because Ed was busy with a customer.

It had been a terrible weekend for Raymond, probably the most extreme emotional distress he'd ever found himself in so far. For the second time in his life, within thirty days, suicidal thoughts floated in his mind. One of those days, he had actually spent over ten hours desperately contemplating an easy way out of life. He had even begun to search for any means at all, regardless of how grotesque.

After considering all options to end life, two grim possibilities had seemed more plausible. First viable option was to hang himself with the institution-supplied bed sheet. However, when he had searched around, anchoring the sheet high enough to suspend his six feet one body became a stumbling block. He thought if he began to struggle at a point of crucial pain, he probably would support himself by standing, effectively aborting his suicide bid. He knew he could kiss population goodbye and spend the rest of his confinement in solitary.

His second option had been to plunge, head down, from the balcony of the third level inside the main lobby. But with only twenty feet elevation, that too suffered an impediment. It wasn't high enough to ensure instant death. He had come to the conclusion that only instant death would do it. If he was unsuccessful in his initial bid, which would be his one and only shot at dying, the unit officer watching would immediately sound an alarm. Backup officers would rush in and the paramedics would be called in for revival. That right there would be all she wrote. Solitary.

Nonetheless, he had chosen taking the plunge, hoping he'd enhance enough gravity by forcing himself to thrust harder.

The bid had taken a dramatic turn when it had suddenly occurred to him that he needed to leave behind a suicide note. His purpose had been to vindicate the Bureau of Prisons and anyone else. He had wanted to make out his will and bid his last good bye to his brother, Ed. He had also wanted to have Ed extend his deepest regrets to the rest of his family, without having to expose his ordeal to the public in Africa. He'd ask to be buried in the United States, without the enormous burden and expense of sending a corpse across the high seas.

When his thoughts had shifted to his little boy, he had buried his face in his hands in a feeling of utter guilt and shame and, silently, had broken down in tears. He had repeatedly cursed himself for engaging in a conduct of abject stupidity.

It was in the process of drafting this suicide note that he had decided it would be in his best interest to first speak directly to Ed, and to bequeath his only brother with his rights and entitlements as the family's first born son. He knew he had to choose his words carefully without a hint of his suicide intention.

Finally, Ed's voice came on the line.

"Raymond," he said impatiently. "I don't think James really wants to help you." He said impatiently. Raymond detected a note of anger and frustration in his voice.

"Oh, why did you say that?" Raymond asked wryly.

"He says he's moving out shortly, making it more difficult for me to arrange any kind of tenancy capable of handling the mortgage. Plus Rebecca, your common-law, ain't going nowhere."

"Did she specifically say that herself or are you just drawing a conclusion out of what you think she meant?"

"From what she said, of course. There's no two ways about that. You should know her well enough by now to realize she has nowhere to go with two children."

Ed was right and his anger became more profound. Both he and James had been particularly careful in avoiding the rumors of Rebecca's flight to shack with another guy. Still, he had more demanding issues to deal with at the moment.

Raymond sighed before speaking. "So you don't see the situation manageable?"

"To tell you the gospel truth, I don't. Ray, you've got to let that house go."

"Eddy, you know how much I have invested in that house. Are you quite sure there's absolutely nothing you could do, no way you can redeem it?"

"You know how demanding my job is and how far away I am from Riverdale".

They paused for a few seconds. Raymond sensed that Ed knew he'd have something to say about that. He contemplated over the hopelessness of the situation. He'd have to inevitably let go of the first major investment and pride of his life. The ultimate American dream.

"Okay," Raymond finally said as reality sank in. "Eddy, listen very carefully: Go to my bank account and withdraw the last of everything in it." He told his brother the particular branch and all the information needed to access his account. He also told him to send their mother back to Africa and to take a trip himself in order to resolve, in person, some of the most crucial family issues regarding land properties that he stood to inherit from their late father.

He went on to instruct that his Rebecca sold everything she could in the house as quickly as possible before foreclosure, and to use the proceeds to re-establish herself.

The properties in his Riverdale home alone, if sold at a fraction of their value, could fetch her as much as five thousand dollars. That, plus the Ford LTD, should enable her find a cheaper place to move in, enough to fix her up until she landed a job.

"Ray, there's a cashier's check you made out to the mortgage company, three of them at five hundred dollars each. What do you want me to do with them?" Ed said.

"What checks are you talking about?" Raymond said and switched the receiver to the other ear. He plugged his index finger inside the other ear to filter some of the noise in the common area.

"Actually, it was a return-to-sender mail. I believe you mailed it long time ago".

He instantly recalled that he had mailed those checks out for an arrears payment of his mortgage. Whatever the problem may have been, the envelope, which he had carefully sealed, addressed and stamped, was sent back. If he were to lose the house anyway, it could be a blessing in disguise that it failed to make it through to the mortgage company. Fifteen hundred dollars could be of great service to him in his current adverse circumstance.

"Send them to me. I'll decide what to do with them later. I know there's a whole lot that can be done," Raymond said, slightly relieved by this latest development. "Send them right away, okay?'

After dictating the prison's address to Ed, Raymond hung up. Fifteen hundred dollars could indeed stretch far enough. For one thing, it could serve for a sizable deposit toward retaining an attorney. If not, it could also boost the financial restraints of his common-law, providing the funds she'd need to rent an apartment to stay. She could then conveniently sell off the household properties, and keep the ones she'll need for herself. His little boy may not suffer much after all.

Raymond knew then he could do better than suicide. He'd temporarily suspend the idea, at least for the moment. If only he could hire a trustworthy defense lawyer, it could be a game changer. He could finally make bond and fight for his freedom.

The daunting task of scouting an affordable but credible attorney was well cut out for him. He'd have to commence immediately. He had a thousand five hundred dollars at his disposal.

Later that afternoon, Raymond began his search for the ultimate lawyer. Information he gathered from other inmates led him to contact a Mr. Walter M. Zeplin of the Law Offices of Foster and Zeplin, at their downtown Brooklyn office.

But he couldn't reach either of the partners immediately, which frustrated him. He resumed his bid to contact them the following day, still without success. They were either busy with another client or inside the courtroom, and inmates could not receive outside calls in lockup. It wasn't until Thursday at around two p.m. that he was able to reach one of the partners, Mr. Zeplin. He had just finished a take-out lunch in his office and, according to him, was snacking on some pretzels.

Their conversation was direct and in conformity with the customary attorney-client cordiality. Mr. Zeplin had told Raymond with firm assurance that whatever the outcome of the case, he would help him to the best of his ability. The concrete assurance made Raymond feel like he was about to be defended by Perry Mason.

Perhaps most humane of Mr. Zeplin, Raymond felt, was the lawyer's understanding of his meager financial resources, and his acceptance to assume representation for a down payment of fifteen hundred dollars. They settled at a fee of five thousand dollars for the entire case.

"Now let me be clear," Mr. Zeplin said emphatically. "The five thousand is only for the case in the district court. If the matter has to go to the appeals court, I will have nothing to do with it. I don't do appeals."

When Raymond was about to respond, a fistfight broke out between two inmates at the lobby, prompting him to pause and look.

The unit officer, a clean-shaven thirty-three-year old American-Indian ex-marine with an average height, sounded the alarm and he knew he had to conclude as quickly as possible. In just a few minutes, the entire unit would be swarmed with correction officers and a mandatory lockdown would be in effect.

Mr. Zeplin, overhearing the commotion, was quick to comment. "Is that a fight breaking out?" he said, his experience and instinct taking hold.

"Yes sir," Raymond said. The excitement from his prospect of hiring a lawyer held back his anger and disappointment for not having his say.

"Why don't you call me back after lockdown is lifted," he said, "I know you've got to go and, depending on how long your lockdown will last, if need be, call me back tomorrow same time."

"Ok," Raymond sighed and hung up.

Lockdown lasted forty-five minutes. The two Spanish fighting inmates had been handcuffed and sent away to Isolation, also known in the institution as *The Hole*. Raymond had inquired from his cellmate to learn that the fight was over television. One had wanted to watch a re-run of Oscar De La Hoya championship bout and the other insisted it had to be the live coverage of Knicks-Hawks game.

Raymond, almost dozing off in his top bunk bed, jumped down, shook himself alert and went straight to the telephone. He dialed and fortunately, he was able to reach Mr. Zeplin immediately.

They exchanged greetings.

Raymond was about to narrate the event leading to his arrest when the lawyer immediately interrupted him.

"Mr. Karr, we can't discuss your case over the phone. Attorney-client matters are privied and I know the phone you're using is an open line."

Oh I'm sorry," Raymond said, feeling disappointed that his eagerness to move it along was cut short. But he was understanding and appreciative of the lawyer's admonishment.

"That's ok," Mr. Zeplin said in a paternalistic voice. "But I'm quite familiar with such cases. Now, how do I get the fifteen hundred?"

Raymond went on to outline how the money was to be sent.

Whenever he received the money orders from his brother, which should be arriving any moment, he'd send them to the lawyer, by express mail, at his office address.

"That's fine, when would that happen?"

"Within a week," Raymond said. Of course he wished the lawyer would receive his retainer within minutes, but it was unfortunately beyond his capabilities.

That was one cash Raymond couldn't wait to spend.

"Send the retainer and we'll go from there. As soon as it gets to my office, I will travel to Otisville to meet with you, or better yet file a writ to have you brought down to Manhattan for an in-person consultation."

With the pen and paper, which he always carried along with him whenever he made phone calls, he wrote down the lawyer's address. They said goodbye and hung up.

Raymond walked back to his cell with a feeling of temporary relief.

One whole week of a daily mail call turned up hopeless. Raymond waited two dragging extra days, and if added the first three days he allowed for the U.S. mail process, it totaled twelve days of continuous uncertainty. After the fifth day when the mail did not arrive, he was certain it would arrive the next day. Each day that passed gave a new heightened assurance to the next. On three occasions, he had rushed forward to collect on a name he was sure was his but that the unit officer must have mispronounced, all to find out that he had heard wrong

He decided he had to telephone Ed to find out what was happening.

After the usual long hold, he got Ed on the line. Ed first revealed yet another shocker. "Dennis was arrested by Dulles International airport customs as he was returning from his trip to Africa," he said.

Shocking as that was, Raymond didn't feel like discussing it, at least not at the moment. It would have to come later. He was more interested in, and needed to discuss the fifteen hundred dollars Ed was supposed to have sent him in the mail.

"Raymond," Ed said. "About the money…, I had been threatened by the credit bureau, who vowed to freeze my bank account and withhold all of my earnings, and have me fired from my job if I failed to come up with the eighteen hundred dollars credit balance owed in my credit card."

Why Ed decided at such critical moment to pay his debt with his brother's money mystified Raymond. The credit card issue began four years earlier when, after graduation from Central State University in Edmond, Oklahoma, Ed wanted to move his family to Washington, DC so the two brothers would live closer to each other. But at that time, Ed had maxed out his credit card, which had a limit of a thousand two hundred dollars, and was hopelessly in default.

"Ray," Ed had said to Raymond, "I'd given up on my MasterCard payment. They just have to charge off on this one. I simply cannot handle it. I can't even afford the minimum payment anymore, and even when I do, it only covers their Interest."

Somewhat more financially stable, Raymond decided to come to the financial aid of his brother and volunteered to undertake the burden of credit repayment, in order that his brother could start anew with good credit establishment. Profoundly proud of his brother's academic achievement, Raymond had figured that Ed would be needing the help to stand on his own and provide for his wife and son. To expedite this, he had to pay five hundred dollars upfront for insurance coverage, which he felt was indirectly a penalty for delinquency. Then he sent payments of three hundred dollars, two hundred dollars, and another three hundred. Gradually, he built up the line of credit to an eighteen-hundred-dollar limit. He had just resumed monthly payments of thirty-five dollars at the time he took on the dooming task of drug courier.

Raymond felt his heart skip a beat. "Eddy," he said, his voice trembling in panic like a voyager in a sinking ship. "What do you mean by the credit bureau threatened to have you fired? Do you realize I'd been in this country longer than you have? I know the limits of bill collectors and they can't do that. Please don't lie to me or try anything phony at a time like this. Kindly send me my money. I really, really need it."

"What are you going to do with money in the prison anyway?" Ed said.

Raymond was so infuriated that he decided it wasn't worth his while trying to explain what he wanted to do with his own hard-earned money.

"Eddy, that's not the issue. The issue is that the money belongs to me. I decide what to do with it. I think as an adult, who knows what he needs to do, it is entirely up to me. The only thing I want you to do is send me those checks. Now one question; are you sending them or not?"

"I just told you what I want to do with them, and that's what I'll do," Ed said coldly.

Furious, Raymond hung up. It seemed like every time he tried to explore a possible solution to his looming problems, some obstacle got on his way. First was Kenny and Clyde who had literally run away from him. Then James disconnected his own telephone line just to avoid contact with him. Now even his brother had joined in the series of impediments, leaving him helplessly prison bound.

Angrily and tearfully, he went directly to his bed and climbed atop. An attempt on suicide again reclaimed his thoughts.

That evening, he skipped dinner to take a mental stock of everything, and to weigh his options. Ironically, the raging anger from the bitter disappointment over everything all of a sudden began to instill in him a burning desire to hang tough, just to surprise and disappoint those who thought he was finished. It must have been some kind of divine intervention.

After carefully weighing his options and deciding he needed to live and get back at his enemies, he discovered that he had never wanted so badly to live and prove himself again. He wasn't such a bad criminal, after all, and therefore needed not to die like one only to leave behind a legacy of infamy.

The rest of the evening, Raymond's thought shifted to Dennis and his ultimate arrest at a point of re-entry. They had claimed that Dulles International airport was the safest entry port. Raymond began to feel sorry for Dennis. He must have mind-wrestled with the temptation of going back to Lagos for a second drug courier errand. He had surprised Raymond when he saw him in Lagos, and now his nightmare had come true.

Still, whatever led to Dennis' demise was less of a concern to Raymond at that point. His hands were full with his own problems, and he would need all his mental resources channeled toward it.

Having slept for two hours, Raymond woke up to the 9 p.m. prison count. After count clear, Raymond sat on a chair in one corner of the common area, away from any distraction, to plan his strategy to deal with the enormous challenge he faced. Now that all hopes of retaining a competent attorney had been finally dashed by his brother, he knew he had to devise a strategy and set it into immediate motion. He concluded would be taking on the daunting task of defending himself in the rap against him. In other words, Raymond Karr, with absolutely no knowledge of criminal defense, will serve as his own lawyer.

First, Raymond would ensure that one wish be carried out. He wrote a letter to Rebecca directing her to do all the things he had planned to relay to his brother. He hoped it would take care of his deep concern on domestic problems and free up his mind to completely focus on his impending legal battle. He felt a bit relieved after mailing out the letter, then got down to business.

Chapter 21

PRE-TRIAL ERROR

Raymond Karr, who was about to take on a daunting task of a masquerade proportion, would caution everyone to never play a game of poker with the court of law. More so for a first-timer, for there may be a Ken Zimmerman, Esq. prosecuting. Raymond would learn that better yet refrain from unlawful conduct, period.

Having gone wobbly from the beginning when he agreed to join in on drug courier run, and down to his decision to take the matter to trial, he now realized how much he had damaged himself.

As soon as he was led inside the courtroom, he quickly informed the judge, through Mr. Cunningham, his court appointed lawyer, that he was waiving his right to a counsel and also his right to a speedy trial. His request on waiving his right to a counsel was quickly struck down by the judge, who insisted that he retained one. However, he was granted the waiver of a speedy trial.

Since he had chosen to go to trial, he decided he would be working with his public defender, Mr. Patrick Cunningham, since he couldn't afford one of his own. His defense strategy was to go along with the story he had told the DEA during his first two days at JFK airport hospital jail.

After being escorted out of the courtroom, he requested from the marshals a need to consult with his lawyer. The marshals, voicing no objection, called in Mr. Cunningham, who obliged immediately.

Mr. Cunningham requested a transfer from Raymond's cell to the attorney-client consultation room and it was immediately arranged and Raymond was in a secured office, where no one else could listing to their conversation.

"Mr. Cunningham," Raymond said, "I'd like to outline our defense strategy."

"Mr. Karr, you're going to plead guilty and that's it. No gimmicks and no waste of judicial resources here. Otherwise you will spend a very long term in prison. I guarantee it."

"No, Mr. Cunningham, not if you come to terms with the disturbing news that in Nigeria, the ruling Supreme Military Council had just decreed retro-actively that serving more than six months in jail in a foreign soil for drug offense mandates five hard years upon arrival in the country."

To make matters worse for him, the U.S. Congress had just overwhelmingly passed a legislation to mandatorily deport all convicts of foreign countries, who had been imprisoned for more than twelve months. What he wasn't going to tell his lawyer was that his real reason to go to trial was that it was the only shot at being set free, of course he could bribe himself out of an African jail. Also that he was so afraid of being kicked out of the country of his dream that he'd go to any length to avoid it.

Mr. Cunningham, uneasy, adjusted his seat and rubbed his chin. This stubborn bastard must be losing his mind, he thought as he looked away from Raymond.

Raymond imagined what it would be like to have to exist in the world for ten years, realizing he had a son, who would suffer the perilous poverty in America, and knowing there was nothing he could do about it. His son would have been meticulously cared for by relative custodians in his homeland, but the little boy's American mother would most probably object to any suggestion of sending him to Africa, and the U.S. laws were heavily in favor of maternal custody. For Raymond, ten years was simply too long a time to wait for anything- rejoining his family and rehabilitating himself.

He firmly chose to stick with his previous statement to the DEA, and for that, he took the initial damaging step. He wrote a lengthy and perjuring letter to the U.S. Attorney's office, standing by his previous statement. Since a plea agreement would send him to prison for three and a half years, and upon completion he'd be deported to do the five years mandatory term in Nigeria, he would rather take a chance on a trial. That could result in one of two alternatives-either he'd be acquitted and his freedom fully restored, or convicted and be sentenced to prison for five or more years, enough time to sit out the governmental era until hopefully a more reasonable and humane regime. From all the horrifying stories Raymond heard from his prison colleagues about incarceration, one came away better off spending ten years in a U.S. prison than a year in Kirikiri Maximum Security Prison in Lagos. Other drawbacks were the high chances of contracting tuberculosis or leprosy. That was if bedbugs did not eat one alive.

Since the prosecution was in possession of the hard evidence of the drugs, Raymond thought his best defense would be exactly what he had told the DEA, which was to lead them to Washington where they could apprehend Clyde the intended recipient of the substance. He was meant to believe that he had swallowed a substance that could improve his manhood, therefore unwittingly became a drug courier. He had never been a criminal defendant before, but from keeping up with the news of famous defendants and their lines of defense, he felt he'd have some chance of convincing one or two jurors.

There was one pressing issue to be resolved though for Raymond… he will need to try to convince his public defender, Mr. Cunningham, a task he knew would require a lengthy audience with him. However, Mr. Cunningham had declined to discuss the case with him, only insisted that he enter a guilty plea in court. Raymond had been warned by other inmates to not go to trial with a public defender if he was to have any chance at all, but he had no other choice than to stick with Mr. Cunningham.

Choosing to write a letter to Mr. Cunningham, he detailed his own dogmatic stance.

There was another important issue that Raymond had to consider before sticking with his story. He needed to avoid a perjury rap piled on his indictment by changing his testimony before taking to the witness stand. If he was to successfully convince at least one or two jurors, he couldn't change his story. Consistency, he reminded himself, would be crucial, especially considering the overwhelming evidence against him.

Raymond spent two days researching in the institution's makeshift law library only to inevitably find out he stood little or no chance of being acquitted. Still, it didn't seem to matter to him if he was also trying to avoid being released from a U.S. prison in three to four years to be deported and face another five hard years in Kirikiri. He just had to give himself a chance at survival. He felt he had already exercised a life-threatening poor judgment by caving in to becoming a drug courier, and now he had to fight to avoid prison in Lagos. It was a decision that would make a positive difference in the long end of this entire ordeal. To Raymond, it amounted to planning for future if the present was doomed.

Later in the week, which was the first week of November, Raymond received a formal Grand Jury indictment notice via US mail from Mr. Cunningham's office. It charged him with two counts of drug related offenses- one count of Importation of Controlled Substance and one count of Importation with Intent to Distribute a Controlled Substance. The docket stated on the plaintiff-defendant column as United States vs. Raymond Karr. The language of the indictment bugged his conscience. His dream had been a scenario that would have read 'United States' Raymond N. Karr, perhaps as a representative in some official capacity. The impending court appearance, which had been scheduled for one week from his receipt of the indictment, was to formally enter a plea. As far as Mr. Cunningham was concerned, he would be pleading guilty. But for him, it would be a plea of not guilty that would set the stage for the battle of his lifetime.

Raymond utilize the few days before his appearance to gather as much information as possible and prepare himself for the dreaded appearance in a Brooklyn federal courtroom.

The stone–faced duty officer's voice roared forcefully. "Okay, everyone, line up against the wall, turn around, spread your legs and place your hands on the wall. Move it!"

Raymond and his fellow inmates obeyed. All thirty-two of them lined up inside a narrow hallway, and were intensely frisked by six other correction officers. The inmate's names had been called out earlier at 8 p.m. to be marched in a single file from one unit of the prison compound to another. One hour later, the thirty-two inmates scheduled to appear in Brooklyn courtrooms at eight o'clock the next morning, had declared their properties that were to be shipped in cardboard boxes.

The protocol of leaving Otisville prison was the same as leaving MCC New York. Raymond and his fellow inmates were frisked and strip-searched, locked inside the cold bullpen for hours. All along clad only in prison jumpsuits, they were shackled and jam-packed in the Bureau of Prison's heavily fortified transport limo, which drove three hours to MCC jail.

Unlike in Otisville prison, where arrival prisoners had at least a day's rest, inmates arriving at MCC jail, usually at five-thirty a.m. remain in the bullpen until court hours when they were carted away to face the judge.

Raymond, exhausted from the all-night travel, and without a rest period, would be making his court appearance that morning.

His day's ordeal did not end there. He was held in the court's cold bullpen for some agonizing hours, and when he was finally called to take the defendant's stand, the courtroom clock struck at two p.m. But five minutes before he was led out of the bullpen, Mr. Cunningham had casually strolled in to see him. He desperately wanted to speak to the public defender, who couldn't even reply his letter or accept his collect calls.

"You're gonna see the judge, you're gonna formally enter a plea," he had whispered and crushed the remnant of a peppermint in his mouth. He carefully avoided looking at Raymond directly in his eyes.

Raymond was so angry at the sight of his court appointed lawyer that he resisted the urge to curse loudly at him. He wisely chose to ignore him in protest. Mr. Cunningham, unmoved, opened his suitcase and produced a vanilla folder that he labeled his client's name, before exiting the bullpen.

"Counsel, are you ready?" the judge said, lowering his eyeglasses to look at Mr. Cunningham.

"Yes, your honor," Mr. Cunningham said and cleared his throat.

The judge then turned to Mr. Zimmerman, who was sitting by the prosecutor's desk. "Counsel?"

Mr. Zimmerman stood up immediately and acknowledge his readiness to proceed.

Mr. Cunningham immediately apologized to the judge for his late arrival, and after a few discussions, he hurriedly came to sit beside Raymond. Raymond had now come to realize that his all morning, agonizing stay in the courthouse cold bullpen was because his lawyer had been late on the first call, which was at ten a.m. He imagined that he could have been in his cell sleeping off the all-night grueling journey but his damned lawyer's action punished him pretty severely.

In a confidential low voice, Mr. Cunningham whispered and began to educate Raymond on the process of entering a guilty plea. Raymond wished he could punch him and get away with it.

But he was too worn out and sleepy to fully pay attention to the proceeding.. Having to stay inside the cold bullpen all morning and afternoon had sapped the edge off his ability to comprehend. All he could indicate to Mr. Cunningham was that he wanted to enter a flat out not guilty plea.

Mr. Cunningham was highly infuriated over his client's desire to enter a not guilty plea, but managed to conceal his enraging demeanor from the seemingly mild-mannered judge. The District Judge, Honorable Simon Boscolo, demanded to be briefed on the method by which the drug was imported. Mr. Cunningham glanced at the Assistant U.S. Attorney Mr. Zimmerman, and both men grinned mockingly at each other before Mr. Zimmerman finally replied,

"Via stomach ingestion, your honor."

Raymond only stood and watched helplessly, humbly joining his hands in front as the proceedings progressed. Though feeling surprisingly comfortable with the new judge, he wasn't confident in his ability to put up a strong defense, but he at least felt that regardless of the outcome, there'd certainly be fairness from the judge, a welcoming feeling.

Bespectacled and in his late forties, and with curly hair that showed signs of grayness, Judge Boscolo was the perfect image of judicial prudence. Throughout Raymond's first six months of agony, appearing before Judge Boscolo was his only bright moments.

At the conclusion of his appearance before Judge Boscolo, Raymond was sent back to MCC at 4 p.m., and just like the previous court attendance, had to remain in the bullpen for two hours awaiting the clearance of the institutional count. As soon as the big iron door opened, the officer on duty conducted a thorough search and then made him undergo the ritual of prisoner intake, before handing him a large Express mail envelope addressed to him. It was from his common-law. She had received his letter of instructions on what to do with his household properties, and had just replied.

Raymond carefully opened the envelope and retrieved a roughly folded white sheet carelessly scribbled on both sides. The sight of the sheet warned him there was unpleasantness waiting. The letter simply began with. "Raymond, how stupid can you be?"

Throughout the first page of the letter, Rebecca went on to accuse him of using the "F" word during the argument that had preceded her departure. She clearly indicated that issue as priority in the letter, stating she only decided to write him at all because she had his son. She would repeat, "How stupid can you be" three more times in the letter.

But the letter also revealed more troubling developments. James had paid Rebecca only a hundred dollars for the China wooden, six-sitter dining table that had cost Raymond twelve hundred dollars just four months earlier, and had moved out of the house, leaving no trace of contact. He had lied to Rebecca about how much the dining table had cost, convincing her Raymond had paid only two hundred dollars for it, and then offered her half of that amount as a deposit, and failed to show up with the other half as agreed upon.

Furthermore, another close friend had beaten Rebecca to the Ford LTD sedan, falsely claiming Raymond owed him an unspecified amount of money, therefore, he had to inherit the automobile as restitution. The news kept unfolding about Raymond's expensive properties being sold to friends at ridiculously giveaway prices.

Finally, Rebecca accused Raymond's friends of repeatedly attempting to take sexual advantage of her then followed with the most mind boggling news. The rumor spread around was that Raymond gave out the information that aided Dulles International airport Custom agents in apprehending Dennis, and that Raymond had also tried to set up Kenny to be apprehended by the same agency.

The entire content of the letter brought back the idea of suicide. He was in deep trouble, and not only he had been deserted by his brother and friends, but had also been taken advantage of. He couldn't wait to be transferred back to Otisville prison where he had initially thought of committing suicide. In his thoughts, the journey to Lagos had been not only the loss of freedom he so dreaded but had evolved to an unmitigated disaster.

Raymond thought about Dennis during the bus ride to Otisville. All evening since reading the letter, Raymond's agony of what his common-law wife stated happened to his properties, and his thoughts of his planned suicide, overshadowed any interest he could have had about the ludicrous allegation of him giving Dennis away to Dulles airport Customs authorities. Even the pain from the so-called bullpen therapy and the all-night journey, was undermined by the deluge of heartbreak Raymond had incurred from reading Fran's letter. He was bewildered as to why his common-law had treated him so poorly. After all they once loved each other. Despite her deserting Raymond for another man, Raymond had literally willed all his belongings to her. She seemed to completely lack any compassion. Raymond's brother and friend displayed insensitivity by cashing in on his unfortunate situation.

He had probably unwittingly contributed to Dennis' arrest. It occurred to him that when he was ordered by the DEA to list three of his closest friends and their contact addresses, he had included Dennis Metu, and by so doing, had compromised Dennis' own security. It was customary for the DEA to track down individuals who traveled abroad, and if the names Raymond had listed showed that one of the individuals had traveled outside the country, there was a probability he had left for the same purpose as Raymond did. Moreover, Raymond had told the agents that if he knew the substance he had swallowed was drugs, he would have flown Lufthansa Airline through a less secured Dulles International airport. After a careful calculation, Raymond conceded he may have indeed been guilty of the rumored allegations.

Every conceivable notion pointed to Raymond's conduct during the interrogation by the DEA. At the moment, Raymond had a lot to think about. Dennis had no child to worry about, and no investment property to lose. He would probably lose his BMW, but what was a sixty-five hundred dollars car compared to a nearly fifty thousand dollars cash investment in his house? Dennis had profited from drug and had purchased his car, while he hadn't spent a dime he didn't work hard for.

Raymond and the other prisoners went through all the normal harsh realities of Otisville, and at about 9 a.m., were finally resting rather comfortably in their warm cell beds. For the despondent young man, it was time to plan for the end of his life.

His first attempt came at lunch. His colleagues had tried unsuccessfully to persuade him to go along with them for lunch.

"Come on, Raymond," one of them said. "Stop being a coward and let's go eat. Put it all in the hands of God. Why kill yourself over something you don't have control of."

What an eerily prophetic statement.

He wouldn't go along with his friends because he needed to be alone. He knew he could conceal and smuggle out a hard plastic knife from the chow hall. After his fellow inmates had left for the dining hall, which was located in a large building three minutes walk outside from inmate housing units, Raymond slowly walked far behind until he arrived and chose a secluded corner, surrounded by other dining tables mostly occupied by a group of Haitians, who knew nothing about him. It was a table for six but only Raymond and one other inmate, a stranger, sat and ate quietly.

Carefully Raymond took the plastic knife and tucked it inside his sock on his left leg. It occurred to him he might need two just in case, and when he attempted to steal the knife from an adjacent vacant table, he noticed an officer was watching. He panicked and had to let go.

As most inmates had finished dining and left the hall, he stood up and proceeded to the exit, where a group of officers stood guard, routinely conducting random searches. If Raymond went alone, there'd be a good chance he will be frisked, therefore, he fished out a group of Spanish inmates and joined them.

As they marched out of the main exit, one of the officers yelled out. "You!" he said, pointing directly at Raymond. "Shake it down!"

He knew he was in trouble. He faced a possible lock down in the Special Housing Unit for a solitary confinement if the knife was searched out. That could really be damaging to his ambition, as well as traumatizing to his state of being.

Raymond assumed the normal search position of hands-on-the-wall and spread his legs. The officer began to pat him down, and surprisingly when he found the knife, he simply confiscated it and said rather jokingly, "You're taking a knife to the housing unit, who are you trying to get rid of?"

It was a hard plastic knife, and posed no serious threat, except for a well calculated suicide plan like Raymond's.

"I forgot I had it," he mumbled in sheer panic.

"Yeah right," the Correction Officer said and waved him through, half-jokingly offering a stern warning.

Disappointed but unrelenting, Raymond planned another try at dinner. Despite his methodical approach toward the triple manned exit, he was scouted by a stone-faced officer, who immediately blocked his efforts. Once again, he escaped with a verbal warning. He'd have to try again the next morning after breakfast.

He went to sleep that night, forced by the institution's 11:30 p.m. m lockdown. In the heart of sleep Raymond was awakened by the nightmarish dream of the life he suddenly found himself in a desperate hurry to exit. In the dream, his little son stood crying vehemently, while his father was being dragged to a cop car by two bulky uniformed policemen. Raymond pleaded with the unrelenting henchmen to allow him to secure his son's well-being before being executed.

"Why can't I have my daddy like everyone else?" he heard his son yell in the dream. "Daddy, please don't leave me. Can't you see I love you?"

Raymond was helplessly subdued and his heart was totally shattered by the mesmerizing look and sadness of his son's weeping. A deluge of fear engulfed him and he woke up for good, thanking his God it was all a dream, but also saddened he was strictly confined in reality and was in no situation to hug his beloved son.

Raymond was glad it was only a dream. His son was still a baby, and strong and happy, and would one day re-unite with his daddy. At the moment, he wasn't aware of the troubles daddy had brought on himself.

Raymond prayed, entrusting everything in the hands of the Almighty. He followed with series of unanswerable questions. Why would he want to take his own life and leave his beloved son an orphan? How would that weigh in the hearts and minds of relatives and acquaintances? He couldn't escape the questions.

Sometime along the eventful night, Raymond once again decided against suicide. That dramatic reversal would signal the core of his renewed ambition to put on a strong fight on two fronts - to battle in court for his freedom, and if he lost, to sum up the courage to serve a lengthy term in a U.S. prison.

The month of November was hard. Christmas songs echoed from radios and television sets. Santa Claus could be seen making his preparations for his annual journey from the North Pole to across the heartland of America. Raymond had stumbled into the wrong America, and wouldn't be there to visit Santa with his son, something he had always done with neighbors' children, and wanted so badly to do it with his own son.

Meanwhile Raymond's letter to the United States Attorney denying a clause in his indictment, which stated that he knowingly and intentionally committed the crime, was copied and given to Judge Boscolo by Mr. Zimmerman the Assistant United States Attorney. As a result, he was scheduled for an impromptu courtroom appearance the last week of November. All his prison colleagues exerted an insurmountable pressure on him to accept a plea for sentencing of a minimum of forty-one months, and a maximum of fifty-one months. Raymond had carefully weighed his options and subconsciously tilted toward heeding their advice. He was still very much terrified by the prospect of a lengthy prison term. Much more troubling was the Lagos prison and the new Nigerian Decree 33. The thought of that alone made it easier for him to decide to risk a courtroom battle.

Raymond stood before judge Boscolo, with Mr. Cunningham standing beside him exchanging legal documents with the court clerk and Mr. Ken Zimmerman. Raymond's jaw was still sore from a sucker punch that morning in the MCC bullpen when he tried to mediate in a fight between a macho Panamanian and an African-American body builder, both inmates at the MCC jailhouse.

Somehow inside the court's holding cell, he changed his mind again about taking his case to the jury and decided on the plea bargain. As he sat alone, cold and tired from the all-nighter, he was looking forward to meeting privately with his lawyer, Mr. Cunningham, so as to go through the fine prints, but Mr. Cunningham never showed up. As usual, Mr. Cunningham met with him after he had been escorted inside the courtroom to stand before the judge. To Raymond's surprise, Mr. Cunningham made a shocking statement to the Judge Boscolo.

"Your honor, Mr. Karr had already entered a Not Guilty plea," Mr. Cunningham said.

Raymond turned his head to look at Mr. Cunningham. Mr. Cunningham, who avoided eye contact with him, turned the other way to face Mr. Ken Zimmerman the AUSA. Raymond felt he had been purposely betrayed. No wonder Mr. Cunningham didn't show up for their usual brief attorney-client consultation prior to court appearance. He had always thought defense lawyers should sit longer than mere two minutes in holding cells with their clients, especially when their freedom is on the line. In a letter Raymond wrote to Mr. Cunningham, he had indicated that he would be willing to plead guilty if the clause, "Knowingly and Intentionally," was deleted from the indictment since he actually did not know it was containing heroin. Whether or not that was a plausible cause to plead in a court of law was supposed to have been determined by his lawyer. In any case, he hoped the public defender knew what the hell he was doing.

However, he was now stuck with an eleventh hour decision of a Not Guilty plea in the wake of Mr. Cunningham's pre-emptive statement. AUSA, Mr. Zimmerman, alerted Judge Boscolo that the government had decided to sustain the two charges levied against Raymond, even if he eventually decides to plead guilty. That was in sharp contrast with the offer Raymond thought was infinitely open to him, which stressed that the second count, "Intent to Distribute' would be dropped upon Raymond's acceptance of the plea bargain. For Mr. Cunningham, it was yet another frustrating moment, and it was most evident when he immediately requested a speedy trial.

At the conclusion of the court session, Mr. Cunningham called Raymond in for a brief consultation. Immediately he approached Mr. Cunningham inside the narrow conference room, the public defender yelled at Raymond like an angry dad.

"You're going down the drain, Mister," he said.

As Raymond was about to explain, Mr. Cunningham cut him off.

"Okay, okay. Next week we pick a jury," he said, still livid.

Mr. Cunningham had repeatedly told him he would be laughed at by the jury who would certainly convict him in seconds if he went along with his defense strategy.

"Mr. Karr, you're a grown man. You know there's no way you couldn't have known what you had inside your stomach. Your incredible story of juju doctor and whoever his priest is, who would perform a miracle you claim could improve your manhood, if I tell you for a second I believe you, I'm a damned liar. And so would anyone else. Don't do this to yourself."

Raymond was thrown into confusion as his lawyer, who had just entered a not guilty plea on his behalf, would scream at him with such venom and wouldn't even want to listen to what he had to say. And now he's telling Raymond how he was doomed.

Mr. Cunningham was right though. Still, Mr. Cunningham didn't know Raymond was secretly keeping to himself his real intention. Mr. Cunningham wanted to help him negotiate a minimum prison sentence for what he truly deserved. For Raymond, it was a bid to take a long chance on being found not guilty, and if not, receive a lengthier jail term to avoid having to go to another jail in Lagos. It was becoming a circumstance of hallucination for Raymond Karr.

"Mr. Cunningham, I have an article I'd like you to read," he said and reached in his legal file folder for a report on male organ grinding in Nigeria he had clipped off of a Philadelphia Inquirer daily newspaper.

Raymond found it and handed it to Mr. Cunningham, who glanced at it before he reluctantly accepted the news clip. "Perhaps sir, if you grew up in a society that believed in bizarre practices like this, you wouldn't be such a damned liar if you say you believe my story."

Mr. Cunningham took out his glasses and wore it. After reading the headline, he quipped,

"Oh!" he said. "Maybe we should go to trial then."

Mr. Cunningham went on to read the entire article, which was in a short column.

The article narrated reports of mysterious disappearance of genitals among some men in a city in eastern Nigeria, an incident that led to the accusation that some wealthy businessmen were complicit. According to the article, luck ran out on a prominent wealthy chief who was allegedly responsible for the disappearance of two people's male organs. The wealthy chief became a victim of vigilante justice when he was clobbered to death, along with his chauffeur, by the people he ruled over.

"This is definitely a strong evidence of the culture," Mr. Cunningham said and rested his back on the chair then removed his eye glasses and rubbed his eyes with the back of his hand.

After digesting the article, Mr. Cunningham took a deep breath and exhaled. He seemed stunned by the article he had just read. He was totally convinced, in Raymond's opinion, but still wouldn't strategize with him for the upcoming trial. Mr. Cunningham inserted the article in a file in his briefcase. "We'll see," he concluded.

Mr. Cunningham closed the briefcase and cradled it. "Well, we pick a jury in a week or week and half."

"Mr. Cunningham, what's new with my money, which the custom agents are still withholding? I believe I explained the circumstance in the letter I wrote you," Raymond reminded the public defender.

"I've not had the opportunity to look into that. I'll have some information on that by the day of jury selection," he said casually.

He stood up to signal the end of the meeting and opened the door. The Marshal strolled in immediately to handcuff Raymond. After securing the cuffs, he escorted him back to the bullpen, where a zoo of angry prisoners yelled and cursed at no one in particular, protesting over the harsh condition in the cold holding cell. Soon all inmates who came to court were all transported back to MCC, and the severe headache that was triggered by Raymond's aching jaw escalated. Raymond rested his head on the jail's flat bed, and dozed off to end another day of the life as an apprehended criminal.

The jury selection was meticulously conducted, a process quite typical of Judge Boscolo's usual professionalism. The selection began at 2 o'clock Wednesday. Earlier that morning, he had made a brief appearance in the courtroom at which point Mr. Cunningham, in introducing his line of defense, revealed to Judge Boscolo he would be calling to the witness stand a New York college professor of arts with specialty in African culture. The professor was to testify that a situation occurred in Nigeria, whereby a vast majority obsessively believed in the spiritual works of traditional juju cult priests, who ultimately enjoy government recognition.

Mr. Cunningham's cheer and surprising benevolence instantly lit up Raymond's weakened spirit. Raymond was, as usual, extremely tired from the all-night journey from Otisville, and finally had something to cheer for. Moreover, it helped erase some of the doubts he had about the public defender's enthusiasm in defending him, although he was still very much concerned that they hadn't sat down together to iron out the key elements of their defense strategy. He still hadn't asked Raymond for his side of the story, and he could sense trouble coming out of it.

With the notion that Mr. Cunningham actually discussed his case with someone outside the Brooklyn courthouse, Raymond assumed the public defender knew what would be necessary to effectively put on a defense strong enough to sway at least one or two jurors. Suddenly, Raymond began to see Mr. Cunningham on his side.

Opening statements was scheduled to commence at 10 a.m. the following morning. Raymond was back to MCC where at 8 o'clock that evening, he was shockingly called up again to pack up his properties for a transfer back to Otisville prison.

He was in the worst state of body and mind as the long awaited trial began with opening statements from both Mr. Zimmerman and Mr. Cunningham. It had been a horrible forty-eight hours, having been transferred to both prisons six times. When he was called up the previous night for the transfer back to Otisville, he had protested vehemently, explaining to the female Correction Officer that he would be appearing in Brooklyn court in the morning for a trial. But she wouldn't budge, and no other officer could override her decision. Raymond had no choice than make himself available for the so-called bullpen therapy.

Upon arrival at Otisville prison, he was immediately notified he would be staying behind in the holding cell to be returned back to MCC for his court appearance. Raymond was a criminal, and therefore couldn't raise his voice beyond a certain limit, despite the outrage. He felt like a dried shrimp in the courtroom when the trial began – and he was completely worn out.

Before his courtroom appearance in the usual security protocol, he and Mr. Cunningham had met briefly inside the attorney-client chamber.

"Mr. Karr, this is Bob Vickerman, a law student at the New York

University. Bob would be assisting in your defense."

Raymond shook his hand and went directly to the matter.

"I hope you raise the issue of Agent Jacobo's refusal of my appeal to monitor a phone call from Clyde, or have Clyde visit me with undercover police in Washington to pick up the balloons," Raymond said. He felt it would be crucial to establish the fact that he had tried to prove to the agents his story was the truth, and that he was unduly denied the opportunity.

Back in Otisville before the day of jury selection, he had prayed hard to his God to help make a final decision on whether or not he should take his case to trial, or simply accept the plea offer. It was a special prayer, and in the end, he asked his God to lead him from there onward. At a certain point, he was reconsidering his options since it was the last chance to accept the plea offer. If he sought for restitution, he would probably have it if Mr. Cunningham pushed hard as he had promised he would.

Just about the time all inmates to be transported to New York City were to check in their properties, he ran into an inmate, who showed him a Washington Post article. According to the article, some students apprehended for drug trafficking in Nigeria were executed by firing squad in a retroactive law decreed by the military government. According to the article, the law was decreed one year after the students were arrested for their crimes and imprisoned.

Foolery for Raymond was the order of the day in the whole mess. He foolishly interpreted this coincidence as a signal from his God for him to go ahead with the trial, and that decision became final. Although not quite confident with the public defender, he'd have to go along with him. That was all he had. With some luck, the public defender would be able to sway a juror or two.

Chapter 22

JUDGMENT DAY

The trial was a circus. The courtroom was called to order, although it was scantily occupied. Only three women and two men were in the public area. Four other lawyers, who were awaiting their own cases, occupied one side of the front row seats, leaving the other side completely empty. Opposite one end of the jury box sat about ten casually dressed NYU law students, notes and pens on hands. Two interns sat at the prosecution's desk, along with Mr. Zimmerman the lead attorney, and a male assistant counsel, a fiftyish Asian-American wearing a bow tie. Almost every lawyer present in the courtroom dressed in a black or blue suit.

The male US marshal doubling as the court's bailiff, white, dressed in a crisply ironed black and white uniform, ordered all to stand and the judge briskly walked in and sat in his high bench. The marshal then ordered all to be seated. The court stenographer, a chubby white woman in her late forties with a red hair, adjusted her eyeglasses, which she tied with a string to hang around her neck when it wasn't needed, stretched her fingers right above the machine in readiness for action.

It all began with opening statements from Mr. Zimmerman, the lead attorney for the prosecution, and then Mr. Cunningham on behalf of Raymond Karr. When it was his turn, Mr. Cunningham outlined to the seated jury a very brief summary of the differences in culture between the American people and African people, and their traditional belief in cults. He concluded by admitting to the jury that the defense would not deny the evidence shown to them by the prosecutor, Mr.

Zimmerman, but that everything would come into clear picture once the defense took its turn. His nervousness was so obvious, depicted by his trembling hands and rattling voice. Raymond hated himself for the embarrassment that he was feeling on behalf of his unworthy counsel, even in the face of his own demise.

The prosecution was scheduled to call their witnesses to stand that same day, and the defense the next day. Mr. Zimmerman called up Agent Jacobo, who testified he suspected Raymond's conduct at the Customs gate, and had to call him up for interrogation. He went on to narrate the rest of the story, twisting it a little bit to soothe.

Mr. Cunningham's cross-examination of Agent Jacobo further highlighted the defense folly. First, he stood up and asked the agent a question no one in the courtroom couldn't understand. Naturally, the agent admitted he didn't comprehend, but managed to restate something he had said during his testimony. It was enough for Mr. Cunningham, who then spent minutes of silence trying to search his mind to frame another question. If there were motives behind his questions, only he understood them.

"Mmmm... Mr. Jacobo..." Mr. Cunningham looked down and scratched his forehead, nervously pacing up and down in front of the jury box. "When you suspected my client at the Custom gate, did you also...scratch...scratch the question," he equivocated, waving off his right hand, the left hand in and out of his side pocket.

Mr. Cunningham managed to ask another aimless question and then ended with, "Scratch it." He tried a couple of more times before admitting he had no further question. He never raised the issue he deemed crucial for his defense—why the agent declined Raymond's request to go to Washington and track down Clyde.

Raymond watched Mr. Cunningham with utter dismay. In his mind, he was thinking of all the freedom expectations that were vanishing rapidly. He thought he had a good chance of avoiding time in prison. Sitting, cross-armed and thinking deeply, he envisioned ahead to the next few years and saw nothing but time.

Another customs agent took the stand to testify that he personally witnessed Raymond when he was using the toilet, and saw the balloons being released from his anus. He recounted how many he had ejected at each interval. The agent, Raymond recalled, was the same guard who denied him a request to speak with an attorney, dismissing him and emphatically insisted that he would be pleading guilty. As the Agent made his way toward the witness stand, Raymond had immediately reminded Mr. Cunningham of the Agent's outrageous remark, and urged that the issue be raised before the court. Mr. Cunningham nodded approvingly.

Mr. Zimmerman told the judge he had no further questions for the witness. Raymond, unsure what to expect, looked at Mr. Zimmerman and inwardly admired his youth and professional accomplishment, surprised that he had not yet developed any traceable hatred for the young prosecutor. Never mind that this was the man who was vociferously trying to take away his freedom. But that was just inside the courtroom. Outside when he was waiting in the bullpen, he had been outright jealous of him. For one thing, the prosecutor grimly reminded him of his own imminently failing ambition to go to George Washington medical school and become a doctor.

Mr. Cunningham stood up from his chair and walked to the jury box, looking confused. "I have no further questions, your honor," he said.

Finally for the prosecution, DEA Agent DiGiovanni took the stand and testified that Raymond had, in his statement in the Agent's office, fabricated the story of the juju cult, and narrated how he came in contact with a fictitious name "Ike." After the agent's testimony, Mr. Cunningham asked the first full question and then gave a few more aborted attempts, before asking the court to excuse Agent DiGiovanni.

One member of the jury hinted to another sitting next to him that the case was not going too well for the defense. Upon overhearing that comment, Mr. Cunningham immediately called the judge to attention. Judge Boscolo, who evidently was determined to conduct a fair trial, dismissed the juror, and the court proceeded with twelve jurors and one alternate.

The government rested their case pretty soon. Raymond was somewhat relieved for the fact that there was no smoking gun. No surprising witness had come forward to testify he saw him in Lagos swallowing the drugs, and none came out to say that he or she saw Raymond accepting the task of flying to Lagos for the purpose of ingesting drugs. Most of the telephone log had been pulled to link him with a drug transaction. It meant to Raymond the government hadn't proven he had knowingly and intentionally swallowed drugs to bring them into the country. That he was caught ingested with balloons of drugs wasn't the issue in this case. The bone of contention was whether he knew the substance was heroin, and if he intentionally accepted importing them into the United States for distribution. It would be up to him to prove his own side of the story.

Judge Boscolo asked Mr. Cunningham to choose between continuing the case to call in defense witnesses and postponing the case until the following day, as originally scheduled. The government witnesses had been as brief as possible, leaving enough time to continue if they decided. However, Mr. Cunningham had scheduled the professor for the following morning, and to continue with the defense that day would amount to dropping a crucial witness.

The judge excused the jury for a break, while the defense considered its options, prompting Mr. Cunningham and the law student to have the U.S. marshals escort Raymond to the attorney-client chamber.

Inside the chamber, Mr. Cunningham and the law student he had brought along to help in his defense insisted they continue the trial without the professor's testimony on his behalf.

"If I call him to stand, the prosecutor's gonna ask him if African tradition includes wrapping drugs in black electrical wire tape and swallowing them to be brought inside the United States," Mr. Cunningham said, guessing Raymond's reaction.

Mr. Zimmerman had used the term "black electrical wire tape" several times during his opening statements to undermine any future testimony from the defense that would characterize the balloons as resembling a fruit the size of a walnut, just like he had claimed earlier.

Mr. Zimmerman's strategy apparently took its toll on Mr. Cunningham, and might as well have done likewise on the jury. Raymond's two defense attorneys brought him to reasoning with them.

There was also another obstacle to their proceeding with the trial, one that he alone could weigh—his being called to the witness stand. He was so tired and worn out from the sleepless nights that he couldn't even stand upright for more than two minutes without leaning against the wall, or for that matter, make any sense if Mr. Zimmerman's flurry of questions began to unravel during cross-examination. Again, Mr. Cunningham and his aide were hell bent on speeding up the proceeding and found excuses enough to support their advice.

"Well, as I've said repeatedly, the jury will convict you in a second. You're worse off now than you were before the trial even began, and if you take the stand, you'd be worse off than you are right now. Why don't you let me use my summation to argue out the second count, since the first's already lost? You'd save your ass from perjury by not taking the witness stand to tell your lies under oath," Mr. Cunningham said to Raymond.

Raymond was adamant. "Mr. Cunningham, if we've got to proceed today, I must take the stand to testify on my own behalf." He felt he was in bad enough shape that he was compelled to take on the case himself. Not taking the witness stand would obviously signal to the jury that he was hiding incriminating fact. Any juror would return a guilty verdict on a defendant, who remained tight-lipped. If nothing else, he could win an emotional plea to the jury if only he could eloquently narrate his social status and the life threatening predicament of the aftermath if he was sent to prison. Mr. Cunningham was out to derail his chances of securing a not-guilty verdict. Mr. Cunningham had even failed to question the agents about his efforts to persuade them to pursue an undercover plot in order to track down the real owner of the drugs, their refusal to grant him a telephone call to an attorney, and the rest of the inhumane treatments he encountered.

Not only had Mr. Cunningham cancelled the anticipated crucial testimony from the college professor, he was persuading Raymond to further rest the entire defense on his sore shoulders. In Raymond's calculation, there hadn't been any defense whatsoever, and he figured he'd be better off without Mr. Cunningham dismal *scratch it scratch it* defense strategy.

The nervous fever of having to lie under oath suddenly caught up with Raymond, just after Mr. Cunningham gave up his efforts. In a few minutes of further thought, Raymond felt like he was totally in control of his every motion, thought or word. Still, especially intimidating was the fact that not only did he have to place his right hand on the Holy Bible but would also be looking Judge Boscolo straight in his eyes while lying. That thought watered down his courage, and the pressure to reverse his decision to mount the witness stand drastically increased as he was being escorted back to the courtroom by the two marshals. For some reason, the marshals displayed open hostility toward Raymond, cruelly gripping his wrists with tight cuffs and pushing and dragging him from door to door, cursing at him. Mentally, he cursed Mr. Cunningham, who took a different route to the courtroom, for deciding that they proceed with their defense the same day. He probably would have chosen not to take the witness stand had he felt that nervous and thought the whole thing over one more time.

However, it was an irreversible situation and firstly Raymond had to do his very best to arrest the nerve wreck.

The real circus began with lead questions from Mr. Cunningham.

"Mr. Karr, you traveled to Lagos for a visit with your relatives. What happened?"

Raymond wasn't quite sure what Mr. Cunningham wanted out of his lead question, but rather than appear dismally confused, he simply began to tell his story. He visibly trembled and spoke timidly as his case began to unravel. He did everything wrong, from wrestling with his memory to explaining the concept of juju cult practices, down to not speaking directly into the microphone. Even when he made his initial comments, he noticed that almost all the members of the jury strained to hear him. He felt like a clown amidst a grief stricken audience. He felt his accent become a huge impediment. A couple of jurors shouted out loud "excuse me?" a number of times to signal they were having hard time comprehending.

Meanwhile, the miscuing lead questions from Mr. Cunningham had Raymond working real hard just to make out what he was thinking in his lead questions. Just when Raymond thought they finally would be in sync, Mr. Cunningham fired another confusing question. "What's the distance from Lagos to Owerri as measured in Nigerian metric system?"

Mr. Cunningham was probably trying to prove the journey took only few hours, allowing Raymond's return to Lagos the same day. But Raymond estimated the five hundred miles to be more than eight hundred kilometers.

"Five hundred miles…. I'd say about eight hundred kilometers,"

Raymond said.

It was a wrong answer considering Mr. Cunningham's motive was to have him clarify that it was five hundred kilometers, not miles. Raymond realized that rather too late.

"That's almost a whole day's journey," Mr. Cunningham said rather rhetorically.

At the conclusion of Mr. Cunningham's questions, Raymond delivered a long, aggravating speech that made him an object of further hatred. He read a three-page statement which he had prepared one day before his first departure from Otisville prison for the jury selection. He had showed a copy to Mr. Cunningham during one of their brief attorney-client meetings.

Raymond began by addressing the judge, and then moved on to ladies and gentlemen of the jury.

"My case is not just a case of one of many Africans who are looking for means to circumvent punishment for their offenses. This is the case of Raymond Karr, whose misguided effort to improve himself made him a victim of a diabolical plan to export illegal substance into the United States."

Raymond could clearly see the look of disgust in the faces of the jurors when he paused to sip on the water. As he followed with the story of his background, he noticed most of the men and women in the jury box had stopped listening, facing the other way. But he continued anyway.

"My lifestyle was out of place with many people. I trusted those I said were my friends, but was deceived many times. Bribery and corruption was the name of the game."

Raymond went into details of his stay in the United States, his education, marriage, and on and on. All were so irrelevant of the criminal charges against him.

To solicit sympathy from the jury, Raymond read, "Back in 1985/86, I joined the American Cancer Society in a program called 'The Road to Recovery.' Under the program, we volunteered our time to help transport cancer patients to area hospitals and back to their residences using our personal cars."

Still when Raymond paused to observe, the jury reaction was simply cold. Some of them made disgusting gestures at him, while others mockingly pretended to be yawning.

Perhaps the most outrageous came when Raymond read examples of other incidents.

"Ladies and gentlemen," he read. "Think back at a time in the past when a friend or relative of yours had made you do something that you really did not want to do. Think of when you did something just because a friend had recommended it to you, and you failed. Yes, my story sounds ridiculous, but so was the story of an innocent man in Chicago not too long ago, when he was arrested and subsequently charged with the murder of a man and his pregnant wife. Can you imagine what could have happened if the true story didn't come out from the brother of the accuser? An innocent man would have wound up in jail just as the prosecution wants me to wind up in jail, since they don't believe my story..."

Mr. Zimmerman's impatience and outrage manifested in his facial expression, and he quickly interjected. "Objection, your honor, the defendant's stories are irrelevant to this case."

"Objection overruled. Are you almost finished, Mr. Karr?" the obviously kind-spirited judge said, looking at Raymond. He was sure Judge Boscolo was hoping he'd come to his senses and read between the lines.

It was only at the end of the day that Raymond realized Judge Boscolo had rather ended his foolery, but was being careful not to undermine his self-defense before the jury. But Raymond said he had a few more words and went on to read another page and half.

He concluded with, "Thanks your honor, thank you ladies and gentlemen of the jury, and God bless your great country."

Later that day, Raymond pictured himself in a jury box at the end of a long day of sitting and watching a criminal tell such insulting untrue story. He would be cursing the defendant by now. Right from the start of his speech, he noticed a lady juror hatefully roll her eyes while turning her head the other way, mumbling a silent curse at him. He believed she said 'bastard' but could have been wrong. He just wasn't so sure. Whatever it was, he was it. After the first minute or so, each time he looked up to face the jury, all the men and women turned their heads away.

Mr. Zimmerman's brutal cross-examination of Raymond felt like a heavy weight boxer's punch, and exposed Raymond's poor defense strategy for what it was. The feisty AUSA was readily handy with all the physical evidence needed to prove beyond every reasonable doubt Raymond had planned ahead to visit Lagos on a drug courier mission. Surprisingly, he also had the receipt for the one night at the Hotel Wentworth. Raymond, nervous as he was, couldn't wait to find out the evidentiary value of a common hotel receipt. Mr. Zimmerman's exhibition of the receipt slip was meant to incriminate him with the signature he nonchalantly signed only manifesting his first and middle names, attempting to convince the jury Raymond intended all along to hide his true identity by deliberately skipping his last name. Raymond's credit card, which Raymond used to pay the hotel bill, also had his first and middle names, but that was because Raymond personally had requested it in that order when he was legitimately approved by the issuing bank.

Mr. Zimmerman also presented as evidence Ed's credit card, which Raymond had restored and taken over its payments, as further evidence that Raymond had a dubious character. To further but highlight his prosecutorial evidence, Mr. Zimmerman produced Raymond's District of Columbia driver's license bearing a residential address other than his Riverdale, Maryland home address.

Having portrayed Raymond as a complete habitual criminal, Mr. Zimmerman then returned to the key issue of the purpose of his journey to Lagos. He introduced two flight tickets into evidence. One of the booklets was Raymond's, which he used to board the Nigerian Airways flight, date of return clearly indicated to the jury. The other, which Mr. Zimmerman summed up to the jury to soothe his presentation, was the booklet from the Lagos bound flight. Furthermore, he produced the two receipts from both the Federal Palace and Eko Meridian hotels, in order to prove that at no period did Raymond leave Lagos for a five hundred-mile journey to Owerri, and stayed more than one day, contrary to the defendant's claim during his false testimony that he had stayed two days in the small city.

Finally, Mr. Zimmerman asked Raymond, "Mr. Karr, do you have a friend by the name of Dennis Metu?"

Raymond's eyes lit up. His face flushed and he was visibly rattled before responding, "Yes."

After cross-examination by Mr. Zimmerman, Raymond gladly but begrudgingly stepped out of the witness stand, feeling like a debutante comedian who had no single laugh from his audience. The AUSA's attack on his profile had stuck deeply, and the wounds manifested as guilt all over Raymond's face. His entire false testimony was, to say the least, an utter disgrace.

During his closing arguments, Mr. Cunningham again failed to show the obviously insulted jury the clip from the Philadelphia Inquirer, which he had hoped could have at least added some semblance of credibility to his testimony. Even if Mr. Cunningham indeed wanted to mount a serious defense, there was no way he or any attorney could defend such a blatant lie. Mr. Cunningham had shown frustration throughout the proceeding, especially when the court recessed. Mr. Cunningham had come to the courtroom holding cell to mock Raymond. During the first recess, he had looked at him and then clenched his right fist and punched his left palm. The next time, he put his hand around his throat in a "choke 'um" mockery. Finally, he had positioned his fingers on imaginary gun-holding and pretended to be shooting at him. These were much to the amusement of the marshals.

Mr. Zimmerman, on the other hand, was relentless in his quest to paint Raymond as a hardened criminal. As he sat dejectedly alone in the bullpen, waiting for the jury to return their predictable verdict, Raymond began to recount some of the key highlights, perhaps lowlights, of the trial. Now all of a sudden, he'd become a credit cards fraudster, all because he had declined a plea bargain. His awe of being branded a credit card fraudster in his mind outweighed the felony rap, ironic especially since a credit card fraud conviction carried a penalty of six months or less in the slammer, far less than the minimum 5 years he faced for drug trafficking. But for Raymond Karr, who could not pick up a lost penny that did not belong to him, it was disingenuous not uncharacteristic.

Almost fifteen minutes went by before the marshals were dispatched to escort Raymond back inside the courtroom, to listen to the inevitable, perhaps largely ceremonious guilty verdict. The jury, so insulted by an obvious criminal, combined with Raymond's ridiculous and awkwardly told false story, would return nothing but a guilty verdict. In Raymond's mind, he speculated on the slim prospect of the jury coming down with a not-guilty verdict. But he came away with the surety that in light of his bizarre defense approach the only not-guilty verdict would have to be by reason of unmistakable insanity.

It was quick. The verdict was pronounced by the jury foreman, and sentencing was immediately scheduled for the 13th of February – Friday the 13th.

Chapter 23

RELEASE BARABBAS

Raymond learned to never fight for what you did not earn.

He had become increasingly angry at himself from the moment he stepped down from the witness stand. Five days after the trial and the subsequent guilty verdict, he was back in Otisville prison, still trying to recover from the trauma of becoming a convicted felon. The extent of that dejection never seized a moment to surprise him, primarily because he thought he had emotionally readied himself for what was to follow. Mr. Zimmerman's questions under cross undoubtedly had much to do with it.

He was very much convinced Dennis had given the government the details of the clandestine operation. No wonder Mr. Zimmerman was able to present such a convincing argument during his summation. If indeed Mr. Zimmerman had known all along from a reliable source that Raymond had actually been part of a plot to import heroin into the United States, the AUSA must have been expecting him to be squirming at cross-examination. His lawyer, Mr. Cunningham, didn't even mention any pre-trial motions, which might have included a motion for discovery of all evidence against him. Such knowledge, he thought, would have undoubtedly forced him to rescind his decision to go forward, and would have spared the government the time and taxpayers the cost of a trial.

He was also still bothered by the comments made by one of the two U.S. Marshals after the verdict when they were escorting him back to the basement cell. It didn't matter at the time, but as he recalled it, everything weighed in heavily.

"Life's over for this one; he's now an ex-con," one Marshal had said to the other. "You think he'll adjust by the year two thousand, Freddie?"

"How in the hell anyone would choose this way to end his life, I don't know," Freddie said and shrugged.

Marshal Freddie's comment was prudent in Raymond's opinion. He couldn't think of an answer either. When the marshals had freed his wrists from tight cuffs, he had walked inside the holding cell.

"Say hi to your folks in the big house, ex-con," the first marshal had said.

Raymond was emotionally devastated by their insensitive comment, though it wasn't the first of its kind since he'd been imprisoned. That comment particularly stung hard. He began to question himself. Was life really over for him? Could it be that he would be receiving a longer prison term than he thought come sentencing day? Their insensitive comments had hung in his mind for two dreadful days.

Following Raymond's arrival at MCC after the verdict, he constantly engaged the one-way telephone service, trying unsuccessfully to reach Mr. Cunningham, who yet again wouldn't accept his collect calls to his lawyer's central office. He placed more calls to special Agent DiGiovanni at the DEA offices at JFK airport, but each time was told the agent was out on special assignment. He desperately wanted to come clean with a more sincere confession, and render whatever assistance he could to help the government track down whoever they wanted to prosecute. A liar and an ex-con, he would need to regain some of his reputation, and he couldn't find a better means to achieve that purpose.

Just one week later, a surprising announcement from the institution's loud speakers called out Inmate Karr for departure back to MCC, New York. Raymond knew immediately he'd have his opportunity to speak with Mr. Cunningham. For a change, he couldn't wait to be transported to the dreadful MCC jail. His only worry was the fast approaching Christmas in the jail. However, the fact that he'd have the opportunity to try to regain some of his tarnished credibility consumed all of his thoughts. This time around, he wouldn't mind being shackled and driven away by the two Bureau of Prison's special task force men.

Unlike the previous times, Raymond wasn't scheduled this time to be transported to Brooklyn U.S. District courthouse that morning. It had always been court on arrival at MCC, but fortunately this time he was quickly notified he needn't go back to the R & D office on the third floor to be routinely processed for court appearance. For the first time, he would rest after an all-night journey.

He slept until noon. When he woke up he was finally able to reach Mr. Cunningham over the telephone in his office, marking the first and only time Mr. Cunningham had accepted his collect call.

"Hello, Raymond," Mr. Cunningham said, sounding unusually upbeat. "How are you?" The enthusiasm, he thought, could have been that he had finally disposed the nagging case of United States v. Raymond Karr, and now free from a grossly aggravating client.

"Fine, Mr. Cunningham, and you?" Raymond said as his body began to heat up.

"Oh well, I know, you want to come forward and try to… to… to fix some of those screw ups. We have your folks in custody. What's his name? I think his name is Kenneth."

"Kenneth Mba?"

"Yes! And the other one too."

"Clyde… D.C.?"

"Is that his name? I don't think that's him. I can't remember his name, but we also have him in custody."

"You're not talking about Dennis Metu, are you?"

"Yeah that's him. Would you be willing to talk to the government about them?"

How Mr. Cunningham knew Raymond desperately wanted

to discuss this issue remained unclear to Raymond. He, however, welcomed the possibility that turning over the information he had might have a positive effect on his sentence, at least some reduction from his jail term.

"Mr. Cunningham, I think something ought to be done soon, otherwise it may be too late. I have a hunch some of these guys might be trying to flee the country," Raymond said.

"Well, in that case, hold on just a few seconds let me see if I can reach Mr. Zimmerman in his office," Cunningham said with a sense of urgency. He placed Raymond on hold.

After a brief pause, Raymond heard the line come alive with the sound of telephone ringing, presumable in Mr. Zimmerman's office. Mr. Zimmerman took the call directly and greeted Mr. Cunningham.

"As you can guess, Mr. Zimmerman," Cunningham began, "the background noise you hear is the prison atmosphere, and I have Mr. Karr on the other line."

Mr. Cunningham went on to relay Raymond's message while Mr. Zimmerman listened attentively, intermittently uttering sounds of approval.

"Hi, Mr. Karr, how are you?" Mr. Zimmerman said enthusiastically.

"It could be better, how about yourself?"

"Fine, thank you. Do you have any names for us?"

"I learned you already have two of them in custody, so now I'm speaking of the man behind the entire affair.

"Yes, we do have Dennis Metu and Kenneth Mba in custody in Virginia. Who's the other guy? What's his name and we'll take it from there?" he said with resounding optimism.

"I can't think of his last name because I'm having a little difficulty remembering it. But his first name is Clyde and he goes by the nickname of "D.C." I believe I have his full identity written in a piece of paper in my folder inside my suit jacket."

"If I'm not mistaken, that's your luggage that the customs agents seized while you were coming out from the airplane," Mr. Cunningham said.

"Yes."

Zimmerman was silent for a while. He probably suspected Raymond was withholding Clyde's full identity as a bargaining chip. But Raymond knew he was being sincere. Mr. Zimmerman decided to abruptly end the conversation by setting up an open-ended appointment for all parties involved to meet in his office. He would send for Raymond when he was ready.

It was the weekend before Christmas. Instead of Christmas shopping or a birthday party for his son, who was born on the eighteenth, Raymond was planning to endure many Christmases behind bars. There was a seasonal bonus of greeting cards available to all inmates who wished to take advantage, but Raymond couldn't since he'd have no address to send them, assuming his house, the only address vivid in his memory, had already been foreclosed.

The attorney general didn't give a damn how miserable it felt to be in such predicament and so Raymond's emotional problem would stay with him. Instead, Raymond chose to send season's greeting cards to Mr. Zimmerman, Mr. Cunningham, and Judge Boscolo. Naturally none acknowledged.

The meeting with Mr. Zimmerman and everyone else took place the next Monday after Raymond had been intensely interviewed by a female probation officer, whose duty it was to make recommendations to the judge regarding penalty. In attendance at the meeting was Mr. Cunningham, who stood and said he'd be leaving right away, and advised Raymond of the strict conditions of the immunity granted him in order to tell all.

"Make no mistake about it, Raymond, this immunity only prohibits the government from prosecuting in the event of new information that may expose you in a criminal activity. It will have nothing to do with your last conviction," he said wryly.

Raymond, sitting in an armchair and wagging his restless legs, felt a cold blood rush to his head. What did the public defender mean by what he had just said? Other inmates who were debriefed by the government always had their sentences reduced. Could this be another case of taking advantage of ever gullible Raymond Karr? Why should anyone in his right mind bother to volunteer information if the only reward is a waiver of prosecution? Heck, who gets prosecuted for saying nothing anyway?

Disingenuous as it may have sounded, he knew he had very limited options if any. Keeping his information to himself meant quietly going away to prison for whatever number of years. However, telling all could potentially touch some heart or at the very least, be a good future ammunition in seeking some kind of redress. In his situation, doing nothing, he reasoned, yields nothing but doing something has, at least, the potential for stirring up something – good or bad, hopefully good.

"My advice to you would be to co-operate first and then hope for the better. There at least you stand a shot at sentence reduction." Mr. Cunningham said as he began to slowly walk away.

Raymond was staring blankly at the ceiling. Mr. Zimmerman stood up from his chair and approached him. Mr. Cunningham stood and waited.

"This office will not guarantee your client anything for his cooperation He can at any point choose to withdraw from his decision to tell all," Mr. Zimmerman said emphatically.

"I already made that clear to him," Mr. Cunningham said and quickly walked away. Raymond suspected there might have been a rift existing between the two lawyers before he re-focused his mind to what brought him to that office.

Also present was a clean-shaven white American, who Mr. Zimmerman introduced as Donald Wessel, a U.S. Customs Agent from Chantilly, Virginia. Raymond did not understand, nor did he give a damn, why the prosecutor failed to introduce an African-American woman in her late forties, who sat and took notes.

When everyone was seated, the stage was set for Raymond to tell it all, this time the whole truth and nothing but the truth. A few minutes into his confession, Mr. Zimmerman interrupted to excuse himself, claiming he had other essential engagements to tend to. But first he wanted to learn how the juju doctor story came into the picture, and he was quick to ask Raymond to enlighten him on that before his departure. Since he wasn't in the mood to satisfy the AUSA's minor curiosity, he wryly told the AUSA it was orchestrated by Ike in Lagos. Mr. Zimmerman smartly read Raymond's lack of enthusiasm and left, having exchanged greetings with Donald Wessel.

Raymond left no stone unturned, narrating how Dennis had come to his house one Sunday evening and showed him two Nigerian passports. He told of James' business travel to Nigeria and his tenant's return to wake him up one early morning to reveal his business engagement, and how he flew in the same Lufthansa aircraft with Dennis. Everything.

Donald Wessel's baffling questions about Dennis' involvement, at the conclusion of Raymond's briefing, revealed there had been some crucial information about the number of times Dennis took to Lagos that was withheld from him. Several times he questioned Raymond if he was completely certain Dennis had made a previous trip to Lagos, and to further try to comprehend Raymond's answer, he came out openly.

"Dennis told us it was his only trip to Lagos, as far as heroin was concerned. No wonder he declined later to come up and testify against you," Donald Wessel said and studied Raymond's reaction.

To Raymond, that was further indication that he had been dismally counseled by his court-appointed lawyer, Mr. Cunningham. If Mr. Cunningham had filed a motion for discovery of all evidence against him, perhaps Raymond wouldn't have gone to trial. Raymond would have known about Dennis' information to the government.

Wessel also revealed that Dennis had been promised a recommendation for a downward departure—a legal maneuver that allowed judges, at the government attorney's request, to consider a reduction in prison sentence for a defendant who aided the government in the successful prosecution of other indicted suspects. In the provision, the government attorney would submit a favorable recommendation generally known to inmates as 5k-1 letter. The letter would then unbind the judge from the strict sentencing guideline for a more lenient prison sentence, sometimes to no jail term at all. Dennis had apparently concealed his first trip and his purchase of a BMW automobile to the government, and had decided to pull out of his commitment to testify against Raymond, perhaps fearing it might result in him revealing the whole affair, which ultimately could earn him a perjury rap. Also Wessel revealed Kenny had been arrested but released for lack of evidence, while Clyde had not been targeted, since Dennis had confessed he didn't know much about Clyde except that they had briefly exchanged greetings when Kenny and Dennis ran into Clyde in a carry-out restaurant in Langley Park, Maryland.

Wessel reached in his briefcase and brought out Raymond's wallet, which was still in the custody of the government prosecutors, and emptied its contents on the table.

"We're gonna go over all these cards and pieces of papers you have in here, see if any of the numbers written on them is relevant to the case," he said.

Principally, Wessel was hoping Raymond could find Clyde's telephone number lying around somewhere in it. As Wessel flashed the business cards and other handwritten pieces of papers, one by one, he saw him hold out the card where Laura had written her phone number for him, and asked him if he thought the number was of any relevance to the drug smuggling enterprise. Raymond chuckled a little before saying no. It was quite a memorable moment for him.

Mr. Zimmerman walked in the moment he was about to be handcuffed to be escorted back to the holding cell.

"So how did it go, anything positive?" Mr. Zimmerman asked Wessel while reaching for the telephone on his office desk.

"So far so good, I guess," Wessel replied with a mild smile that was most likely driven by nicety.

The two men chatted for a few minutes before Wessel double-locked the cuffs on Raymond's wrists and shook hands with MR. Zimmerman, who was about to engage the telephone dial. He then shook hands with the lady, who had remained mute all through his debriefing, walked closely behind Raymond through several offices, and back to the holding cell.

At the U.S. Marshal's custodial affairs desk, Wessel took out from his breast pocket a business card, while one of the marshals stood up to re-assume custody of Raymond, and handed it to Raymond.

"Here, Raymond, this is my card. If you remember anything you may have forgotten to tell me, please feel free to call me at the office number," he said.

"How do I look so far?" Raymond asked Wessel in desperation to hear something bright for a change about his future.

"Well, I'll check your information out and if something good comes out of it, you'll surely get the credit."

He thanked Wessel and followed the slight shoving of the marshal to the bullpen, where he was temporarily released from handcuffs to re-join his colleagues.

Sitting down and neglecting the noisy prisoners already inside the crowded bullpen, Raymond began to assess the situation. He was embittered by the fact that Dennis, whom he considered his closest friend, had sold him out. Dennis could be in more trouble than Raymond was if, as Wessel had indicated, further investigation revealed Dennis had actually made two trips to Lagos and had admitted to only one of them. Raymond also became very much concerned that Wessel and Mr. Zimmerman weren't exactly enthused with his debriefing. He had expected a more enthused atmosphere, where at least Mr. Zimmerman's anger toward his infamous speech during the trial would be lessened. Instead, Mr. Zimmerman, who was the lone power broker in any bid to lower the young man's sentence, coldly sat and warned Raymond before hand, and in the very presence of Raymond's attorney, that he wouldn't promise Raymond anything, and that he didn't have to talk to them. The world for Raymond Karr still seemed very much on the dark side.

The cold December wind blew hard against the U.S. Marshal's security van that was transporting eight inmates, himself included. There were also three female prisoners, who were all being transported back to the Metropolitan Correctional Center. As usual, the busy Brooklyn-Manhattan rush hour traffic reminded Raymond of the most precious possession of mankind that he had just lost—freedom. Watching motorists as they blew their horns became a sickening reminder of the preciousness of freedom and liberty. In his non-status as an inmate and ex-convict, he couldn't even raise his voice beyond certain low level if he had an opinion, or for that matter, dared question any direct order either by a youthful U.S. Marshal or arrogant Correctional Officers.

Very much evident in the outside world was that unmistakable sentiment of the approach of Christmas day. Once again, the thought reminded him of his son and his birthday, and all the wonderful things that could have come had he not engage in an illicit trade.

After clearing routine security at MCC, all inmates, who just returned from the court house collected their cold macaroni dinners on disposable plates, and were back inside the ever noisy MCC jailhouse. Raymond would remain inside this fifth floor prison cellblock until Christmas night when he was called to pack up his property for a transfer back to Otisville prison.

Upon arrival in Otisville prison, Raymond was greeted with the shocking news of the Christmas spirit-of-the-season gesture accorded to other African inmates charged with the same drug courier adventure as he did. They were being released from the jail as a reward for turning into government witnesses and were to become immunized from prosecution. A secret legal maneuvering among African inmates had emerged during his absence. In the scheme, a group of African inmates numbering about eleven had secretly met and unanimously agreed to share damaging information against one of their colleagues charged with a king pin status. Subsequently, they fed the same damaging information to the US attorney prosecuting the case, who stood to gain the coveted chance of winning a conviction against a king pin, and he had bought it.

The rumor swirling among inmates was that the United States Attorney's office was so desperate in searching for and winning the conviction of drug kingpins that they would go to any length to achieve it. The Assistant U.S. Attorneys were mobilized to battle the drug lords, and they aggressively hunted down any incriminating information that would lead them to indicting one. From most accounts, the U.S. Attorney's office wouldn't hesitate to release a Barabbas if he would aid them in winning a conviction against a defendant they had labeled and charged with the kingpin status. It was generally believed to be their ladder to a successful carrier with the Justice Department, and to achieve that, a government attorney would have to win as many convictions of kingpins as possible. Qualification to becoming "government witness" required one to have been a heroin courier with proven track record of several oversea trips.

The mechanism of the deal was simple. The U.S. Attorney naturally would call in for debriefing an inmate indicted for notoriously frequenting the clandestine operation. If deemed credible, the inmate would essentially be guaranteed a recommendation to the judge allowing a deviation from the sentencing guideline, via the almighty

5K-1 letter, as inmates fettishly dubbed it. In most cases recipients were credited with time-served and walked straight home. The inmate would sign the deal with his attorney and representatives of the U.S. Attorney's office. The inmate would then go to court to testify against the kingpin. He'd do a "good job" and would be credited with the time-served sentence. But first-time felons, the likes of Raymond Karr, had no chance of any such deal since they lacked enough experience to effectively convince a jury to slam suspects charged with the kingpin status.

But Raymond witnessed some of his fellow inmates exploit the unique opportunity further. Some first-timers paid a certain agreed cash amount, usually in thousands, to a prosecutor-recognized frequent courier well positioned to testify against an indicted kingpin. Payment would be transacted by both parties' allies or relatives outside of the prison confine. The money was kept for them to re-establish themselves after gaining freedom. In exchange, the recipient would detail the first-timer on the drug running apparatus of a king pin. Every detail about the unfortunate kingpin would be explained, including, among others, the king pin's home address, the scope of his assets, drug dealership history and physical description. The first-timer would subsequently call up his attorney and would have him set up a meeting with the U.S. attorney's office. The deal would be sealed. That's all, he's in as a witness.

Raymond was keenly aware that those inmates apprehended and charged with drug kingpin status may have actually been guilty of the charges against them, not all who testified or agreed to stand as witnesses against them had dealings with them. It was only a means to "cop out," a dubious method of escaping jail term by using those who were irreversibly destined to prison—the kingpins.

The first to hit Raymond with that astonishing revelation was none other than his newly re-united old high school pal, Dave Amadi. Dave was staging his own campaign to have the DEA and the AUSA sit down and "deal" with him. The government lawyers had given a cold shoulder to Dave's offer of cooperation because Dave had shouted derogatory insults at the Customs agents and DEA Agents at the time of his arrested at Kennedy airport, and the AUSA had records of those rude encounters.

"Ray, listen," Dave said as they sat on the lunch table. "Some of these guys, who had been freed don't have the slightest idea of the identities of the guys they're agreeing to testify against. They just gathered information from others and corroborated their stories."

"That's too dangerous and unfair of them, isn't it?" Raymond asked wide eyed.

"And look at me who had been going to "market" for them since 1980. My prosecutor doesn't even want me to testify and go home," Dave said.

Raymond revealed to Dave his own call to New York City to debrief the agents, and how he came forward with what little knowledge he had about heroin courier operation.

"If you want, Dave, I'll hook you up with the special agent from Virginia. He's obviously an aggressive drug crime hunter. He'd do anything for a valuable info." Raymond said with a slim hope he would somehow benefit from such arrangement.

"Why don't you do that as soon as possible, Ray, the big guys in this deal have all been apprehended, and I'm their worst nightmare. I'm quite certain that if any of them finds out I've turned a government witness, he'll immediately cop out."

"So you're the man behind their network, huh?"

"Since 1980. In fact, there was a period when I flew to Lagos almost weekly. Just tell them to talk to me. They'll be glad they did. I'm serious."

"No problem. I tell you what… why don't you just come up to my housing unit and I'll telephone Mr. Donald Wessel and have you speak with him?"

"I can't come to your cell unit. You know it's against the law here. Just tell him to contact my attorney or try to convince New York DEA or my prosecutor. Those idiots are still mad as hell at me."

Raymond knew the agents had every right to be angry at Dave. He had reportedly kicked, shoved, and cursed at the arresting agents, and they had vowed to have him severely dealt with. Now he desperately needed their cooperation and they refused to deal.

"Well, I'll see what I can do, Dave."

"Should I trust that you'll do that for me?" Dave said.

"You know me."

Dave wrote down his full name and prison number, his attorney's name and telephone number, and names of the DEA agents assigned to his case.

"Do it, George. I'll make sure you're taken care of," Dave concluded and patted Raymond on his shoulder.

"We'll do."

Raymond didn't telephone Donald Wessel until three weeks after New Year day, on the twentieth of January, 1991. Wessel enthusiastically jotted down all the information he gave him regarding Dave's proposal. Raymond also discussed his own case further. They talked about Clyde and his two residential addresses. How Wessel could trace the seller of the BMW automobile, which Dennis had purchased.

They agreed to speak again in another week or so to check up on the developments.

That same day, Raymond wrote letters of apology to Judge Boscolo and AUSA, Mr. Ken Zimmerman, for his gross misconduct and for unnecessarily dragging the inevitable to trial. He also hinted Mr. Zimmerman in the letter about Dave, and stressed that Dave was someone they'd need to talk to about some highly sought after heroin traffickers.

Dave disappeared a few days after, and was rumored to have been taken to MCC, New York. Raymond's further inquiry revealed that Dave had pleaded guilty of the charges against him, and was to be sentenced sometime in March or April. Dave's sudden disappearance from Otisville signaled to Raymond his messages to Donald Wessel and Mr. Zimmerman had been delivered accordingly and they had acted upon it.

Raymond's sentencing day was re-scheduled and moved up to the fifteenth of March, thankfully, from the previously scheduled Friday the thirteenth of February, an ominous date that always signaled bad luck to him. Any date except when thirteenth fell on a Friday. Topping the eventful harsh winter was the riveting news of the commencement of massive air strikes on Baghdad by allied coalition forces, and the subsequent annihilation of Saddam's forces in a textbook ground assault that freed Kuwait in just a matter of days. Raymond had his work cut out for him in trying to convince his fellow inmates that the allied campaign was justified.

"If I may ask, why do you like George Bush?" an astonished African-American inmate said during one of Raymond's heated debates with them.

"Because he has all the qualification I'd like my country's president to possess—a man who had defended his country, putting his life on the line," he said. Each time, Raymond's answers seemed to further infuriate his fellow inmates.

"But he put you in prison," they would say.

"Wrong. I put myself in prison. He didn't ask me to break the law."

The victory of the Gulf War so aggravated Raymond's opponents that he was drawn into physical altercation with an African-American facing a 20-year prison sentence, a Spanish Bush hater, a Trinidadian Muslim fanatic, and two Nigerian Saddam freaks—one of whom was Raymond's cell mate. Raymond was also struck with a severe virus. His high temperature lasted over three weeks, and he lost a whopping twenty-two pounds. There was also a pandemonium of snitching for freedom among some Nigerian heroin couriers. More and more defendants were simply being educated by others about the drug activities of those apprehended and charged with king pin status. Most of these would-be government witnesses were later rewarded with bail bonds of personal recognizance on grounds they would oblige. Raymond would later learn that some of them never had to testify because of subsequent plea bargaining by the intimidated alleged heroin kingpins, but were rewarded anyway with 5K-1 letters.

Raymond had also kept in constant touch via the telephone with Donald Wessel, who confirmed he had promptly delivered his messages about Uzoma Amadi to the New York jurisdiction. Nothing, according to Wessel, was coming Raymond's way to alter the outcome of his sentencing in March.

"I'm still working on the information you gave me. If anything happens, I'll let you know," Wessel said.

Finally, about three weeks before Raymond's sentencing day, he received yet another depressing package from the probation office.

The probation officer had been displeased with Raymond's false testimony in the court and had strongly recommended to the judge a charge of perjury. According to the statement, he stood to receive a prison sentence ranging between sixty-three months and seventy-eight months, but because of her recommendation, the judge could, under the sentencing guidelines, go as high as twenty years, certainly no less than the sixty-three months minimum sentence.

The news gravely troubled Raymond, despite the encouragement from his colleagues that district court judges didn't approve of unnecessarily lengthy prison sentences mandated by the new law. Just three years earlier, drug couriers apprehended in the same crime category as Raymond's would've been given a second chance and slapped on the wrist with probation, and the judges were wary of the senseless new lengthy penalty but could do absolutely nothing about it since it was an act of Congress.

Following the discouraging probation report, Raymond had intensified his willingness to cooperate with Donald Wessel, but it would lead him to nowhere. The only word from Wessel was that Clyde had been tracked down, but not yet arrested. Wessel had also successfully traced the fact that Dennis had actually purchased a BMW, and that Dennis had also made a previous trip to Lagos on heroin courier run. Wessel also told Raymond his information so far hadn't led to anything completely fruitful, therefore wouldn't help with reduction of his sentence.

On the day of sentencing, Raymond felt like he was about to be executed. He was taken to a narrow holding cell, adjacent to the main courtroom where he would soon appear before Judge Boscolo for sentencing. Sitting outside and keeping close eyes on him were two U.S. Marshals and poised for adverse action if need be. Soon Mr. Cunningham came in.

"Raymond?" Mr. Cunningham inquired in a low voice as he visually searched inside the cage-like cell.

Raymond answered in the same low voice. Mr. Cunningham, satisfied with his verification, said okay before withdrawing back toward the courtroom, and silence befell again. He apparently came to ascertain Raymond's presence.

Soon the silence was broken by a Jamaican Zionist prisoner, who was meditating outrageously loudly, and limping on a deformed left leg, as he was escorted inside the same cage-like cell Raymond was in. Two other U.S. Marshals dragged him along. Raymond observed the prisoner he would temporarily share the same cell with had a Jewish bible snugged under his arm. As the Marshals sternly warned him while locking the caged door, to keep his meditation to himself, he stood next to him. But finding their warning wasn't doing any good, they resorted to a friendly plea. The Rastafarian, who immediately loudly proclaimed his Jewish affiliation, stopped and apologized to the marshals for his misconduct, but then resorted to intermittent audible meditation, each time as though he was possessed by spirits. Each loud meditation was equally met with a hush warning by the marshals. He would stop to apologize in a humbling manner, repeating the very same apologetic words he had used before.

Under normal circumstance, he would have found it extremely funny. But it was no ordinary times. Raymond had to concentrate on his own humongous problem as he was enduring belly butterflies. He called the attention of a marshal and requested an audience with his lawyer. The marshal quickly went inside the courtroom to fetch Mr. Cunningham. Moments later, the public defender walked out, with the marshal following behind.

On the approach of few feet away from the cell, Raymond immediately fired his question.

"Mr. Cunningham, am I getting any credit from Mr. Zimmerman for my cooperation?" Raymond said as the seemingly tensed public defender approached the cage-like holding cell.

"Nope, nothing," Mr. Cunningham replied, paused for a few seconds, and then slowly began to withdraw back to courtroom entrance.

"Well, did you try to ask Mr. Zimmerman?" Raymond pressed on.

"Haven't even heard from him since we last met in his office back in December."

"How come, though?"

"What am I gonna speak to him about? It's all up to him, and if he determines you'll get something, he'll tell the judge, but I don't think he's in the mood. Do you want to speak with him?"

"Yes, please."

Mr. Cunningham went into the courtroom, and in a few seconds walked out with Mr. Zimmerman. Raymond's heart pounded as he saw the AUSA approach the cage. The Rastafarian, who was facing as many as forty years, as revealed by one of the marshals, cursed at the two lawyers, but they chose to ignore him.

"You wanted to talk to me, Mr. Karr?" Mr. Zimmerman said to Raymond, who placed his hands against the cage cell to speak.

"Yes, Mr. Zimmerman. I just want to find out if I'm getting any recommendations before the judge," Raymond said with uncertainty.

"There's nothing I can do for you now. You had the opportunity to accept a plea offer and you chose to go to trial."

He reminded the Assistant US Attorney of the day he had changed his mind to accept the plea offer and the AUSA had declined and had told the judge the government would no longer drop the second charge, even if Raymond decided to plead guilty. Mr. Cunningham interjected in a demonstrative anger, which also revealed his frustration.

"You're now asking for a sentence reduction after I did all I could to try to convince you to plead guilty? You'll be worse off when you step out of this courtroom than you were when you got here. I kept telling you that. Remember, I guaranteed you this situation when you chose to tell the jury your big lie."

"I'll have to go back now. I have no time to waste. I've got a lot to do inside," Mr. Zimmerman said as he slowly walked backward to the direction of the courtroom.

Raymond choked back tears. No disciplined or educated person had been so mean to him ever before. But he recognized he put himself in such a lousy predicament, so in his conscience he did not blame the lawyers.

"Mr. Zimmerman," Raymond called out again.

Mr. Zimmerman stopped to listen.

Raymond paused briefly before continuing, "You know, I promised to do anything for the government, and you know I can. Why don't you just give me this break and I'll make myself available for anything... anything, Mr. Zimmerman, anything."

"I just can't do it, Mr. Karr. You chose to go to trial. Deals are for those who make my work easier for me. If I give you a recommendation, what would it look like to those who accept their responsibilities? Moreover, why should I consider you?"

"I didn't give any of your men any troubles. I cooperated with them and even volunteered for them to come to Washington to help me track the culprits of the drug I had. Plus I didn't involve myself in a violent crime, and no guns involved in my first..."

"The crime you committed is a violent one, remember?" Raymond's lawyer, Mr. Cunningham, angrily interrupted.

"How so?" Raymond asked, turning to face Mr. Cunningham.

"When you were bringing drugs into the United States, did you not know you were bringing in items that will kill American children?" the public defender asked.

Raymond was unsettled at what he heard his lawyer say. He felt his public defender had reached a new low. Though shocked but Raymond was not entirely surprised that his own defense counsel would make such a damning comment to his own client, at least not in the very presence of the prosecuting attorney.

"Well, you have a point there, Mr. Cunningham, but remember one fact had clearly been established here, and that is that this is not just my first time of being caught, but my first time of engaging in any criminal activity of any kind."

"What does that have to do with your running drugs?" Mr. Cunningham said, "Even one run can cause serious harm to an American's health."

"Would you conscientiously say that I have contributed to anyone's harm by importing drugs, since this was my first attempt, which didn't make it through, thank God, across the border?'

The two lawyers looked baffled and silenced by his question. Mr. Zimmerman again excused himself and continued his way back to the courtroom. Mr. Cunningham stayed behind and coached him on what to say, during convict's acceptance of responsibility, before Judge Boscolo. According to Mr. Zimmerman, the judge would need sincere contrition in order to stay within the original sentencing guideline, and ignore an upward departure as recommended by the probation officer.

Soon after Mr. Cunningham left to go back inside the courtroom, the court bailiff came to fetch Raymond.

"Raymond Karr, you're up next," the bailiff called out.

Raymond stood up as one of the marshals unlocked the cage door. He almost fainted out of nervous wreck and stomach butterfly. That very dreadful moment only provided him with the unenviable opportunity to experience that in some predicaments one could actually shit in his pants. In Raymond's experience, it was the closest ever to actually happen. Raymond had always thought it was a hyperbole when he heard people express it while describing how they reacted from an extremely scary situation. The moment at hand brought it all to reality to him. In fact, he started to cover his buttocks with his hand and marched his legs up and down to force back the bowel pressure.

The two marshals and the bailiff marched him toward the courtroom entrance door. The judge was wearing an ordinary checkered shirt and a pair of jeans pants, no tie.

The sight of Judge Boscolo sitting on the bench without a judicial robe was a miracle. It immediately restored Raymond's consciousness, and literally wiped out the ravaging scare in him. He was so surprised that there were no group of enraged government lawyers and a group of angry community drug crusaders present to persuade the judge to throw the book at him. Now he could confidently address the casually dressed judge for a lenient sentence based on his minimal participation in the drug crime escapade.

When the proceeding began, the judge first heard from both Mr. Zimmerman and Mr. Cunningham. Naturally, Mr. Zimmerman reiterated how unconscionable Raymond's engagement in drugs dealing had been, firstly by attempting to import heroin into the United States, and secondly perjuring himself by his false testimony before the court. Mr. Zimmerman concluded by asking the judge to take it all into consideration when sentencing him to rightfully consider the probation officer's recommendation for an upward departure in his sentencing guideline. As for Mr. Cunningham, Raymond was so distrustful of the public defender to pay attention to whatever Mr. Cunningham said to the judge.

Judge Boscolo then asked him if he had anything to say before sentencing.

In pleading to Judge Boscolo, Raymond briefly stated how he had tried to help the government and the extent of his cooperation with Donald Wessel. Raymond finally submitted himself to the mercy of the court, having stated how remorseful he was for involving himself in such disgraceful illicit activity.

Mr. Zimmerman, who had the final say before the bench, told the judge he wouldn't recommend a reduction in his sentence, and that if and when his information yielded a fruitful result, he would then consider such recommendation.

"Well, is his co-operation determined to be in good faith? I think that's the essential question here," Judge Boscolo said.

I'd say so," Mr. Zimmerman admitted. "But just like I stated, nothing can be done unless it's fruitful."

"What I'm trying to iron out here is that the three months on top of sixty months is unnecessary. However, would there be any objection if the three months is waived because of Mr. Karr's established co-operation in good faith?"

"I have no objection to that, your honor," Mr. Zimmerman said.

"Good… I therefore recommend him for sixty months in the custody of the Attorney General." The modest judge concluded and signed a paper on file, no gavel. He went on to also recommend, at the inquiry of the court clerk, four years of probation for each of the two counts to run concurrent.

It was obviously all over for Raymond. But did he still have legal remedies to explore?

Chapter 24

AFTERMATH

The dramatic events following Raymond's sentencing to five years imprisonment changed him forever. The moment he walked out of the courtroom, escorted by the two U.S. Marshals, he knew immediately that life would never be the same again. Among all, it would be devoid of trustworthiness and compassion from the society. He also realized belatedly that good name was a major component to a life of fulfillment.

This first experience of lack of compassion came from the two U.S. Marshals, who marched him to the courthouse basement bullpen. They mocked as they were walking along the hallway, and despite Raymond's emotional exhibition of sadness about his impending journey to the big house, he overheard one of the two marshals angrily criticizing the judge's lenient sentence.

"You see." he said. "That's what I'm beefing about. We spend all this time, put our lives on the line hunting down these damn criminals, and what do you know? An asshole judge literally slaps them on their wrists. Some of these so-called judges really need be probed for possible ties with these asshole drug dealers."

Inwardly, Raymond knew that the Marshal's reference to five years of his life in the prison as a slap on the wrist exposed a common person's anger, and a clairvoyant sampling of the insensitivity of the society toward drug convicts.

"Well, sonofabitch, you're lucky I'm not the judge. Your ass would've been really creamed for life," he said to Raymond.

The young convict could not think of an appropriate response for the Marshal's comment. He knew he had lost his place in the free society. He simply glanced back at the Marshal and said, "Yes."

The grim news of Raymond's five-year prison sentence stunned virtually all African inmates, both in MCC and Otisville prison, who heard of the new development. It was the longest prison term dished out to any of the African inmates in both holdover jails. Most of these defendants, who were in the same predicament as Raymond, usually either copped out to become government witnesses or cajoled into plea agreement and received lesser sentence for helping preserve judicial resources. Sentencing guideline for a plea agreement usually chunked off a sizable number of prison time. For most inmates, who were either considering proceeding with trial or already undergoing the preliminary processes, the shock of Raymond being slapped with such high number of years in the slammer for blowing a trial intimidated them into total submission. He had made himself a devastated scapegoat.

As days went by, he began to realize and somewhat appreciate how much of a break he had had receiving only the five years. First, he had perjured himself and was recommended by the probation officer to be severely punished. Secondly, there was his outrageous speech when he mounted the witness stand, which infuriated the government counsels and the jury, and which also should have angered Judge Boscolo. That consideration actually eased his emotional agonies. The few inmates he had tried to convince about his supposed good luck stared at him as if he was insane, and to some, who never even considered a trial, he appeared indeed a complete lunatic.

Raymond's arrival in Otisville prison, this time as an ex-convict, felt more dreadful than the previous ones. Upon clearing the institution's standard routine check-in, a stone-faced desk sergeant, a fat Puerto Rican with a clean-shaven round jaw and a turkey neck, barked in a deep husky voice. "We're basically gonna declare your will right here, got the gig, bro?" he said and reached for the pen tucked in his breast pocket.

Raymond remained expressionless but his eyes caught the sergeant's name tag that read 'JESUS PAPANTONIO.' He cursed him in his mind, hoping the fatso had blasphemed.

When the sergeant was set to write, he began to pose unsettling questions that scared the daylights out of Raymond, quite different from the previous times. This time around he had to answer such eerie questions as who his next of kin was, if he had secured a will, what he would like done with his corpse if he died in custody. Questions that made him feel like he was heading directly to his coffin.

On the first Sunday of Raymond's weekend after sentencing, Uzoma Amadi, who was highly appreciative of his efforts to connect him with his prosecutors for negotiations, invited him for a one-on-one chat at the games lounge. When they met, Uzoma secretly expressed his unyielding eagerness to see his buddy cut a deal for himself too. At least salvage some of the damages he had done by going to trial.

"Ray, I really insist that you join in on a couple of guys I know all too well and turn a government witness against their guy," Uzoma said casually in a very low voice, studying Raymond's expression, unsure what to expect.

Raymond was jolted but managed to hold the shock in perfect check. He wrestled with his mind to come up with a response but was betrayed by complete emptiness.

Uzoma, figuring out Raymond's silence meant he had been caught in an indecisive moment, pledged to thoroughly educate him on the kingpin defendants' past drug activities, and to personally urge his prosecutors to call him in, but contrite as he was, he just didn't have the guts to participate in such treachery. It simply was not in his nature to bear false witness.

"Why don't you just sleep on it and let me know by Tuesday. I know you. This might not be something you agree with, but we're talking freedom here. There's no time for self-righteousness here. The man is gone big time, whether you're in or out. I'm figuring why not seize an opportunity while it's knocking?"

"Ok, I'll let you know by Tuesday then," Raymond said and managed a smile.

When Tuesday came, they met and Raymond vehemently declined Uzoma's offer but thanked him for his care and concern.

The next day, Wednesday, he was assigned to his first prison job as a garbage remover. His job description was discarding garbage into the dumpster as collected by inmate sanitary workers all units and other facilities of the institution. The pay was eleven cents per hour.

The job itself was enough to occupy the huge void during daytime. The next step for Raymond was his expectation that at any given moment his name would be announced over the institution's loud speakers, a usual signal that one was about to be designated to a federal prison facility, where he would be serving out his prison sentence.

Prison designation prospects proved to be mind-boggling itself for him. The Bureau of Prisons was highly secretive about which institution around the vast country an inmate was to serve his time in, primarily for security concerns. As explained to Raymond by a fellow inmate, who had been in and out of the system several times, it was implemented to deter potential plans by prisoners to plot an escape route. If a prisoner was knowledgeable of his transport route, he possibly could plot to have the prison vehicle hijacked. He thought it was such a ludicrous expectation, but indeed it happened all the time. Given his personality, Raymond Karr would not jump prison even if the gate was blown wide open in the midnight. Life on a lam was equivalent to death in his conscience, therefore not an option.

The uncertainty of Raymond's designation to a prison facility loomed in his mind until the middle of April.

One windy morning, when he was just about to report to his job site, he was called to attention of a note posted on the bulletin board, listing five names of inmates required to pack up their properties and report to the Receiving and Discharge office. Sure enough, Raymond's name was listed. All of his attempts to try to find out where he was being designated were futile, and it further depressed him. He knew he was about to experience the same nightmare other inmates, who had experienced the ordeal of horror, in transit. Friends in prison, who had been designated, had written them to confirm the horror. Admittedly, those inmates' communications were quite contrary to the Bureau of Prison's law prohibiting such contacts among federal inmates, especially convicted felons.

The temperature was in the low sixties, the sky brightly blue, and the gentle breeze that blew reminded him of a typical spring in Washington, DC. The fifty-two passenger seat Bureau of Prison bus Raymond was shackled inside drove off, destination unknown to all twenty prisoners. All of a sudden, Raymond again began to recall his fun-filled life in the Capital City. He wondered if he'll ever get to see it again. Five years in the slammer, and a one-way ticket to Lagos Kirikiri Maximum Prison for another five, would certainly wipe him clean of positive thoughts, and life was no longer a guarantee, much less good health.

Raymond was emotionally overwhelmed with a bitter feeling. All the usual questions- why did he ever think of running a drug errand, succumbing to the natural pressure of a temporary impoverishment? Why did he take his case to trial? Why did he not humbly accept his attorney's advice to plead guilty and accept his responsibility? That would have knocked off almost nineteen months in incarceration. Now he had to go to prison for his first mistake. During some of their many gatherings back in MCC and Otisville jails when most of his inmate colleagues told tales of their own exploits in the illicit operation, Raymond had heard how they had stashed away enough wealth to retire when freedom came back. Some had admittedly had enormous exhilaration from the spread of wealth and had proclaimed they wouldn't mind sacrificing as much as ten years behind bars for the many years of wealth enjoyment. Others in a similar category to Dave Amadi's, had had so much expeditions that it turned out in their favor, and no time in prison or deportation to serve the decreed five additional years in a Nigerian prison.

There he was, Raymond that is, on his one and only attempt in a criminal activity, headed for his own Waterloo. He didn't even keep the properties he had spent all his adulthood legally sweating for. It was a prime example that crime never pays and in most instances would leave the criminal dismally crippled. He always metaphorically equated this ordeal as having to eat a penny worth of food and outlandishly excreting a dollar worth of shit.

Nearly six hours into the ride, the bus veered off and headed for a very large concrete wall, about a quarter of a mile long and fifty feet high. From the front view, the top of the wall had four dome-like constructions lined up from one end of the wall to the other. Raymond was told by the inmate seating next to him it was the great wall of historic Lewisburg's U.S. penitentiary, and that what looked like domes were the guard's posts, which also were mounted in all four corner walls.

"Is this where we'll do our time?" Raymond inquired from his fellow inmate, his heart slight thumping.

"I don't know. I doubt it though, but these cracker heads will never tell you where the fuck you're gonna be going until you get there," the inmate told him and then turned to answer more questions from other equally curious prisoners jolted by the sight of the huge confinement arena.

The African-American inmate's vivid explanation of the nature of life in the "big joint," as he called it, cast no doubt in Raymond he had once been a resident. The experienced inmate was right when he said he doubted they'd be housed there. It was a prison for the more violent criminals.

Once he and other inmates underwent the extraordinarily vigorous processes of inmate reception, they were told where they would be serving out their prison sentences, and that they only would briefly stay in the big house's twenty-four-hour lockdown "K" dorm for as much as one month.

Raymond learned he would be serving his five-year prison term at a one-year-old Federal Correctional Institution in Fairton, New Jersey. The African-American, who lectured Raymond on the nature of life in the Lewisburg Penitentiary, would remain in the "big joint" to serve his big time.

Two long, hard weeks in the penitentiary's holdover dormitory and Raymond was transported, along with about nine other inmates, to Fairton, New Jersey prison where his new agonizing life would commence.

Raymond's first six months at F.C.I. Fairton, New Jersey was nothing short of devastation. When credited with the previous six months from his arrest at JFK Airport through trial and sentencing, he had already spent one full year in custody. Soon after inmates' usual one-week long institutional orientation, Raymond began to attempt to adjust himself to prison life. Two months later, Raymond received a reply of a letter he had written to his common-law, informing him that his son and stepdaughter had all been forced into the custody of the foster care child program. The Prince George's County, Maryland Department of Social Services had deemed her incapable of providing for the welfare of the kids after she left them alone for a night shift work assignment. Two gunmen had broken into the house, where they were sleeping. The gunmen had left without harming the eight-year-old girl and her sixteen-month- old half-brother. Under the program, the children would remain indefinitely in the custody of the agency and could be put up for adoption. Raymond's initial assessment of the news was with a mixed feeling. Inherently, it would remain his main concern for the rest of his stay in the federal prison, and perhaps at Kirikiri too.

Following the forced custody of his children by the Department of Social Services, he became even more desperate to assist Donald Wessel in his pursuit of Clyde. The same man who had reneged on his promise to throw money at him both for his legal expenses and financial support for his family, were he to be apprehended. Raymond also wanted to turn in Bryan Jason, and if necessary, Dennis, who had given out the information that he thought compromised his defense. He felt if he could get more involved and have more "valued information" for Donald Wessel, Mr. Wessel could help shorten his period in jail, which could mean less suffering for his son and stepdaughter.

Raymond telephoned Donald Wessel, who at the time was on the trail of investigation of Clyde and other wanted heroin traffickers in the Northern Virginia and suburban Maryland area. Mr. Wessel surprised Raymond with the news that Dennis had been sentenced to eighty-eight months in prison.

"How come?" said a surprised Raymond.

"Cause he chose to go to trial," Wessel said.

"I thought you had him co-operate with you guys. What led to his going to trial?"

"Well, he didn't like the deal he was offered and...."

As Wessel paused, Raymond could detect his reluctance to go into details with him. Wessel told Raymond he was too busy to talk at the moment, and frustrated Raymond into giving up his intrusive questions. Raymond wondered how one who had given the government details of his illicit engagement would turn around to go to trial. What in the hell would be his line of defense?

In concluding his plan to have Clyde nabbed at the right time, Wessel restated Raymond would definitely benefit, but at the moment nothing whatsoever could be credited to him. When they hung up, Wessel's conclusion left Raymond with nothing but hopelessness.

Chapter 25

SURPRISING TIMES

By the summer of '91, Raymond was just beginning to accept and adjust to the inevitability of prison life. He had stopped thinking much about sex and Laura, as well as his very last fling at the Eko Meridian hotel in Lagos with Manuella. In fact, he had experienced his first wet dream, which occurred while he was dreaming about sex with his common-law. When he woke up from that dream, he felt a bitter disappointment and tears ran down his cheek.

Raymond also began to adjust to his assigned prison job, UNIBASE, as a data entry clerk. The job itself was rare to land since it paid a whopping forty-six cents per hour, much more than the eleven cents per hour general duties assigned to the majority of inmates. He was fortunate to have been randomly assigned to it.

Working one day, his supervisor called him up to inform him he was needed in the institution's visiting room.

"I'm not expecting any visit," he said, surprised.

Raymond knew it was such a strange development, especially since he had chosen to isolate himself from his relatives and the rest of the world out there. He felt worthless and too embarrassed to face anyone and he also knew he had no plausible explanation for his action that landed him in the slammer.

"Well, you are Raymond Karr, aren't you?" his female supervisor said sarcastically.

She handed him the institution's emergency movement pass and Raymond paced hurriedly to the visiting room, wondering along the way whoever would want to visit him.

Raymond was extensively frisked by the attending correctional officer. When the C.O. was satisfied that he was clean, he waved him by and told him to proceed to the room marked "Legal Visit."

In the room sat six white Americans, all men and dressed in suits, sitting around a conference table with one vacant chair.

"Sit down, Mr. Karr," the man who looked like he was the oldest said and waved Raymond to the lone vacant chair.

Raymond sat down and curiously stared from left to right, looking to see if he could recognize any of the six men. He looked hoping to see Donald Wessel but was disappointed that he was not there. All were strangers to him.

"Mr. Karr, I'm John Theilmann, the United States Attorney for the Baltimore, Maryland district," the older man said, and then introduced the rest of the panel. The others were two Customs Special Agents, one DEA Agent, and two, as Raymond recall, were of narcotics related task.

Mr. Theilmann and his colleagues were apparently on a trail of series of investigations, and have stopped by F.C.I. Fairton with hope of convincing some drug convicts to aid in identifying fugitive dealers. They had met with several other inmates, and when Raymond was seated, he was shown over a dozen photographs to try to identify anyone of them and tell of the fugitive's activities regarding drug trafficking. Clyde and Richard weren't in any of the photographs, and he didn't recognize any of the others.

"Mr. Karr, I've spoken with your attorney, but I'll try to contact him to notify him about this meeting with you," Mr. Theilmann said. "If I'm not mistaken, you had indicated to New York your willingness to cooperate with the government. Do you still wish to do that?"

"Yes sir," Raymond emphatically answered.

"Are you sure you don't know any of these men?" Mr. Theilmann said and carefully watched Raymond's reaction.

"Well, as you may have already known, I never had previous involvement in a drug deal, so I don't know a whole lot. I had already articulated to the AUSA in New York the extent of my involvement and those who worked with me. I'd be glad to restate their identities to you guys if you're interested. But I'd like to first inform you that I've given out much information about the guys involved to a Virginia based Custom special agent, Donald Wessel, who is still investigating."

"If you don't mind, could you give us those details?" Mr. Theilmann said while his entourage looked on.

Raymond detailed them the same information he had told Mr. Wessel in New York. After Raymond's testimony and several questions and answers by the visitors centered on the whereabouts of Clyde and Richard, Mr. Theilmann made his final comment.

"You know that if any of the information you just gave us ever yielded any result, it would work toward your time reduction?"

"Looking forward to that, sir," Raymond said without enthusiasm.

"Well, thank you, Mr. Karr. We'll be in touch, and we'll work on your information," he said. Raymond shook hands with all of the men, then left to be strip-searched again before reporting back to his coveted forty-six cents per hour prison job. The whole incident would be swallowed by time and hence forgotten.

One cold and windy, early morning in December of "91, Raymond was awakened by the unit's midnight shift Correction Officer at exactly 4:30, and told to pack up his properties and be ready to leave the institution.

"Are you sure I'm the right person?" Raymond lazily asked the officer, hoping he wasn't so he could go back to a wonderful sleep.

"What's your prison number?" the C.O. said, raising his hand to read the identity card he was holding.

Raymond recited his federal prison number and the officer reassured Raymond he was the inmate the message was for.

"Well, where am I going?" Raymond asked foolishly before quickly realizing he wasn't privileged to such information.

"I don't know, man. Just pack up and be sure you're in R and D before six."

At 6 a.m., Raymond had already said goodbye to his friends and collected their names and numbers for future contacts. He wasn't sure where he was going but was quite certain it wasn't home. Transfer was his primary suspicion, but he didn't foresee any reason for that either. he had waived his right to appeal, and that ruled out going back to any court for any reason whatsoever.

At R&D, the duty officer told Raymond he'd been placed on a

writ, purpose or destination unknown to them. All Raymond knew was that he was about to taste a worse hell, riding in the van with shackles and chains all over him again.

The agony of being transported as a prisoner never stopped tormenting the mind, and Raymond's journey to Montgomery County Detention Center in Maryland via Baltimore was indifferent. The prison limousine van, having left F.C.I. Fairton at approximately 10 o'clock that morning, reached Harrisburg International airport at noon, where all six of the inmates occupying the caged back seats sat handcuffed until the Bureau of Prisons airlift aircraft arrived at about 6 p.m. There was no restroom, and no food or drink. At the airport's special terminal, all transit prisoners from the region were transferred either to the BOP's Boeing 727 aircraft or to another prison vehicle. Raymond was transferred to another limousine van for his journey to Rockville, Maryland.

The Montgomery County Detention Center was a complex county holdover jail located in Rockville, Maryland. It also served as a temporary holding jail for federal government inmates, who were on trial or for other judicial obligations around the Baltimore-Washington region. Raymond would be housed in that jail for ninety days and ninety nights, along with some of the most undisciplined human beings he ever saw or encountered.

Having been taken through the normal but slightly different vigorous prison intake routine, Raymond was issued a thin mattress and directed to a narrow unit where he settled inside a room with iron beds nailed to the wall. It was off to sleep, exhaustion overshadowing the killer hunger that made him stagger and savor swallowing his saliva.

Early the following morning, Raymond was awakened by the noise of the loud speaker announcing the names of inmates scheduled for court appearance. Raymond's name was called along with three others, to be picked up by the U.S. Marshals. Raymond had missed breakfast and would be headed for Baltimore on an empty stomach.

The marshals arrived at 9:30 a.m. to pick up all five of the inmates, who had gotten used to the long wait inside crowded bullpens. In twenty minutes, the marshal limousine van rolled out through the custodial exit.

Raymond couldn't bear the sight of the good old route I-270, the beltway and all its exits—Wisconsin Avenue, Connecticut Avenue, Georgia Avenue, New Hampshire Avenue, and the colossal and emblematic Mormon temple, which hung the great sculpture of David Smith blowing a trumpet. Raymond strongly resisted the temptation to look up. He wiped off tears as he just couldn't bear the sight and had to face down to tried to sleep it all off until they reached the city of Baltimore. That would be the same routine all through the five trips he took to Baltimore for duration.

Raymond had guessed right during the transit from New Jersey. Clyde had been taken into custody, and so was Bryan Jason.

Steve Malik was the assistant U.S. attorney prosecuting Clyde, while Bryan Jason's case was being prosecuted by Mr. Gilbert Saltzman and Ms. Hillary Abrams.

Raymond's first meeting was with Mr. Malik inside his office in the courthouse building. Also in attendance was Vic Badanjek, a DEA agent, who reminded Raymond he was an entourage with Mr. John Theilmann when Raymond was questioned in Fairton, New Jersey. Step by step, Raymond recounted his story, and without reservations, gave all the details of the only operation he was involved, from the Sunday evening, when Dennis visited to hint him of an exploration deal, down to the pay-off by his high school colleague, Richard, who flew in from Atlanta to collect the drugs, and ended with his arrest at John F. Kennedy airport.

After the meeting, Raymond was returned to the holding cell, where he waited until 6 o'clock when the marshals came in to transport them back to Rockville. The meeting itself raised Raymond's hopes as Steve Malik had reassured him he would be called to the witness stand on behalf of the government, probably in the last week of December or first week of January.

There was no doubt Raymond would be spending another Christmas in a much stricter confinement, but he didn't care since it was for the sake of freedom – his freedom. As it was, Raymond would be anywhere, be it purgatory or hell, if it meant his ticket to freedom. Moreover, the Washington Redskins were having a Super Bowl strength season, and the fans inside the county jail were going hog-wild.

On the Sunday of the week before Christmas, Steve Malik and

agent Vic Badanjek visited Raymond at the jail, this time to strategize with him on his upcoming performance on the witness stand. During the second meeting, Raymond cautioned, rather respectfully, of his intention to state all the facts as they were and not try to exaggerate in order to appear believable, since his false testimony in New York federal court during his trial would undermine his credibility as a witness. Steve Malik hailed Raymond's personal commitment and advocated it was the exact quality that the department needed to maintain its high standard of justice. After concluding their meeting, Mr. Malik reassured Raymond he would most probably be putting him on the witness stand, and the two discharged him to head back to Baltimore.

Granted, Raymond had a pretty good Christmas. On the eve of the big day, he was called up for another visit, and astonishingly present was his common-law, along with his son and stepdaughter. Also visiting was his long time friend who brought along his wife and two children. Apparently they had been tipped off by Dennis Metu, who was, for some strange reason to Raymond, transferred from the F.C.I. in Kentucky, where he had been designated to serve his prison time, to stay in Prince George's County detention center in Upper Marlboro, Maryland.

Raymond's two-year old was healthy and so was his half sister. Their mother, whom Raymond expected to be worn out from the daunting task of regaining custody of the children, looked equally as good. They spoke through the intercom, and only saw each other through the bullet proof glass, but it was enough to find out all that had happened.

"How did you manage to get the kids out of child welfare?" he asked her.

"It was hell. The baby cried so much, and they couldn't handle it. I had to undergo through so much with respect to counseling to get them back. When are you coming out?" she said.

"I don't know yet. But I know it's gonna be a long, long time. So don't look to me being free anytime soon."

"What am I supposed to do then? I can't wait indefinitely."

"Do whatever you have to do. Just assume I'm dead, 'cause that's what I am—dead," he said.

The visit was concluded in two hours, and Raymond was never

happier, for that day perhaps will undoubtedly be the happiest all through his stay in prison. However, it also brought him to the brink of shedding tears when was watching them as they were on their way out of the visiting room.

Raymond would receive yet another message few months after he got back to New Jersey, that the kids again had been snatched back by the same county social welfare department.

He remained in Montgomery County detention center for almost a month and half without testifying or hearing from the government attorneys, and found that greatly troubling. He wondered what had happened with Clyde's trial, if it was already over. The happiness of seeing his family now faintly hung in the air, and the euphoria from the Redskins' victory in the Super Bowl was beginning to fade away in the darkness of his predicament.

Raymond had to phone Mr. Theilmann for some kind of update.

Mr. Theilmann came on the line after a brief hold.

"Mr. Theilmann," he said, "I'm wondering why I haven't been called up for testimony. No one gave me even a hint of what's going on."

"You have nothing to do with the on-going trial of Clyde, except if they want to talk to you about Bryan Jason. They should be calling you up in a couple of days. And if they're not gonna use you, I'll send you back to New Jersey."

"I see. Well, thank you so much, sir," Raymond said and angrily hung up, once again feeling utterly disappointed.

He stood miserably still by the telephone to contemplate Mr. Theilmann's message. He felt the sentiment of being struck out after all. It left no doubt in his mind it had everything to do with his conduct in the New York courtroom, and that poor judgment to go to trial probably would keep him behind bars for the entire five years, no matter what he did or how he tried to help the government. During one of their meetings, Steve Malik had cautioned Raymond that it would be difficult for him, Raymond, to sound believable to the jury as a witness since he had perjured himself in a New York federal court. Now the big question for Raymond was if the attorneys for the government would still recognize him as the chief source of the information that netted them Clyde and Bryan Jason, and reward him for his endeavor. Mr. Theilmann's statement that Raymond didn't have anything to do with the on-going trial did not strike the chord he was hoping for.

As he sat in his iron bed, his spirit slowly dissolved into chaos and desperation. If all their talk about rewarding him when his information led to something was only a means to con him into giving up the information, he was in for a big shock. They had sounded very sympathetic and friendly toward him when he met them in their office, but now look what they're turning into, he thought.

Raymond fell asleep, heavily perturbed by the freedom threatening development.

The wakeup shake by his cell mate was to collect his dinner tray of four teaspoons full of green peas and meat loaf, and a slice of wheat bread. After dinner, Raymond went back to seclusion to think about how to overcome the trauma from his dashed hopes. He suddenly began to feel it was all beyond his control, and therefore shouldn't have been something he'd allow to cause him a heart attack. After all, he thought, when he initially decided to come forward with the truth, it was for the pious purpose of eradicating some of the damage he'd done to his credibility, and had less to do with his prison time reduction. The hype of being rewarded had been generated by the authorities he had talked to, and escalated by how his adverse situation had affected his family. Now his son and stepdaughter were no longer separated from their mother, and he would pray to God to be with them until his ordeal was over - whenever.

Raymond's efforts to put Mr. Theilmann's negatively resonating message out of his mind were futile, but he had to live with the situation until he was again called up few days later for another trip to Baltimore.

Just after he was freed from handcuffs to be led into the Baltimore courthouse holding cell, he was jolted by the sight of one of five prisoners sitting on the iron bar. It was Clyde.

That incident constituted by far the most embarrassing moment since his trial. Clyde stood up from his seat, and with a mocking smile on his face, paced nervously up and down the cozy cell, murmuring and uttering, "betrayer, ingrate, snitch, Judas." He fixed his face toward him from every direction.

Raymond, though stupidly embarrassed, managed to wave to Clyde after sitting down. He was overwhelmed with shame and fear, but Clyde snobbishly ignored Raymond to continue his soliloquy.

"Clyde," he said, feeling compelled. "Don't you recognize me?"

"Raymond, please leave me alone. Why should I say anything to you? Can you just tell me why after you betrayed me?" he said.

Other prisoners had begun to listen in. It was such a dangerous situation for him because inmates were known to be extremely hostile to known snitches, and it often led to fatal consequence. Raymond also knew that a dangerous label as a snitch tagged along and spread quickly from prison to prison. If that became his fate, he'd be doomed, for he no longer would be housed with the prison general population. He'd be housed in a special housing unit, which would restrain him in what would amount to solitary confinement. It was either that or his life and he couldn't imagine the latter.

"Even Dennis Metu, whom I hardly knew, only meeting once, took the witness stand against me to testify that I, Clyde Ibe, sponsored him twice, and paid him to collect the 'market' he brought. Did I even know Dennis that much to know of his whereabouts, or his 'market' involvement?" Clyde said, obviously angered.

Raymond knew he just had to get to the bottom of it all, and Clyde was more than willing to explain it all to him, unaware he had full knowledge of the origination of Dennis' real drug courier sponsorship.

"Wait a minute," Raymond said, astonished by the revelation. "You mean Dennis took the witness stand against you?"

"I swear to Almighty God he did, and his false testimony is weighing heavily against me. The jury is now deliberating, and in a few minutes, I'll be called in for their inevitable guilty verdict. I'm facing a lot of time if they believe his lies. As for you, Raymond, aren't you going back to the same country? We'll see what you'll earn for singing about me to DEA. Do you think I'm a dummy? Everything was okay until your stupidity sank you like a sailboat, and now all of a sudden Dennis got rocked, triggering a domino effect."

Clyde continued to pace up and down, vehemently lamenting on Dennis' false testimony against him. Meanwhile, Raymond was gladly picked up by the Marshal to be escorted to a large office, where the prosecutors, Mr. Saltzman and Ms. Abrams, were waiting to meet with him. Just as they left the cell, Raymond heard scattered shouts of 'snitch bastard' coming from other neighboring holding cells, a testament of what was to come for him.

Having to be locked in a cell with Clyde and to be called a snitch infuriated Raymond beyond emotional control.

"My safety is compromised, be it here or elsewhere," he said to the government lawyers.

"Why did you say that?" Mr. Saltzman was quick to ask.

"You guys really have no concern for me, and I don't blame you for that. But would you please not lock me in the same cell with Clyde again?"

"What's the problem, George?" Ms. Abrams said. The thirty-something lady, who appeared to be limping over a major leg injury, looked concerned, and so was Mr. Saltzman, who listened attentively while Raymond explained.

"Your guys really did it to me, locking me up in the same holding cell with Clyde Ibe. Now I know why I wasn't called up to testify against him. Quite simple… they used Dennis as a witness against Clyde, and if I were to testify, my testimony would've conflicted with Dennis', and I know my account of what happened is the truth."

The two government prosecutors were startled by his comment.

"Did Clyde tell you that?" Mr. Saltzman said.

"He certainly did, but most importantly, he bitterly embarrassed me in front of other prisoners, calling me all kinds of names, and I'm highly upset at that. Now every inmate out there will label me a snitch"

"We're really sorry about that. Did he threaten you or anything?" Ms. Abrams said.

"No, he didn't threaten me," Raymond said sarcastically "Of course he did, and I don't think it was a bright idea to have used a false witness against him. If he's guilty, it should be from a real witness source and not a false one. I know, first hand, about all the Dennis' two trips to Lagos, and who sponsored him. There's no confusion about that. Dennis was sponsored by Richard on both his trips."

"But you know it's also possible that they may have done something else and turned around to confuse you, right?" Mr. Saltzman said.

After a few arguments with the two prosecutors, he decided it didn't matter what he complained about, he couldn't possibly benefit from it. He wisely chose to end the matter.

"Anyway, you're right, and I think I know well enough that I shouldn't meddle in a matter that is none of my concern. I have too much trouble right now to be looking for more. I'll just seal my mouth on that one."

"Someone screwed up, but I wouldn't worry about it. It won't happen again. I'll be sure of that," Mr. Saltzman said apologetically. The two attorneys deplored the mistake by the Marshals before they began with the story he had told several times.

Raymond was scheduled to mount the witness stand for the trial of Bryan Jason to testify to the extent of his involvement with the American-born drug courier. Raymond detailed every incident to the prosecutors, from the no-show of Jeff at John F. Kennedy airport, to the delivery of ten thousand dollars to Ben in Lagos, and up to the time when they dropped Bryan Jason at the hotel, where Ben had chosen for him to stay in Lagos. In turn, Raymond was debriefed by the two government attorneys, who encouraged him to state the facts only, and not try to exaggerate anything as it would be contrary to their profession's ethics.

"Hopefully, You'll come across believable to the jury," Mr. Saltzman concluded.

The DEA agent, who marched Raymond from the bullpen to the office, cuffed him again and escorted him back to the bullpen. The next day, Raymond would mount the witness stand.

Chapter 26

The Final Fate

On the ride back to Rockville jail, Raymond was becoming increasingly concerned about the government attorneys' story on Clyde. The whole affair, after thinking it all over, didn't sit well with his conscience. He wondered why the prosecutors put Dennis on the witness stand against Clyde, after he had repeatedly debriefed them of his narcotics involvement with Dennis Metu. His thinking was that Dennis had lied to them, probably because he had become too desperate to regain his own freedom.

Raymond also suspected that Dennis may have had difficulty fingering Richard, who actually flew in from Atlanta to pay him and Kenny for the heroin. Since he only met Richard once and did not know much about his identity, enough to feed the eager feds, it was only convenient that his only ticket to freedom was to limit his fingering on Clyde. Scapegoating Clyde alone sounded uncomplicated.

Still, Dennis might have been coerced to bend the truth on the witness stand by the aggressive prosecutors, who were out to nab drug kingpins. Whatever happened behind closed doors between Dennis and the government attorneys remained a mystery to him. Every perspective indicated that something was missing somewhere.

Raymond knew he had accounted to the best of his knowledge every detail of his drug courier involvement to the government attorneys. It seemed unsettling to him that prosecutors were well aware of the true story but could have decided to look the other way. They may have figured since Dennis, having made more than just one trip to Lagos, would make a more formidable witness in the eyes of the jury. Raymond's first and only trip wouldn't be enough evidence to tag a kingpin.

He wondered how Dennis explained Richard's involvement. If

Dennis and he were on the same side for the government, he couldn't comprehend why they were in separate holdover jails. Having both men locked up in separate courtroom holding cells only fueled his suspicion of a hanky-panky. No matter what, it was quite accurate to say that if both he and Dennis were to be called to the witness stand, their testimonies would be incoherent. That, Raymond surmised, must have been the reason why only one of them had to be called, and it had to be one with a more damaging account - Dennis.

In the morning of Raymond's day to mount the witness stand against Brian Jason, two marshal vehicles, one that he was transported in and another from the Prince Georges County detention center in Upper Marlboro, Maryland, had just emptied their inmate passengers. Raymond was caught by surprise at who stepped out of the vehicle – Dennis Metu. Raymond was flabbergasted when he saw how elated Dennis became at seeing his old buddy that he, Raymond, was ready to bury whatever hatchet there was. Both men quickly exchanged love for one-another since it was unlawful for inmates from one federal prison to communicate with those from another federal prison.

In their brief encounter, he found, perhaps not surprisingly, that Dennis still maintained his good sense of humor. As when he asked Dennis what his prison stay in Michigan was like, Dennis was still his old self.

"Commissioner," Dennis said, "these people hammered me with eight whole years of my life and some change. It's so frustrating, but as frustrating as it is, I wouldn't mind them tacking on an extra year for a six-pack of green bottles."

Raymond chuckled aloud, alerting the marshals, who stared briefly and continued with their discussion.

"Did you ever hear from your girlfriend, Annette, or did you pretty much cast everyone away?" he asked Dennis after their discussions on the matter that brought both of them together.

"I don't even want to think about her anymore. Every time I think about her, all I get is nothing but sheer frustration and an unstoppable erection. What benefit is that for me? She called me twice and I had to tell her to stop. I'm gonna be in jail for such a long time I don't even want to communicate with any woman. Commissioner, I'm so hungry for sex that, if I come across anything that even remotely resembles a vagina, honestly speaking, I'm shoving in penis."

Raymond sank right into the land of laughter. Dennis laughed nearly as hard too, inevitably attracting the attention of the two marshals, who hurried over to admonish both men. To ensure it did not happen again, they immediately hauled Dennis away. Raymond laughed because he knew he felt the same way about sexual starvation but couldn't have expressed it any better.

Raymond was again called to Mr. Saltzman's office for what they told him was a final strategy. Steve Malik, who prosecuted Clyde, came in to speak to him about his status in his case. Also present was Ms. Abrams, who reported to Steve Malik about his incidental run-in with Clyde in the bullpen.

"That's a major mistake," Malik said. He seemed shocked and inwardly angered about the blunder. He apologized repeatedly before telling Raymond the news he had been waiting to hear.

"We didn't need to put you on the witness stand after all, because we already had overwhelming evidence against Clyde. But your information was extremely important in winning a conviction, and I'll be sure to recommend that to Mr. Zimmerman in New York. I just had to come down here to sincerely thank you for your cooperation."

He smiled happily, feeling there couldn't have been a moment looking brighter since his ordeal.

They shook hands before Steve Malik left the office. Raymond was escorted back to the bullpen to await his turn to testify against Bryan Jason. He would get the call at about 2 o'clock, and on the witness stand, he meticulously narrated the incident, led by the AUSA Mr. Saltzman, before answering humiliating questions from Bryan Jason's extremely aggressive lawyer. When Raymond took his seat on the witness stand, he saw Bryan Jason for the first time since the day they met after arrival in Lagos. The man he saw in Lagos had changed. He had gained weight mostly in his face. Bryan Jason sat next to his lawyer and stared fixedly at Raymond with a combination of pure hate and astonishment.

Bryan Jason's lawyer's questions mostly focused on Raymond's credibility and false testimony during his trial in New York, and Raymond admitted his fault, accepted his responsibility for the mischief, and called it unfortunate and regretful.

After Raymond's testimony, he was escorted again from the bullpen to attorney-client room, where Mr. Saltzman took time off to come in and extend sincere thanks for his composure and believable testimony on the witness stand.

"I want to assure you that Mr. Zimmerman is an old friend of mine, and I'll be sure to let him know of your extreme value to our region, okay?" Mr. Saltzman said, obviously enthused as if something screwed up had been unscrewed.

"I thank you, sir. If I may ask, would you please send me a copy of any letter of recommendation you send to Mr. Zimmerman?" he said enthusiastically.

"No problem. I'll do that as soon as possible," Mr. Saltzman said

Raymond was led back to the pen where he sat until evening transport back to Montgomery County jail.

The agony of staying in the county jail lasted until the tenth of March, almost a month and a half from the middle of January when he was told he had completed his writ obligation. He couldn't wait to be transported back to New Jersey prison because of the increasingly intolerable environment in the county jail. He had incurred a broken nose for mediating a shouting match between a Cuban inmate and a white American bully, who summoned three of his young African-American commissary dependents to rush him. Raymond obviously hadn't learned from the last brawling incident in MCC bullpen. This time around, it had been more serious, and medically Raymond had been improperly cared for and had emaciated to almost beyond recognition.

However, the euphoria from the thought of receiving a letter from the U.S. attorney's office recommending him for a sentence reduction overshadowed his pain and suffering. He was looking forward to a day, any moment, when he'd stand before Judge Simon Boscolo to hear the Judge tell him he'd be free in a month or two, or for that matter, pronounce "time-served."

Meanwhile, during their ride back to New Jersey prison, Raymond would suffer a two-day physical and mental torture from the marshals escorting him. When he arrived at the institution and released into the prison population, it felt like home.

His dream of achieving freedom sooner vanished a few months after his arrival back to F.C.I. Fairton, New Jersey. After the traditional 4 p.m. standup count, Raymond received a shocking letter, a copy of the recommendation sent to Mr. Zimmerman in New York by an attorney from the Baltimore region. In the letter, Mr. Saltzman simply reminded Mr. Zimmerman of their previous telephone conversation, advising him of the cooperation that Raymond had rendered their office regarding Clyde and Bryan.

The letter mentioned that in the case of United States Vs. Clyde Ibe, Raymond Karr was debriefed by the attorneys trying the case and that Mr. Karr strongly indicated his willingness to testify to the facts he knew about Clyde's involvement in heroin trafficking. It cited that because the case against Clyde was an extremely strong one, however, the attorneys handling the case made a tactical decision that his testimony would not be necessary.

The letter further stated that Raymond subsequently testified, however, in the case of United States vs. Bryan Jason, which was tried February between18th and 26th, 1992. Mr. Saltzman admitted in the letter that Raymond was extremely cooperative in preparing for his testimony in the matter, and that he thought Raymond's testimony on the stand was truthful. Also that he did not appear to exaggerate the number of his contacts with the defendants, and he set precise limits on what he did and did not know about Bryan's involvement in the heroin smuggling ring that was the subject of the case. Mr. Saltzman's word that did not particularly please Raymond in his letter was that Raymond's testimony, though, was not of central importance to the case. Although Mr. Saltzman did mention he believed that the testimony usefully corroborated that of several other cooperating witnesses, and he was glad that Raymond's testimony was available to the government. He stated also that he would certainly say that his testimony made a significant contribution to the conviction of Bryan Jason.

The conclusion of the letter decided everything.

"As we discussed over the phone, I realize that there is a serious question as to whether the district court still retains any authority to reduce Mr. Karr's sentence in light of the period of time that has passed since he was originally sentenced. If there is anything that you or your superiors believe you could do at this stage to reward Mr. Karr for his cooperation in the cases brought by this office, I would be glad to have this letter considered by the court in that regard."

Not a thing came Raymond's way, and he never heard from Mr. Zimmerman or his attorney, Mr. Cunningham. If he survived prison, he knew he would face imminent deportation to oblivion, for which he faulted no one but himself. He had come to realize with absolute conviction that when it came to immigration, it might be easy to remove a person from America but difficult, if not impossible, to remove the American in a person.

Six months after he returned from his Writ of Testificandum in Maryland Federal District Court, his hope to re-gain his freedom sooner was slowly fading away. He was mentally poised to serve out his entire five-year prison sentence, which felt like a lifetime. But whenever his thoughts went to all he suffered in Maryland, a renewed determination to fight on took hold. It was one of his inhibitive acquisitions during his decade stay in America to never quit fighting for a good cause.

Raymond devised other plans to gain freedom and went right at them. Each day after work at his UNIBASE job site, the institution's dinner call blasted in the loudspeaker. His agenda was to go straight to the institution's law library for research. His colleagues would persuade him to join them in either soccer practice or in a game of spade, but he would decline, instead would spend his recreation time sifting through thousands of pages of law books. He would thoroughly investigate the validity of any that had anything to do with the American jurisprudence.

The one thing Raymond was certain about was that he had a very fair-minded judge during his trial, and so to leave no stone unturned in his quest for freedom, he decided to communicate his disappointment with the US Attorney's office to Judge Boscolo. In his letter to the judge, he detailed his co-operation with the US Attorney's office in Maryland, his disappointment with his lawyer in not adequately representing him in his quest to timely receive the sentence reduction's 5K-1 letter. He also attached a copy of the communication between Assistant US Attorney, Mr. Saltzman in Maryland and Mr. Zimmerman the Assistant US Attorney in New York, who prosecuted his case. He inherently felt that Judge Boscolo should be informed but was well aware the judge, who must have been overwhelmed with numerous dockets on his calendar, must have forgotten who he was. Still it did not deter him from making such move.

Midway through his second year in the slammer, it was all an emotional roller-coaster to him, sometimes furtively composed, ready to ride out the five years, and sometimes torturous and tormenting. There had been no visits from any relatives or so-called friends, which frankly was something he never wanted anyway. He had had some time to think through all his past friendships, male and female. It had finally come to dawn on him that the circle of friends he had during his early years in America was his true friends. They were all academically inclined and highly motivated toward success. They were also the no-nonsense one-strike-and-you're-out individuals, who would have nothing to do with a person in Raymond's current predicament. And so he was well aware he was morally impeded from re-joining that category of fine social friendship and it sickened him to his stomach whenever he thought about it. He would sit and think about how shocked they will be if they learned of his fate. Not only they knew him personally, but they knew his very popular family in Nigeria and well aware of his untainted family background of doctors, lawyers, nurses, engineers, etc. Raymond knew his later circle of friends earned him the ugly spot he was in and to reside for the next four years and so he began to regret everyone he had met from five years before prison.

He had endured the confinement of his second summer in incarceration, when in early September he received an official letter from the US Attorney's office in the Eastern District of New York. It was such an uncertain moment, for he knew it could have been anything. Certainly there was a prospect of being slapped with a superseding indictment for whatever reason so he knew not to open it immediately in the very presence of curious fellow inmates. He impatiently waited until the next ten-minute on the hour inmate movement and when it was finally announced he rushed back to his unit. Fortunately his cellmate was absent, which pleased him quite enormously. He shut the steel door behind him and immediately opened the big brown envelope with a heightened sense of caution. Inside it pulled out a four-page letter signed by Mr. Zimmerman. In the letter, Mr. Zimmerman was responding to an apparent letter written to him by Judge Boscolo asking Mr. Zimmerman if he would object to the judge's vacating of Raymond's original sentence to re-sentence him in light of his substantial co-operation with the government prosecutors despite the lapse of time. Mr. Zimmerman had agreed not to object to Judge Boscolo's suggestion but cautioned the judge to not overly compensate Raymond since the judge had, during sentencing, already sliced three months from his sentencing guideline.

Raymond was ecstatic at the prospect of returning to Judge Boscolo for a sentence reduction. Once again, the kindness of the Honorable Simon Boscolo was coming to his rescue. He knew right at the moment that he wasn't going to spend all five years in jail. He welcomed any reduction, even if it was for a day. Anything that could at least acknowledge his sincere effort to self-rehabilitate would be fine with him.

He climbed atop his double-bunk bed to relish the entire unfolding episode and the excitement grew more and more. The thought of a lenient Judge Boscolo, legally empowered to arbitrarily decide his new sentence, was titillating. He felt like break-dancing. For the first time the man, who had been plagued by one predicament after another, had a reason to celebrate. He had also been losing his appetite over impending dooms, but now, suddenly, he'd lose one for what felt like a super good news.

In the weeks following the arrival of the letter, he read and re-read it almost every day and discerned every wording to avoid any possible misinterpretation. He wanted to ascertain that there would be no undue expectation on his part, a bitter lesson he had learned, time after time, in other experiences in the past. The moment the letter arrived, he had read it frequently, even as frequent as at the top of every hour. Then the reading routine had spanned to the end of every meal, and then to at least once or twice a day. It never bored him to re-read the letter, for it was like a gift of endless pleasure. The excitement never subsided in him. He became so familiar with all the wordings of the letter that he could quote a large portion of it without even looking.

His obsession with the letter from the US Attorney's office was equally accompanied by the expectation that he'd be called to pack his property for his journey back to the federal courthouse in the Eastern District of New York. He wasn't quite sure how that worked. He'd never before experienced a circumstance such as sentence reduction, nor had he spoken to an actual person who had been issued with such letter. He certainly could not discuss it with anyone else, lest he compromised his own security were he to be labeled a snitch.

Three months after the letter, Raymond's cellmate rushed in to inform him that his name was one of about six others listed to be transferred to another federal correctional facility in Loretto, Pennsylvania. Disappointed and confused, he climbed atop his bed, reached under his mattress and retrieved the letter and read it once again. Still it was unmistakable. He had been recommended by the Justice Department for a sentence reduction. The question should've no longer been if but when? Since he had to keep the letter a top secret for several reasons, mostly his own security, it frustrated him that he just couldn't seek an opinion from anyone. He constantly reminded himself it was something that could not slip out of his tongue. Sentence reduction meant a person must have snitched to merit such gratuity and therefore could lead to inmate hostility, and that was deadly in the prison world. The jailhouse cliché, *Snitches End Up In Ditches With Stiches*, always hung in his mind.

He folded the letter in its original form and replaced it under his mattress. He reached out to his locker and took out the lone can of orange soda he had been reluctant to expend, opened and sipped to a certain degree of savory. He placed the soda can between two iron rods guarding the window and relaxed back on his bed, now becoming his sanctuary, facing the ceiling.

The sound of his cellmate flushing the toilet awoke him. He knew right away he had dozed off, and it slightly angered him. When he looked at his wrist watch, it was almost 9 p.m. He had not showered and last call for bathing was at 8:45 p.m. He lifted his arms to smell his pits. Sure enough they registered, prompting him to damn himself. He reached for the remnant of his orange soda and gulped it down. His cellmate was already lying in his lower bunk bed listening to the music from his Walkman. He climbed down from his top bunk bed, trash the empty can, before making for the door. He was just about to reach for the door handle when he heard the all too familiar click sound. It was the correction officer locking the door for the day. Frustrated, he climbed back atop his bed, where he spent most of the night regurgitating in his mind the events that led to the state he found himself.

The entire last week of June went by and nothing happened with the inmate re-designation to Lorretto, Pennsylvania. Raymond had a very restful weekend, mostly staying indoors, and was looking forward to a week that was to see a pay day. His commissary account was nearly empty and he needed to re-stock his locker with items such as Oodles and Noodles soup, soda, crackers, and stamps for communication. He also badly needed a can of shaving powder. He had borrowed for his last three shavings and it was beginning to worry him that he was likely a subject of gossips as being a ward of his fellow inmates, a thin-veiled status as a leech. And so he had endured without most of his unavailable needs.

Early Monday morning, the unit officer opened the door. "Inmate Karr, pack up your properties, you're leaving the institution, possibly for re-designation," he said and re-examined the sheet of paper he was holding. "The same goes to you too," he said, with his flashlight, pointed at Raymond's lower bunk cellmate.

There was no indication that it was about his trip back to New York for re-sentencing, but he held out the hopes of being separated from other re-designated inmates for that subject matter. As he and his cellmate were packing their belongings, he kept relishing the prospect of re-sentencing. He was speculating how much time Judge Boscolo was likely to shave off his five-year sentence. Three months maybe? Five? He knew that six months off his original sentence was less likely, but his little knowledge of Judge Boscolo re-assured him it was not farfetched. That would really excite him. He mentally calculated his time. He'd serve eighty-five percent of his time if he remained in good prison standing, which was fifty-one months out of the sixty months. He had already served 19 months of that, leaving him with only thirty-two more. If Judge Boscolo were to shave off another six, he'd be sitting pretty at only twenty-six months left in his time in prison.

Suddenly Raymond began to dwell heavily on the prospect of six months sentence reduction. Although he cautioned himself several time not to be overly optimistic, he still subconsciously factored it in his mental calculus. The correction officer came in to warn him and his cellmate they were taking too long to come out and join the four other members of the unit leaving for FCI Loretto. Two laundry bags substituted for suitcase. Basically all inmate properties consisted of books, family photo albums, sweat suits, and commissary items. That was all. Inmates could not take any item issued from the institution. They must all be surrendered to the correction officer.

When Raymond and his cellmate finally came out hauling along two laundry bags containing their properties, the correction officer hurriedly matched all six inmates straight through the grass field to Receiving and Discharge office about two hundred and fifty yards away from Unit D, Raymond's housing unit. He and his fellow inmates were kept in a holding cell, where they would undergo the twelve grueling hours of inmate discharge protocol, before finally transported to FCI Loretto.

Officer Ivan Foster, in charge of FCI Loretto UNICOR operation, rushed in soon after lunch hour to personally escort Raymond to his unit. This came unexpectedly four months following his arrival at the lowest security level institution. All inmates, capacity of seven hundred, had a year or less to go in their sentences. They posed virtually no flight risk at all, and no record of physical violence. The housing units were more like a college dorm and the windows had no iron bars. The compound was thinly fenced that one could easily jump over. The only count was the Bureau of Prison's 6 p.m. mandatory count. Food was great with more variation. Inmates could sense and breathe freedom at FCI Loretto after so many years of confinement in other higher level institutions. Raymond was introduced to several such high-profile inmates as former lawmakers, former Wall Street executives in for insider trading, ex-movie stars in for tax evasion, even law enforcement officers and ex-judges and lawyers mostly in for bribery and corruption. All on the verge of serving out their time and walking free.

He could not read any meaningful cause out of the fact he still had over three years left in his jail time but nonetheless was re-designated to such a low-level institution. If Raymond didn't care, he sure loved the much relaxed confinement. He loved the fall atmosphere and there was a certain wind which blew that ushered in him an aura of freedom. Perhaps it came from the fact that he no longer had five years of prison time ahead of him but less than half of that if his prison term was reduced.

Raymond counted days but he knew he was also passing some of his jail time as he waited for the impending sentence reduction. He had grown so obsessed with the sentence reduction that he once even had a wild speculation that Judge Boscolo could go as far as a whole year grace. But he quickly shut down that speculation as senselessly improbable if not impossible. He chose to stay with the hope that six months was not farfetched and three or four months reduction was more likely.

It took him just twenty minutes or so to pack and be ready for a journey to New York City. He harbored some doubts that, after his reduced sentence, he was going to be designated anywhere else other than FCI Loretto. He left notes to a couple of his cellmates, asking them to hold on to the books and other items he lent them. He hoped to be assigned to the same unit but he knew it would be an uncertain prospect. He also was well aware he might not even be returning to the same correctional institution. But the savory about it all for him was that inmate transit with the Bureau of Prisons took time and that by the time he'd be back to FCI Loretto, it could take as much as six months in transit. Factor that with whatever sentence reduction he would be receiving, it meant almost a whole year off his jail time. That to him was very exciting.

As Raymond was awaiting the institution's discharge protocol, alone in a holding cell, he reflected on everything that happened, from his acceptance to run a drug courier through the exhibition of the ninth photograph to his arrival at MCC holding jail in Manhattan. As his reflections reached MCC, he began to dread being housed in Otisville prison. Otisville almost always brought him to instant agony whenever he remembered his botched trial, the sickness that almost killed him, the nightmarish journeys to and from MCC New York. They were all flashbacks he never wanted to re-live but one that kept creeping in from time to time in the prison

It was not until 7:35 p.m. that FCI Loretto officially released Raymond to the custody of two US Marshals, who came to transport him to New York City. This time, Raymond was sitting comfortably alone in the back seat of an unmarked black Chevy sedan with heavily tinted windows. Although Raymond was shackled, he found the ride relatively smooth, no turns. His only wish was that the ride on his way back to FCI Loretto remained as comfortable – with a shortened jail term.

In just two and a half hours, Raymond was back in MCC New York, the very dreadful first jail nearly two years back, where he was initially housed following his arrest and where tears in his eyes flowed like river. There were virtually no changes at all. Everything looked the same, correction officers and intake officials were still the same except that inmates in his eighth floor unit were total strangers. He saw no Nigerian inmates, although at 10 p.m. it was almost lockdown and most could have already been back in their cells and ready to call it another day. He arrived at MCC too late for dinner and so he woke up the next morning to find out that food still sucked in the jail.

While in MCC, Raymond remained low-keyed, absorbing the bitter memories, and there were many. He avoided the usual cellmate questions and answers about what brought inmates there and how long they'd be incarcerated. He never asked his new cellmate, a chubby Ecuadorian in his forties, any questions at all. He mostly listened as the inmate rambled about how he was unjustly framed and arrested over some bullshit drug and gun possession, how innocent he was and how he planned to beat the charges. It was the same usual posture most inmates portrayed of themselves as if no one in the jail committed any crime. He was surprised at how composed the Ecuadorian was in his ninth day of lockup. He remembered his early days of being apprehended and how dreadful it was for him, for he could barely eat in a bitter loss of appetite.

Three nights sleep in the MCC jail, Raymond was awakened 4:30 a.m. the fourth morning by the unit's correction officer for the routine inmate readiness for a 10 a.m. court appearance just across the Hudson River to Brooklyn's United States courthouse in the Eastern District of New York. Raymond was reminisced by the dreadfulness of going from one crowded bullpen to another, standing room only for a prolonged period and being ordered around like the villain he had become. The reminiscence was unsettling but the prospect of some months off his prison term provided recompense.

While waiting in the bullpens, he repeatedly deliberated on the prospect of prison sentence reduction. Could Judge Boscolo really shave as much as six months off his time? Raymond though it really would be way too much and hoped that even if the ever so kind judge went that distance, Mr. Zimmerman the AUSA wouldn't appeal it. Six months off seemed too generous. At the end of every deliberation, Raymond would conclude he'd rather stay with the pessimistic approach of hoping for three months or four at best. He hoped that Judge Boscolo possessed the judicial fortitude to slash six months though. Whichever one it was, he couldn't wait to be back to FCI Loretto to serve out the remainder of his time.

The clock on the desk officer's wall struck at 8:45 a.m. when a jail officer unlocked the court-bound bullpen. Inmates in that particular bullpen had already been inspected and shackled, awaiting transportation to various courthouses. He marched along in a seemingly familiar routine to an elevator that took them to the jailhouse's basement, where they boarded the Ford van equipped with siren and bullet proof windows. The bus meandered its way to the street level and sped off, escorted by a siren-blowing squad car in front and another behind. Raymond, through the limited view of the windows, saw the river end buildings of Manhattan and hated it even more than he hated it during his trial days. If it wasn't for the purpose of sentence reduction, it would have triggered a renewed sense of awe, which inwardly by the way seemed to be somewhat lurking in the horizon of his mentality. In his thought, he hoped it would be his very last such awful trip and that he would receive his six months sentence reduction and return to a more homely FCI Loretto to serve out his remaining prison term.

Just when the van reached the final turn from the ramp from Park Row overlooking One Police Plaza, and entered the ramp that led to Brooklyn Bridge, Raymond realized he had subconsciously assumed he was going to receive six months sentence reduction. He inwardly chose to believe this could indeed happen. If that would be the case, he told himself he was going to dance all the way back to FCI Loretto. He closed his eyes and said a prayer, making an impassioned plea to God to grant his wish of receiving as much as six months grace from his jail term. He imagined what it would feel like to be back in FCI Loretto with only two years and just a few months left to serve and came away with a feeling of optimism and euphoria.

The van raced across Brooklyn Bridge and veered off to the service road that led to the courthouse on Cadman Plaza East by the end of the bridge. Raymond's heart began to thump as the van turned right just before Tillary Street and unto the ramp that led to the court's special underground parking. What if Mr. Zimmerman strongly objected? Raymond was certain six months grace was simply too much to ask for and it was sure to raise a solid objection from a shrewd AUSA. He cautiously and deliberately chose to fall back to the hopes of three or four months as his big hope for six months jail time grace was rapidly fading into guarded optimism, and quite frankly sometimes approaching outright doubt. It came to a point where his hope for that much grace required a willing suspension of doubt. Not certain what to make of the mind-boggling question, he chose to leave it all in the hands of God. Since he as a Catholic was shackled and could not lift his hands for the sign of cross, he managed to place his hands on his lap and with his index finger drew a cross on his right thigh.

Shortly, thereafter, Raymond was in one of several courthouse holding cells, along with criminal suspects undergoing their own legal due process. As he looked at them he was always reminded of his own ordeal nearly two years back. The unpleasant reminiscence was ever present. Every now and then, he would shrug and vow never to plunge himself into such a horrific situation ever again. This time around, he never wanted to establish any rapport with other prisoners. In his thoughts, all he wanted was to conclude his purpose of the trip and quietly return to FCI Loretto.

At about 11:45 a.m., one of the marshals came to escort him to the courtroom holding cell, the same one with the size of a small elevator he was always held in during his trial days. Raymond's heart pounded even harder as he waited to be called inside Judge Boscolo's courtroom. Moments later, Mr. Cunningham, his undesirable court-appointed lawyer, casually strolled in and peeped through the cage.

"George?" Mr. Cunningham called out in a low voice.

Raymond almost did not answer. But on a quick second thought he decided to handle it politely. So after a moment of hesitation, he quipped, "Yes?"

That was as polite as Raymond could find himself achieving at the moment. Whether or not Mr. Cunningham figured out his lack of enthusiasm to communicate with him was of no discernable significance to Raymond. This was the man who couldn't fight for him in his most vulnerable time. Raymond thought about his lost luggage, his money that was seized by the agents of the US Customs that was never returned to him, the court-appointed lawyer's lackluster performance during trial and refusal to help secure a downward departure during sentencing in the wake of his client's co-operation with the law enforcement. Raymond found it all reprehensible to warrant a chat with him. In fact, he was so glad a handshake was impossible since he was unreachably caged in.

Mr. Cunningham was about to speak when the courtroom marshal hurried in, yelled out Raymond's name and unlocked the door. Raymond gladly walked out and led by the courtroom marshal toward the courtroom, avoiding looking at his defense counsel. Cunningham silently followed behind and everyone walked inside the courtroom after a brief stop by the court entrance door to remove his handcuffs. Raymond, not waiting to be told, took the position he was accustomed with at the defendant's stand. Mr. Cunningham closely stood next to Raymond, who contemplated the mild and ridiculous urge to punch him in his face but was easily tempered by the inevitable repercussion.

The Honorable Simon Boscolo was already seated. He was concentrating on material he was reading. The sight of Judge Boscolo seating behind the bench instantly reminded Raymond of how friendly the court had been to him in the past. All of a sudden, he felt the thumping of his heart significantly subside. But the sight of Mr. Zimmerman walking up to take the prosecutor's stand concerned him. Raymond was well aware Mr. Zimmerman stood between three to four month credit he thought he could receive and six months credit he wished he would receive toward his sentence reduction. Whichever one it was to be, he was then ready to get it over with.

Moments later, Judge Boscolo removed his glasses and looked up at the general direction of both the prosecution and the defense.

"Good morning, Your Honor," Raymond greeted loudly.

Judge Boscolo ignored Raymond's greeting and it left him pondering in his mind what the judge was up to. He had been responsible for Raymond's presence in his courtroom for sentence reduction, so why the cold shoulder? Raymond guessed that the prospect of a six months sentence reduction was virtually out the window. Judge Boscolo then briefly turned his head to the stenographer, a bespectacled middle-aged lady in a gray pants suit, to ascertain she was ready to proceed, and turned to the clerk.

"You may proceed, Mrs. Zahn," Judge Boscolo said in a very gentle tone of voice familiar to Raymond, re-arranging the docket sheets scattered on his desk.

The clerk began her routine re-introduction of the case in the United States versus Raymond Karr and recited the docket number. Raymond's heartbeat felt completely normal and he was calm and wildly speculative. In his mind he urged the judge to go ahead and make or break his day. How about only one month sentence reduction or nothing at all…why not six months…while at it, why not nuke 'um and reduce a cool year, that would surely make a sound fairytale? It would be nice to have only a year left to spend in FCI Loretto, wouldn't it?

Judge Boscolo turned to Mr. Zimmerman the Assistant United States Attorney.

"Counsel, would you like to proceed with your motion?"

Mr. Zimmerman stood up and reiterated that as per the direction of the court whether his office would characterize Raymond's assistance as sufficiently substantial to warrant a reduction of sentence were it not time barred pursuant to Rule 35(b) of the Federal Rules of Criminal Procedure. If so whether the United States Attorney's office would object to an order vacating Raymond's judgment of conviction for the limited purpose of permitting a resentence. That he would not object to sentence reduction for as long as it did not exceed a measured reward.

Raymond, who was looking down, turned his head to face Mr. Zimmerman and hated him even more. This was the man who really didn't want him to ever leave jail any time soon. He thought Mr. Zimmerman would surely object to a six months sentence reduction, let alone anything more. But he also knew he would stand at a legal advantage if he received the six months grace while the AUSA appealed, so it was a preferable outcome.

After Mr. Zimmerman concluded his motion introduction, Judge Boscolo paused.

"The defendant has served a year and nine months in prison," the judge said and searched the docket, looking to corroborate his assertion with actual record.

"Correct, your honor, a year and nine months," Mr. Zimmerman quickly confirmed.

"Thanks counsel,"Judge Boscolo and briefly consulted his diary before he continued.

"Well then, the defendant, having rendered substantial assistance to the government in their prosecution of suspected criminals, and having already served a year and nine months in prison...."

After another brief pause, Judge Boscolo turned to face Raymond. "Before I continue, Mr. Karr, do you wish to say anything else?"

Raymond wasn't ready for that question but he wisely chose to address the court.

"Yes, your honor, I just want to say that I'm truly sorry for my misconduct and I promise to be of good behavior and a model citizen for the rest of my life, be it in prison or when I regain freedom."

Once again Judge Boscolo looked down and studied one of several documents on his desk before coming down with his decision on how much credit he would receive for his co-operation with the government counsels.

"I therefore resentence the defendant to... time served."

Raymond's jaw went slack. He was instantly plunged into a mix of sheer panic and unanticipated euphoria. Eyes dilated he looked to the right at his lawyer and further right to Mr. Zimmerman, both of whom were expressionless, just listening attentively to the judge as he continued with his instructions.

"The defendant has an INS detainer on record and therefore shall be turned over to the custody of US Immigration and Naturalization Service." Judge Boscolo signed a document then continued.

"Record also indicates the defendant has an outstanding warrant with the State of Maryland in which case he must serve out the warrant accordingly."

Raymond instantly recalled his inability to show up in Maryland traffic court in the wake of his detention at JFK airport. He doubted that the State of Maryland would want to waste enormous resources on a traffic violation warrant.

After a long pause while he was writing, Judge Boscolo looked up and asked, "Anything further?"

"Yes, your honor, the government requests that the originally imposed probation period on the defendant remain the same," Mr. Zimmerman said and cleared his throat twice.

"How many years on record?" Judge Boscolo questioned, looking at his secretary.

"Four years, your honor," Mr. Zimmerman quickly said.

The secretary searched out his original sentence sheet and confirmed to the judge that four years was indeed accurate.

Meanwhile, Raymond, smiling, his eyes scanning everything, was mesmerized by the unexpected freedom from a US prison. No more questions about four months or six months of jail time reduction. Not even one year, and no FCI Loretto either. He felt his emotion running uncontrollably wild, so wild he almost hugged his lawyer, Mr. Cunningham, whom he loathed so much. Sonofabitch, I forgive you, he thought in his euphoric mind as he looked at Mr. Cunningham's direction.

Judge Boscolo continued. "The four years of probation shall remain the same as stated by counsel for the government, thank you counsel for reminding me of that," Judge Boscolo said.

Raymond could care less about how many years of probation he was to receive. He couldn't wait for an opportunity to dance in celebration of an unexpected freedom from humiliating shackles, miserable bullpens; he hated bullpens with a passion, macho C.O's who tested the height of their meanness, nagging count times, forced lockdowns, constant frisking, the whole dehumanizing prison world. Suddenly without warning, Raymond was staring at freedom from all. He dreamed of a chance to redeem himself and that opportunity had finally come. And so as far as he was concerned, probation for life meant nothing to him. All he needed to do was become the Raymond Karr he was before undertaking his journey to Lagos, Nigeria.

"The court would stand in recess," Judge Boscolo concluded, gaveled and exited the courtroom.

A female marshal, contrary to the usual two males, escorted him back to his bullpen, this time without the usual handcuffs at the door. And just likewise, with only a set of handcuffs and no shackles, Raymond was led down to the basement bullpen via the elevator, where he was to await the arrival of an immigration field officer for an official prisoner handover.

Late that afternoon, several hours after he had been set free, he sat sometimes alone and sometimes with other due processing inmates, some of whom he chatted with and some he chose to ignore. He mostly listened, but when pressed to discuss his own plight with the law, he simply and wisely told them he was in for income tax evasion, a highly complicated legal subject that so bored bullpen inmates that they didn't want to hear another word on it. Culturally, inmates never talked about their imminent departure from prison as such disclosure could prove deadly. At least so he learned during the course of his time in prison. Jealousy was known to be the driving force. An inmate facing life in the slammer, who would have nothing to lose could take it all out on the bragger.

Raymond spent some of the time he was alone in the bullpen relishing his new freedom. Only at that point in his lifetime had he fully imagined and fully appreciated how magnificent it must have felt like the day freedom broke out of slavery. He had read about slavery in history class and how abolitionists like British Thomas Clarkson and William Wilberforce and a host of other pioneers of antislavery fought relentlessly to end the unconscionable practice. He knew that slavery was finally abolished and freedom reigned, but until his release from jail he never really thought much about the feeling of the individuals who were directly impacted by the abolition. His own freedom from prison had given him a snippet of the momentous nature of freedom from slavery. He was totally convinced it must have been a wildly ecstatic experience.

At 7:35 p.m. that evening, he was still being held, alone in the bullpen, for pick up by the Immigration field office. He was extremely tired and despite the happy mood that blocked his appetite for food for most of the day, it was becoming apparent he needed to eat. His stomach was growling and he was beginning to feel weak. He called out for a marshal, who responded and told him they'd release him if no one came for him by 8.

"Did you get a sandwich?" the marshal, a slim white male with red hair, asked Raymond.

"Nope, none at all," he responded hoping the marshal would offer one.

"I can't understand why not, but you should be heading outta here shortly," the marshal concluded and started to walk away.

Raymond looked at the clock hanging on the wall where the desk clerk sat and it showed it was only about 20 minutes before it struck 8 o'clock. Raymond thought he might be walking out after all and not did have to deal with the Immigration detainer immediately. But the moment he was about to resume his seat on the concrete bench, the content of the conversation he overheard was crushing disappointment.

"Oh, there you are, what took you guys so long?" the voice of the red-haired marshal was unmistakable.

"Sorry about that, we had a busy day today," replied the other male voice with a certain distinct accent.

"Well, let's look at it this way, at least you're here," the marshal said and both men laughed in a mutual agreement. "C'mon over, your man is sitting right over there."

Raymond was very disappointed as he heard the two men's footsteps approaching his location, but he was still upbeat from the bargain re-sentencing of time-served he had just received from Judge Boscolo and did not mind the civil process of immigration litigation. It was no criminal process that could result to prison.

The immigration field officer, a Korean about five feet five inches height, light skin and usual Asian jet-black short but full hair, handcuffed Raymond and led him out through the main entrance of the federal courthouse with no scrupulous security measures the likes he had almost grown accustomed to in the past couple of years. As Raymond stepped outside, darkness had fallen and the entire park in front of Cadman Plaza was free of people. It was a welcomed sight for Raymond, who was once again, even as he was still handcuffed, getting a taste of freedom, at least so he felt.

The short walk to the officer's white Toyota Camry parked by the metered curb somehow made Raymond feel like he was unauthorized to do so. Walking in shackles and chains became the new normal in his life and he never envisioned walking along the street for a foreseeable future if it wasn't for Honorable Simon Boscolo's justice that was tempered with mercy.

Raymond respectfully, with full appreciation of almost anything, sat quietly next to the Immigration field officer, who drove toward Brooklyn Bridge. The feeling ironically reminisced the day he first arrived in the United States and boarded a Lincoln Continental taxicab at JFK airport. He began to think seriously of what to do next with his new freedom. Immigration detention might take a day to book him and release him and so he was eyeing two, three, maybe four days at the most in whatever detention center they may place him. Predominant in his order of priority was to see be with his son and assume full custody of him. He knew his academic ambition was indispensable but he didn't want his son to spend a day he needed not to in a foster home. And so he was certain his academics was mandatory and that he would soon be back at school pursuing his ultimate goal of becoming a medical doctor. There was no doubt in his mind that becoming a doctor was one awesome machine that was capable of vacuuming away all the nightmarish experience that stemmed from his long journey to Lagos. The subject of sex briefly crossed his mind but he immediately suppressed it. He knew that was to come in a natural order of daily encounters. Besides, his libido had been so suppressed he must have been feeling like a Catholic priest.

The Immigration field officer exited the Brooklyn Bridge in Manhattan, looped out to the front of City Hall and turned left onto Chambers Street. At Church Avenue, he veered right and followed it until it became Sixth Avenue. Raymond had no idea where he was or their final destination, and chose not to ask any questions. He simply sat and appreciated the bright city lights he was about to be released into. Unlike during his trial months, he no longer fantasized on walking alongside the pedestrians he was witnessing. It will be happening real soon. He was having a sweetheart moment and in his mind, he contemplated on a paraphrased famous quote by a US President, who aptly observed that only from the bottom of the valley can one fully appreciate how magnificent it is to be on top of the mountain. When he was being shackled and shuttled back and forth across the Brooklyn Bridge he was at the rock bottom of the valley. He was beginning to feel he was close to mountain top once more and he swore never to blow it again.

At West Houston Street, the officer veered left and proceeded across Seventh Avenue and pulled the Toyota Camry inside the loading dock of 201 Varick Street, where four Pinkerton security guards started to get busy with their version of prisoner intake, a much relaxed protocol than the federal prison. Raymond followed the immigration field officer to the fourth floor of the building, where he was booked and assigned a top bunk bed inside a large dormitory-style jail.

Raymond saw diversity in the federal prison but the sight of diverse foreign nationals he was witnessing in the Immigration detention center physically gave him his first impression of a general assembly gathering at the United Nations. They were from Israel, England, Sierra Leone, Togo, Romania, Uzbekistan, Iran, Russia, China, Haiti, Jamaica, Nicaragua, Dominican Republic, Zambia, Pakistan, Marshal Island, United Arab Emirate, you name it. In Raymond's honest personal assessment, every country was represented. Those immigrants regarded as illegal aliens, most of who were never incarcerated in any county, state or federal prison, were simply there either for illegally accepting employment without authorization or overstaying their visas. Others were detained because they attempted to enter the country illegally.

Raymond's imagination ran wild as he observed from one end of the large dorm to the other. In his mind he concluded that if the United States was the second best country on earth, the first must be heaven. All detainees had one common goal – a shot at American dream. He could not imagine any other country in the world with that many different nationals struggling to get in. Especially given that some hid inside the boat engine, some swam, some came as stowaway, others scaled leg-breaking high walls, and many were sacrificing as many as six years of their lives in detention just to leave no stone unturned in their quests to taste the American dream. Raymond hoped he had not entirely blown his own opportunity. Two years of confinement seemed like eternity. Six years was downright scary and inconceivable.

"God forbid," he quipped and made a cross sign.

He slept like a baby that night, and when he woke up the next morning for breakfast, he was quickly engaged at the breakfast table by four of the many Nigerian detainees desperately fighting deportation. Prison was hell-on-earth but the immigration detention center felt like purgatory. One of the Nigerians, a thirty-five-year old Yoruba tribesman, knew something about everyone in the detention center. He had seen detainees come and go – bonded out to the streets or sent to dreadful home. He spoke most of the time and everyone seemed to be paying great deal of attention to whatever he was saying. Raymond was shocked when another Nigerian hinted the Yoruba man had been detained at the center for more than six years. He was seeking a relief under asylum, claiming to be fleeing Nigeria for religious persecution, which he thought was ludicrous. All detainees proclaimed and called him 'Mayor,' which he proudly acknowledged. He seemed to be relishing the degree of reverence accorded to him by some of the detainees, who offered him commissary items. He also gained the friendship and sometimes fellowship of security officers manning the detention center.

Over the next few days, Raymond learned a few valuable tricks in fighting deportation from other detainees. The knowledge he thought was most important was to never consent deportation under his status as an aggravated felon. Aggravated felons by virtue of his narcotics conviction were statutorily barred from re-entering the United States forever. With his son living in a foster care program in the US, coupled with the mere fact he had not lived in Nigeria with its double-digit unemployment and economic woes for the past twelve years of his life, such an ill-advised move to avoid lengthy detention stay would certainly end up in a debacle.

On his fifth day of detention at the immigration facility, he filled out a request sheet seeking an audience with an immigration officer. He was hoping to discuss his case status and to determine his course of action. The request was granted and scheduled for 2 p.m. the following day, which was his sixth day of detention.

He was walking along the corridor toward the main office on the same floor of the building when he saw 'Mayor' and about four other foreign national detainees, including another Nigerian, standing and discussing deportation issues. Raymond stopped to greet 'Mayor' and decided to kill the ten minutes he had left prior to his appointment with the immigration officer. 'Mayor' embraced him as was becoming customary and continued with his lecture on the importance of having a good lawyer in deportation matters. 'Mayor' was discussing the overkill story of how one of the detainees, a young and well-connected Nigerian detainee hired the very awesome Theresa Suarez, a seasoned immigration lawyer, who had recorded a whopping thirty-three cases of precedence in the immigration law books. Theresa Suarez's other litigation accomplishments included a successful asylum for Dmitry Zhukov, a convicted Russian mobster, who served a twenty-year prison sentence, quashing of deportation proceeding against Ricardo Gonzales, a Colombian immigrant, who had just concluded a thirty-year sentence for his connection with the Cali cartel. She was widely acclaimed to not only defend immigration cases but wrote some of its laws. She also shuttled to Boston on Saturdays to teach law at Harvard.

Raymond had read much about the inimitable Theresa Suarez and her vaunted knowledge of US Immigration defense even before he was incarcerated. At fifty-four, five feet seven inches tall, light skinned and brunette with a patch of signature gray hair slightly to the left of her forehead, she was born of a Peruvian immigrant father and an Irish-American mother. Early in her career, she served as a government counsel then was appointed an immigration judge, before going into private practice. Immigration prosecutors sarcastically concluded that Theresa Suarez penetrated brains, and they had reasons to. In litigation case after case, Theresa Suarez, with her brilliant instinct, accurately predicted what a prosecutor was thinking in a case, where the prosecutor would proceed, where he or she should effectively proceed and where he or she would actually proceed, and Theresa Suarez would be dead set to tackle them. Raymond also knew that hiring the litigations whiz would cost an unimaginable fortune, and so whoever 'Mayor' was talking about must have had a pocket deeper than the Atlantic Ocean.

Two minutes shy of his 2 p.m. appointment Raymond left the group and proceeded to the office specifically designated for audience with immigration officers. As Raymond approached the office, he could see the seated officer through two glass sides of the door busy writing on a log. The officer looked up before Raymond had the chance to knock and beckoned him to come in.

"Good afternoon, sir," he said and took the seat opposite the officer, who kept on filling out log.

"Good afternoon, Mr. Karr, just a second please," the officer, a slightly heavy set white, clean-shaven male in plain clothes, acknowledged and continued his writing.

Raymond turned his face to the wall behind the office and silently critiqued the photos of the president of the United States and the

Director of Immigration and Naturalization. Moments later, the Immigration officer stopped his writing, dropped his pen on the table and looked up to face him.

"I'm Ron Bradshaw with the Immigration and Naturalization office. Your case had been assigned to me, but before I begin, do you have an attorney representing you in your deportation matter?"

"No, not yet," Raymond answered, unsure of where the officer was coming from.

"Do you plan on retaining one?"

"I have no money to hire an attorney," he said.

"Well, Mr. Karr, I suggest you retain one because you're under Exclusion based on alleged conviction for aggravated felony," the officer sternly warned and reached inside the top drawer to retrieve a blue sheet of paper.

"Here is a list of pro bono lawyers in the area you can call to assist you in your defense."

Raymond received the paper and glanced at it. He read the list of organizations, including Catholic charities, then folded and held paper in his hand.

"Do you have any further question for me today, Mr. Karr?"

Raymond thought for a moment.

"Yes sir, what does being under Exclusion mean for me in this case and do I have a chance at bond?"

"I cannot address those specific issues with you. Only your lawyer can give you such advice. The decision about bond can only come from the judge. Contact those in the list I just gave you and you definitely will find one who can advise you and protect your interest before a judge. As for the Exclusion, it means you are prohibited from re-entering the United States. However, as I said only your lawyer can advise you as to what your rights are."

Raymond had a thousand more questions but he decided to withhold them all since he knew he wouldn't be getting any plausible answers from the officer.

"Ok, thanks, sir," he said and stood up to leave the office.

"Just one more thing, Mr. Karr, I need your signature right there," the officer said, with his ink pen pointing on a dotted line in his log. "This is just to acknowledge we held this discussion and I have advised you of your rights as a deportable alien."

Raymond quickly signed, received a carbon copy from the officer and immediately exited the office. He walked directly to his bunk bed. Weighing heavily in his mind was that the immigration battle wasn't looking as simple and easy as he had initially thought. Being told he was under Exclusion was no mincing of words. With such plain language, he felt he was in deeper immigration trouble the magnitude even Theresa Suarez likely couldn't get him out of, and he was likely to never ever become free to walk the streets of America.

As Raymond was contemplating his next course of action, his mind touched on the issue of his son in foster care, who was likely to be heavily impacted by his doomed plight. If Exclusion from the United States was truly his immigrant status, adoption was next in his son's future. Tears filled his eyes and depression forced him to fall asleep.

Eight days after he was detained at the Varick Street holding jail, Raymond had acquired some knowledge about 'Exclusion' status by asking around. 'Mayor' provided much of the insight. Raymond learned with dismay that the cold air that constantly blew from all the vents in the building was unstoppable despite the fall weather that was turning unusually cold. The uncomfortable effect was a brutally cold environment that approached human cruelty and had detainees hauling along their blankets and hoarding some more just to achieve some degree of warmth. But most of all, 'Mayor' had promised to introduce Raymond to the popular young man he called Sylvester, who retained Theresa Suarez. So the morning of his ninth day at the detention center, 'Mayor' decided to make good of his promise.

And so as Raymond followed 'Mayor' to Sylvester's corner, Raymond was merely trying to show gratefulness rather than enthusiasm on meeting a youngster he knew was of no meaningful use to him. But as soon as he saw Sylvester, Raymond's eyes almost popped out and so did Sylvester's eyes. Another shocking recognition encounter was taking place. Sylvester was Emeka's young brother, who fed Raymond with the balloons of heroin shortly before Raymond's flight back to the United States. Raymond never knew his name. He was so fearfully overwhelmed by the prospect of swallowing drugs that he never asked during their down-to-business drug-swallowing encounter in Lagos.

Sylvester stood up from his bed to shake Raymond's hands but Raymond sluggishly stretched his hand to shake Sylvester. 'Mayor' watched in amazement, smiling as the two facially and vocally expressed their surprises at encountering one another in an immigration detention center in America. A group of five Lithuanian detainees sitting around a bunk bed next to Sylvester's corner were distracted by the aura of re-union. They observed with equal appreciation then kept on with their discussion. From the outlook Raymond's reticence for a handshake with a member of the very clan that got him into the jam he was in was completely shielded. But in the inside he was mighty resentful for many reasons, one of which was his ratting out their brother, Clyde, and testifying against Bryan Jason a key asset in their drug smuggling ring, both men receiving lengthy prison sentences.

Emasculating all the resentment in Raymond was his curiosity to find out how in the hell Sylvester wound up in a US immigration detention center two years later, and perhaps more. And so Raymond flimsily reciprocated the hug from Sylvester. 'Mayor', looking increasingly isolated wisely decided that the best course of action would be for him to depart.

"Gentlemen, go ahead and rejuvenate with each other while I go take care of some business," 'Mayor' said, burped aloud and shook both men before leaving with full appreciation of his re-unification of what he wrongly perceived was two old friendships.

"What in the world brings you here?" Raymond turned away from departing 'Mayor' and asked Sylvester.

"Raymond…that's your name, right, Raymond?" Sylvester said in a distinct Nigerian accent.

"Uh huh, Raymond it is," he said and both men simultaneously decided to shake hands again.

"It's a long story, Raymond, but why don't we wait until after dinner to really sit and discuss."

Dinner was at 6 p.m., just twenty minutes away, and Raymond knew it was the right call.

As all detainees gathered in mess hall and sat around on wooden tables reminiscent of a fast food restaurant, Raymond collected his food tray of shredded chicken stew over white rice and one apple fruit and was walking toward a vacant spot on a table at the far end of the hall. A loud hiss came from behind and when he turned to observe, it was 'Mayor' trying to get his attention. 'Mayor' beckoned Raymond to come sit with the group of Nigerians he accompanied. Raymond briefly struggled with his decision before joining them. His reluctance to caucus with Nigerians in the jail stems from his unwillingness to feed their curiosity over what led him, a twelve-year resident in the United States, to be subjected to deportation proceeding. But there was no doubt in his mind that Sylvester's knowledge of his ordeal would be a hindrance to his desire to keep any secrets. Sylvester was certain to hint 'Mayor' and Raymond somehow believed 'Mayor', despite his goodwill intentions, gossiped a little bit.

'Mayor' invited Raymond to sit next to him on a table that sat a total of six people, three on each side. He filled the lone vacancy on the table and exchanged greetings with the three Nigerians and a Ghanaian that were already seated and eating. Around the hall, other detainees juggled for available vacant seats preferably close to their compatriots.

"Where did you know our home boy from?" 'Mayor' asked Raymond as he positioned himself to eat.

Raymond, sensing 'Mayor' must have known something about Sylvester, pretended he heard nothing and concentrated on his food. He wasn't sure how to approach the subject of his encounter in Lagos with Sylvester, nor did he want to discuss his reason for being placed in deportation proceeding period.

'Mayor' did not repeat his question all through and that pleased Raymond, who pretended to be completely focused on his hearty meal. At the conclusion of their dinner, 'Mayor' invited him to walk back to the dorm with him and Raymond obliged. As both men slowly walked side by side along the corridor that led to the dorm, Raymond mistakenly answered the question that opened the door for a flurry of inquiries from 'Mayor.'

"I can't believe I met Sylvester here of all places," Raymond said before realizing he was on the verge of blowing a cover.

"Oh yeah? Where did you know him from? 'Mayor' repeated his question.

Raymond knew he couldn't escape 'Mayor's' curiosity.

"In Lagos."

"Are you two related?"

"Not really. I had a business relationship with his older brother."

"He is so rich, that kid, and I know he's well connected. Look at who he has for a lawyer. Quite frankly, I don't know what he's still doing here with a big shot attorney like that."

It was the initial informative clue for Raymond that perhaps 'Mayor' did not know a thing about Sylvester's background. In the hopes that Sylvester was smart enough not to discuss his legal problems with anyone, Raymond falsely narrated a story of how himself and Sylvester's older brother, Emeka, jointly engaged in a luggage import business from Italy. Raymond, after telling his false story, wasn't sure and didn't care if 'Mayor' bought into it. His only hope was that Sylvester did not reveal the drug supply affair. He knew he was to meet Sylvester that evening for further discussion and therefore was not to dive into any hot-button issues that could spread throughout the detention center.

"Oh I see, so that's how you met him," 'Mayor' said in a dragged vocal. "How long ago was this?"

Raymond sensed it was a gotcha question.

"Years back, when Sylvester was still a little boy," he managed to answer immediately.

"He seems to have lots of valuable information for you, you should speak with him. He knows a thing or two about each and every African, not just Nigerian, but African in this jail," 'Mayor' said and fixed his eyes at him to gauge his reaction.

Raymond wisely remained indifferent in his demeanor.

"Ok, I'd love to hear from him. One of these days I'll consider having a real meaningful chat with him," he said.

"You should do it as soon as possible because you could be transferred to Oakdale soon. Try to do it today latest tomorrow."

"Why? Where is Oakdale anyway?" Raymond asked with heightened curiosity. He knew whatever 'Mayor', who had his own reliable means of gathering information regarding the plight of detainees, had some truth to it, at least some element of truth.

"Louisiana."

"Why would they send me to Louisiana? Isn't JFK Airport the closest for a trip to Nigeria?"

"Oakdale is where immigration has their largest jail. Most people transferred to Oakdale face imminent deportation. Generally, it is known as a point of no return."

As horrible as Varick Street detention center was, Raymond, after more than a week was not enthusiastic about leaving New York City without his freedom. As they walked close to Raymond's bunk bed, which was near the middle of the whole floor, 'Mayor' explained briefly before separating from Raymond.

"Don't worry, I'll find out more about it for you say tomorrow or next, okay?"

"Okay," Raymond said and immediately climbed atop his bed.

While resting on his bed, he thought about 'Mayor's explanation of the possibility of having to be flown to Oakdale, Louisiana. He knew he needed some more information but he was reserving it all for whichever pro bono attorney he would be speaking with.

Close to half hour after resting on his bed, Raymond decided it was time to meet and discuss with Sylvester. He stood up and went directly to Sylvester's corner toward the far end of the unit. Sylvester, whose Bulgarian bunk mate was resting on his top bunk bed and reading a book, was sitting upright on his lower bunk bed listening to his Walkman radio with a headset. When he saw Raymond, he quickly stood up and removed his headset.

"Good evening, sir," Sylvester humbly greeted with a tepid smile.

"Good evening to you, buddy, what's brewing?" said Raymond, who wasn't at all certain how to approach the meeting prospect. Sylvester was Emeka's little brother, the very one who, despite his well-groomed appearance and a slight weight gain, was still looking like the teenager he was just two years back. Sylvester still showed signs of respect for Raymond just as he did in Lagos.

"Have a seat, sir," Sylvester said and pointed to the bottom end of his bed.

"Why don't we just walk to the rec room, there we'll find some privacy on one corner," Raymond said in a seemingly suggestive manner.

"Okay," Sylvester said and immediately lifted his pillow and placed his Walkman radio under it. He then excused himself from his bunk mate and left with him.

At the recreation room, all three ping pong tables had been dismantled for the day and all sitting tables had been cleared of monopoly board games. Only a few detainees were sitting and Raymond could sense from their language they were Austrians. Raymond led Sylvester to one of the many vacant tables and both men sat down facing each other.

"First of all, I hope you did not reveal to 'Mayor' or anyone else in here our Lagos affair," he said to Sylvester.

Raymond knew he needed to be smarter than his old self in dealing with the youngster. He needed answers to many disparaging questions and he knew if he had to successfully arrive at those answers he had to be extremely crafty, even if it meant twisting some arms a little bit.

"No. No one here knows me and I don't know any of them. However, I had discussed about you to 'Mayor' about a month ago. Whether or not he knows it was you I talked about I can't say for sure"

"That was a big mistake. You don't talk loosely around here. I could wreck several people here and I know much more than you think I do, but I will reserve my knowledge to myself for now. I spoke to 'Mayor' but I'll give you a chance to tell me what's up," Raymond said with slight anger. He hoped his lie about discussion with 'Mayor' could force Sylvester's hand.

It worked and played right into young Sylvester's naivete. Sylvester began to spill his guts, but before then he demanded that Raymond kept it an ultimate secret as things could get a little complicated with him. Raymond obliged and they both shook hands on it.

"Tell me what you want to know," Sylvester asked and locked his fingers on the table.

"First of all, how did you end up here?"

"About eight months ago, my brother and I were vacationing in London, when Scotland Yard stormed my room and took me into custody. They seized everything I had and told me I was wanted by DEA in America. They extradited me to New York and detained me at MCC. Fortunately, I had a good lawyer and they gave me six months, which I served at MCC."

"But no one serves time at MCC, what federal prison did you serve time in?" Raymond curiously inquired.

"No. By the time my case was over it was already a little over six months so the judge gave me time-served. In fact, I was extremely lucky that my brother gave me a good lawyer otherwise I could have been in a lot more trouble. I went to London with a passport that showed I'm twenty years old. When they brought me to America and charged me with conspiracy to distribute drug and several other charges, my lawyer was able to prove that I am actually seventeen years old so they could not charge me as an adult in America. So we cut a deal that I do six months and be sent back to Nigeria. That's why I'm here."

"And who was your lawyer?" Raymond inquired aware Sylvester's lawyer must have been too damn good.

"R. John Masulo."

Raymond almost chuckled. R. John Masulo was one of the most powerful high-profile criminal defense attorneys in the nation. He craftily argued and handily worn a mistrial in United States vs. Canachio. In that case, Vito Canachio, an alleged violent Capo in the Bartolo crime family, who faced multiple murder and racketeering charges with incriminating evidences and eyewitnesses that included mob turncoats and law enforcement covert operatives, was freed and could never be tried again on those charges under the Fifth Amendment's Double Jeopardy clause. Five of Canachio's co-defendants, who were each charged separately with the same criminal counts, were all convicted and sentenced to life imprisonment. So arguably, standing between freedom and ten feet concrete walls of prison for Vito 'Good Fella' Canachio was R. John Masulo. That was Sylvester's chosen lawyer.

"If I may ask, how much did it cost you to hire R. John Masulo?"

"My brother hired him. The lawyer said he wanted a hundred thousand on an account he will bill on for his services and my brother wired him the money. So after the case, he said we had thirty-two thousand dollars coming back to us and my brother told him to use it to hire an immigration lawyer."

Raymond was infuriated with the revelation. One hundred thousand dollars wired like ordinary paper, whereas he could not even receive a hundred dollars in commissary money from the very people he risked it all for. The idea of vengeance started to trickle into his mind. His brain was processing all when Sylvester continued.

"The reason for wanting to burn out the money here was because my brother was afraid that DEA could be tracing to find who would collect the money and arrest him. They're desperately looking for him."

"Okay," he said. "Now how do I stand in your brother's eyes, are we enemies? What happens if I am deported to Nigeria, will he support me financially?"

Before replying, he chuckled in sarcasm. "No matter what you do, never step foot into Nigeria unless you can hide for the rest of your life. They know everything about you, your family and old friends. They know where to find you and how to locate you even if you run inside a rat hole."

Raymond shifted his chair and adjusted himself, folded his arms and rested his back on the chair, successfully hiding the flaring scare in him.

"Why? because I crashed?" he said, extremely eager to find out.

"Nope, for several other reasons. As for the 'market', you never stood a chance. You were doomed from the get go. You see, you were used only as a distraction for five women in the same Nigerian Airways flight, who had multiple times more 'market' with them. As soon as you boarded the flight, they called JFK Customs and informed them you had 'market' inside you and gave them all information they needed to track you down. They described your luggage too. That way Customs will concentrate on finding you and all the ladies will easily cross with lots of 'market'.

Raymond, shocked and surprised, then knew why his luggage did not make it from the conveyor belt. He remembered waiting impatiently for his luggage at JFK airport and being the odd man out as every passenger picked up their luggage and left. He thought he was a fool not to have realized it was the long wait for his never-arriving luggage that gave him away. He also thought he should have known that Customs agents held out his luggage at the back in order to accurately identify him. Although he was still scared about Sylvester's dreadful advice not to return to Nigeria, he was so furious that his life and freedom was so casually dispensed so some jerks could nefariously acquire excess wealth. He'd been disposed like a sacrificial lamb.

"So they brought me all the way from Washington, DC to Lagos in order to use me like that?" Raymond asked Sylvester.

"No. It was because you associated with a guy by the name of Ike, you remember him? He was a known undercover for the Nigerian Security Organization, which co-operated with DEA in America to track our guys. So they didn't want to take a chance with you"

"Now wait a minute, you mean the guy I first met at Murtala Mohammed Airport?"

"It must have been him but I'm not sure. I heard my brother say his name was Ike."

Each revelation shocked Raymond even more. He just found out Ike was never his friend after all rather someone looking to score a promotion in his job as an undercover agent.

"So how come they allowed me to swallow all those punishing balls of heroin, and why did Emeka take me to the juju priest?"

"You see, they did not find out about you and Ike until two days before your flight. That's when they seized the opportunity to make even more money at the expense of your freedom. As soon as it was learned your security was compromised, all the ladies, none of who had satisfactorily spent the mandatory one month travel stay, were quickly told to get ready for a trouble-free flight back to New York. They even received good money from other 'market' running groups that they tipped off about a flight where a decoy had been planted. That's the nature of the business. Sometimes they use decoys but you were not supposed to be a decoy until two days before."

"How much do they pay the decoys to go to jail?"

"Decoys never know what they're being used for and never paid. They just be gone, sorry. It's cold but it's not in my hands. My job is to just encourage our guys to swallow as much 'market' as possible. That's my business."

"And how about allowing me to swallow all those balls?"

"That's just so Customs would be so convinced that they would never question the credibility of the source of the tip off. Otherwise, they will find out: they're very smart."

Raymond was about to ask another question when Sylvester interrupted him.

"The real reason why they want you quenched is that they think you have some critical information that you shouldn't have gotten. I don't know much about it but Goddy mistakenly showed you the wrong batch of photographs. I don't know much about that since it was not my department but I believe it had to do with the batch of photographs you saw that was supposed to be shown only to Bangkok, Thailand 'market' runners. America 'market' runners were only shown Nigerian guys quenched in Thailand for stealing money or 'market'. I really can't tell exactly what it was but it went something like that. They're not expecting you to come out of prison so soon. I think they're also intent upon quenching you anyway they can, so I'd advise you to hide in Ghana or Sierra Leone or any other remote country other than America and Nigeria."

Raymond knew immediately Sylvester was talking about the dreadful photo of the dead Isaac Dellum, III and his young daughter. He recalled when Goddy requested the photos, his partner that spotted a walrus mustache struggled a little with which envelop to retrieve from his briefcase. The anger again shifted back to fright. He knew he definitely possessed the knowledge he should never have acquired.

Last call for shower was announced through the loud speaker. Raymond thanked Sylvester and stood up to leave. Sylvester stood up and was ready to follow Raymond.

"Raymond, I hope everything I told you will never be heard by anyone else. It's for your own good so you can use it to make your way out to hiding for good. And you look out for me too because if DEA finds out I supplied you with 'market', they will definitely void my plea bargain and throw me back in jail," Sylvester concluded.

Raymond looked at Sylvester and marveled over his youth and inexperience and total naiveté over law and self-incrimination. He did not ask but the guy had retroactively armed Raymond with a bargaining chip. However, it was the knowledge Raymond no longer needed since he had gotten all the information he wanted, plus much more. He shook Sylvester's hands and assured him it was all between the two, before each man went to his bunk bed.

Detainees who waited for the last minute to shower were all rushing to the shower room. Raymond needed one, for he skipped the day before because of depression over his immigrant status as an excludable alien in a country he so dearly loved but had violated its priority law. He grabbed his toiletries and made his way to shower for the evening.

Raymond went to bed at 9:30 p.m. with even more concerning issues. Sylvester's revelation about how the heroin lords had utilized him to their own advantage and to his doom was coming across to him as grossly unfair. Not only that, they had him on their Wanted Dead list because of their inadvertent photographic revelation of their complicity, if not total culpability, in the death of Isaac Dillum, III and his young daughter. Above all, facing imminent deportation was harboring, to a certain degree, an illusion of a death sentence. Freedom, after all, was not coming anytime soon for Raymond Karr.

Early the following morning, Raymond was awakened by the night shift security officer to pack up his belongings and be ready for a transfer to the point-of-no-return Oakdale, Louisiana federal immigration detention center, with the crushing weight of his legal problems squarely rested on his shoulder.

In making the call as it appeared, Raymond had no choice than to acknowledge something he hated to admit in the wake of his ordeal—when it came to crime and punishment, he was a hell of a coward and by no stretch of imagination, a masquerade.

END